Hugh Bicheno was born in Cuba and educated in Chile, Scotland and Cambridge. He has had careers as an academic, an intelligence officer and a kidnap and ransom negotiator and now devotes his time to writing about men at war and those who make wars happen. His previous books include the bestselling *Rebels and Redcoats*, written in conjunction with the TV series presented by Richard Holmes, the critically acclaimed *Crescent and Cross*, and *Gettysburg* and *Midway* from the Cassell Fields of Battle series.

D1147191

RAZOR'S EDGE

The Unofficial History of the Falklands War

HUGH BICHENO

FOREWORD BY

Richard Holmes

PHOENIX

A PHOENIX PAPERBACK

First published in Great Britain in 2006
by Weidenfeld & Nicolson
This paperback edition published in 2007
by Phoenix,
an imprint of Orion Books Ltd,
Orion House, 5 Upper St Martin's Lane,
London WC2H 9EA

1 3 5 7 9 10 8 6 4 2

A CIP catalogue record for this book
is available from the British Library.

ISBN-13 978-0-7538-2186-2

Printed in Great Britain by
Clays Ltd, St Ives plc

The Orion Publishing Group's policy is to use papers that
are natural, renewable and recyclable products and
made from wood grown in sustainable forests. The logging
and manufacturing processes are expected to conform to
the environmental regulations of the country of origin.

www.orionbooks.co.uk

To the memory of my friend,

ROLO FERNÁNDEZ PONDAL

disappeared on 5 August 1977

'Oh no, you cannot write a novel about the experience we are living. Novels are works of the imagination, and what is going on around us exceeds the limits of even the most extravagant fiction.'

Manuel Mujica Láinez
(Argentine 'magical realism' novelist) to the author, February 1978

Contents

Maps and Diagrams

* *with additional Photo Diagram*

Acknowledgements

My Thanks To:

My old friend and colleague from dire days together in Buenos Aires, now H.E. the Governor Howard Pearce, CVO, whose wedding in Stanley Cathedral to the delightful Caroline, née Thomée, was the occasion of a heart-warming demonstration of community spirit and the never-to-be forgotten highlight of my second visit to the Falklands.

Patrick Watts MBE, Tony Smith of Discovery Falklands and Ken Greenland QPM, of Darwin House for their guidance during my study of the terrain, Terry Peck MBE, CPM and Trudi McPhee of Brookfield Farm for their part in Longdon, Don Bonner BEM, Steward of Government House during the occupation, Councillor Roger Edwards of Sulivan Farm (Fox Bay), Ailsa and Tony Heathman of Estancia House, Pat Short, ex of San Carlos Settlement and Rob McGill of Carcass Island.

Alex Blake for the aerial photographs and his parents, Sally and Tim, OBE, JP, ex of Hill Cove Farm, for their hospitality. Vera Bonner for making everything work and finally Anita Alazia and the staff at Government House for making it feel like home.

Sonia my revered agent, Ned, mentor and dear friend, Ian Drury and Keith Lowe of Orion/Cassells, to all of whom I owe so much.

Maggie for her indomitable example, Scott and Shaun, Katty and Jack for the hope they represent, Robin for lighting up my life and whatever gods there be for sparing me to bear witness to the events I chronicle, despite my efforts to the contrary.

Acronyms and Abbreviations

2 i/c Second in Command

.30-calibre 0.3-inch (7.62mm) machine-gun

.50-calibre 0.5-inch (12.7mm) machine-gun

66 66mm (2.6-inch) AT weapon

84 84mm (3.3-inch) AT weapon (Carl Gustav)

AAA Anti-Aircraft Artillery

AT Anti-Tank

BEM British Empire Medal

BIM Argentine Marine Battalion

C-130 Hercules transport aircraft

Carl Gustav See '84'

CGT Argentine equivalent of TUC

CO Commanding Officer

CPM Colonial Police Medal

CSM Company Sergeant-Major

CVO Companion, Victorian Order

DINA Chilean counter-terrorist agency

ERP Argentine People's Revolutionary Army

ESMA Argentine Navy Mechanics' School

FAL Argentine semi/fully-automatic rifle

FCO Foreign and Commonwealth Office

FIBS Falkland Islands Broadcasting Service

FIC Falkland Islands Company

FSB Fire Support Base

GA Argentine Artillery Group

GAA Argentine Airborne Artillery Group

GADA Argentine Army Air Defence Group

GDA Argentine Air Force Air Defence Group

GPMG British General Purpose MG

GR3 RAF Harrier, ground attack variant

HMG Heavy MG (.50-calibre)

HMNZS Her Majesty's New Zealand Ship

HQ Headquarters

IOR Vatican bank

KC-130 Aerial refuelling tanker

LCU 100-ton load Landing Craft

LCVP 5-ton load Landing Craft

LMG Light MG (magazine-fed Bren converted to 7.62mm)

LPD *Fearless* class assault ships

LSL *Sir Galahad* class logistics ships

MAG Argentine GPMG (also MMG)

M&AW Mountain and Arctic Warfare

MBE Member, British Empire Order

MG Machine-gun

Milan Wire-guided AT missile system

MMG Medium MG (.30-calibre)

MoD British Ministry of Defence

NCO Non-Commissioned Officer

NSA US signals intelligence service

OBE Officer, British Empire Order

OC Officer Commanding

O Group Task-defining meeting of CO with subordinate commanders

Ops Operations

P 2 Italy-based secret association

PNR Process of National Reorganization. (Argentine military régime 1976–83)

PRT Argentine Worker's Revolutionary Party (front for ERP)

Psyops Psychological Operations

PTSD Post Traumatic Stress Disorder

QPM Queen's Police Medal

RA Royal Artillery

RAF Royal Air Force

RAOC Royal Army Ordnance Corps

RAP Regimental (First) Aid Post

RCL Rocket Launcher

RCT Royal Corps of Transport

RE Royal Engineers

REME Royal Electrical and Mechanical Engineers

RFA Royal Fleet Auxiliary

RI Argentine Infantry Regiment

RIM Argentine Mechanized Infantry Regiment

RM Royal Marines

RMP Royal Military Police

RSM Regimental Sergeant-Major

SAM Surface to Air Missile

SFMG Sustained Fire MG – Abbreviated from the correct GPMG (SF)

SLR British semi-automatic rifle

UXB Unexploded bomb

VT Variable Timing

Timeline

MARCH – JULY 1982

MARCH

28   Argentine invasion fleet sets sail.

29   Decision taken to send Royal Navy nuclear attack submarines.

APRIL

1   *Spartan* and *Splendid* sail from Faslane.

2   Argentine invasion of the Falkland Islands.

3   Argentine invasion of South Georgia.

4   RAF transport aircraft deploy to Ascension Island. *Conqueror* sails from Faslane.

5   *Hermes* and *Invincible,* nucleus of the British Task force, sail from Portsmouth.

9   Requisitioned liner *Canberra* sails from Southampton with 3 Para and 40, 42 and 45 Royal Marine Commandos.

11   *Splendid* and *Spartan* arrive off the Falklands.

12   *Conqueror* arrives off South Georgia. Britain announces 200-mile Maritime Exclusion Zone around the Falklands. Destroyer *Antrim,* frigate *Plymouth* and tanker *Tidespring* with M Company, 42 Commando, depart Ascension to recapture South Georgia.

14   South Georgia Task Force rendezvous with *Endurance,* already on station.

16 British Aircraft Carrier Group arrives at Ascension.

18 Task Force sails from Ascension, *Brilliant, Coventry, Glasgow, Sheffield* and *Arrow* race ahead to have credible military force in place to strengthen diplomatic pressure.

21–22 Helicopters from *Antrim* insert and extract SAS from Fortuna glacier in South Georgia.

24 *Brilliant* arrives off South Georgia.

25 Argentine submarine *Sante Fé* caught on the surface emerging from Grytviken, disabled by Royal Navy helicopters. Royal Marines and SAS put ashore by helicopter and Royal Navy ships fire warning bombardment to persuade Argentine garrison to surrender.

26 Nun-killer Astiz and his 'sworn to die' detachment at Leith surrender without fighting. 2 Para departs Hull on board requisitioned ferry *Norland.*

27 Argentine Navy sails from Puerto Belgrano and Ushuaia to mount pincer attack on British Task Force.

MAY

1 British Task Force enters Maritime Exclusion Zone. RAF Vulcan bombs Stanley airfield followed by Harrier attacks from *Hermes. Glamorgan, Alacrity* and *Arrow* shell Argentine positions around Stanley. First air battles. Insertion of SAS and SBS parties.

2 *Conqueror* sinks the cruiser *General Belgrano.*

3 Royal Navy helicopters disable Argentine patrol vessel *Alférez Sobral.*

4 *Sheffield* set on fire by an Exocet, sinks 10 May. Sea Harrier shot down at Goose Green.

6 Two Sea Harriers collide in bad weather.

9 Sea Harriers sink Argentine spy trawler *Narwal.*

10–11 *Alacrity* sinks Argentine supply ship *Isla de los Estados* in Falkland Sound.

12 Fifth Army Brigade of 2nd Scots Guards, 1st Welsh Guards and 1/7th Gurkha Rifles sail from Southampton on requisitioned liner *QE 2. Glasgow* and *Brilliant* shoot down three Argentine Skyhawks, *Glasgow* disabled by a bomb. San Carlos selected as landing site.

14 SAS from *Glamorgan* raid Argentine air base at Pebble Island.

16 Sea Harriers damage supply ships *Bahía Buen Suceso* and *Río Carcaraña.*

19 Transfer of troops at sea preparatory to landing. Twenty-one SAS lost when their helicopter crashes.

20 Insertion of SAS team in southern Argentina goes wrong, helicopter burned in Chile.

21 San Carlos Landings: *Ardent,* three British and fifteen Argentine aircraft lost.

23 *Antelope,* one British and five Argentine aircraft lost

24 Logistics ships *Sir Lancelot* and *Sir Galahad* hit by UXB, four Argentine aircraft lost.

25 *Broadsword* damaged, *Coventry* sunk off Pebble Island, three Argentine aircraft lost. Exocet sets *Atlantic Conveyor* on fire, sinks 28 May.

27–28 Battle of Darwin/Goose Green.

29 Sea Harrier lost over the side from *Invincible* in bad weather. Tanker *British Wye* hit by UXB from an Argentine C-130 Hercules.

30 Last air-launched Exocet attack fails. 3 Para and 45 Commando reach Estancia and Teal Inlet, 42 Commando reinforces SAS after battle for Mount Kent.

JUNE

1 Royal Marines Mountain and Arctic Warfare Cadre attack Argentine Special Forces at Top Malo House. Argentine C-130 transport shot down by Sea Harrier.

2 Two Para airlifted to Fitzroy.

5 Scots Guards shipped to Bluff Cove by *Intrepid.*

6 Bungled shipping of Welsh Guards to Bluff Cove by *Fearless.*

8 *Sir Galahad* destroyed with many men lost, mainly Welsh Guards. *Sir Tristram* and *Plymouth* damaged by air attacks. Three Argentine aircraft lost.

11–12 Battles of Longdon, Two Sisters and Harriet. *Glamorgan* damaged by a land-based Exocet.

13–14 Battles of Tumbledown and Wireless Ridge.

14 Surrender of Argentine forces in the Falklands.

20 British remove Argentine military presence from Southern Thule in the South Sandwich Islands, first established in 1976.

JULY

13 Six hundred officers and specialists repatriated to Argentina after Buenos Aires tacitly accepts an end to hostilities.

Foreword

THIS IS A VERY unofficial history, whose author is uniquely well-placed to write it. I first met Hugh Bicheno when we were undergraduates at Emmanuel College, Cambridge, a lifetime ago. I often quip that he taught me the most valuable lesson of my early life, the management of the *bota*, or Spanish wineskin. Like so many friendships, ours hinged on the fact that that although we were strikingly different in many respects (I had short hair and was an enthusiastic member of the Officers Training Corps, while Hugh's mane proclaimed another outlook as he strode on confidently with conviviality never far away), we had a fundamental common interest.

In our case it was military history, although I could not have imagined, in 1966, that we would both end up making a living from it. Not only are we now in the same profession, but often find ourselves collaborating. Acting as general editor to *The Oxford Companion to Military History* would have broken me without the support provided by Hugh and my colleague Chris Bellamy. When I made the BBC series *Rebels and Redcoats* I could not spare the time to write the book as well as present the programmes, so Hugh did it, and I was delighted that, though we had had precious little time to discuss detail, my series and his book struck precisely the same tone.

Yet if we were dissimilar in the 1960s, we are no less different now. I have been a professional historian (with breaks spent as an amateur infantry officer) all my working life, and have rubbed shoulders with the

Establishment cheerfully enough. I usually keep my politics out of my books. Indeed, when sheer exasperation at my subject matter drove me to political comment in my recent *In the Footsteps of Churchill* there was tut-tutting from some reviewers, based more on the fact that I had actually ventured an opinion than that they disagreed with it.

Hugh could not be more different. He stayed on to do research at Emmanuel, but then went off to serve as an intelligence officer in Argentina and elsewhere in the 1970s. This was in itself not surprising, for he is bilingual in English and Spanish, and his upbringing makes him a natural traveller. Even now, living in Cambridge within a few miles of the bones of his ancestors (do not be misled by his Latinate name for it is a contraction of Birchenhaugh, old English for Birch Hollow) he radiates the feeling that he is *in* a place but never quite *of* it. He and government service were never destined for a long and happy marriage, and as I flick through my address book I see an assortment of addresses in Central America and latterly the United States – testimony to a lifetime spent as a security consultant in dangerous places. If Hugh has not been in battle, he has looked death in the face, and his own understanding of the 'Dirty War' in Argentina is sharpened by the memory of a personal encounter with 'a mestizo Guatemalan police sergeant who just liked to hear white men scream.'

Hugh started writing history on his return to the UK eight years ago, and it was clear that he had lost none of the intellectual sharpness which had earned him a First Class Honours degree. *Crescent and Cross,* his account of the battle of Lepanto was remarkable, not least because he took the trouble (as he does with all his books, and as readers will shortly see for themselves) to map the microterrain, in that case the complex and changing coastline of south-west Greece. His prose rose memorably to its epic task. I shall never forget his image of how Don Juan of Austria 'under a clear blue sky, in the sight of the Christian host and in the face of an enemy fleet that stretched from horizon to horizon… danced a carefree galliard on the foredeck of the mighty *La Real* with God's following breeze ruffling his hair.'

While I may be reluctant to transgress the borders of what I deem judicious academic comment, Hugh quickly makes it clear that for him Clausewitz was absolutely right. War is indeed 'the continuation of politics with the admixture of other means.' Not only are its causes, course and consequences shot through with politics, but the way that we interpret it is often political, and so historiography too is a political act. Yet, as he observes at the conclusion of his book, he did not find 'in all the academic literature on the Falklands War, a single book in English that explores the social and cultural currents that move politics like flotsam in the Gulf Stream.'

The book also provides the most detailed account yet of the conduct of military operations on and around the Falklands in 1982. It is neither a British nor an Argentine view, for Hugh's mastery of Spanish and familiarity with Argentina ensures that he is comfortable on both sides of the line. There are many occasions on which he dissects small-unit combat so effectively that we can see exactly how men fought and died. Thus at Goose Green, the war's first major land engagement, Lieutenant Colonel H. Jones of 2 Para was hit as he moved into a re-entrant covered by a machine-gun manned by Lance Corporal Ríos, who was himself killed soon afterwards by the direct hit of a 66mm rocket fired by Corporal Abols. At the very end of the war, when the Scots Guards took Tumbledown Mountain, an Argentine soldier known only by the post mortem nickname 'Pedro' fought on long after the position had collapsed, firing and moving to new positions until some members of the fire support team advanced round the base of an area known as 'the Terrace' to acquire a better firing angle, and killed him. Hugh's account brings the Argentines within measurable distance of being able 'to identify and honour the memory of a very brave man lying in an anonymous grave in Darwin Harbour cemetery.'

The attention to terrain detail is remarkable and unparalleled. Hugh has walked and climbed all the battlefields of the war, and his own scrupulously-drawn maps make it clear that a good deal of what has been written about the fighting (sometimes by veterans, who may be forgiven if their *post hoc* reconstructions of a series of episodic and harrowing events are inexact) simply cannot be true. In the dangerous grammar of infantry battle the ground imposes its own hard rules. He is spot-on in so many of his judgements on the timeless truths of battle. In combat you never get a second chance to make a first impression, and the first action of a campaign, or the first clash in a particular engagement, often sets the tone for what follows. Furthermore it is idle to imagine that men behave normally in the midst of battle, and wishful thinking to imagine that we can impose the standards of civilised behaviour upon them in the very eye of the storm.

That said, some men behaved with remarkable decency when all the pressures might have promoted a lapse. Corporal Watts of 42 Commando was killed while disarming three conscripts huddling in a trench. One of the terrified men shot him, but all were nevertheless permitted to surrender. When the Royal Marine Mountain and Arctic Warfare Cadre took Top Malo House, a wounded Argentine officer shot one of his attackers in the stomach and narrowly missed another. He was astonished to have his wound treated and to be given morphine by his adversary, who remarked, 'No problem, it's war,' before returning to the battle.

'Friendly fire' incidents can involve even the best-trained combatants, and are an inevitable consequence of poor communications. Benevolent assumptions about units' readiness for operations are no substitute for rigorous preparation. Real warriors – hard men who thrive on battle – make a disproportionate impact, even if armies and the societies they defend can find them hard to love. Corporal Stewart McLaughlin of 3 Para led his section to the attack on Mount Longdon 'standing up on a rock, tracer everywhere, shouting: "Come on lads, I'm fucking bulletproof, follow me!"' He received no posthumous award, doubtless because severed ears were found in his ammunition pouches after he was killed.

I have never written about the Falklands. Too many of my friends fought there: H. Jones, killed under controversial circumstances at Goose Green, was my syndicate instructor when I learned how to be a company commander at the School of Infantry. I would find it impossible to take a balanced (and thus at times necessarily critical) view of men I have known for most of my life, and I do not always agree with Hugh's deductions about them. Moreover, I could not jettison my academic carapace to make Hugh's uncompromising political analysis. But I am delighted to see a historian of his skill and flair take on this subject, and to have so many of our assumptions about this much-described war challenged so vigorously. If reading this fiery, hard-hitting book leads to raised blood pressure in London and Buenos Aires, then that is no bad thing at all.

Richard Holmes

Introduction

A GENERATION HAS GROWN up since the war fought between Argentina and Britain for possession of South Georgia, the Falkland Islands and Dependencies, known as *las Malvinas* to the Argentines. It began with the Argentine invasion of East Falkland and South Georgia on 2–3 April 1982 and ended with the surrender of all their forces in the theatre seventy-four days later. Hundreds of books later, the cosy belief it was 'unnecessary' has become set in stone. If the Argentine reality is factored in, however, it becomes clear the war was the product of a clash of cultures and consequently far less easily avoidable than many profess to believe. The greatest surprise for English-speaking readers may be to discover that ideological issues most regard as the defunct relics of a bygone age were – and to a considerable degree remain – alive in Argentina. Terms like 'Fascist' and, particularly, 'Liberal' have lost their historic meaning in a welter of Anglo-American hyperbole, but they must be used and understood with precision when discussing the deep background.* The enemy Britain fought in 1982 was the same as in 1939–45, on a smaller scale but no less poisonous. Although nothing short of conquest and prolonged occupation is likely to modify the principles on which a nation organizes itself, one result of the war was to cut another head off the Nazi/Fascist hydra, as worthwhile an outcome as any war could have.

* See **Appendix A** for a regrettably necessary clarification of the basic terminology.

In between cause and effect lay the war, like the neck of an hourglass through which grains of sand pass to a new configuration. Brigadier Julian Thompson, commander of the British Landing Force, judged the defining feature of the war to have been that the Argentines should have won – the odds were always stacked against the British recovering the islands before being forced to abandon the enterprise by the onset of the South Atlantic winter. Thus the neck of this hourglass is unusually interesting, for small variations in the performance of the combatants could have altered the outcome.

Although there is little evidence victory paid an electoral dividend to Prime Minister Margaret Thatcher, defeat undoubtedly would have forced her resignation, desire for which led some (mostly anonymous) politicians and civil servants to leak information designed to bring it about. Her refusal to compromise in the face of a gratuitous international crime was indispensable, as was the ability of the British armed forces to cobble together a rapid deployment at the extreme limit of their resources. But the crucial factor was that time pressure forced a normally stolid military culture to take hair-raising risks, dislocating the expectations of an enemy confident they lacked the guts to do so.

The sand at the bottom of the hourglass, until the Argentine military regime turned it over, was laid down by the erosion of international respect for Britain. The men who decided to invade the Falklands would not have done so if they had believed the British morally capable of reacting as they did. They were in good company. Few in the British political nation – by which I mean not merely the political parties but also and particularly the Civil Service, the media, and to some extent the academic community – believed it either. I spent much of my life alternating between spells abroad and at 'home'. On return, I was always struck by an atmosphere of cultivated hopelessness quite unlike anywhere else. Somewhat naturally the rest of the world accepted the British at their own poor self-estimation. Even today public opinion polls reveal widespread desire to get away from the burdens added to daily life by a uniquely British combination of oppressive institutional arrogance and often sadistic incompetence. The mood was deservedly much gloomier twenty-five years ago: but as one who was abroad to experience it I can testify that international perception of Britain as a self-defeated nation was changed, almost overnight, by the Falklands War.

Military operations are often conducted on the basis of subjective assessments of enemy morale. A basic assumption underlying the conflict was that the British were, in the opinion of the war's main architect, Admiral Jorge Anaya, unworthy heirs to a glorious heritage, the men mainly *maricones* and the women, consequently, *putas desesperadas* (frantic sluts). Much hangs on the nuances of the term *maricón*: although the direct translation is 'queer', it is widely used to describe timidity or, more precisely, the absence of Latin *virtus* (manliness). Thus a woman may describe herself as a *maricona* without any hint of Sapphic inclinations, and to call a man a *maricón* does not necessarily question his heterosexuality: but it definitely impugns his physical and moral courage.

Anaya was Naval Attaché in London from January 1975 to January 1976, when he was fawned on by officials anxious to win contracts for re-equipping the Argentine Navy. He returned to Argentina, making no attempt to conceal his contempt for all things British, to become Fleet Commander under the politically ambitious Admiral Massera. What elevates Anaya's words above the anecdotal is that he spoke them in early 1977, after he and Massera installed a military base on Southern Thule in the South Sandwich Islands, easternmost of the Falkland Islands Dependencies. Prime Minister James Callaghan's government sent an attack submarine to the South Atlantic (under orders not to respond if attacked but to 'surface or withdraw at high speed submerged'), but since the Argentines did not know about it until after the 1982 invasion, the gesture served no deterrent purpose whatever.*

What mattered to Massera and Anaya was that Foreign Secretary Anthony Crosland and, upon his death in February 1977, his successor David Owen, resumed negotiations on the sovereignty of the islands without insisting on the removal of the Southern Thule base, while feebly begging for the usurpation to be kept out of the public domain. It was the British request not to publicize the deed that drew Anaya's scathing comment, which should have been highlighted in British intelligence assessments after he became head of the Navy and a member of the ruling Junta in September 1981. It was unwise to dismiss his words as the ranting of a *boludo* – one whose balls, meaning no compliment to them, are bigger than his brains.

I first learned of the Falklands invasion in a hotel bar in San Salvador,

* In 1982 Callaghan alleged he had used SIS channels to let the Argentines know about it in 1978. He lied.

where contract CIA personnel and Argentine military advisers were cheering the news. What I was doing at the time demanded anonymity and I checked out of the hotel at once, lest the members of what I had silently christened the 'Quadruple A' (Argentine–American Anti-Communist Alliance) should identify me as one of the pinko-faggot Brits whose defeat they were prematurely celebrating. I also wished to get back as soon as possible to my Anglo-Argentine wife, one half of whose cultural identity had now attacked the other. Furthermore we were at the time living in Guatemala, governed by another military dictatorship and nurturing its own dispute with Britain over Belize.

Although the fraught circumstances in which I learned of the invasion may have coloured my perception, nothing I have read in the intervening years has modified my conviction that the deepest causes of the war were guilt, complicity and shame: a desire by the Argentine military to expiate their guilt for the 'Dirty War' they had waged against insurgents as a means to affirm their right to rule; US complicity in Argentina's attempt to export its infamous means of combating subversion, which misled the Argentines into overestimating their leverage in Washington; and the shame of a Britain forced to look in the mirror held up by a 'tin-pot dictator', to see how negligible she had become in the eyes of others.

Of course the guilt was not all Argentine, nor the complicity exclusively American, and not only the British felt ashamed. But as general explanations they hold up better than the reasons most cited by those who flinch from the reality of an irrational world: namely that the invasion was the expression of deeply felt Argentine outrage at the British 'usurpation' of Argentine sovereignty over the islands in 1833; that the USA tried to act as an honest broker; and that Britain acted to uphold sacred principles enshrined in the Charter of the United Nations – also of truth, justice and the right to drive on the left. Not to mention the wild-eyed explanations put forward by conspiracy theorists, chief among them that the war was deliberately provoked by the USA, in order to oblige Argentina and Brazil to abandon their nuclear weapons programmes, and/or by the wicked witch Thatcher, in order to strengthen her hand for the task of destroying the wonders of Socialism in Britain.

I knew how shocked Americans were by the long series of homosexual/

espionage scandals in Britain, but until that day in San Salvador I had not understood how it all came together in a certain kind of mind. According to the conversation overheard at the bar, the British were *maricones,* which explained both why they would bend over and spread 'em, and also why they were crypto-Communists. From what I had observed at the Buenos Aires Embassy in 1974–78, it seemed very likely the British government would indeed assume the position. After the Argentine base on Southern Thule was discovered and in response to a request for an up-to-date assessment for a pending session by the Joint Intelligence Committee (JIC), an all-agency embassy group war-gamed a number of Argentine options, including invasion, all of which projected British humiliation. Our reasoning was that even in the unlikely event of a robust British response, the Argentines, who pride themselves on clever rascality (*viveza criolla*), would simply return to the mainland and jeer at us, having made their point. Because it was so laughably improbable, we never considered the possibility that they might stay and fight it out if the British political class were to bestir itself to do something other than talk. Tactfully sanitized, this underlay the JIC assessment of 31 January 1977.

And yet . . . back in April 1975, when Callaghan was Foreign Secretary, he sent the Argentine government a formal warning that an attack on the islands would meet with 'a military response'. During 1976 my reporting from Buenos Aires on the methodology of the Dirty War provoked a (non-archivable) private letter to my Head of Mission from the head of the Latin American Department. The PL complained that my reports had prompted Callaghan to reject concessions on sovereignty with the trenchant words: 'I'm not handing over a thousand eight hundred Britons to a gang of fucking Fascists.' Not for nothing are senior members of the Foreign and Commonwealth Office (FCO) known as 'Mandarins', a caste immune from the mundane concerns of democratically elected politicians. They subverted Callaghan's correct assessment of what the British people would tolerate by encouraging successive junior ministers to believe they could square the circle of uncompromising Argentine demands and the adamant refusal of the islanders to be handed over to their appallingly misgoverned neighbour. The FCO judged that British politicians might talk the talk, but when it came down to it, would not walk the walk: therefore an explicit commitment to meet force with force was abandoned. Instead a policy of appeasement was adopted and, just as it did in the 1930s, it encouraged aggression.

There was no 'intelligence failure' – the British government was well served with hard information from technical and human sources about Argentine actions and intentions. There was, however, an intellectual failure systemic to the political nation. The Chinese Nationalist leader Chiang Kai-shek once quipped that British officials wore monocles so they should not see more than they could understand, and it is hard to decide whether the British genius for 'muddling through' is the consequence or the source of a chronic reluctance to think things through. The causes of this aversion may be debatable, but the result is that inconvenient facts are routinely brushed aside or, worse, deliberately misrepresented in the formulation of policy, which then becomes set in stone because of a paramount concern to deny the possibility of error, even long in the past. The outcome is an incoherent and arbitrary political culture that gives the impression of being wrapped in a cocoon of impenetrable conceit.

The attitude still dominates British public life, but it was even more clueless a generation ago. Talk of 'moral leadership' independent of economic and military power was still common, the National Health Service was supposed to be the 'envy of the world', and so on. With regard to the Falklands, such analysis as took place prior to the war was further conditioned by the same Cold War considerations that led US Lieutenant General Nutting to call it 'the wrong war in the wrong place at the wrong time and with the wrong participants'. Of course he did not mean it could ever be wrong to make war on a murderous regime that has attacked you, only that he wished it had not become necessary.

From wishing to believing can be a very short step. Astonishingly, the narrative most frequently cited remains a book written by the journalists Max Hastings and Simon Jenkins in 1982–83, the best of the post-war flurry but a snapshot of partially observed reality nonetheless. Unfortunately much of the subsequent literature in English dug no deeper, and the virtual exclusion of the Argentine dimension nurtured a facile judgement that the war was 'unnecessary'. On taking power in 1997 the Labour government commissioned an 'Official History', opening confidential government files exclusively to Professor Sir Lawrence Freedman in breach of the thirty year rule: a harbinger of the use they were to make of their anaemic Freedom of Information Act to break with the convention that an incoming government shall not use material from classified files to discredit its predecessor. Presumably the intention was to demystify the 'Falklands Factor' they believed kept Labour out of power for eighteen years. Now, with plenty of skeletons piled up in their own cupboard, they no doubt regret their decision, which may explain why publication of Freedman's book was delayed past the date of the 2005 General Election. I think it unlikely another Anglocentric account of events a generation ago, however authoritative and compendious, would have swung a single vote: but a neurotic concern with information control is the distinguishing characteristic of New Labour.

For one who can read both Spanish and English, the main obstacle to writing a balanced history is that with one brave exception no Argentine author, not even those who denounce the mass murders of the Dirty War, concedes that their 'rights' in this matter may be questionable.* Félix Barreto, one of the Argentine conscripts interviewed by Vincent Bramley – both veterans of the savage fight on Mount Longdon – realized as battle drew near that: 'the English were not just here to reclaim something they thought was theirs, they were coming to take back what belonged to them.' The majority of his countrymen, however, appear to believe that shrilly repeating the mantra *las Malvinas son argentinas* is sufficient argument, and that if they keep it up for long enough the islands will eventually be given them. In the opinion of the brave and resourceful islander Trudi McPhee – who deserved more than the Commendation she received for the assistance she gave 3 Para before Longdon – that is precisely what will happen, because 'the Foreign Office will just give us away. I mean, we are just an absolute pain in the arse [and they] spend every waking hour trying to think of some devious way to get rid of us.'

I'm sure she's right, but I doubt if there is much conscious thought involved. FCO prestige took a hit in 1982 that still rankles. As an institution it blames the Falklanders for unreasonably refusing to be handed over to a genocidal dictatorship: for to do otherwise would be to admit gross, contumacious error, and an assumption of institutional infallibility is the psychological underpinning of the type of personality drawn to the Civil Service.

★ The honourable exception is Carlos Escudé – see **Chapter 2**.

But it should never – ever – be forgotten that until 1982 British policy was to hand over the islanders to what Whitehall knew very well was a thoroughly evil regime. The manner in which the policy was implemented betrays at best self-deception, at worst the hypocrisy for which British policy-making is famed. Even if one accepts that a dishonest ability to make a virtue of necessity is the essence of diplomacy, that still leaves necessity to be defined. There is a very clear line beyond which willingness to accommodate another's point of view ceases to be a virtue and becomes moral cowardice.

Unfortunately that line is seldom drawn. It was with some astonishment that I read an interview in 2004 with Dr Rowan Williams, the new Primate of the Church of England and allegedly a 'formidable theologian', in which he said suicide bombers' sincere faith in the rightness of their cause in some way redeemed their actions, without the morally catatonic British media so much as raising an eyebrow. The same formidable theology appears to have animated the priests who blessed the torture and murder of thousands in Argentina. I have met several Dirty Warriors, but my only personal experience of their stock-in-trade came at the hands of a *mestizo* Guatemalan police sergeant who just liked to hear white men scream. I shudder to think of falling into the hands of the soldiers of Christ the King who ran the Argentine Dirty War, for they would have tortured me until, unscripted, I confessed whatever it was they wanted to hear, with the added horror of anonymous death to follow. But of the sincerity of their belief there can be no doubt.

There is an oppressive amount of literature on the diplomatic background to the war, most of which fails the test of Ockham's Razor. An attack by a vicious militaristic regime on a political society that gave every indication of soul-deep poltroonery is not a particularly complicated issue. Furthermore, the extremely narrow window of opportunity for British military success shines a cold light on those who sought to thwart or delay the counter-attack. Despite a patriotic lead by party chief Michael Foot, a few Labourites broke ranks, and among the Conservatives the faction associated with ex-leader Edward Heath was spitefully defeatist. Their motives were obvious. The main harm was done by the BBC, which gave disproportionate prominence to those who opposed the war and falsely projected significant divisions within the country. It also broadcast operational details, courtesy of never-investigated leaks from the Ministry of Defence (MoD), which might have cost British lives. Ironically, the Argentines did not believe an outfit called the British Broadcasting Corporation would do such a thing and dismissed it as disinformation. To what degree the BBC's misrepresentation of the national mood encouraged the Junta to overplay its hand is hard to say. It certainly left me, far away and cut off from public sentiment in Britain, convinced there would be a last minute sell-out.

As time went on, however, I wryly noticed the BBC was paying the war decreasing attention as evidence of British success began to mount: and I was delighted to see every key assumption of the 1977 embassy conclave proved wrong. It was logical to assume the Argentines would sail home after demonstrating their ability to seize the islands whenever they wished. Yet they stayed. We assumed the Soviet bloc and 'the South' would prevent any UN resolution in our favour. They did not. We assumed Washington would broker a face-saving formula to permit London to wriggle out of an inconvenient commitment. Well, we almost got that right. We did not believe Britain could mount a successful counter-invasion. Yet it did.

If the Argentine Junta can be forgiven for believing the British government would accept the invasion as a *fait accompli*, everything else the Argentines did could scarcely have been better designed to ensure defeat. Far from becoming the beneficiaries of worldwide anti-British feeling they found themselves isolated, not realizing the negative historical associations evoked by the sight of a dictator haranguing a baying mob from a balcony. Argentina had only one military ally during the war – the Peruvian government, with which it had been planning a joint war on their common neighbour Chile. Knowing they were next if the Argentines won, the Chileans lent the British all support short of going to war themselves, fear of which kept most of the Argentine troops best conditioned and equipped to fight in the Falklands guarding the long Chilean–Argentine frontier.

Few things more clearly illustrate the culpable ignorance of British 'Progressives' than their insistence that a last minute Peruvian proposal, designed to delay operations until winter made a landing impossible, was a viable alternative torpedoed by Thatcher when she authorized the sinking of the *General Belgrano*. That Defence Secretary Nott exaggerated the imminent threat posed by the cruiser in a gratuitously false statement to the House of Commons, and that Thatcher defended the falsehood, is another matter altogether.

Beyond sketching in the usually overlooked wider context of the war, my concern has been to pay proper attention to those sent to redeem the failures of their respective political nations. If in the following pages I dwell more on the Argentines than some may judge their efforts deserve, it is to redress the balance of a story so far told, in English, almost exclusively from the point of view of the victors. But above all I have sought to emphasize the importance of the seldom adequately valued third party: the terrain. Topography not only conditioned how the battles were fought but is often the only truly reliable witness. The tunnel vision of combat, compounded in the Falklands by the fact that all but one of the major land battles were fought entirely at night, makes it more than usually important to recreate the framework on which to assemble the patchwork quilt of memoirs and after-battle reports. Having spent many days exploring the battle hills around Stanley, and after months working to trace the outlines of the quartzite ridges running along them onto the uncertain contours of the Ordnance Survey map – using aerial photographs and over 200 of my own taken from ground level – I am confident my maps are a close approximation to reality.

The officers who planned the battles had only the Ordnance Survey map to work with and lacked the precise details of enemy deployments available to the historian. Hindsight, of course, reveals a number of things that might have been done better, but even in the light of all the information now available the British campaign remains an extraordinary triumph over natural and man-made adversity, and a remarkable epic of arms. Brigadier Thompson's modest memoir insisted the war was *No Picnic,* but it has suited a broad range of commentators to portray the outcome as a foregone conclusion once the British landed. It demeans both sides to portray the Argentine troops as sheep to the slaughter: they fought well enough when they were properly led, and sometimes when they were not.

Zigzagging like a spavined goat up the steep sides of the battle hills, I could only wonder at the fortitude of the men who assaulted them heavily laden, in sodden boots and impossibly awkward combat webbing, with grenades raining down and in the teeth of fire from snipers, machine-guns, mortars and bazookas. Even more amazing that so much lethal ordnance could have been thrown at so many to kill and injure comparatively few, particularly on Mount Harriet, where only one Marine was killed and thirteen others wounded during an attack on an entrenched battalion. Caught by a hail-laden katabatic wind in the saddle where the Scots were pinned down for hours on Tumbledown, I realized why the defenders usually did not see the attackers approaching, and why many of them wore dust goggles: the strong prevailing wind, like the British advance, comes from the west, straight into the streaming eyes of anyone trying to peer into the menacing darkness.

When I took shelter in a naturally formed rock sangar (defensive position), it was likewise apparent why British artillery was not as murderous here as elsewhere in the wars of the twentieth century. Possibly not even a direct hit by a 105mm shell could have destroyed my shelter. I was to find only one clearly pulverized Argentine bunker, on the saddle between Mounts Tumbledown and William, probably the command post hit by the first laser-designated bomb dropped in anger by British forces. The other reason for the relatively low incidence of artillery casualties was the dense peat overlying rock or clay strata, giving new meaning to the term 'groundwater'. Although annual rainfall in the Falklands is less than in Britain, water lies at or near the surface even on the steepest slopes, seeming to defy the pull of gravity and the physics of soil absorption alike.

The islanders and returning veterans have marked a few of the spots where individual exploits took place. No visitor can fail to be moved by the cairn marking the spot on Darwin Hill where Lieutenant Colonel 'H' Jones, CO of 2 Para, was mortally wounded while winning the Victoria Cross. There should perhaps also be a marker at the nearby place where Argentine Sub-Lieutenant Estévez won his country's highest award for gallantry, ful-filling a premonition that he would die in battle. Only a meagre stick marks the trench from which the undecorated Lance Corporal José Luis Ríos of the 12th Infantry Regiment shot Jones, to be killed in turn by a rocket from a 66mm anti-tank weapon fired by Corporal Abols DCM. On the other side of the feature, a small pile of stones placed by his comrades during the South Atlantic Medal Association pilgrimage in November 2002 marks the spot where Corporal Prior, likewise undecorated, died helping to rescue the gut-shot Private Worrall.*

---

* British ranks used for both sides throughout. Except in the case of men with common surnames I omit christian names and, for the Argentines, their second (matronymic) surnames.

Another cairn and a cross marks where Sergeant Ian McKay of 3 Para fell while winning the Victoria Cross on Mount Longdon, the spot also immortalized by the haunting *Daily Express* photograph of his back-lit helmet on an upturned rifle. Not far away seventeen-year-old Private Burt, the youngest soldier killed on either side, died following him. Fifty yards away the characteristic tuning fork shape of the .50-calibre heavy machine-gun bunker that held up 3 Para for hours can still be seen. The gun was manned by Marine Private 1st Class Scaglione and three others, killed when Corporal McLaughlin (later wounded by a rocket and then killed by artillery when walking to the Regimental Aid Post), calling on his section to follow him because he was bulletproof, climbed an exposed ridge above the bunker to attack it with grenades. Within 40 yards of each other along the jagged rocky rim of the ferociously defended summit 'bowl', memorials mark where Private Laing was killed trying to rescue the dying Lance Corporal Murdoch soon after the start of combat and where, nine hours later, a rocket killed Corporal McCarthy and Privates Hedicker and West.

This was an intimate war in which other, less celebrated incidents were often well enough described to enable me, with the indispensable help of local guides Patrick Watts, Ken Greenland of Darwin House and Tony Smith of Discovery Falklands, to identify where they probably took place. On Tumbledown there is a rocky alcove, carpeted with old 7.6mm bullet cases, which looks out on the crest where Lieutenant Mitchell and two other Scots Guards were shot when incautiously admiring the view from the newly won summit. Only the nickname 'Pedro' given to him by visiting Falklanders identifies the tenacious soldier who died holding up the Scots from the crags at the eastern end of Tumbledown, so inaccessible that his body was not recovered until the Royal Pioneers came with a team of civilian morticians in January 1983. Like C.S. Forester's *Brown on Resolution*, 'Pedro' could have sat out the battle; but instead he fought on alone and it is sad his name is not known and honoured.

The great Argentine novelist (and Anglophile) Jorge Luis Borges dismissed the war as 'two bald men fighting over a comb'. Not a lot of hair has grown since then, although some of the implants in the British pate seem to have taken root. In 2001-02 Argentina went through five presidents, three in one week, and declared the largest sovereign debt default in history. Her political culture remains as corrupt and strident as ever, and is likely to doom the current economic revival as it has all its predecessors. Meanwhile, the British belatedly recognized that the terms 'industry' and 'nationalized' form a tautology, but in the struggle to establish this self-evident fact the Civil Service was bought off with additional privileges that loom over posterity with the finality of a headsman's axe. Britain has enjoyed a long period of prosperity, but with the windfall revenue from North Sea oil and gas running out and the friction of ever-increasing regulations and taxes discouraging domestic enterprise, it remains to be seen for how long productivity gains in the private sector can continue to hold the line against the 'British disease' resurgent in the morbidly obese state apparatus.

But a short, tightly limited war was never likely to affect long-term trends in the combatant nations. This one was fought very specifically to return the islands to the form of government desired by their inhabitants, and the prosperous tranquillity enjoyed by that small community today confirms the wisdom of their choice. However it came about, in the end it was an honourable deed to rescue the Falkland Islanders from tyranny and, consequently, to reverse the policy of malicious neglect that had for so long threatened their survival.

NOTE TO THE PAPERBACK EDITION

The response to my request for comments by participants was gratifyingly favourable. I spoke to none when researching the book, and still believe that memoirs and interviews are decreasingly reliable the greater the time elapsed. However I have made a few significant changes, to correct poor wording that seemed to suggest Professor Sir Lawrence Freedman was a new Labour stooge, and to moderate the harsh verdict I reached about Admiral Sir John Woodward on the basis of his peers' memoirs. For the first, I regret what was collateral damage in a blast against the shameless mendacity of the New Labour regime. For the second, it is unwise for officers to depend too much on their campaign diaries, particularly where they 'vented' their frustration at the pressures of the moment. I should not, however, have based my judgement on the first editions of the memoirs in question: first-time authors, in particular, do not appreciate that strongly worded statements often jump off the page and acquire a life independent of the modifying context within which they were written. I have no such excuse and in the following pages have edited those passages where I previously failed to make sufficient allowance for these factors.

1 Casus Belli

THE 'KELPERS' WERE what it was all about. A small community of people from many backgrounds, eking out a living on an archipelago where the wool trade was the sole significant economic activity. Unsophisticated and shy, what they wanted above all was to be left alone. That may not have been why their ancestors first came to the islands: but it was why their descendants remained, and many of the newer arrivals specifically came to the islands in order to get away from government interference. Some believed the Falklands would be a safe haven in the event of a third world war, among them the Canadians Bill and Barbara Curtis, who with their two young children took up residence in what they fondly believed would be a sanctuary of peace in March 1982, just weeks before the Argentine invasion. Even if Argentina had not been so criminally misgoverned throughout most of her history, the attraction of British sovereignty exercised lightly from 8,000 miles away would still have been strong. However there was also a deep historic and cultural commitment. In the Commons debate following the invasion, Michael Foot, Leader of the Opposition and a lifelong pacifist, spoke to the heart of the matter:

> There is no question in the Falkland Islands of any colonial depend-
> ence or anything of the sort. It is a question of people who wish to be
> associated with this country and who have built their whole lives on

Map 1
ATLANTIC THEATRE
OF OPERATIONS

Canada

USA

45°

30°

Cuba

15°

0°

Perú

15°

Bolivia

Santiago

Buenos Aires

ARGENTINA

Bahía Blanca

30°

Com. Rivadavia

45°

Falkland Is.

Stanley

×1914

Ushuaia

Cape Horn

South Shetland Is.

© Hugh Bicheno

Venezuela

Colombia

Brazil

Paraguay

Uruguay

Chile

Patagonia

1914

Montevideo

×1939

Mar del Plata

Rio de Janeiro

Guyana

Sur.

Fr.

Equator

Tropic of Cancer

Azores

Madeira

Canary Is.

Cape Verde Is.

Bissau

Mauritania

Guinea

Sierra
Leone

Liberia

Gambia

Ivory
Coast

Ireland

UK

N

B

France

Sw

Port

Spain

Gibraltar

Morocco

W. Sahara

Mali

Burkina
Faso

Ghana

Togo
Benin

Nigeria

Eq. Guinea

Gabon

D

Sw

Germany

Poland

Czech

Austria

Hun

Yugoslavia

Italy

Tunisia

Algeria

Libya

Niger

Chad

Cameroon

C.A.R.

Congo

Zaire

Ascension Is.
4260 miles from Britain
3915 miles to Falklands

St Helena

Angola

Tropic of Capricorn

Namibia

S. Africa

Cape Town

Tristan da Cunha

Grytviken

South Georgia

South
Sandwich Is.

Southern Thule

S. Orkney Is.

0°

15°

0'   250   500   750

0°   0°

15°   15°

30°   30°

45°   45°

60°   60°

0   250   500   750   1000

Statute miles

60°   45°   30°   15°

0°   15°   30°   45°   60°

Latitude

the basis of association with this country. We have a moral duty, a political duty, and every other kind of duty to ensure that it is sustained . . . So far, they have been betrayed . . . The government must now prove by deeds – they will never be able to do it by words – that they are not responsible for the betrayal and cannot be faced with that charge.

When in the islands I was appalled to learn that post-war visitors from Britain used to ask the Kelpers if they thought they were 'worth it'. One doubts visitors would dare ask the same question in Northern Ireland. I found a representative example of the attitude in a book by a retired Army officer, who quotes an unnamed source to describe the pre-war islanders as 'a mainly drunken, decadent, immoral and indolent collection of drop-outs', which sounds like Admiral Anaya on the subject of the British in general. The author goes on to write of the islanders 'relying on the generous teat of British tax money' and of a 'small, self-centred and fragile society'. As to small and self-centred, a product of the military womb really should choose his words more carefully. With regard to 'the generous teat', the one constant in Falkland Islands history before 1982 was official neglect and the dis-couragement even of the ship repair, chandlery and bunkerage services they were well located to provide. In most years the islands produced more in tax revenues than they cost to run, and the Kelpers' present day self-sufficiency in all matters save defence has a long history. But even if they were as described, in what way could that diminish their right to the normal protection of British custom and law? If the armed forces do not exist to defend British citizens against armed aggression then let us by all means abolish them, dismiss the bloated bureaucracy that nominally exists to support them and install an answering machine that says 'We surrender'.

A number of authors who treat the Kelpers as objects to be negotiated away seem to believe they are an imperial hangover and thus a distraction from Britain's true destiny in an ever-closer European Union. It is a peculiar fact of modern political life that in Britain, alone among the members of the EU, the Europhile case goes hand in hand with vicious denigration of the nation's historic character. The premise seems to be that an identity forged in opposition to Spanish, then French and then German visions of a pan-European empire must perforce be hostile to the Union, but the phenomenon is quite a bit older than the Treaty of Rome and was decried by Winston Churchill in 1933:

> The worst difficulties from which we suffer do not come from without. They come from . . . a peculiar type of brainy people always found in our country, who, if they add something to its culture, take much from its strength. Our difficulties come from the mood of unwarrantable self-abasement into which we have been cast by a powerful section of our own intellectuals.*

Those who consider themselves 'right thinking' often impugn the intelligence of people who obstruct their vision of a perfect world. The Kelpers have collected a lot of flak from people like that, yet one must ask if it was not extraordinarily stupid to expect them to put their fate in the hands of Argentina, a state that has no respect for international treaties, does not pay its debts and does not even abide by its own laws. The 1982 war came about for the same reason industrial relations in Britain reached a nadir during the preceding decade – if you reward bad behaviour, you will get more of it. The British Civil Service is full of clever people, who, like the fox of the adage, believe they know many things. Meanwhile, like the stalwart hedgehog, the Kelpers know one big thing: Argentina will settle for nothing less than dominion over them and no meaningful negotiation can take place when the minimum demand of one party is greater than the maximum concession the other can make.

It is a good question whether Kelper society had much in common with modern Britain, but even their British citizenship was under threat by the Immigration Act of 1971 and the British Nationality Act of 1981, the first creating the concept of 'patriality' or right to abode and the second denying it to the islanders as well as to the hordes of Africans and Asians from the old colonies supposedly anxious to immigrate. Denying automatic right of abode to British passport holders made them in effect stateless persons, in breach of international law. It put the Kelpers against the wall, as unless they returned to Britain to give birth, which most could not afford to do, their children would not even have the right to a British passport. The injustice

---

* Speech to the Royal Society of St George, 24 April 1933.

was corrected after the war, which begs the question why an exception was not made for them when the 1981 law was drafted. There can be little doubt the intention was to force them into the arms of Argentina. They were already required to hold an Argentine identity document in order to travel, which thanks to the Communications Agreement of 1971 required passage on Argentine aircraft through Argentina. The next step was to take away their British passports.

SO, WHAT HAD THE Kelpers done to deserve being treated like a dog turd on the British shoe? A few moments in Stanley's quintessentially English Christ Church Cathedral should make any 'patrial' Brit blush. On the right-hand side of the nave is a plaque to the memory of Rear Admiral Sir Christopher Cradock and the men of the obsolete armoured cruisers *Good Hope* and *Monmouth,* who sailed from Stanley on 23 October 1914 and nine days later were lost in battle with a modern squadron under the command of Vice Admiral Graf Maximilian von Spee, off the coast of Chile at Coronel. The plaque was paid for by subscription of the islanders and crew of the pre-dreadnought battleship *Canopus* at a memorial service for the fallen on 29 November 1914, when they also prayed for reinforcements to arrive from Britain before Spee.

Canopus, whose mechanical unreliability caused Cradock to leave her behind, was deliberately grounded in the inner harbour, her light armament unshipped and mounted around the eastern peninsula to repel a landing.* The entrance to the harbour was mined and observers for her 12-inch guns posted on nearby high ground, known ever since as Canopus Hill. Hurricane force winds hampered these preparations and another plaque commemorates seven members of the Falkland Islands Volunteer Force, drowned on 1 December when their boat swamped on active duty. On 7 December 1914 the lookouts reported warships approaching, soon revealed to be Vice Admiral Doveton Sturdee's fleet of eight, including the battlecruisers *Invincible* and *Inflexible,* specifically built to destroy fast armoured cruisers like Spee's *Gneisenau* and *Scharnhorst.* Spee, meanwhile, had decided to destroy the wireless station on Hooker's Point and, less than twenty-four hours after

---

* One of the 12-pounders, in remarkably good condition, can be seen at Gypsy Cove. For the geography around Stanley see **Diagram 3** (p. 108) and **Maps 4, 6** and **21** (pp. 120, 125 and 201).

Sturdee steamed into Stanley, the domestic servant Christina Goss, posted along with a boy messenger as a lookout on Fitzroy Ridge, spotted smoke to the south. She sent the boy running down to Fitzroy Settlement, whence her employer Muriel Felton reported the news to Stanley on one of the first telephones installed on the islands. Sturdee, caught with crews ashore, fires banked and both battlecruisers coaling, needed two hours to make ready for battle and was saved by *Canopus,* which opened fire at maximum range. Live rounds from her fore turret fell short, but her aft gun crew had loaded dummy shell the night before in the expectation of a competitive practise shoot in the morning, and one of these ricocheted off the waves to hit *Gneisenau.* Spee turned away at full speed, but *Invincible* and *Inflexible* were five knots faster and, after a long chase and prodigious expenditure of ammunition, sank Spee's armoured cruisers, while the light cruisers *Cornwall, Kent* and *Glasgow* sank their opposite numbers *Nürnberg* and *Leipzig.*

The islanders built a galleon-topped monument to the victory on a promontory jutting into Stanley Harbour, and a few hundred yards away in the Museum can be seen the patent of the extinct baronetcy of Sturdee of the Falkland Islands, donated by the admiral's granddaughter in 1973. The next ship to bear the name *Invincible* was the light aircraft carrier the Argentines believed they sank or severely damaged on 30 May 1982, her return to port in apparently impeccable condition being taken as indisputable proof of limitless British guile and duplicity. *Glasgow,* the sole survivor of Coronel, was the sixth of that name and has a street named after her in Stanley. True to the ship's motto *Memor es Tuorum* (Be Mindful of Your Own) the eighth *Glasgow* returned to fight another Battle of the Falkland Islands in 1982, and was no less lucky to have a 1,000lb bomb pass through her without exploding on 12 May.

The archaeology of remembrance on these once-forgotten islands includes two 6-inch gun turrets on Canopus Hill, overlooking Stanley Airport, one with a rusty 'Fuck the Argentines' scratched into its flaking paint. These guns were dismounted from *Lancaster* in 1916 and originally installed on Mount Low and Sapper Hill. They were moved to their present location by a battalion of the West Yorkshire Regiment stationed in Stanley during World War II, against the threat of an Argentine attack while Britain was otherwise engaged. It is an eerie feeling to stand under the old guns and look south over Hooker's Point, where the wireless station once stood, and beyond to where Spee's squadron was annihilated. The station was later moved to Moody Brook valley, where the old concrete anchors for the transmission tower provided some precarious cover for Argentine artillerymen in 1982. Eerier still to realize that Hooker's Point was the place from which the Argentines fired the Exocets that near-missed *Avenger* on 27 May and hit *Glamorgan* in the early morning of 12 June, killing thirteen of her crew.

The area also saw action during World War II. On 13 December 1939 three cruisers under the command of Commodore Harwood gave battle off the mouth of the River Plate to a German 'pocket battleship' named for the admiral killed off the Falklands twenty-five years earlier. *Graf Spee* quickly put the medium cruiser *Exeter* out of action and she limped to Stanley for repairs, too badly damaged to keep her crew on board. On her way she passed the heavy cruiser *Cumberland,* racing from Stanley to join Harwood's light cruiser *Ajax* and her sister ship, the New Zealand *Achilles*, off Montevideo, where the German warship took refuge. Unlike her namesake, *Graf Spee* did not go down fighting but was ignominiously scuttled and her crew ferried to pro-Axis Argentina. The next warship to bear the name *Exeter* was the best equipped of the British warships for air defence in 1982 and shot down four Argentine aircraft between 30 May and 13 June. One of the battle ensigns flown by HMNZS *Achilles* in 1939 hangs over the Cradock plaque in the cathedral, and on 6 May 1982, following the loss of HMS *Sheffield,* Prime Minister Muldoon of New Zealand offered to send HMNZS *Canterbury* to replace her.

During World War I, as well as sending many of their sons to serve in the Royal Navy, the miserably poor Kelpers not only donated an aircraft to the Royal Flying Corps, but also thousands of pounds to a number of war-related charities. They also voted 10 per cent of their annual customs revenues to help pay off Imperial War Loans. During World War II, 150 Kelpers served with the British armed forces and in addition to £30–40,000 donated to a number of war charities, the little community gave over £70,000 to the British government, some of which paid for ten Spitfires flown by 92 Squadron from Biggin Hill during the Battle of Britain. A plaque in the cathedral records that Kelper Flight Lieutenant Donald Rafur was killed early in that battle, on 8 August 1940.

Then there is the potent metaphor of the great Victorian engineer Isambard Kingdom Brunel's *Great Britain,* the first iron-hulled, steam powered, propeller driven and – when launched in 1843 – the largest ship in the world. In 1886, by then a purely sail-powered freighter, she was damaged off Cape Horn and limped into Stanley, where she was condemned. Bought by the Falkland Islands Company (FIC), for the next fifty years she was used as a storage hulk. The FIC wished to scuttle her at sea in 1937 but at the insistence of the Kelpers she was driven aground in Sparrow Cove, whence she was salvaged in 1970 and towed back to Bristol for loving restoration, now on permanent display in the dock where she was built. It is almost unbearably apt that the rusted, battered hull of the *Great Britain* was removed not long after Whitehall decided the islanders should be sold out to Argentina.

THE FUSE FOR THE Falklands War was lit in 1968, when Michael Stewart, Foreign Secretary in the Labour administration of 1966–70, agreed a Memorandum of Understanding with Nicanor Costa Méndez, Foreign Minister to President Juan Carlos Onganía, first among nominal equals in the Military Junta that toppled civilian President Illia's democratically elected government in 1966. Onganía's regime was a dress rehearsal for the *Proceso de Reorganización Nacional* (PNR) of 1976–83. Congress was dissolved, political parties suppressed, executive and legislative power vested in the president, and the public administration shared out among the three armed forces. The key passage in the Memorandum stated that when it could be shown to be in the *best interests* of the inhabitants (my italics) 'the Government of the United Kingdom as part of such a final settlement *will recognize* Argentina's sovereignty over the Islands from a date to be agreed.' The best summary of the legal and diplomatic background to the dispute was written at this time – by an American.* He concluded that 'on the basis of history, or equity, or international law, therefore, it would appear that Argentina would experience some difficulty in obtaining a settlement satisfactory to her national pride.' But, the author went on, Argentina's best ally was British officialdom. Of the Memorandum he commented:

* J.C.J. Metford's introduction to the 1982 edition of Julius Goebel's *The Struggle for the Falkland Islands.*

Whether the Falklanders will be allowed to say that they approve of such benevolence, or whether it will be imposed upon them, remains to be seen. They themselves know exactly where they stand. Rather than accept Argentine rule, for which they have no respect, they will leave the islands from which, against considerable odds, they and their predecessors have contrived for over 130 years to extract a livelihood.

Why, then, not settle the matter with a compulsory purchase and a generous resettlement? Anyone who has worked for government knows the answer: it was cheaper to cheat them, and bureaucrats are always strong to the weak and weak to the strong. Pursuant to that philosophy, while no money could be found to improve the security of the islanders, no price was too great to appease Argentina. Stewart and the FCO even sweetened the pot by throwing in South Georgia, a separate crown dependency to which Argentina had no claim whatever, as well the uninhabited Falkland Islands dependencies of South Shetland, South Orkney and South Sandwich Islands. And at whose feet did they wish to lay these offerings? None other than Costa, who when he returned to the Foreign Ministry in 1981, was second only to Anaya in urging the invasion. Costa's character and the absence of principle in Argentine diplomacy was displayed during his first spell in office, when he threatened war with Uruguay over Martín Garciá, a small island very close to the Uruguayan bank of the River Plate. Costa rejected Uruguay's case for possession on grounds of geographical propinquity – although this lies at the core of the Argentine claim to the Falklands – and asserted the Argentine right on grounds of historic possession: the very principle he denied in the case of the Falklands.

Costa left office in 1970 convinced the British could be bullied into giving up the Falklands. What he failed to evaluate properly was that after Stewart was roasted in the House of Commons when he tried to defend the Memorandum, to the mortification of the FCO henceforth the paramountcy of 'the wishes' of the islanders replaced the weasel words 'best interests' in the formulation of policy: a gallows on which to hang any British government that sought to renege on the commitment. Despicably, having failed to sell out the islanders by command, the FCO determined to manoeuvre them into a position where they would have no choice but to accept Argentine sovereignty 'voluntarily'. The man most prominently associated with this policy was Hugh Carless, head of the Latin American Department in 1973–77 and Chargé d'Affaires in Buenos Aires in 1977–80: but the arrogance was institutional. The result was to encourage Argentine aggression, exacerbate Kelper distrust and to mislead ministers into believing that hard decisions could be fudged indefinitely. Carless was a personable, intelligent and experienced diplomat, who was fully aware that Argentina had imperialist designs in the South Atlantic (in Mandarin, a 'forward policy'), and who sincerely believed in the policy he advocated. His efforts irresistibly draw to mind the old ditty:

> They told him the job couldn't be done
> And he laughed and said 'Lead me to it!'
> So they showed him the job that couldn't be done
> And he couldn't bloody well do it.

The supposedly stupid islanders were right and the 'best and brightest' wrong about the possibility of squaring the circle with Argentina. At the time I did not share in the delusion that the Argentines could be appeased, but I admit to having been too much of an apparatchik to concern myself with the human consequences. But if we are not wise or humane before, we should at least try to be after the event. While Argentine authors have been morally blind in their accounts of the war, many of their English-speaking peers have also adopted a view akin to Talleyrand's on the murder of the Duc d'Enghien by Napoleon – 'worse than a crime, it was a mistake.' As a result, those responsible for the 'mistake' were never obliged to answer for the fact that Falkland Islands policy pursued prior to 1982 was not flawed because it failed to prevent a war, but because it was intellectually dishonest and ethically indefensible. Rather than wondering if the islanders were 'worth it', one should ask instead: how could a once great nation have got itself into a situation of such deep moral debt to this little community, so much so that it had to fight a war it might easily have lost in order to redeem its own honour?

2 Guilt

GUILT IS WHAT NORMAL people feel when they have done something wicked. Those who feel no guilt for evil actions were once called psychopaths and regarded as a menace to society for as long as they were at liberty. Now they are said to suffer from 'an antisocial type of personality disorder' and are therefore supposedly capable of rehabilitation. Psychopathic regimes enjoy much the same dispensation because there are always those in the wider world who argue they can be reformed through 'engagement', usually in order to obtain commercial advantage but also from a belief that any successor regime is likely to be as bad or worse. In fact anybody with the slightest historical awareness knows such regimes are unreformable and respond only to coercion. But it requires politically suicidal intellectual honesty and moral courage to argue the case in democratic societies, where voters invariably prefer emollient falsehood over objective truth: until confronted with the consequences of living a lie, at which point they no less invariably blame the politicians for having pandered to them.

The international community was confronted with a profound moral conundrum on 24 March 1976, when a military coup in Argentina overthrew the elected but chaotic government of 'Isabelita' (María Estela Martínez de Perón), vice-president and successor to her husband, the *caudillo* Juan Domingo Perón, upon his death on 1 July 1974.* Pitifully inadequate,

---

* *Caudillo* is the Spanish equivalent of *Duce* in Italian or *Führer* in German.

Isabelita depended heavily on the advice and moral support of her spiritualist guide, Minister of Social Welfare José López Rega (known as 'The Warlock'), and was completely lost when the military forced his resignation and exile in July 1975. Burned by previous efforts to govern against the will of the Peronista popular majority, the military were reluctant to assume direct responsibility for a society where the hallucinatory had become commonplace. They tried to govern through Isabelita but, provoked by terrorist attacks and near-total breakdown of law and order, they were drawn into the void of authority they had helped to create. The timing of the coup was also influenced by a desire of the other service chiefs to pre-empt an attempt by the Commander-in-Chief of the Navy, the handsome and charismatic Admiral Massera, to become Isabelita's main man and thus, he hoped, to don the political mantle of her late husband. There was always a degree of madness inherent in Massera's ambition – the Army would never have allowed the emergence of another Perón from its own ranks, still less from one of a different branch of the armed forces.

Nonetheless the palpable, almost electric aura of a society completely out of control during the latter months of Isabelita's presidency helps to explain why nobody in Argentina protested the coup, and why it was greeted internationally with a sigh of relief. It did not seem possible for the new regime to be worse, and diplomats permitted hope to triumph over experience in welcoming the 'Process of National Reorganization' (PNR), announced by the original Military Junta of General Videla for the Army, Massera for the Navy, and General Agosti for the Air Force. I recall drafting a Despatch for my Head of Mission, in which I inserted the caveat that a period of submission to arbitrary authority reduces the probability of responsible behaviour by the governed thereafter. But overall the stated objectives of the PNR seemed unexceptionable. If they had, as promised, strengthened the rule of law, put the public finances on a sustainable basis, and had then presided over an orderly return to civilian rule, they would have deserved the heartfelt thanks of their countrymen.

Unfortunately, to have hoped things would improve was to fall into what the Argentine sociologist Carlos Escudé regards as the fundamental error of employing rational criteria to assess a pathological culture. Escudé convincingly argues that the pathology dates back to the early twentieth century, when the extreme Nationalist ideology that animates Argentine public education and political debate was invented. Originally a construct of reactionary Roman Catholic Conservatives, subsequently adopted by their nominal opponents in the Radical Party, then by the military rulers who overthrew them and finally by Peronismo, '[the Nationalist construct] represented a certain consensus in an otherwise deeply divided country: it was and still is like the white of the eyes, shared by all men and women without realizing it . . . a continuity that quite possibly represents the very identity of the new and artificially generated nation that is Argentina.'

In 1941 Perón returned from a spell as Military Attaché in Italy enthusiastic about Fascism, which has tended to obscure the domestic roots of the political movement named after him. Peronismo is merely a symptom: the disease is a sedulously fostered, radical irrationality. Perhaps the most illuminating aspect of Perón's enthusiasm for Mussolini's system is that it was undimmed by having seen it militarily humiliated in 1940–41, by the despised British to boot, in the gratuitously self-imposed test of war.

The Argentine Nationalist myth was created to 'de-Europeanize' the mass of mainly northern Spanish and southern Italian immigrants that transformed Argentine society between 1880 and 1916, when the population increased from 2.5 to 8.25 million, less than half of it by reproductive growth.* But along with it came a hatred of Liberalism, which in Italy and Spain led to the emergence of, respectively, *Duce* Benito Mussolini in 1922 and *Caudillo* Francisco Franco in 1938, while Italo-Hispanic Argentina alternated between populist and conservative dictators interspersed with ineffectual elected civilians from 1930 to 1983. The crucial difference is that Argentina offered the de-Europeanized immigrants no genuine collective memory or traditions to respect, only polemical versions of history rough-hewn to serve the purposes of propaganda. Much that is so uniquely strange about Argentine politics arises from the widespread belief that the community remains undefined, and a society lacking a secure identity is highly vulnerable to the idea that a 'New Man' must be created. To understand what happened in Argentina in 1973–83 it is essential to bear in mind that many of those tortured and murdered during the Dirty War fully shared

---

* Between 1821 and 1932 Argentina with 6.5 millions was second only to the USA as the destination for European immigrants, although its smaller population baseline made it proportionally by far the largest recipient.

their executioners' belief that the birth of the New Man could only be bloodily violent.

While it in no way excuses the Dirty War, the Nationalist commonality does explain why, after the Trotskyite ERP (Revolutionary Army of the People) was all but exterminated in 1975–76, there were no significant ideological differences between the remaining warring parties. Both the armed forces and the leading faction of the ultra-Peronist terrorist group called Montoneros (from a mounted guerrilla group active in the independence struggle against Spain in northern Argentina/Southern Bolivia), were unequivocally Fascist with some elements of Nazism. It is highly germane to the deep background of the Falklands War that Montoneros traced their modern existence to 'Operation Condor', the forced landing of a hijacked Aerolineas Argentinas DC-6 on Stanley racecourse in 1966. The hijacking was the work of Tacuara, an unapologetically neo-Nazi group, whose first battle honour was the murder of the Jewish Communist Raúl Alterman in 1964. Ex-members of Tacuara were on all sides during the 1970s. Its founder Alberto Ezcurra (d. 1993) became a fanatically Counter-Reformation priest and a leading apologist for state terrorism, while his 2 i/c Joe Baxter (d. 1973 in a bizarre accident at Paris–Orly airport) became a leading figure in the PRT (Revolutionary Party of the People), the political front for the ERP. But the true successor to Tacuara was Montoneros, an ideological ragbag united around a common belief in the regenerative power of violence, whose founding acts were kidnapping, murder and – a uniquely Argentine touch – body snatching.*

The third party to the genocide was the trade union movement created by Perón, directed by gangsters who began to run death squads of their own after Montoneros assassinated José Rucci, the Secretary General of the CGT (the Argentine Trade Union Council) on 25 September 1973. Acting together with the Federal Police, the Peronista trade union bosses led by Lorenzo Miguel, head of the hegemonic Metalworkers' Union and of the '62 Organizations' (the Peronista trade union coordinating body), launched a pogrom against their opponents under the *nom de guerre* of Argentine Anti-Communist Alliance, the infamous 'Triple A'. Others involved in the Triple A were Isabelita's warlock, José López Rega and both Italian and Argentine

---

* Not content with the kidnap/murder of Lt Gen Pedro Aramburu in June 1970 (a deed applauded by Perón) they grave-robbed his body in October 1974 to demand the return to Argentina of Evita's embalmed corpse.

members of the shadowy ex-Masonic organization known as *Propaganda Due* (P 2), on which more later.

Possibly the main reason why English-speaking commentators have failed to explore the Argentine side of the Falklands War is that to do so requires stepping through the looking glass, into a reality too weird for most to comprehend. There is no adequate historical analogy for what happened in Argentina in 1976–82, but it might help to imagine the Italian armed forces in the 1930s seizing power following the death by natural causes of Mussolini and taking over from the Fascist labour movement a ruthless persecution of the no less Fascist youth movement, itself lethally divided between those tending towards Corporativism and those flirting with Socialism. To round off the analogy, the military would then have sought to unify the country behind them by invading Malta, amid rapturous popular acclaim.

Muddying the water yet further, in the years since 1983 all too many US and British commentators have tied themselves in knots while trying to find a formula condemning the massacres perpetrated by 'right wing' governments, while finessing the pile of skulls on which the Soviet Union and kindred regimes were founded. Thus the Guardianista Iain Guest in *Behind the Disappearances: Argentina's Dirty War Against Human Rights and the United Nations* blithely states that 'there is no record of political kidnapping and clandestine murder in the Soviet bloc,' and that 'in Uruguay dissent had been stamped out far more thoroughly and ruthlessly than in most countries of Eastern Europe.' But the main disqualifying flaw in Guest's argument is his acceptance of moral equivalence between economic exploitation and genocide. The deliberate blurring of what should be an unequivocal moral line (as Guest's own research convincingly demonstrates to anyone – except, it seems, the author himself) was what enabled Gabriel Martínez, Argentina's able UN representative at Geneva 1974–83, to run rings around those who were trying to make the UN Commission on Human Rights more effective. At another level, Martínez and his masters got considerable mileage from the argument that societies such as the British, with 150–180,000 abortions carried out at public expense every year, lacked the moral authority to lecture anyone else on the sanctity of human life. The *tu quoque* (you're one too) defence may be a logical fallacy, but it is emotionally effective.

The great Conservative thinker Edmund Burke wrote: 'When bad men combine, the good must associate; else they will fall one by one, an unpitied sacrifice in a contemptible struggle.' I played a tiny role in the work of one such association in November 1976, as the embassy-designated interpreter for the visit to Buenos Aires by Lord Avebury (once the Liberal MP Eric Lubbock) and the Jesuit US Congressman Robert Drinan, in representation of Amnesty International. The British government hoped its support for the Amnesty visit would send a message. It did: it said 'we want to appear to be doing something about human rights.' In 2003 I contacted the researcher who accompanied Lord Avebury during the visit, seeking to discuss the Amnesty report published in 1977. She refused, with the po-faced comment that my attitude 'appeared at the time somewhat ambiguous'. So was that of the government I represented – however, she may have had in mind my suggestion that the report should make a clearer moral distinction between torture and murder. The military were not going to cease torturing suspects, and instead of releasing those unfortunates 'sucked up' by mistake would erase them rather than risk adding to the Amnesty case files: precisely what happened two months later to the Swedish–Argentine teenager Dagmar Hagelin, wounded and kidnapped in error by naval officer Alfredo Astiz (on whom more later), and then disappeared for the sake of deniability.

Inside Argentina, the Amnesty report was counter-productive. Despite the presence of Drinan, the military portrayed it as an attack on true Latin defenders of the Roman Catholic faith. Banners, window posters and bumper stickers appeared all over the country with *Los Argentinos Somos Derechos y Humanos* written across the national flag – a play on words, as *derechos humanos* means 'human rights', but the slogan translates as 'We Argentines are Upright and Human.' The Amnesty report was also dismissed as a gullible repetition of propaganda disseminated by opposition groups – who are indeed and inevitably the most likely sources of information on human rights abuses. All nationalities tend to close ranks against criticism by outsiders and the report, soberly accurate as to the facts of human rights abuse, was violently criticized for failing to address the context of a failed society. In other words it was strong on what should be, without offering any suggestions on how to get there from the dreadful place in which Argentina found itself in 1976. But had the Amnesty investigators sought to do so, they would have been denounced for grossly exceeding their brief, like the UN Human Rights group that reported on Chile in 1978, which contaminated its report by denouncing the Pinochet regime's 'right wing' economic policies. Amnesty simply reiterated the self-evident truth that civilisation rests on the rule of law, and that you cannot uphold the law by breaking it.

Governments and their security forces should – must – be held to a higher standard of behaviour than insurgents: but it is as unrealistic to expect them to consent to their own overthrow because they lack the means to fight armed subversion 'cleanly' as it is to propose that insurgents should wear uniforms and fight out in the open. Also, the whole point of terrorism is to provoke overreaction from the authorities: most terrorist campaigns target the police, magistrates and other officials without whom a 'clean' counter-insurgency campaign cannot be conducted. This said, the likelihood is that whoever wins a struggle between terrorists and counter-terrorists will continue to use the same methods to hold power. The classic example is the Communist Party of the Soviet Union, which remained a terrorist organization throughout its existence despite unchallenged control of an all-pervasive state apparatus. Thus also the PNR, which institutionalized the techniques of counter-terror instead of rebuilding the civic culture and legal infrastructure in whose name it claimed to have fought the Dirty War.

There is no way of finding out what proportion of those 'disappeared' participated directly or indirectly in the many assassinations, bombings and kidnappings that precipitated the 1976 coup. Nor any way of knowing how many were betrayed by their rivals – most find it highly suggestive that the leaders of the Corporativist wing of the Montoneros survived virtually intact, while most of their Socialist-leaning comrades and their Marxist–Leninist peers in other armed subversive groups died. It does not help that human rights organizations commonly cite the figure of 30,000 dead, when the list prepared by Grupo Fahrenheit, building on the work of the National Commission on the Disappeared (CONADEP), totals not far short of a still appalling 11,000, of whom no less than 800 were Jews. What can be said without qualification is that since the security forces only suffered 492 fatal casualties during the same period, to call it a war is grotesque and I use the term 'Dirty War' only because it is the identifier in general use.

I was personally unenthusiastic about the Amnesty visit because I thought it likely someone would shoot at us to discredit the authorities, during what

I expected to be an exercise in bleeding heart ineffectuality. The tough-mindedness of Avebury and Drinan made a convert of me, which I remain, while noting that history over the last quarter century tends to support the view that the main difference between oppressors and oppressed is opportunity. The danger was always that Amnesty would be hijacked by those with an ideological axe to grind, and so it has proved. Meanwhile those who style themselves Progressive have moved on to other causes, and Amnesty reports are now not only ludicrously biased but also lost amid the competing claims of an obscene proliferation of alleged charities doing well out of seeming to do good. The climate of opinion that Amnesty shaped is gone, and today Progressives refuse to condemn regimes every bit as vile as the PNR because they fear being accused of cultural imperialism – which is what the Junta and much of the Argentine middle class called it. If such it is, so be it.

In the end, though, the PNR was only likely to be influenced by domestic pressure such as that generated in Britain by the late eighteenth and early nineteenth century movement to abolish slavery. The abolitionist movement was driven by religious faith, but the only church that could have played a similar role in Argentina was overwhelmingly pro-Junta, while the voice from the heart of Roman Catholicism was silent. The Papal Nunciatura in Buenos Aires was the first port of call for relatives of the disappeared and by 1980 the Nuncio had compiled a list (subsequently destroyed) of some 6,000 names. The few lives he may have saved through discreet interventions weigh little in the balance. The contrast with the role of the church in Chile could not be more stark. Across the Andes, Cardinal Raúl Silva Henríquez took on the secret police of the Pinochet dictatorship in 1975, when he formed the Vicariat of Solidarity to replace the banned Committee for Peace, an all-faith group linked to the UN High Commission on Refugees and the World Council of Churches. There was no similar display of principle or pastoral leadership by the Argentine Roman Catholic hierarchy.

Father Federico Richards, a third-generation Irish–Argentine priest and pastor at the parish of the Holy Cross in Buenos Aires, fearlessly attacked the ongoing Dirty War in his newssheet *The Southern Cross*. Interviewed in 1995 he confirmed that Papal Nuncio Pio Laghi kept a list of the disappeared, as did Bishop Adolfo Tortolo, Vicar-General of the Armed Forces, of whom Richards comments 'he always had an excuse for everything the military did.' Richards belonged to the conservative Passionist Order, at the time of the Dirty War under the direction of the Irish–American Bishop Theodore Folley. During a visit to Buenos Aires, Folley received a letter from the Argentine Primate, Cardinal Antonio Caggiano, denouncing a Richards editorial entitled 'The Silence of the Bishops'. Folley ignored Caggiano's letter and publicly praised Richards for his stand. To the lasting dishonour of the church in Argentina, its involvement in the Dirty War went far beyond mere silence: priests acted as informers and gave spiritual comfort to torturers and murderers at their hellish places of work.

Father Richards' niece Gloria Keogh was among those disappeared (on 15 June 1978), but before that he witnessed the incident that synthesizes the miasmic nature of those dark years. In the evening of 8 December 1977 two of the Mothers of Plaza de Mayo (who demonstrated daily outside the presidential palace to demand news of their disappeared children), plus the French nun Alice Domon and four others, meeting in Richard's church to prepare the text of an appeal to be placed in the broadsheet *La Nación,* were 'sucked up' by a team from the Navy Mechanics School (ESMA), the most notorious of the Dirty War 'processing centres'. Two days later Azucena Villaflor, the founder and first president of the Mothers of Plaza de Mayo, and 62-year-old Léonie Duquet, another French nun, were kidnapped separately. Some weeks earlier a young man claiming his brother had been disappeared had joined the group, accompanied by a woman he introduced as his sister. He was Navy Lieutenant Alfredo Astiz and the woman was the Montonera Silvia Labayrú, kidnapped when pregnant and 'turned' by her captors with the promise that her baby and her husband's kidnapped family would be spared if she collaborated. Her child and in-laws survived, and Labayrú herself was released unharmed in 1979.

It is worth stressing what a compound assault this operation was on everything the military claimed to revere: motherhood, the integrity of the family, the sanctuary of the church and, last but not least, institutional and individual honour. It was also very far from being an isolated 'excess'. The Navy, and in due course the civilian political/legal system after the restoration of democracy, continued to promote Astiz and defend him against domestic and international prosecution for these and several other crimes, including the above-mentioned case of young Dagmar Hagelin. During the

Falklands War Astiz led a select group of Marines 'sworn to die' in defence of South Georgia: but when the time came to fight he surrendered without firing a shot. Despite his abject performance he was for many years lionized as a hero, with chic young women lining up to be serviced by a man they knew to be a murderer.

There is no evading the conclusion that something was, and remains, deeply rotten in the state of Argentina. No easy explanations emerge for the chronic failure of a society with a broadly educated population character-ized by a sharp, ironic sense of humour, a diverse, thriving press, the smartest capital city and (once) the highest standard of living in Latin America. It is difficult to understand how a nation that nurtured the socially acute and irreverent cartoonists Joaquín 'Quino' Lavado (*Mafalda*) and Roberto Fonta-narrosa (*Inodoro Pereyra*) can have been for so long in thrall to the person and legacy of a posturing blowhard like Perón. Argentines tell wickedly self-deprecating jokes (the best deal in the world is to buy an Argentine at cost and sell him for what he thinks he is worth), yet collectively they exhibit what Hannah Arendt believed was the defining flaw in the naturalized Argentine Adolf Eichmann's character: 'an inability to think from the standpoint of someone else'. Above all, they have failed to reach an agreement among themselves on how to live together within the ample possibilities of an otherwise richly endowed territory, as recognized in another popular quip: the Archangel Gabriel asked the Creator why he was giving Argentina such a cornucopia of natural resources. 'Wait and see the people I'm going to put there,' God replied.

Successive British administrations did not ignore the crimes of the PNR, but with the Falklands and tens of thousands of dual nationals potentially hostage they judged discretion the better part of moral indignation. Nor was it necessarily wrong to believe that trade, including arms sales, might smooth the edges of bilateral relations. The error was to forget that unbridled regimes are no less unconstrained in their international dealings and to overlook the extremely small part cost-benefit calculation plays in Argentine foreign policy. The latent menace of the PNR's religiosity was likewise discounted because religion plays so little part in modern British life. Having assumed the mantle of the Inquisition, it was a welcome step for Argentine officers – who thought only Roman Catholics were true Christians – to strike a blow against England (they never call it Britain), a state born of rebellion against Rome.* The invasion was code-named 'Rosary' at the urging of the CO of the Army component (RI 25), an extreme Roman Catholic mystic whose name, Mohamed Alí Seineldín, suggests he was a disappointment to his parents. Stanley museum preserves a copy of the hallucinatory leaflet Seineldín distributed among the incredulous Kelpers:

PEOPLE OF THE MALVINAS
[Crude picture of a crowned Virgin and Child]
You have been liberated from the illegal colonial government
The People and Armed Forces of Argentina embrace you as brothers
JOIN US IN FORGING A GREAT FUTURE FOR THE ISLANDS
Join us in giving thanks to the Blessed Virgin Mary
for the success of Operation Rosario.

The Roman church itself was in crisis at the time, amid circumstances that seemed to confirm the wildest conspiracy theories. Connoisseurs of scandal agree a benchmark was set by the cascade of revelations, starting in 1974 and running well into the 1980s, concerning the close association of the 'Vatican Bank' (IOR) with Michele Sidona and Roberto Calvi, two fraudulent Italian financiers, and with Licio Gelli, the head of the Italy-based worldwide web of corruption and crime known as *Propaganda Due.* Members included most of the Christian Democrat oligarchy that ruled Italy since 1945, many Argentine generals, leading Mafiosi, Nazis exfiltrated by the Vatican to South America and 'Black Hand' terrorists. Narcotics smuggling and arms trafficking, real and faked suicides, assassinations, hetero- and homosexual orgies, links with the secret intelligence services of Europe and the CIA – it had the lot. If to this we add the attempted assassination of Pope John Paul II on 13 May 1981 by a Turkish right-winger recruited under an Islamic false flag by the Bulgarian Secret Service on behalf of the KGB, it is fair to say that it was an apocalyptic time for the faithful.

Since it was unthinkable that Holy Mother Church could be the *casino* emerging from these revelations, she must necessarily be the victim of a

---

* Army chaplains were drawn preferentially from the Dominican Order, *Domini Canes*, the 'hounds of God' forever associated with the Inquisition.

conspiracy. Enter the Christ-killers, arm-in-arm with the Bolshevik hyenas and the English Masonic sodomites. Two books published at this time, *El poder en la sombra: el affaire Graiver* by Ramón Camps, ex-Chief of Police of Buenos Aires Province, and *Dope, Inc: The Book that Drove Kissinger Crazy* by Lyndon LaRouche's Executive Intelligence Review, outline the same worldwide conspiracy linking Jewish-run world capitalism and Soviet communism, directed by a network of English aristocrats who had been laundering drug money since the days of the Opium Wars. The aim being, of course, to destroy Western Christian Civilization in general and its Argentine paladin in particular. Variants of this self-contained 'Explanation of Everything' featured in the belief systems of Isabelita's banished warlock López Rega, all branches of the Argentine military and the Tacuara continuity represented by Montoneros leader Mario Firmenich.

Although it is dangerous to leap from the frying pan of neo-Nazi psychopathology into the fire of its leftist equivalent, it isn't paranoia if they really are out to get you. Not only those involved in armed subversion but also those believed to have been too soft on them were the target of the joint venture code-named 'Condor' among the secret services of Argentina, Bolivia, Brazil, Chile, Paraguay, Perú and Uruguay, to share intelligence and to permit hit teams from one country to operate freely in the others. I do not subscribe to the idea that Latin Americans are incapable of organizing this sort of thing without the encouragement and assistance of Uncle Sam. But as we shall see in the next chapter, US Secretary of State Henry Kissinger gave tacit approval to Condor as a temporary expedient, only to have it blow up, almost literally in his face, when a car bomb planted by the Chileans killed Orlando Letelier and his American assistant on Embassy Row in Washington on 21 September 1976.

Thanks to the Letelier hit and also because the Soviet propaganda machine concentrated on Chile, the Pinochet dictatorship attracted, and continues to attract, disproportionate criticism by comparison with an Argentine regime that committed the same crimes on a greater scale, and was also closely tied to the wider web of intrigue emanating from Italy. As I write, there is a move afoot in Britain to criminalize any suggestion that a pathological culture might have something to do with the religion it professes. Yet whether or not one believes that the teachings from which they draw their authority are the Word of God, the institutions that have grown up to mediate between mankind and the Word are human creations, and as such not only fallible but also self-interested. Just as it is not possible to discuss the Dirty War without reference to the Argentine church, so it is not possible to overlook the historic role of conspiracy and counter-conspiracy in the long and savage struggle between the Roman church and Liberalism in Latin countries. The term 'Latin America' itself dates back to the dream of French Emperor Napoleon III and his devout Spanish wife to create a Roman Catholic counter to the Liberal Protestant hegemony of the United States. This is not to pursue an anti-Catholic agenda, merely to remind those reared in a freethinking environment that personalities shaped by Liberal democracy, free speech and scientific enquiry are *hard-wired* differently to those raised in less open traditions, and that language is the least of the barriers to mutual understanding. As Samuel Huntington put it in his seminal article 'The Clash of Civilizations':

> Differences among civilizations are not only real; they are basic. Civilizations are differentiated from each other by history, language, culture, tradition and, most important, religion. The people of different civilizations have different views on the relations between God and man, the individual and the group, the citizen and the state, parents and children, husband and wife, as well as differing views of the relative importance of rights and responsibilities, liberty and authority, equality and hierarchy. These differences are the product of centuries. They will not soon disappear. They are far more fundamental than differences among political ideologies and political regimes.

On a visit to the Córdoba hills early in 1978 I was introduced to the 'magical realist' novelist Manuel Mujica Láinez, who confirmed a rumour that cadets graduating from the Córdoba Air Force Academy were brought to the hills for an initiation ceremony into the fraternity of the 'Baptised by Fire'. The ceremony involved parading around a bonfire and swearing a dagger-oath to defend the holy soil of the fatherland with their blood – the Nazi *Blut und Boden,* probably a legacy of Hans Ulrich Rudel, the outstanding Stuka pilot and unregenerate Nazi appointed Chief Instructor to the Argentine Air Force by Perón in 1947. I suggested Mujica might wish to write about it and his reply is the epigraph to this book. He added that writing about it probably would get him killed. One cannot imagine RAF or USAF cadets doing something like this except as a drunken joke – or flying into battle with crucifixes and rosaries hanging from their gunsights and the words 'Long live the Fatherland' on their lips. Not the least of the chips on Latin shoulders is the knowledge that Anglos regard them as melodramatic buffoons. Thus a paean of praise addressed to the Argentine pilots of the Falklands War by the Free French pilot Pierre Clostermann, much decorated while serving with the RAF during World War II, ends with the words (my italics): 'To the fathers and mothers, the brothers and sisters, the wives and children of the Argentine pilots who went to their death with the most fantastic and astonishing courage, I say that they honour Argentina *and the Latin World.*'

Another area of Latin cultural sensitivity was revealed by the Argentine withdrawal of ambassadors in January 1976, the given reason a British message in reply to some bellicose huffing and puffing by Argentine Foreign Minister Arauz Castex in which the sovereignty dispute was described as 'sterile'. The Argentine Foreign Ministry chose to translate that poor choice of word with the literal but loaded *estéril* (impotent) rather than the neutral *improductivo,* and the Buenos Aires tabloids beat drums and hairy chests. In February Massera ordered a destroyer to arrest the British research vessel *Shackleton* in Falklands waters and to fire into her if it could be done without causing casualties. *Shackleton*'s skipper ignored shots fired across his bows and the Argentine captain chose not to escalate the incident further. In response the British government warned that the islands would be defended if the Argentines resorted to force, but it also resumed negotiations in which sovereignty was once more put on the table. Since this was not accompanied by a strengthening of the islands' minimal defence capability, the Argentines concluded that the promised resistance would be perfunctory.

Instead of discussing deterrence, however, the MoD stressed how difficult it would be to *retake* the islands without *Ark Royal,* the last remaining Royal Navy fleet carrier, which was due to be scrapped. She was axed anyway, but in trying to save her the MoD, no less keen than the FCO to be rid of the Falklands commitment, deliberately slighted the far cheaper option of putting some teeth into the British military presence on the islands.

It is now clear that to have reinforced the Falklands garrison would have been doubly effective, at once making it plain that an invasion would be contested and also showing respect. By doing nothing the British made it clear they thought the Argentines were all talk. To follow up 'sterile' with a display of indifference towards what was in effect Massera's vigorously waved penis was asking for trouble, but I doubt if British governments will ever accept that 'fortress Falklands' works as much to assuage Argentine egos as it does to deter adventurism. It might help to post personnel to the Buenos Aires Embassy with prior experience in the Far East, where nobody doubts the overriding importance of 'face'.

The first half of Horacio Verbitsky's *Malvinas: la última batalla de la tercera guerra mundial* (Falklands: the Last Battle of the Third World War), unfortunately not available in translation, is the most fascinating writing on the war to emerge from Argentina. It is dedicated to Rodolfo Walsh, like 'Che' Guevara the descendant of Irish immigrants,* which takes us through the looking glass once more because Walsh was an armed revolutionary killed in a gunfight with security forces, as his daughter had been killed a few months earlier. Somehow Verbitsky finds it possible throughout the book to combine condemnation of the utter folly of those who provoked a war they could not win with adulation for one of them, and so on throughout the book. Still, few others can hit the nail on the head like this:

> The sick logic of the [Dirty War] led both sides to become like the caricature each made of the other. The guerrillas, who were not the spearhead of worldwide [Communist] aggression, ended up isolated like foreign bodies in a community that for many years disowned them while they were persecuted and murdered. The soldiers, who were not an occupying force, acted as though they were, and once the terror was past they experienced the lasting rejection reserved elsewhere for colonial armies.

I was born and spent my childhood in Cuba, later lived in Chile, Bolivia, Colombia, Guatemala and Perú as well as Argentina. Only in Argentina did I regularly experience what I call 'Manchurian Candidate moments', when you are reading or conversing with people who seem to be sensible: and

---

* 'Che' (roughly, 'pal') is a verbal tic unique to River Plate Spanish (although the Kelpers also used to call each other 'chay'), thus a nickname commonly given to Argentines elsewhere in the continent.

then they segue seamlessly into something so irrational that your jaw drops. For example another talented Argentine journalist, Rogelio García Lupo, after chortling at length about the delusions of grandeur entertained by the military, writes that on the day after Roberto Calvi – he of the Banco Ambrosiano/*Propaganda Due*/IOR/Mafia connection – authorized a loan of 200 million dollars to the Peruvian Central Bank for the purchase of arms to be sent on to Buenos Aires, Calvi appeared hanging from 'the only bridge over the Thames painted in the blue and white colours of the Argentine flag'. Calvi was murdered on 17 June 1982, three days after the Argentine surrender in Stanley, and it requires a staggeringly unrealistic estimate of the importance of Argentina to imagine he would have spent his last day investing in a lost cause. Or that MI5 would indulge in Rococo symbolism in the wildly improbable event it could get clearance to commit an assassination in the heart of London.

This said, Verbitsky's seemingly far-fetched account of how the plan for the invasion of the Falklands was incubated is well sourced and entirely credible. He reports that during 1977 a group of Montoneros prisoners in the ESMA saved their lives by developing a project for the political apotheosis of Massera, exploiting the fact that the Navy was put in charge of the Foreign Ministry following the March 1976 coup. The 'big idea' was to revive the vision of the Liberator San Martín for a Southern Cone empire. Argentine territorial claims, based on a spurious right of succession to the Spanish Viceregency of La Plata, extend far beyond the Falklands. They include all of Uruguay and Paraguay, Bolivia, the northern provinces of Chile, the whole of southern Chile, and a sizeable bite of the southern provinces of Brazil. A book by the head of the Council of National Security during the Onganía regime, who coined the phrase *Argentina Potencia* (Argentina World Power), juxtaposes a map of 1778 with present-day frontiers. In fact Argentina as a modern state dates from 1862 and country maps made in 1833 (the year of the so-called Falklands 'usurpation') did not even include Patagonia.

The Montoneros' ESMA think-tank identified three border conflicts that could be exploited. The first was with Brazil over the utilization of the Paraná river: a non-starter because Brazil was too strong and the other armed forces would never consent to it. The second was with Chile over three islands in the

Beagle Channel. Border disputes with Chile, by treaty, were subject to binding arbitration by the British Crown, which put the hot potato in the hands of the International Court of Justice at the Hague. A panel of international jurists found unanimously for Chile, hardly surprising when even official Argentine maps from earlier in the century showed the islands to be Chilean. Massera's men in the Foreign Ministry repudiated the treaty and the judgement, cynically claiming it was flawed by British bias. The Navy, backed by the Air Force, overrode Army objections and geared up for war around Christmas 1978, the plan being to seize the islands and then negotiate from a position of strength (*ocupar para negociar*). The Marines in Tierra del Fuego had received the order to attack when Pope John Paul II intervened and sent an envoy to defuse the situation.* Tension remained high until 1985, when the two parties signed a treaty recognizing Chilean sovereignty over the islands while limiting the projection of Chilean territorial waters into the South Atlantic. In the articles collected in *Diplomacia secreta y rendición incondicional,* Rogelio García Lupo astutely observed that the rhetorical excesses of December 1978 were extremely ominous, for they went far beyond merely territorial ambition:

> Those close to the Argentine generals over the past few years have heard them say that war would be the forge of the new Argentina. Many years of peace had softened the Argentine people, they said. In 1978 when war with Chile seemed to be a matter of hours away, enthusiasm was rampant among chiefs and officers who shared the same chimera: that the war would produce a race of Argentine supermen. Thus the calming mediation of the Pope, which postponed the explosion, was also felt deeply by the military, for whom the prolongation of peace was an unforgivable coitus interruptus.

Which left the Falklands and Dependencies, and the projection of *Argentina Potencia* across the South Atlantic, to create the territorial basis for a declaration of Argentine sovereignty over the nominally British segment of Antarctica. This calculation has been grossly understated in the plethora of books written in English about the causes of the war, yet it is the single most

---

* Thereby giving the cruiser *General Belgrano* an extra three and a half years of life. The Chilean submarine *Simpson* was shadowing her as the deadline approached.

illustrative factor in play. All territorial claims had been declared in abeyance and Antarctica internationalized since 1961 by a treaty to which Argentina was one of the original twelve consultative members, which included the USA and USSR. The preamble states (my italics) 'that it is in the interest of all mankind that Antarctica shall continue *forever* to be used exclusively for peaceful purposes and shall not become the scene or object of international discord'. Despite this declaration, the treaty was not regarded as an obstacle to the hallucinatory geopolitical project elaborated by the prisoners in Massera's charnel house.

Those of us at the British Embassy in Buenos Aires whose duty it was to analyze the political situation were aware that some – as we thought – 'turned' ex-Montoneros intellectuals were working for Massera in the ESMA. But we were so oppressed by the difficulty of making the Argentine reality come alive to incredulous readers back in London that the item was not, initially, selected as particularly significant. The truth – that Massera's head had been turned by the Montoneros' geopolitical fantasy – was quite simply incredible. Nonetheless alarm bells should have rung loudly and insistently in Whitehall after the embassy reported a widely commented speech by Massera on 10 June 1978, in which he appropriated the Montoneros slogan 'sovereignty is not negotiable':

> The Malvinas are an open wound in the dignity of the Republic and we Argentines are disposed to correct what negligence, cultural submission and a mistaken concept of international good manners have kept segregated from the metaphysical map of the Fatherland. The Malvinas are not a fragment of soil. The Malvinas are a piece of our soul and we must go forth to find them because sovereignty, like dignity, is not negotiable.

My friend Rolando Fernández Pondal (to whose memory I have dedicated this book), whose newssheet *Ultima Clave* had been for some time the preferred outlet for off-the-record Navy briefings, was probably killed because Massera decided he had revealed too much to him. What I now know about the paranoid atmosphere within the ESMA think-tank makes it seem likely that although Rolo and I met openly in restaurants, it may still have been interpreted as trading with the enemy. His widow, child and countrymen should know ours was a perfectly normal, overt exchange between a diplomat and a journalist, one of many we both had, and that without prejudice to a warm friendship based on personal affinity, he never told me half of what he must have known, as I only told him what I was prepared to see in print. The thugs who killed him should have looked among their own number and to their own procedures for the many leaks in their rotten ship. In retrospect Rolo and I failed to take the ideological delirium at the heart of the PNR seriously enough. If we underestimated it, those far from the febrile atmosphere of Buenos Aires can be forgiven for not perceiving the pattern behind the bizarre and barbaric details of the deranged reality of life in Argentina.

Perón himself would never have been so foolish as to invade the islands. A territorial claim is politically useful as something to be trotted out at need to distract the masses from whatever may be exercising them. The downside is that it creates an issue others will exploit to question the Nationalist credentials of whoever is refraining from recovering the lost lands. This was the game Massera got into with the Montoneros, aggravated by his delusions of grandeur. He had set his sights on becoming the new Perón ever since 1974, but his control of the Navy was such that his fellow Junta members did not dare move against him for fear of repeating the near-civil war of 1963 between military factions for and against an accommodation with the Peronistas.

Not long after the March 1976 coup an exasperated Videla told Massera to stop talking about invading the Falklands and to produce a plan for a combined operation – which he never did. Instead he entrusted Anaya, his Fleet Commander, with the task of pursuing purely naval initiatives, one of which was the symbolic occupation of Southern Thule. Another was an incident on 22 September 1977 when Massera/Anaya ordered the capture of four Soviet trawlers fishing in Falklands waters, which were fired on and a crewman killed. It was a carefully calculated act designed to assert sovereignty and to demonstrate that *Argentina Potencia* could stand up to a world power: also to show the United States that Argentina could be a more dependably robust Cold War ally in the South Atlantic than the feeble British.

However the other members of the Junta were never going to allow Massera to reap unilateral political gains from playing the Falklands card.

Once he lost his power base on retirement from the Navy and the Junta in September 1978, he rapidly discovered that he had no following in the country, despite the enormous boost to Argentine pride (and to his own and the Argentine Navy's finances) from hosting and winning the 1978 Football World Cup. Lest we forget, the international football authorities went ahead with the competition in a country governed by a genocidal dictatorship and also turned a blind eye to the bribery of the Peruvian by the Argentine Football Federation to lose extravagantly at the end of the second round, and so permit Argentina to sneak into the final ahead of Brazil. In *The Land That Lost Its Heroes*, sports journalist Jimmy Burns commented that 'not since the Berlin Olympics of 1936 had sport been so transformed into a political circus' – but he failed to note that Massera was not speaking of football when he said 'we have lost too many times for any Argentine to be satisfied with a draw. *This time we are going to win.*' As Verbitsky observes, a plan of action intended to bring about the political apotheosis of Massera survived his departure from power like a slow-ticking time bomb, to blow up on the eve of the next Football World Cup in 1982.

While I have implied that language is the least of the barriers to understanding between cultures, it is the first. Failure to breach it has led to a serious imbalance in the English literature on the causes of the Falklands War, focusing too much on the miscalculations immediately involved and not at all on the matrix from which they sprang. Yet without exploring the deep background it is impossible to understand not only why the invasion of the islands came to be seen as a political imperative, but why the Argentine military chose to risk all on a trial of arms rather than to seize the substantial diplomatic gains on offer from a US-brokered deal with the British. For the men who launched it the invasion, like the Dirty War, was simply a means to an end. The contrast between the military and the militarist way was pungently defined by General George Patton when he said nobody ever won a war by dying for his country; he won it by making the other poor dumb bastard die for his. Although from the Argentine side the war did fulfill Clausewitz's dictum of being the continuation of politics with the admixture of other means, the purpose was the purification of the national character through sacrifice rather than the efficient application of military force to achieve realistic objectives. The commanders of all three armed forces used the suggestive phrase *cuota de sangre* (share of blood) to describe the contributions made by their respective services during the war: the language of atonement.

Although I would like to see an independent psychiatric report on Massera, I do not believe his fellow Junta members were psychopaths in the strict meaning of the term.* Only men who knew they were guilty would have lied so much and invented so many justifications for their actions – and only a guilty society would have accepted them. No survey of the reasons for the Falklands War can ignore that the Argentine officer corps – no member of which could claim ignorance of the kidnapping, torture and murder of thousands of men, women and children – had an urgent collective need for expiation. Argentina's Dirty War went on much longer than similar 'house cleaning' in Uruguay and Chile. The guilt was systematically generalized throughout the armed forces as well as the police, and spread out to corrupt a sizeable proportion of the whole population. The subject seems to be too painful for most Argentines to deal with, just as it seems too alien for most outsiders to grasp. Understandably so, for what is one to make of urbane, churchgoing officers with an elevated concept of personal honour, who directed the repeated electrocution and partial suffocation of helpless prisoners prior to dumping their still-living bodies into the ocean from aircraft, who married women they had 'turned' by torture, and who adopted the infant children of parents they had murdered? And of the civilians who knew their fathers, sons, husbands and friends were doing this?

The barbaric totem of the Dirty War has obscured the no less shocking ideological continuity linking the genocide and the invasion of the Falklands. Thus the author Nigel West – no stranger to wheels within wheels – misunderstood the reason why Elena Holmberg, the Argentine Cultural Attaché in Paris, was abducted and murdered in January 1979, shortly after her return to Buenos Aires. It was not, as West believed, because she had prepared a dossier on the counter-terrorist activities of a group of naval officers operating under diplomatic cover (including the notorious Astiz), but because it revealed the group's purpose was to liaise with the Montoneros' exiled leadership on behalf of Massera's presidential ambitions. Iain Guest, who gets that right,

---

* Not so those who actually did the dirty work. See *www.yendor.com/vanished/junta.html* and note that Acosta, head of Massera's hit squad, was an employee of the Ministry of the Interior under President Menem in 1996.

footnotes without comment the astoundingly significant fact that Licio Gelli, the spider at the centre of the *Propaganda Due* web (who had been an honoured guest at Perón's inauguration in 1973), brokered a meeting in Italy between Massera and exiled Montoneros leader Mario Firmenich in 1978. Within the minds of those involved, they represented a 'Third Way' hostile alike to Anglo-American economic and social Liberalism and Soviet Communism. They were perhaps too stupid, and certainly too impatient, to notice that the social organization they advocated was the organizing principle of the Economic and Social Committee of the European Community, the posthumous triumph of the ideas worked out by leading Nationalist and Roman Catholic intellectuals in Italy during the 1920s.

I do not believe the Falklands War represented a brave new dawn for Britain, but it undoubtedly doomed the PNR. There are few regimes so disgusting that the 'international community' will bring effective pressure to bear on them, and when individual governments attempt to do so they will always see their efforts undermined by others seeking to profit from the situation. In practise a regime may do whatever it likes so long as it pays its bills and does not attack the interests of another strong enough to punish it. Even when a regime resorts to armed aggression, the UN Charter limits the right of self-defence to proportional retaliation, which precludes regime change as a specific war aim. Given all these constraints, those who claim to care about human rights should logically applaud any legitimate measure to erode the power of a murderous regime. In the matter of the Falklands War that applause was not forthcoming at the time or since, because the most obvious political beneficiary was Margaret Thatcher. In any apportionment of guilt, some must attach to those who cannot summon up the moral integrity to admit that the Argentine invasion of the Falklands was the work of evil men expressing the sick aspirations of a failed society, and that regardless of previous equivocations the British response was both necessary and just.

3 Complicity

HERE'S WHERE WE blame everything on the Americans. Actually, no: here's where we review how the USA elected President Jimmy Carter, a decent, well-meaning soul, and how the rest of the world, scarcely believing its luck, rushed to take advantage of it. Four years later American voters replaced him with Ronald Reagan, a notably harder-edged chief executive, amid international wailing and gnashing of teeth. Carter sought to introduce an overtly principled dimension into US diplomacy after the long tenure of the highly pragmatic Henry Kissinger as National Security Adviser and Secretary of State to Presidents Nixon (1969–74) and Ford (1974–77). Carter failed to win re-election in 1980 thanks mainly to severe economic dislocations, but there was also widespread feeling that his foreign policy had been disastrously misconceived. His successful challenger and successor asked voters whether they were better off than four years ago and whether America was as respected throughout the world – fair questions to which the answer was, unequivocally, no. The reason for the verdict was not so much the geopolitical gains made by the Soviet Bloc in 1977–81 as it was the revealed weakness, opportunism and disloyalty of America's allies.

With regard to the Falklands, the election of Carter was the main reason why Massera's South Atlantic strategy was put on hold in 1977. The next step was to have been a repeat of the Southern Thule technique, only this time to occupy South Georgia in order to negotiate from a position of strength (*ocupar para negociar*), which the British would not have been able to brush under the carpet as they had the Southern Thule occupation. In June 1976, in an exchange with the Argentine Junta's first Foreign Minister, Admiral Guzzetti, Kissinger expressed the view that just as the Royal Navy had been unable to prevail in the 'Cod War' with Iceland in 1975–76, so over the Falklands 'the British Admirals will be forced to settle.' It was a dangerously careless remark, but with the advent of Carter to the White House seven months later, US–Argentine relations became icy and not even Massera thought it possible to proceed. However, far from supporting the US embargo on arms for the Argentine military, the British redoubled their efforts to sell the Argentine Navy six Type 21 frigates to go with the two Type 42 destroyers sold in 1970, following the first round of appeasement. The sales effort extended to government-sanctioned training and equipment for Argentine special forces, including 100 sound-modified Sterling sub-machine guns, some of which featured in the pictures flashed worldwide of Argentine troops posing in triumph over the prostrate forms of the Royal Marines who surrendered to them on 2 April 1982.

The six-frigate deal failed because the British did not offer a substantial off-the-books payment to what the Argentine Navy negotiators coyly called their pension fund. Presumably the West German government was not so fastidious, despite the disappearance of forty-eight of their own nationals in Argentina, because Blohm und Voss got the contract. The French also chose to overlook thirty-six disappeared nationals including the two 'Flying Nuns', so-called (from the popular TV series starring Sally Field) because they had been thrown from an aircraft. The French sold the Argentine Navy three corvettes originally built for South Africa, combat helicopters, Super Étendard strike aircraft (beating out the British Harriers) and Exocet missiles. The Italians, with 304 nationals disappeared, the Spanish with 164 and even the Swiss with six also eagerly contributed to the Argentine ability to wage war, as did the Belgians through their Bolivia-based arms salesman Klaus Altmann, widely known to be Klaus Barbie, the Gestapo 'Butcher of Lyon'. During the Falklands War the Belgian government halted delivery of artillery ammunition to Britain, but secretly continued to honour the Barbie contracts with Argentina.

More surprisingly, Israel developed a cosy relationship with the neo-Nazis of the Argentine Air Force, supplying aircraft, missiles and training to fill the void left by the Americans, who only completed deals already in the pipeline for Neptune and Tracker maritime surveillance aircraft, unarmed helicopters and transport aircraft. Countless books in Spanish and English seek to blame the USA for the behaviour of Latin American military dictators, yet it was not Washington that fed the ruinous arms race in which the dictators indulged during the 1970s. British-made Hawker Hunters attacked the presidential palace during the Chilean coup of 11 September 1973 because in 1966 the US State Department vetoed the sale of Northrop F-5As to the Chilean Air Force, arguing that they would be regionally desta-bilizing. Had State not done so, leftists would no doubt still be citing the F-5As as further proof of US complicity in the coup. To anyone not intent on blaming the USA for the chronic and often murderous misgovernment that has characterized most of Latin America since its independence, the common denominator for much of what happened in the continent during the 1970s was the breakdown of US authority in the region, which the Europeans no less than the Soviets sought to exploit.

It was a long-established principle of US diplomacy to discourage extrav-agant military spending in Latin America, and much of the training at the US Army's School of the Americas in Panamá was intended to increase pro-fessionalism within Latin American armed forces and so diminish their proclivity towards coups d'état. In the vexed matter of interrogation tech-niques, the use of field telephone generators to apply graduated electric shocks and the technique of half-drowning or half-suffocating suspects (known as the wet or dry submarine) were pioneered by the French in Algeria. The Israelis and South Africans also contributed their expertise in this area. Milder procedures found few takers among the Latin American military: they considered sensory deprivation to extend the shock of arrest, as de-veloped in Northern Ireland by the British, to be too tame and ignored the School of the Americas doctrine that information obtained by physical torture was unreliable. Alas, the better trained the Latin American military became, the more contemptuous they were likely to be of the corruption and disorder of civilian politics, and the less disposed to accept low pay and obsolete equipment. The match to the tinder was civilian politicians' Gadarene appeals to the armed forces to act as the final arbiters of their disputes, all of which worked against the US desire for stability in its back yard.

It was not as apparent then as it has become since the collapse of the Soviet Empire how anti-Americanism is cultural and not ideological. Even if the USA at all times demonstrated Christ-like compassion and forbearance, there will always be those who will define themselves in opposition to it, be it in the rather pathetic snobbishness with which many British intellectuals wrap their resentment, with lofty opportunism like the *énarques* of the Elysée, or in self-ruinous acts of rage like the 2001 attack on the World Trade Center. Comparable in intent to 9/11 was the 1976 assassination of the Chilean Orlando Letelier, previously Minister of Defence in the Socialist government of Salvador Allende. The killing was carried out in Washington by DINA, the same Chilean counter-terrorist agency that had tried the previous year to assassinate Bernardo Leighton, Minister of the Interior in the Christian Democrat government prior to Allende's. Letelier's assassins clearly intended to show contempt for the US Congress, which was using the Chilean coup as a stick with which to beat the Ford administration. Neither Letelier nor Leighton posed any serious threat to General Pinochet's regime. What infuriated the dictator was that both had tried to enlist the military, respectively in support or opposition to the Allende government, and were thus in his opinion morally unfit to point the finger.

But what angered Pinochet even more was the hypocrisy of the Americans. He disliked them, regarded the performance of their armed forces in Vietnam as contemptible, and mounted his coup to pre-empt a characteristically over-complex plot sponsored by the CIA, designed to put in the US-favoured faction of the Christian Democrats. It is only a slight exaggeration to say that the bankrupt and discredited Allende regime overthrown by Pinochet was of secondary importance to him: like most military men he despised all politicians, and as a patriot he felt murderous anger towards those who had turned Chile from the most stable and sober republic in the continent into just another Latino disorderly house. Largely forgotten today is that Chile's *Carabineros*, by some distance the least corrupt and most competent police force in Latin America, took the opportunity to wipe out previously untouchable criminals and their mouthpieces, including the 'Chilean Connection' for Bolivian cocaine. But Pinochet was not just another man on horseback. He installed a government of apolitical technocrats to show how unnecessary professional politicians were, and as a result the military were actually less involved in government after the coup than they had been under the hapless Allende.

There is more complexity in the affairs of men than a left/right mindset can accommodate, and it is discouraging to find banal oversimplifications of this period in Latin American history unchallenged in the material available to students on the internet. No mention, for example, of the fact that the Soviet Union, badly burned by the cost of maintaining Fidel Castro's Cuba and by the unpaid bills of populist anti-American dictator General Juan Velasco Alvarado in Perú, offered Allende little beyond moral support. Or that Kissinger had very little clout with the dictators of the Southern Cone because he was a Jew, an American and, in their eyes, a liberal, playing a very weak hand amid a rising tide of isolationism in the USA. Consider the following, said by Kissinger to Argentine Foreign Minister Admiral Guzzetti in the June 1976 conversation previously alluded to (my italics):

> Let me say, as a friend, that I have noticed that military governments are not always the most effective in dealing with these problems . . . So after a while, many people who don't understand the situation begin to oppose the military and the problem is compounded. The Chileans, for example, have not succeeded in getting across their initial problem and are increasingly isolated. You will have to make an international effort to have your problems understood. Otherwise, you, too, will come under increasing attack. *If there are things that have to be done, you should do them quickly. But you must get back quickly to normal procedures.*

These words are usually cited as Kissinger giving the 'green light' to the Dirty War, whereas an objective reading of the full exchange reveals that he knew the Junta was committed to it and nothing he said could turn them aside. Furthermore the CIA's programme of carefully targeted assassination (Operation Phoenix) in Vietnam had been highly cost-effective and he was in no position to condemn the technique when employed by others. Kissinger was simply giving warning of the inevitable political repercussions in Washington if it went on for too long. As a German–Jewish refugee, Kissinger could not be indifferent to Human Rights: but unlike his critics he was dealing with the real world, begging the Argentines to behave sensibly if they could not behave decently, and incidentally to refrain from adding to his own troubles with a Congress out for his blood. The Argentines ignored him, just as they were to ignore Patricia Derian, Jimmy Carter's Assistant Secretary of State for Human Rights, and they celebrated their defiance of both as gestures of independence from the hated *yanquis.*

Carter was no less a Cold War zealot than his predecessors and successor. He simply took the basic premise that the USA is a force for good in the world to what seemed to be its logical conclusion and made it the centre-piece of a strategy based more on moral and less on military confrontation. People tend to judge themselves by their intentions and others by their actions, but the USA is particularly prone to formulating policy in terms of overarching idealism, which the other inhabitants of the planet find hard to swallow. President Kennedy's vow to 'pay any price, bear any burden, meet any hardship, support any friend, oppose any foe, in order to assure the survival and the success of liberty' led to the Vietnam War, anti-American riots all over the world and violent anti-war demonstrations at home, alter-nating with the wrenching violence of a long-postponed reckoning with the racial apartheid that had for so long mocked the principles on which the nation claimed to stand. Kissinger's attempt to wean US foreign policy from messianic rhetoric and his ruthless liquidation of Kennedy's open-ended commitment continues to attract fire from (small 'l') liberals in the USA, who at the same time condemn the revival of that rhetoric and its attendant overseas military involvement by President George Bush Jr. A little intel-lectual coherence is long overdue from that quarter.*

The ignominious, televised evacuation of the US Embassy compound in Saigon in April 1975 encouraged attacks on US interests all over the world, while a flood of revelations about the CIA and FBI fed the traditional American belief that the world of power is inherently evil. The process was crowned by the election of Carter, which proved a lamentable error of collective judgement. Instead of applauding his efforts to put his own house in order, critics divided evenly among those who were aghast at his dangerous naivety and those for whom it provided extra ammunition for their view that no sparrow ever fell without being shot by the agents of

---

* The British transplant Christopher Hitchens is perfectly consistent in attacking Kissinger and supporting Bush.

American imperialism. By making respect for human rights the cornerstone of his foreign policy, Carter undermined authoritarian US allies without in any way pacifying those for whom the USA was 'the Great Satan'. The term was coined by the theocratic despot who took over after the Shah of Iran fled in January 1979, following his disavowal by the Carter administration on grounds of Human Rights violations. Far from being put on the defensive, the Soviets greeted Carter's inauguration by starting a build-up of intermediate range missiles to achieve a first strike capability in Europe. They also installed a puppet regime in Afghanistan and, when it proved unsatisfactory, they invaded the country in December 1979. A month earlier the US Embassy in Iran was seized by a semi-official mob and the staff held hostage while shredded documents were reassembled to reveal the extent of CIA liaison with the deposed Shah's hated secret police. Further humiliation followed when a rescue mission was bungled in April 1980.

In *Falklands: Britain Versus the Past in the South Atlantic,* Daniel Gibran argues that the war occurred at a time of 'international anarchy', there being no supranational power to maintain law and order. There is much merit in the thesis, and those who wish the United Nations fulfilled that function should ask themselves what shred of moral authority remained to a body that elected Idi Amin's genocidal Ugandan regime to its Human Rights Commission in 1976. The UN was brought into being to serve generally laudable US foreign policy objectives and could be effective as an international peacekeeper only when it fulfilled that purpose. During the 1970s the UN bureaucrats lost sight of this and devoted themselves to departmental empire building, with consequences wretchedly apparent a generation later. However, although Gibran's thesis is generally true for the period there can be little doubt the Argentines would not have invaded the Falklands if Washington had warned them it would back Britain militarily. The main reason Washington did not is because, since the British had not themselves made it clear they would fight, there was no reason for the Americans to commit themselves in advance. Also, the pattern of British diplomacy was not such as to justify doing them any favours, a sharp reminder that loyalty works both ways. The effect of this on British foreign policy was salutary and lasting.

When President Reagan took over in January 1981 the Soviets were in the ascendant and international respect for the USA was at its lowest point since it first stepped onto the world stage in 1899. Two months later Reagan was shot by a young man seeking to make an impression on a film star he had never met. Six weeks later came the KGB/Bulgarian assassination attempt against the new, fiercely anti-Communist Pope John Paul II, after which members of the new US administration could be forgiven for concluding the rot had to be stopped by any means possible, even by restoring the covert action capability emasculated by Congress. Such operations are called 'deniable' when it cannot be proved whence they come: 'untraceable' (where the unseen hand is not even suspected) is not normally an option for the CIA, which will be accused of responsibility even for manifest acts of God. The conundrum for the Reaganauts was how to get around the financial oversight of Congress in order to reinstate programmes that were, following the moral fervour of the early to mid-1970s, explicitly illegal. Direct action was out, making indirect financial support for covert action by proxies the only deniable option.

Argentina's independently developed programme of counter-subversion in Central America was so ready-made for this purpose that policy towards Argentina began to change even under Carter, who was concussed by the boomerang his Human Rights policy had become. It is easy in hindsight to see that the immediate costs of the Carter doctrine had been paid and that its slower-arriving benefits, including the restoration of stable democratic forms of government across Latin America, were in the long-term interest of the USA. It is likewise obvious, now, that the military build-up, begun by Carter and continued by Reagan, exerted python-like pressure on the Soviet Empire, causing it to collapse a decade later. However the eventual success of these policies was by no means apparent in the early 1980s. Consequently the Reagan administration embarked on a number of adventures designed to produce a clear-cut contrast with its predecessor. Prominent among these was a convoluted effort to counter the upsurge of guerrilla activity in Central America following the July 1979 overthrow of the Somoza clan, rulers of Nicaragua for forty-two years, during which Washington's view was summed up by President Franklin Roosevelt's quip that although the first of the dynasty was a son-of-a-bitch, he was *their* son-of-a-bitch. Diplomatic pressure to move towards legitimacy (*sic*) having failed, Carter disowned the last of the bastards, who fled in the face of a popular uprising to be assassinated the following year in Paraguay by a group of survivors from the decimated Argentine ERP.

Unfortunately for Nicaragua, the Sandinistas who came to power after the fall of Somoza were not content with appropriating the dictator's vast property holdings, and were misled by Cuban encouragement into thinking they could also milk the Soviet cow. The dreary pattern of corruption and repression continued under a veneer of anti-American posturing, sufficient to convince useful fools in Europe and the USA that real social change was taking place, but failing to convince the Castro-bitten and twice shy Soviets. However the success of the Sandinistas did revive the mystique of armed revolution, somewhat tarnished by Cuba's subservience to the Soviet Union, and attracted failed revolutionaries from all over Latin America: most prominently Montoneros leader Firmenich, who attempted to use the money obtained from kidnappings in the mid-1970s (including the sixty million dollar ransom paid for the Born brothers in 1974) to buy himself a place at the Sandinista high table. The Argentine military therefore had good reasons of their own to become involved in Central America, and sent training cadres to El Salvador, Guatemala and Honduras to instruct the locals in Dirty War techniques.

When Carter lifted the embargo on military aid to Argentina in 1979–80, he knew it would free up funds for the PNR's continent-wide programme of counter-subversion. Unfortunately, the programme included an intervention the USA fervently did *not* want in the rolling catastrophe that was Bolivia. Between July 1980 and August 1981 Bolivia was taken over by an alliance among the cocaine producers, a group of old and new Nazis led by Klaus Barbie (later joined by Stefano Delle Chiaie, responsible for a series of terrorist acts in Italy culminating in the August 1980 bomb-massacre at Bologna railway station), and Argentine military advisers, including Mohamed Alí Seineldín. They were presided over by General Luis García Meza, possibly the most evil man ever vomited into power in the tragic history of that benighted country. The outcome was the clearest possible illustration of the perils of realpolitik, for US policy towards Bolivia under Carter had been to support civilian government and economic reform precisely to prevent the emergence of the narco-military combination. One of the consequences of the Falklands War was to abort an Argentine-backed bid by the García Meza clique to recover power in July 1982, permitting the free election of President Siles Zuazo and the 1983 extradition of Barbie to France, where he was at last brought to book for his war crimes – in a trial that rigorously excluded evidence of complicity in his post-war doings by the Belgian government and many other influential Europeans.

The Argentines saw the lifting of the Carter embargo as a victory for their hard-nosed line on Human Rights, but their obsessions led them to overrate their importance to US policy makers: not in Central America, where their role was indeed valued, but in the South Atlantic, where it was not. They based their self-delusion on the war across the South Atlantic in Angola, where some 36,000 Cuban troops, acting as proxies for the Soviet Union, maintained an avowedly Marxist–Leninist government in the face of two groups of insurgents backed respectively by South Africa and the USA. Soviet objectives were to gain preferential access to Angolan natural resources and to create a base from which their naval forces could threaten the Western jugular: the sea route for oil tankers from the Persian Gulf. The Argentines and South Africans alike convinced themselves that the USA needed their help to counter this threat, whereas the view from Washington was that their bases at the British islands of Ascension in the Atlantic and Diego García in the Indian Ocean were more than sufficient, and that the US Navy could protect the sea lanes without additional shore facilities. The Cape Route was indeed a vital US geopolitical concern, but the Argentines failed to realize that they counted for less than a couple of little British islands in the equation.

It was fortunate for Britain that the remnants of her empire were of such great military value to the Americans, because if 1980–82 was a period during which the Argentine government was suddenly more important to Washington than at any time before or since, it was no less a time when dissatisfaction with the British reached boiling point. From 1964 to 1970 and again from 1974 to 1976, Labour governments inched towards Cold War neutrality under the leadership of Harold Wilson, a man widely believed to be a Soviet agent of influence, while the Conservative administration of 1970–74 was led by Edward Heath, whose commitment to Europe was rooted in a visceral anti-Americanism. Heath was brought down by communist-led strikes, as was Wilson's successor, Jim Callaghan.* There was no reason to believe the Conservative government led by Margaret Thatcher, elected in June 1979, would fare any better than its predecessors, while Britain's chronic social and economic crises led to defence cuts that greatly reduced its value as a military ally. Finally, the first year of the Reagan regime coincided with Britain's presidency of the European Economic Community (EEC) at the United Nations, during which it consistently voted with the other EEC representatives whenever there was a disagreement with the US delegation, most notably over Central America.

There were other, chronic irritants affecting Anglo-US relations. During the Carter administration Senator Edward Kennedy, paladin of American Progressivism, described Northern Ireland as 'Britain's Vietnam', implicitly arguing that since the British had not supported his brother's war in South-East Asia they could not reasonably expect the US government to interfere with the right of his Irish–American constituents to fund IRA terrorism. Andrew Young, Carter's African–American ambassador to the United Nations, pronounced that Britain 'invented racism', while Jeane Kirkpatrick, Reagan's appointee to the same post and a cabinet-ranked member of his national security team, was not only Irish–American but also possessed of that little learning which is a dangerous thing.

In an article written in 1989 Kirkpatrick insisted that 'for Latins, Britain is the historic colonial power.' She made a book of her PhD thesis about Argentina and was, in her own mind, an expert on Latin America. Somehow she failed to notice that Argentina was not in the slightest representative of the rest of the continent, which Argentines regard with racist contempt and by which they are, in turn, despised for their bombastic arrogance. As to the historic legacy, she really should have been aware that although Spain and Portugal were the colonial powers, persistent US interventionism had long ago won it the status of most hated nation. British soldiers, sailors and merchants played significant roles in the independence of Venezuela, Colombia, Ecuador, Perú and Chile – the USA contributed only the 'Monroe Doctrine' of European non-intervention in America, which it lacked the means to enforce. Uniquely in Argentina, the rout of British expeditions in

* In a TV programme not long before his death Callaghan and his long-time KGB liaison agreed there had been nothing improper about their association. It certainly did not help him to deal with the British comrades.

1806 and 1807 – embarked on in the expectation they would encourage the locals to overthrow Spanish rule (which they did bloodlessly in 1810, although only declaring independence in 1816) – became part of the nation's founding mythology. Kirkpatrick's suggestion that the USA and Argentina shared an anti-colonial heritage tells us as much about State Department's long-held delusion that the USA was untarred by the imperialist brush as it does about her own ignorance of history.

Both parties to the Falklands conflict knew the US attitude was crucial and that the British were hag-ridden by memories of the 1956 Suez debacle, when US financial pressure forced them to pull out of a joint exercise of gunboat diplomacy with the French and the Israelis. The Argentines believed they had succeeded in portraying the Falklands issue as a matter of decolonization and that therefore they would be the beneficiaries of a similar US demarche if Britain sought to recover the islands by force, a belief encouraged by State Department for many years. The background explains why – despite President Reagan's personal warning to Galtieri on the eve of the invasion that if it came to war the USA would support Britain – Argentine Foreign Minister Costa in a post-war interview could refer to a 'violent about-face in [US] policy when they lent their support to Britain . . . I think Argentines understand that we were not defeated by Great Britain. We were defeated because they had US support.' Indeed – and State Department bears a heavy responsibility for permitting Argentine Nationalists to believe it would be otherwise.

If it had been left to the diplomats the Argentine calculation would have been proved correct, but State Department, no less than the FCO, failed to anticipate domestic repercussions. Even Edward Kennedy supported Britain, and fellow Irish–American Senator Daniel Moynihan excoriated Kirkpatrick by declaring that 'the hottest places in hell are reserved for those who in a moment of moral crisis maintain their neutrality.' The reaction of US and British diplomats alike was to try to save face by subverting Thatcher's determination to settle for nothing less than a complete and unconditional Argentine withdrawal. Encouraged to do so by Francis Pym, appointed Foreign Secretary to replace Lord Carrington (who was the last Cabinet Minister ever to honour the principle of responsibility for the failure of his department by resigning), British ambassadors lobbied European premiers to urge compromise on her. But the *pièce de résistance* was Pym's initiative to 'internationalize' the islands, which State Department persuaded Reagan to espouse publicly on 3 June. Led to believe that Thatcher wanted him to provide political cover for a climbdown, Reagan was aghast when she vehemently rejected his initiative. Finally, at the UN Security Council meeting of 4 June, Kirkpatrick first joined Britain in vetoing a ceasefire resolution sponsored by Spain and Panamá, only to announce a little later that she had just received permission to abstain if she wished, and that she would recall her veto if she could. It was as perfect a getting-the-worst-of-all-worlds performance as the annals of diplomacy records.

In her excellent comparative study of Suez and the Falklands, Louise Richardson argues that belated recognition in Washington of the harm done to US interests by the brutal yanking on the economic reins to bring Britain to heel over the Anglo-Franco-Israeli attack on Egypt in 1956, followed by the cancellation of the US Skybolt missile system on which the credibility of the British V-bomber force depended, led to the sharing of the Polaris submarine ballistic missile system. The result was such a close working defence relationship that in 1982 Defence Secretary Caspar Weinberger did not feel it necessary to obtain formal presidential approval before author-izing full support for the British. Less persuasively, Richardson sees the shuttle diplomacy performed by Secretary of State Al Haig, in emulation of his mentor Kissinger's successful mediation in the Middle East following the Arab–Israeli War of 1973, as an example of Defence and State pursuing separate agendas. For this to be so it would be necessary to accept the sur-prisingly common view that the shrewd Reagan was a remote and disen-gaged president. Reagan made the US position clear to Galtieri in their private pre-invasion conversation. If the FCO/State combine had not so thor-oughly muddied the waters, he would have followed this with a public dec-laration. What Reagan was *not* prepared to do was come out openly and unequivocally on the British side while there was the slightest chance they were bluffing and might cut a deal at the last minute. Thus as well as creating the preconditions for the original Argentine miscalculation, US and British diplomats ensured the matter would be settled in blood by misleading Reagan about Thatcher's resolve. No doubt all the diplomats involved still think their supposedly good intentions redeemed their crass ineptitude.

The deep background of Anglo-US relations affects the Falklands story in another way. The delusions of grandeur nurtured by the 'special relationship' had Lord Carrington pursuing an insultingly unwelcome peace initiative in the Middle East when the Falklands crisis broke, provoking Prime Minister Menachem Begin of Israel, in his time a vicious terrorist with plenty of British blood on his hands, to rush arms and technical assistance to Argentina. In addition, the 'Europe vs. USA' false dichotomy colours much academic analysis of the war, thus Richardson concludes:

> The 'special relationship' can be seen as a policy coldly, pragmatically and persistently pursued by Britain as a means of exercising more influence internationally than would be warranted by an objective assessment of its power. Just as British nuclear policy can be seen as an inexpensive way of staying 'at the top table', so the British diplomatic policy of maintaining the special relationship can be seen as a means of exercising great power status vicariously through the United States. This relationship has enabled Britain to avoid assuming the role its power and position would seem to indicate for it, that of a leader of an emerging Europe.

What leadership post-war Britain, with all its social and economic miseries, could possibly have offered the booming Franco-German combine at the heart of the EEC is a question Richardson leaves unanswered. In his memoirs, ex-Defence Secretary Nott complains about pressure from State to negotiate a face-saving deal for the Argentine Junta, and alleges that France was Britain's 'greatest ally' in the conflict. Breathtaking. Without US logistical support the Task Force could not have proceeded beyond Ascension Island, and Weinberger even offered the use of a US Navy aircraft carrier should one of the two in the Task Force be disabled.* France merely refrained from delivering the Exocets already paid for by Argentina, and would not even have done that if the Gaullists, who have never forgiven Britain for fighting on while France surrendered in 1940, had still been in power. Nott's misrepresentation is unfortunately typical of the crab-like manner in which the case for ever-closer European Union is commonly advanced in Britain, polluting it in the eyes of many otherwise inclined to favour the project. There was no 'Europe' in 1982: after an obligatory (by treaty) initial show of

---

* Which is why Caspar received a post-war KCB and John – umm – did Nott, although he was knighted later.

solidarity, Belgium, Italy and Ireland did all they could to help Argentina and hinder Britain. Although Spanish public pronouncements seemed to court a British veto of their application to join the EEC, they quietly closed down an Argentine covert operation to attack Gibraltar with a team of divers led by one of the Argentine Navy's turned Montoneros. Finally, if France was such a true ally, one wonders why the British government was so strongly inclined to believe reports that there were black market Exocets available in Europe, to the point that millions of pounds were earmarked to deny them to the enemy. Fortunately it was discovered, at the last minute, that it was a scam by some more than usually shady arms dealers: but it is significant that their opportunistic fantasy was seriously entertained in the face of the truthful denials by the French government and by Aerospatiale, the makers of Exocet, that any missiles were unaccounted for.

All this said, it was not US diplomacy's finest hour. It was not coherent for the representatives of a society that believes itself to be 'the shining city on the hill' to appear to offer mediation on terms of moral equivalence between aggressor and aggressed, particularly when the former was a dictatorship and the latter a democracy. State Department and CIA alike failed to antic-ipate the fall-out from reversing Carter's Human Rights policy, and were unable to give Haig and Reagan objective guidance as the crisis unfolded because they had their own axes to grind. State, anxious to re-establish the low-cost hegemony over Latin America enjoyed by the USA until the 1960s, lost sight of the global picture. They also entertained the idea that support for Britain would result in the loss of Latin American hearts and minds, having failed to note that both were closed to them and would be for as long as the power and prosperity of the USA was a daily reminder of the relative insignif-icance of its southern neighbours. CIA, having reactivated the big brass balls that clang brigade, was obsessed with the idea that if they let a pissant country like Nicaragua defy them, the loss of face would undermine US interests all over the world. American support for Britain in the Falklands War led to the post-war departure from Guatemala, Honduras and El Salvador of what the CIA regarded as its Argentine proxies, which left the Agency scrambling for alternative means to destabilize the Sandinistas. The need to pay, directly, the British and Nicaraguan mercenaries who filled the gap, created the powder trail to the Iran–Contra scandal that bedevilled the last years of Reagan's administration and ran on into that of George Bush Sr., his vice-president and successor.

Hegemonial power has a downside: whether or not you like it, you will be drawn into other people's conflicts, damned if you do or if you don't by those not facing the costs and consequences of being the world's policeman. Though irritating, such carping seems a small price to pay for the privilege of making the rules you enforce. A more self-confident USA would have handled the Falklands crisis more decisively and would have emerged from it with greater credit: but when one reviews the widespread international complicity in the criminal Argentine regime, it is impossible to select US policy for particular blame. In the final analysis the most culpable accomplices were the British, because their policy of appeasement misled not only the Argentines but also the Americans into believing Britain would scuttle.

4 Shame

THERE IS A PROFOUND difference between guilt – which is recognized responsibility for a wrongful act – and shame. Shame is more powerful because it relates to what you are, your very being, and acts to prevent misbehaviour not for fear of getting caught but because it is incompatible with self-respect, the Spanish *pundonor* – personal honour. *Sinvergüenza* (literally 'without shame') describes a person who is wholly outer-directed and will do whatever he can get away with, which accurately describes the character of the men who ordered the invasion of the Falklands. By contrast, shame once had a strong claim to being the defining national characteristic of modern Britain, the common denominator of the best and the worst. As the Anglophile American émigré Bill Bryson put it, in *Notes from a Small Island:*

> What an enigma Britain will seem to historians when they look back on the second half of the twentieth century. Here is a country that fought and won a noble war, dismantled a mighty empire in a generally benign and enlightened way, created a far-seeing welfare state – in short, did nearly everything right – and then spent the rest of the century looking on itself as a chronic failure.

It was not by comparison with previous greatness but with geographically or culturally proximate societies that the British were increasingly convinced theirs was a failed society. That, however, was not the reason for the spiritual malaise Bryson identified. It was the same 'mood of unwarrantable self-abasement into which we have been cast by a powerful section of our own intellectuals' that Churchill condemned in 1933: a defeatist, anti-patriotic and dreary intellectual orthodoxy, which conditioned the transformation of Britain from a place where the practical once reigned supreme to the 'can't do' nation, where reforming even the most evidently dysfunctional institutions became virtually impossible. There was, from the start, something pathological about it. It was never healthy self-criticism but rather a process of both expressing and inculcating envy and resentment, either by negative comparison with a romantic ideal of a pre-industrial past or, more perniciously, by contrast with a New Society to be built by a self-selecting élite. The three twentieth century ideologies with pretensions to answering all the questions of existence were Marxism–Leninism, Nazism/Fascism, and Anglo-American Progressivism (see **Appendix A**). Of these Progressivism, the least offensive, proved the most durable, particularly in Britain, where the New Society has indeed produced a New Man – who looks uncommonly like the old model before he was civilized in the Victorian era.

Stripped of cant, Progressivism is a technique to create a one-party state within the constraints of formal elections. In an unguarded moment US President Woodrow Wilson (1913–21), he of 'a world fit for Democracy' and other resonant pieties of our time, admitted that the Progressive ideal was to become 'the party of government' – that is to create such a large body of people dependant on the state that the classical Liberal ideal of government as the arbiter among competing interests would be buried for ever. However it was in Britain, not the USA, that this vision came nearest to fulfillment, and where 'public' came to be seen as in some way morally superior to 'private' by a large proportion of the population, despite the fact that everything run by the British government, including defence, delivers lower quality service at significantly higher unit cost than comparable institutions elsewhere in the developed world. A generation ago 'public' included utilities, communications and the industries that Harold Wilson (Prime Minister 1964–70 and 1974–76), echoing the Soviet despot Lenin, considered 'the commanding heights of the economy'. Now barely hillocks in the economic landscape, for decades the nationalized industries cast a heavily subsidized and rancorous shadow over the whole society. Subsidies were a post World War II phenomenon, but the classist animosity nationalization was supposed to allay stretched back over a century and proved unappeasable. Unfortunately, the terms of debate about British economic under-performance were set by the Labour Party's doctrinal commitment to 'public ownership of the means of production', a distraction from the fundamental problem of incompetent management and chronically low productivity across the whole society.

The post-World War II 'settlement' in Britain, to which both the major parties subscribed, was based entirely on the Progressive conceit that individuals from academic and Civil Service backgrounds, of whom Harold Wilson was representative, could build a New Jerusalem. A vast increase in government power and patronage ensued, which it is in the interest of no politician to diminish and which changed the character of British society irreversibly. In his 1966 study *Parasitism and Subversion: the Case of Latin America,* sociologist Stanislav Andreski concluded that whereas business was the surest means to wealth in the USA, south of the Rio Grande it was politics: Britain still falls nearer the Latin American than the US end of that spectrum. *The Rise and Decline of Nations,* economist Mancur Olson's no less seminal study of societal sclerosis published the year of the Falklands War, selected Britain and Argentina as extreme examples of countries suffocated by special interest groups devoted to seeking favours from government or to cartelize markets.

The roots of the process reached back to the mid-nineteenth century with the founding of the professional Civil Service. The old system of personal patronage had the merit of tying the interest of powerful individuals to the performance of their nominees, with a healthy flushing of the system whenever power changed hands. The new permanent institution gradually became an independent power in its own right, not least because it enabled people with no managerial skill to strut the political stage, until at last they became the norm and politics ceased to attract individuals with the personality and life experience to impose their will on officials. The result was a creeping bureaucratization of British society, well described in a 1935 lecture on 'Liberty in England' by the novelist E.M. Forster:

We're menaced by . . . what I might call 'Fabio-Fascism', by the dictator-spirit working away quietly behind the façade of constitutional forms, passing a little law here, endorsing a departmental tyranny there, emphasizing the national need for secrecy elsewhere, and whispering and cooing the so-called 'news' every evening over the wireless [at the time a BBC monopoly], until opposition is tamed and gulled.*

Forster was speaking at a time of Conservative Party dominance, which underlines how the growth of statism in Britain was driven by considerations other than Socialist ideology, however much it has become associated with it since then. For decades British governments poured money into the public sector, creating or maintaining non-productive jobs until the economy sagged far below that of every comparable society outside the Soviet bloc. Wage inflation soared along with 'bureaucratic displacement' – the decreased attraction of private employment by comparison with the undemanding work and job security offered by the Civil Service and public corporations. The process had hit the buffers long before the Callaghan government went cap in hand to the International Monetary Fund in 1976, seeking a *deus ex machina* for the monetary discipline his government was unable to introduce on its own authority. The conditions of the loan included deep cuts in public spending, long used to conceal structural unemployment, while the indifference of the trade union movement to public welfare was demonstrated by a succession of strikes culminating in the 1978–79 'winter of discontent', when the dead went unburied and household refuse piled up in the streets.

All who represented Britain abroad during the 1970s can remember being asked 'what has *happened* to your country?' It was a fair question, because economic failure was only one aspect of a more general societal breakdown. At its heart was the crumbling of respect not merely for the lawmakers, but for the law itself. Belief that, however flawed it might be, the law still embodied societal norms and would be fairly applied was more central to national identity than the monarchy, the Church of England, Westminster and the Union Jack put together. However, once the law became the expression of an abstract vision of an ideal society, the evolutionary process of Common Law, which had made the British one of the most self-policing

* 'Fabio' refers to Fabianism, Progressivism by another name. See **Appendix A**.

peoples on earth, was undermined. The assault has continued, and today the administration of justice enjoys less legitimacy in the eyes of the governed than at any time since Common Law began to evolve.

Others will have their own Damascene moment, but for me it came in the late 1970s after a decade in which one corruption scandal after another had destroyed any illusions about the British police, when judges at last began to accept defence lawyers' arguments that their clients had been 'fitted up'. Yet their lordships sternly refused to review the 1974 conviction of the Guildford Four, known by all to be based on false police testimony after the capture of the real perpetrators in 1975.* It was over this issue that Lord Denning, the leading practitioner of Progressive judicial activism in British jurisprudence, revealed his unequivocal belief that the purpose of the law was to uphold the authority of the state and not, as defined by English history, as the citizen's bulwark against over-mighty rulers. It became apparent that judges had knowingly conspired to pervert justice, under cover of which police forensic and investigative skills had become as atrophied as their ethics. A spiral of disrespect created an 'us and them' mentality that incubated further corruption. Perhaps I was naive before, but when my eyes were opened to the degrading facts I not only left government service but also the country.

I was already half inclined to do so by growing contempt for the political class, condensed for me in the akin-to-treasonous Harold Wilson. He received generous 'consultancies' from the Soviets in the 1950s, and the trade agreements he negotiated with Moscow as Prime Minister permitted the Russian intelligence services to establish a presence in London that overwhelmed the resources of MI5. Shamefully but hardly surprisingly, while Wilson was Prime Minister the USA severely curtailed defence and intelligence collaboration. Christopher Andrew's *The Mitrokhin Archive* confirms that Wilson was never formally recruited, but what Lenin described as the 'useful fools' of the West never were. Making it worse, Wilson's reason for permitting the Soviets to roll a Trojan horse into London appears to have been the simmering resentment, common to many of his generation, summed up by Jason Leigh in *The Wilson Plot*:

★ The Guildford Four were not released until 1989. Nobody was punished for the perjury that convicted them.

Wilson shared the sense of bitterness over the fact that the US, with its shrewd terms for war-time 'lend-lease', had not only colonized (*sic*) Britain's lucrative pre-war markets in Latin America, but had also stolen (*sic*) her scientific heritage by getting free (*sic*) manufacturing rights to British inventions in return for desperately needed supplies. Jet aircraft were one of the key technologies Wilson singled out in his later reminiscences, along with nuclear research, radar and antibiotics.

The political alternative on offer in Britain was little better. Anyone seeking a model of anti-charisma could do worse than select Edward Heath, leader of the Conservative Party 1965–74. Although he did permit a mass expulsion of Soviet spies in September 1971, sour anti-Americanism on a par with Wilson's was one of the few passions to animate his tepid personality. Anti-Americanism was the motor of his desperate desire to join the EEC on whatever terms he could get, although in other respects motivated by the same quest for a *deus ex machina* to revitalize the economy that drove Callaghan to call in the International Monetary Fund five years later. Voters generally punish infirmity of purpose and when Heath, beset by communist-led strikes, called a 'Who Rules?' general election in 1974, the British people concluded that if he did not know, then he was the wrong man for the job.

To put Heath and the era that saw him rise to prominence in perspective, he is on record as believing that Tony Blair is 'too right-wing'. Even the idiotic cabal Leigh writes about, which thought to remove Wilson in a coup d'état in the late 1960s, subscribed to the bureaucratic Progressive model, a smothering consensus that drove well-educated Britons to seek fresh air abroad in their thousands. For over two centuries Britain's greatest exports had been capital and people, looking for better opportunities all over the world and in the process, as the historian Niall Ferguson argues so persuasively in *Empire,* creating the modern world. The American jibe that everyone in Britain with get up and go had got up and gone has little merit, but it is less easy to dismiss the possibility that British public life never recovered from the slaughter of a generation of patriotic young men in the volunteer army that fought the first half of World War I. Their sacrifice was widely believed to have been in vain even before resurgent German militarism had to be beaten down again in 1939–45. The 'brain drain' of the 1960s and 1970s represented a similar loss to society, but bore witness to the erosion of faith that Britain was a worthwhile entity: never before had the exodus featured so many who, had they remained, would have enjoyed the best British society could offer. The Progressives had built their New Jerusalem in England's green and pleasant land and the lost tribe, far from celebrating it, fled in droves.

Meritocracy is simply a new word for equality of opportunity, the classical Liberal ideal. Those wishing to explore how a nation that stood alone for liberty in 1940–41 came to repudiate it in the post-war years could do worse than start with Michael Young's *The Rise of Meritocracy* followed by Friedrich Hayek's *The Constitution of Liberty*. Hayek mistakenly thought *The Rise* was a brilliant satire of contemporary ideals of social justice, whereas in fact Young, one of the most influential of the New Jerusalemites, intended the exact opposite. Young believed with all his heart that it was unfair to reward merit because talent and the disposition to make the most of it was randomly distributed, and that meritocracy was more damaging to people's self-esteem than the social inequalities of the past because it left them with nowhere to hide from society's verdict on their usefulness. Although the US academic John Rawls has made the running more recently, Young was I believe the first to propound a philosophy with mediocrity as its ideal.

Among the grosser symptoms of this depressing world-view were the gratuitous maintenance of wartime social and economic controls and the throwing of good money after bad to maintain employment in the unreformable traditional industries. Maybe even more pernicious was the perversion of the Welfare State into what the aptly surnamed social satirist Tom Sharpe contemptuously described as 'a piggy bank for the middle classes and literate skivers, and an incomprehensible and humiliating nightmare of forms and jargon for the provident poor'. Progressives claimed to believe the social pathologies nurtured by their programmes were 'unanticipated consequences' but when, after undeniably adverse results, they persisted in administering them, it became apparent that while the consequences may not have been foreseen, they were not unwelcome. Like the tellingly named Social Security programme in the USA, many provisions of the British Welfare State took from the poor to buttress the middle class. Only the exercise of psychological denial to the point of intellectual hibernation made it possible for 'Progressives' who entered public life at this time to think well of themselves.

It may be that democracy inevitably produces government of the mediocre, by the mediocre and for the mediocre, which may in turn be no bad thing given the adage that a nation may be fortunate to produce great leaders but most unfortunate to need them. However, after most of the tenets of the post-war settlement proved illusory, what happened in Britain was a case of throwing out the baby and treasuring the bath water. Thus the nationalization of medicine was originally supposed to be a self-mortgaging investment, with the cost to society reducing as public health improved. As a result it preserved a host of restrictive practises in the National Health Service, which has proved no more capable of increasing outputs commensurate with increased inputs than any other nationalized industry. The 1948 Town and Country Planning Act also persisted unchanged, despite overwhelming proof that it had totally corrupted local government while failing to provide the affordable housing and sensible land management that was its rationale. No area of public policy was more subject to Progressive dogma than education, and in no other aspect of national life did the gulf between alleged intentions and measurable outcomes grow so steadily. What remained amid the wrack of objectively failed social and economic policies was an ever-increasing class of parasitic government employees.

It cannot be argued that the political class was unrepresentative – levels of electoral participation remained high throughout the period and if in retrospect one may judge that the country did not get the government it deserved, it certainly got what it voted for. The same can be said of the British press: the line of descent from quality journalism crossed the rising line of incestuous self-regard at about this time, testimony to which was the absurd number of books later published about the media and the Falklands War. Circulation figures remained high as the entire enterprise tipped over into voyeurism and gossip. Although public opinion polls regularly show journalists to be by far the least respected occupational group in the country, they are the product of a highly competitive market and must be judged to speak both to and for their readers. With the exception of the outstanding Ambrose Evans-Pritchard, British journalists in several South American hotspots where I was able to check their reporting against reality made no effort to find out the truth. I have heard it said that they were demoralized by lack of British interest in foreign news in general and Latin America in particular, and by the fact that their material was so often spiked. Yet if you consider what you do is pointless, but continue to do it, you cannot fail to dislike what you see – with clear eyes – in the mirror. As in politics, I assume the best people generally got out while the *sinvergüenzas* stayed and prospered, and it was they who set the tone for British journalism, recruiting and promoting others like themselves.

A scene-setting chapter for an account of a military campaign is not the best place to propound a general theory of how the public face of a nation that once defined itself in terms of 'good form' could have become so squalid. But it is necessary, because an intrinsic part of that process has been a striking refusal on the part of British intellectuals to question the organizing principles of their own society. I have not found a British Carlos Escudé, willing to examine the collective mindset shaped by Progressivism in Britain with the same open-mindedness he has shown with respect to Nationalism in Argentina. Yet it can be argued that Progressivism has played the same role in Britain as Nationalism has in Argentina, creating a corpus of assumptions shared by all men and women without realizing it, a continuity that quite possibly represents the very identity of a new and artificially generated nation, quite deliberately cut off from its own historical roots. Consequently younger generations are not aware how Britain became such a wretched place in the 1970s, when the New Society – to make way for which much that was worthwhile in the old one had been destroyed – was revealed to be as bankrupt of ideas as it was of the means for continuing its ruinous policies. No people is ever likely to see itself as others see it, but it is not possible to understand why the Argentines acted as they did, and believed almost to the end that they would be able to dictate the terms of a negotiated settlement, without recognizing that they had good reason to view Britain as a society bereft of dignity and honour.

If the Junta had not precipitated matters in 1982, by the following year Britain would have sold off or scrapped the ships that made the counter-invasion possible. The Junta knew this but went ahead anyway, confident there would be no such reaction. Even after the British landed, the

Argentines believed their garrison in the Falklands would hold out until 'General Winter' came to its relief, based on a calculation that the British soldier of 1982 was not the man his father had been. But he was: and better in attack than history might have led one to expect of an army more famed for stoicism than tactical flair. Nor was the British political class quite as bereft of *virtus* as those who knew it well judged it to be, although the fact that its unexpected moral vigour was expressed by a *femina* added a sting to the sharp dislocation of expectations in Buenos Aires. 'That woman would not dare,' said Galtieri to Haig. But she did, risking a defeat that would have led to the fall of her government and the electoral eclipse of her party, when standard Whitehall operating procedure was to scuttle – proclaiming a victory for common sense and moderation all the while.

Had they been attuned to it, the Argentines might have noticed there was a new sheriff in old London town when Thatcher sent the SAS to resolve the Iranian Embassy siege of early May 1980, and when she let ten Irish terrorist convicts starve themselves to death in May–October 1981. Her toughness marked a change, although not one likely to impress men who knew they could have cleared up 'the troubles' in Northern Ireland in a few months, and who regarded British policy in the province as further proof of spinelessness. They had a point – as soon as the hunger strike was called off, Thatcher's government made all the concessions the terrorists had been demanding. As Martin Dillon confirms in his well-researched account of *The Dirty War* in Ulster (although, given the competition, 'The Murky War' would have been more appropriate), the British authorities knew the Irish Republic's future Taoiseach Charles Haughey and a coven of Roman Catholic priests were the godfathers of the Provisional IRA, but they have never dared say it out loud. Today, seeing murderers and torturers in receipt of handsome salaries paid by British taxpayers while their kindred scum grow fat on smuggling, robbery and extortion, it is tempting to think the world would be a better place if London had indeed waged the Dirty War the IRA and their useful fools in Britain never ceased to denounce. But one has only to look to the legacy of it in Argentina to banish the thought.

With regard to the Falklands, the Argentines had no reason to suspect Thatcher's administration was any more principled than its predecessors. In 1979 and 1980 the Thatcherite Foreign Office Minister Nicholas Ridley made the FCO line his own and set out to do the job that couldn't be done. Not only the Argentines but also to the Guatemalans, who had similar ambitions towards Belize, were offered a 'leaseback' arrangement whereby their sovereignty claims would be recognized but the territories would continue for a defined period under their existing form of government. To crown it, at a public meeting in Stanley in late November 1980, Ridley told the Kelpers they could expect no help from Britain if they were invaded, because 'we do not have the capability.' His proposals were rejected nonetheless, and he flounced back to Buenos Aires. There were two islanders present who were covertly working for the Argentines and one of them had a clandestine transmitter installed in his attic, which may explain why Ridley found the Argentines disinclined to waste any more time on him. Although Ridley was savaged from all sides when he tried to defend the initiative in the Commons, Foreign Secretary Lord Carrington was not similarly roasted by his fellow peers in the Lords and so was not forced to reconsider the bankrupt policy he had inherited.

Thatcher's relative robustness was far from universally admired, even among those whom one would expect to applaud it. In a Yorkshire TV documentary, Brigadier Thompson recalled thinking 'although you don't mind really dying for your Queen and country, you certainly don't want to die for politicians.' But if democratically elected representatives do not have the right to decide when national interests are at stake, who does? In fact there was all-party support for the war, and the majority of the population was fully behind it, including the Royal Family, with Prince Andrew serving as a helicopter pilot on *Invincible.* In fairness, Thompson's comment came in the context of being ordered to advance from the bridgehead before the logistical requirements were in place. However, his anger at being cast on a far shore with inadequate means to perform an extremely demanding job would have been better directed at 'the system', run not by politicians but by senior officers, officials and defence contractors.

Until German Chancellor Bismarck invented the welfare state to bind the lower middle and industrial working classes to his vision of a strongly centralized state, what we now prefer to call defence was the sole pork barrel available to rulers. Consequently there is no government department, in any country, more steeped in corruption and cronyism, or more adept at covering up its errors and omissions. Far be it from me to urge sympathy for politicians, but it might encourage them to tackle substantive issues if political journalists could free themselves from their dependence on the off-the-record briefings with which Whitehall keeps ministers in line, and turned their attention to the workings of the anonymous and self-serving institutions that actually run the country. Any attempt to make the bureaucracy more responsive or cost-effective is countered not only by a blizzard of damaging leaks, but also by ensuring that the first casualty of any funding reduction will be something with a high symbolic value. One such was MoD's determination to scrap the ice patrol vessel *Endurance*, the last symbol of British commitment to the South Atlantic and undoubtedly one of the 'signals' that led the Argentines to believe they could invade with impunity. It had nothing to do with saving the pittance she cost to run, everything to do with raising the political cost of the defence cuts announced for 1982.

All the bureaucratic games aside, the test of a military establishment is whether it is able to rise to a challenge, however unexpected, and to prevail. Sound of trumpets, enter First Sea Lord Admiral Leach. Forty years earlier he stood at the dockside in Singapore searching in vain for his father, captain of the battleship *Prince of Wales*, sunk by shore-based Japanese aircraft. Leach therefore knew, better than anyone, how vulnerable the navy would be off an enemy coast without Airborne Early Warning. Yet when he learned of the imminent Argentine invasion he bypassed the chain of command to tell his Prime Minister that if a counter-invasion were not undertaken and carried through to a successful conclusion, then Britain would be a different country, one whose word counted for little.

But what word was that? For seventeen years Britain's 'word' to the Falkland Islanders had been that if it came to the crunch they would be abandoned. Leach was speaking of what the French call 'the real country', the one to which political parties from time to time must submit their works for judgement. The bedrock underlying all the accretions of petty larceny and gratuitous intrusiveness that constitute the modern state is that those to whom power is delegated will defend their own. Faced with the reality of an armed attack on British citizens, both Thatcher and Michael Foot, the deeply pacifist Leader of the Opposition, understood this immediately. Others did not, and it is they who largely defined the subsequent terms of debate about the Falklands War. If asked directly probably none would dare argue that, as Callaghan put it, the islanders should have been handed over to 'a gang of fucking Fascists': but in their view it would have been an acceptable price to get rid of Thatcher.

The polemical edifice of those who hate the lady and all her works rests on the belief that she had to go to war to save her political skin, and thereafter exploited an easy victory to ride a populist wave in the 1983 general election. Politicians should not, in Churchill's celebrated phrase, 'resent criticism even when, for the sake of emphasis, it parts for the time from reality', and with the graffiti washed away the reality in 1982 was a high-risk operation pursued when politically safer options were available. Furthermore, any government elected in 1979 would have been compelled to continue the process of cutting public expenditure begun by Callaghan. If, as some have argued, the defence cuts announced for 1982 were a 'signal' that precipitated the Argentine invasion, a re-elected Labour government would certainly have made them earlier and would therefore have been unable to respond. Therefore, to pursue 'what if' a little further, if a Labour government had been in power, it would have been humiliated in 1982.

In fact, outright catastrophes aside, voters generally attach little importance to foreign affairs and the Falklands War merely coincided with a jump in government popularity following Geoffrey Howe's 1982 budget, which represented a sharp break with the pessimistic expectations that had informed public policy for a generation.

The electoral facts are instructive. The Conservatives won 339 seats with 44 per cent of the popular vote in 1979 and 397 with 42 per cent in 1983. The figures for Labour were 268 seats with 37 per cent of the popular vote in 1979 and 209 with 28 per cent in 1983. The picture is one of a collapsing Labour vote, not of a Conservative surge. Also noteworthy is that 44 per cent of the popular vote translated into 339 Conservative seats in 1979 and 419 Labour seats in the supposedly epoch-making 'landslide' of 1997. With the electoral dice so loaded in favour of the Labour Party, clearly the voters were rejecting the programme it adopted in 1983, which also split the party. As the Tories pointed out during the campaign, the top twelve policy objectives in the 1983 Labour Party manifesto were identical to those of the Communist Party of Great Britain. If there was a 'Falklands factor' it played

Evil little men with delusions of grandeur: Admiral Emilio Massera (left) and Admiral Jorge Anaya (right). (Reuters and Camera Press)

Royal Marines gratuitously humiliated: the image that galvanized the British. (Camera Press)

Alfredo Astiz, 'sworn to die' in defence of South Georgia, surrenders without firing a shot. (IWM)

Full military honours for Petty Officer Félix Artuso, sole fatal casualty of the fighting in South Georgia, tragically killed through misunderstanding. (IWM)

Lieutenant Colonels Hew Pike (3 Para) and 'H' Jones (2 Para) on flight deck of Task Force flagship HMS *Hermes*, with Amphibious Command ship HMS *Fearless* in the background. (IWM)

Rare daylight extraction of a Special Forces patrol from behind enemy lines: the Mark I eyeball once again proved to be the most dependable source of operational intelligence. (Military Picture Library)

RI 4's Sub-Lieutenant Oscar Silva, MVC, the outstanding Argentine platoon commander of the war. Until he was killed, the Scots Guards made no progress on Tumbledown. (Soldados Magazine)

Sergeant Ian McKay, VC, outstanding representative of the NCOs who won the war on the ground. He died restoring momentum to the stalled 3 Para assault on Longdon. (Airborne Forces Museum)

RI 25 Sub-Lieutenants Roberto Estévez (left), who died, and Juan Gómez Centurión (right) who survived. Both won CHVCs in the fight with 2 Para for the Goose Green isthmus. (Soldados Magazine)

Residue of the formal, mass Argentine surrender ceremony on Goose Green airfield. (Empics)

Paras in Argentine 120mm mortar bomb crater on Longdon demonstrate how dense Falklands peat absorbed the energy and shrapnel, making artillery relatively ineffective. (Military Picture Library)

Major John Kiszeley leading a patrol of Scots Guards with 'war face' firmly in place. (Getty Images)

The entirely preventable tragedy at Fitzroy – it could have been so much worse. (Empics)

The wrack of a defeated army – the centre of Stanley on 15 June 1982. (IWM)

out within the Conservative Party, where Thatcher was able to get rid of the openly disloyal Pym and other 'wets' (a schoolboy expression denoting personal qualities similar to the milder meaning of *maricón*), but the clean-out proved ephemeral. Her most lasting achievement was to force the Labour Party to rethink its reason for being: she was unable to prevail on her own party to do the same, with consequences dismally apparent today.

Although the war may have had little electoral significance in Britain, it did mark a line below which most members of the political factions perceived they dared not sink, and a rare moment when officials were told, not asked what to do. The journalist and historian Max Hastings, whose broad familiarity with things military made his reporting stand out from the rest during and after the war, declared that, 'after so many years . . . reporting on one aspect or another of national failure, it was enormously moving to see and to record a national success.' But, he continued, it was 'saddening to come back to the real world'. That sadness once hung over Britain like a toxic cloud. I am glad to see my sons' generation free of it, but it lingers with those of us who caught a glimpse of a basically decent and astonish-ingly self-regulating civic culture before the social engineers destroyed it. If the war did play a part in persuading the British people there was life in the old dog yet, so much the better. But if so, it was a devastating judgement on the political nation that it took a totally unwilled and deeply unwelcome event to bring it about.

5 Men and Weapons

PERCEPTIONS OF NATIONAL character play a large part in bringing nations to war, but the fighting is done by institutions with personalities of their own. England's political contribution to the world developed in good part thanks to a geography that made it unnecessary to maintain a large standing army, permitting the evolution of a libertarian consciousness that could not emerge in the garrison states of mainland Europe. Defence of the islands rested instead with the Royal Navy, which was doubly beneficial: first because it acted as a distant outpost protecting the peace and prosperity of the realm without being much involved in it; second because it permitted the projection of trade, hence Napoleon's militaristic sneer that the English were a nation of shopkeepers. So they were, a circumstance permitting them to ruin him and other tyrants whose ambitions outstripped their means. Worldwide, the imposition of English rule on anarchical societies encouraged the emergence of peaceful institutions, in due course permitting subject peoples to demand self-government by right. Force, by contrast, was almost invariably met by force whatever the justifying grievances: something the Argentines might have considered before kicking over the beehive, choosing a battlefield where the traditional British combination of a strong navy and a small professional army was most likely to succeed.

The Italo-Hispanic culture of Argentina turned the absence of any invasion threat from a blessing to a curse, with the Argentine Army becoming a Praetorian Guard that saw itself as the embodiment of the nation's higher aspirations. If an armed institution considers itself a school of civic virtue, how it performs in battle will hinge almost entirely on whether patriotism and manliness – assuming these have indeed been inculcated – can compensate for lack of military expertise. Lack of expertise will make itself felt not so much in the conscript who, if properly trained, could achieve an acceptable level of proficiency, but in the career cadre condemned to repeat the basic cycle year after year. Brigadier General Jofre, seeking to explain his passive defence of Stanley, wrote 'our troops were never organized, taught or equipped to confront enemies trained to conduct world-level operations. The cost and effort it would have involved were totally beyond the country's possibilities.' Jofre's excuse was ill-founded. Properly spent, the vast sums diverted to military use under the PNR could have produced just such an army. It did not because of the Argentine Army's political agenda and consequent neglect of professional development.

Peter Dunn, co-author of *Military Lessons of the Falklands War: Views from the United States,* briskly summed up the reasons why the British prevailed:

> Whatever the merits of the Falklands victory, no self-respecting professional military officer should confess to having learned anything from it. To admit that one discovered that superb fitness, high morale, superior fieldcraft, capable and courageous political and military leadership, a sound logistics system, intelligence, a sensible control of the news media, air and naval support, a sound strategy, skilled improvisation and an intelligent use of technology (as opposed to reliance on it) were necessary for victory is to admit that one is in the wrong business.

Dunn's is not an entirely accurate assessment of the British performance. Although the Marine Logistics Regiment and the RAOC and RCT contingents performed certifiable miracles with inadequate resources, and the tiny cadre of Task Force intelligence officers rapidly gained speed from a standing start, the lack of contingency planning or even a basic military threat assessment would have doomed any force not as wearily resigned to 'skilled improvisation' as the British.* Their ability to make do with what they had was the crux of the whole campaign. The Argentines had not considered the possibility that they might have to fight, and by creating a situation that would award victory to whoever 'muddled through' to best effect, they surrendered the initiative to the world's premier practitioners of the art. Buenos Aires never fully recovered from surprise – bordering on disbelief – that the British were prepared to do battle against an equal or superior number of troops on the Argentine doorstep: and thereby hangs a salutary tale of the difference between paper and real military strength (see **Appendix B**).

The Argentine Army had better boots, better cold-weather jackets (but not, oddly, over-trousers of similar quality), better rations, better standard and sniper rifles, some with better night sights, superior passive night goggles and ground radar. On 16 May a short article, 'What is the Enemy Like?' was published in the newssheet *Gaceta Argentina,* distributed to all the troops around Stanley, in which the author stressed the British 'are men like you or I. Tall, short, good and bad tempered, none of them have the attributes of Superman, especially invulnerability to bullets. They are armed with FAL [SLR] rifles like ours, MAG [GPMG] machine-guns, rocket launchers and mortars identical to ours. But they do not have 120mm mortars.' In fact the rocket launchers were not identical and the British had many more of them, in particular the dependable single shot 66mm US M72 but also the longer range Swedish 84mm Carl Gustav, which misfired more often than not in the damp conditions of the Falklands. Crucially, they also had the man-portable, wire-guided Milan anti-tank missile system, fired from the prone position and deadly accurate over 2,200 yards, against the longer range but wheeled ballistic 105mm rocket artillery used by the Argentine Army (equivalent to the British 106mm Wombat, shipped but not used). The Argentines believed their big Brandt mortars could redress the balance for their outranged artillery, and the 120s were indeed formidable support weapons. But their crews were overly concerned that they might be tracked by the British Cymbeline mortar locating radar (which in fact did not live up to expectations) and, because the 120s required hard standing (even the 81mm mortars used by both sides drove their baseplates into the peat, making it

---

* Of which the tsunami of shipping organized at short notice was the most spectacular example. See **Appendix C**.

impossible to maintain continuous accurate fire on a given target), they were vulnerably installed on the rocky ridges rather than concealed on the reverse slopes where they belonged.

However, although at least as well-armed as the British, the Argentine Army lacked the fundamentals. Warriors since time immemorial have formed primary groups, classically groups of ten – the basic bricks of armies – around cooking and eating together. The Argentine Army regarded food simply as fuel and followed the US pattern (which failed so miserably in Vietnam) of treating soldiers as factors of industrial production: interchangeable inputs supposed to respond to impersonal stimuli. Among their infantry only the Special Forces and RI 25 had combat webbing and rucksacks, the rest only awkward kitbags. These deficiencies pale, however, beside the fact that during April and May no programme of physical exercise was carried out and the conscripts were not put through live firing exercises or rehearsed in general combat drills until they became second nature. They did not even test-fire their weapons and draw up range cards.* The conscripts were mostly eager young men in the prime of life, and it was disgraceful to waste their potential by doing so little to prepare them, compounded by the folly of not rotating them back to Stanley for periodic breaks from their cold and damp defensive positions in the hills.

Discipline is instilled by a combination of repetition, physical and mental challenge, and punishment. Absent the first two, the Argentine Army relied far too much on the last, employing nineteenth century field punishments that included staking men out on hillsides and collective beatings. There were no formal executions, but Trudi McPhee saw an officer shoot two men in the head, presumably for theft, near the Distribution Point at the Moody Brook barracks in mid-May, and Don Bonner saw another shot to death near the containers in the paddock in front of Government House. No Argentine accounts confirm these summary executions, but they may explain why the previously rampant thieving of stores abruptly stopped in early may. A lack of discipline intrinsic to Argentine culture also meant the conscripts could not be depended on to take proper care of themselves or their equipment, putting junior officers *in loco parentis* in a way unimaginable in the British army. Many, particularly the

* A plan drawn up for each defensive position showing arcs of fire and distances to aiming points.

newly-graduated sub-lieutenants, rose admirably to the challenge and earned the devotion of their men, and some proved outstanding combat leaders: but when they were killed or disabled their men usually lost heart.

The loss of a subaltern had no such effect among the British because the soldiers were far more self-sufficient and there was leadership in depth. Normally responsibility moves up the pay scale in peacetime and rapidly down in war. During the 1970s the traditional importance of NCOs in the British Army had been accentuated by the long struggle against terrorism in Northern Ireland, which was very much a section leader's war. The sergeants and corporals who went to the Falklands had shown initiative in near-war situations and were accustomed to command. To put the two conflicts into perspective, sixteen members of 2 Para were killed in an IRA ambush at Warrenpoint on 27 August 1979, one more than at Goose Green on 28 May 1982. In contrast there was very little combat involved in the Argentine Dirty War, and the qualities it tended to enhance were pathological.

Although only a crude measure of combat leadership, it is notable that fourteen (8 per cent) of the 177 British killed in ground fighting were officers, while seventy-four (42 per cent) were NCOs. Twenty-three (8 per cent) of the 279 Argentines killed in similar circumstances were officers, but only fifty-eight (21 per cent) were NCOs. As in most garrison armies, many of the Argentine Warrant Officers and top sergeants (SNCOs) were corpulent, bureaucratic and corrupt. Some of the bitterest criticism by returning Malvinas veterans was directed at SNCOs who abused their authority up to the eve of battle, when they remembered urgent appointments elsewhere, not least because those they had abused might wish to settle accounts in the time-honoured way. The phenomenon was far less prevalent in the British Army, but even there one or two deeply unpopular SNCOs prudently found ways not to offer their backs, at night, to men who hated them.

In general, however, British NCOs owed their stripes to the respect of men who were not easily impressed. The cult of hardness in the Paras and Marines was more pronounced than in the line regiments, but although brutality was an ingredient it was not enough, by itself, to command obedience. Young men are merciless judges of character, and although promotion from the ranks depended on the recommendation of officers, the commissioned officers were acutely aware that their own authority depended on good NCOs. In the Argentine infantry the career officers and NCOs were 'us' together against the conscript 'them', whereas among the British 'us' were the privates and the NCOs, 'them' the officers who were regarded with cold-eyed scepticism by their men until they, too, had proved themselves. Junior officers were still expected to set an example but were far from being indispensable. It may be argued that the emphasis on personal leadership came at the expense of the managerial qualities required of the higher ranks, but at the cutting edge it was a fierce meritocracy in which authority was earned, unlike the rest of contemporary British society.

Considerations common to all the land battles are best addressed here. **Diagram 1** shows optimum defensive positions that, thanks to the high water table, were not easily created in the Falklands. The principal factors include the topographical crest, the highest point of a feature, and the military crest, which commands the flattest line of sight for ground-grazing small arms fire. An ideal defensive position will be on the reverse slope (for protection from direct fire), with communications trenches or even tunnels leading to forward observation posts and firing positions overlooking a uniformly gentle slope. Failing this, a defender must move down the hill to achieve grazing fire and to deny an attacker the dead ground. The problem for the Argentines was that they hit groundwater as soon as they dug into the peat at the foot of the hills, forcing them either to build highly visible above-ground firing positions or to move further up the hill and lose optimum fields of fire. At Darwin/Goose Green they had to deal with smooth, convex slopes, and their solution was to dig in halfway up and cover the dead ground with detached trenches firing across the face of the main line. Elsewhere the slopes were generally concave or uniformly gentle, littered with rock formations that could be converted into bunkers relatively easily, but which also gave an attacker good cover from grazing fire. The greatest weakness of the hills around Stanley was that they ran east–west and so were naturally strongest facing north or south. This was particularly true of Longdon and Tumbledown, both of which were attacked from the west and prised open like clamshells.

The standard British infantry advance to contact is 'two up, one back' as illustrated in **Diagram 2**, with the artillery beating a path – a battalion

Diagram 1
TOPOGRAPHICAL v. MILITARY CREST

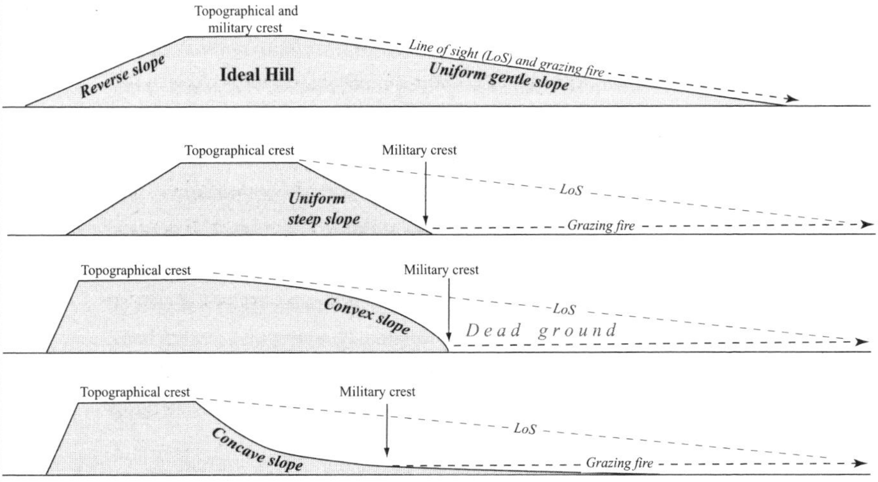

Topographical and
military crest

Line of sight (LoS) and grazing fire

Reverse slope   **Ideal Hill**   *Uniform gentle slope*

Topographical crest   Military crest

*Uniform
steep slope*

LoS

Grazing fire

Topographical crest   Military crest

Convex slope   *D e a d   g r o u n d*   LoS

Topographical crest   Military crest

Concave slope   LoS

Grazing fire

Diagram 2
CANONICAL (WARMINSTER) INFANTRY COMPANY ATTACK
(one up two back for standard arrowhead formation)

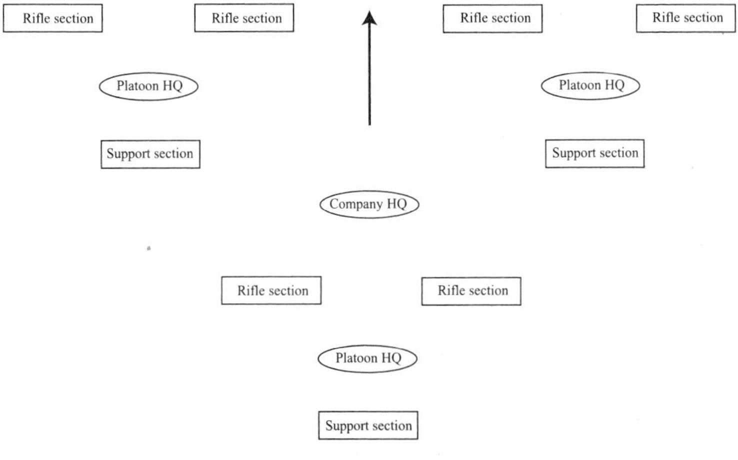

| Rifle section | Rifle section | | Rifle section | Rifle section |

Platoon HQ   Platoon HQ

Support section   Support section

Company HQ

Rifle section   Rifle section

Platoon HQ

Support section

attack would simply multiply the pattern with two companies forward, one back and Tactical HQ in the middle. Once at close quarters, the sections would advance by individuals running forward under covering fire from their comrades, obscurely if charmingly known as 'pepper-potting'. 2 Para was the only battalion to attack twice, on both occasions permitted by topography and enemy deployment to fight a battle of manoeuvre. At Darwin/ Goose Green they spread out and dispersed energy with near-disastrous results, but at Wireless Ridge they reverted to basics with overwhelming success. Another departure from orthodoxy involved the extended line abreast adopted by B Company, 3 Para at Longdon, which degenerated into a bloody stalemate. It is no surprise British troops did best when they adhered to the tactical formations they had practiced again and again in training.

The Argentines shipped or flew 159 wheeled transport vehicles to the islands (seventy-five of them Jeeps), all of which were effectively limited to Stanley, the airport peninsula and the road running south-west in the direction of Fitzroy as far as Wall Mountain. The track running north-west as far as the Murrel Bridge was more rustic (see **Maps 22** and **23**, pp.207–8). Driving off-road in the Falklands, even in a four-wheel drive vehicle, requires a practiced eye for subtle changes of vegetation that indicate swampy ground, or the rivulets that lurk to trap the unwary even on seemingly level moorland. 3 Commando Brigade was able to draw only seventy-six Volvo 'Bandwagon' tracked over-snow vehicles and trailers from UK stores (the majority were in Norway), as well as nine four-wheel drive Eager Beaver fork-lift trucks that were worth their weight in gold at the beachhead. The Argentines discounted the possibility of a distant British disembarkation because their own experience (their Amtraks bogged down during the invasion) led them to believe that even tracked vehicles could not cope with the terrain. Helicopters played an increasingly important role as the campaign developed, but it was the Bandwagons plus the assistance given by Kelper guides and drivers that made it possible for 3 Para and 45 Commando to achieve operational surprise by marching across East Falkland.

The Argentines also shipped twelve Panhard six-wheeled armoured cars to the Falklands. The Panhards had a useful 90mm gun, but proved no more able to operate off-road than any of the other vehicles. The opposite occurred on the British side, where unfounded doubts about the cross-country capability of the eight light tanks (four each Scorpions with 76mm and Scimitars with 30mm cannon) of 3 and 4 Troops, the Blues and Royals, kept them back from Darwin/Goose Green: a battle for which they were ideally suited. At Wireless Ridge they completed the demoralization of the defenders, but before that, all four tanks and their Samson recovery vehicle had driven across the island without difficulty, frequently called on to extract bogged-down Bandwagons, help infantry stragglers to catch up and to relieve others of their burden of support weapons and ammunition.* If the demands of the Household Division genuinely had to be accommodated, it would have saved a lot of time and lives to have shipped the rest of the Blues and Royals in the second wave, instead of the almost useless wheeled vehicles of the motorized Guards regiments.

Perhaps the greatest technical advantage enjoyed by the British was the Clansman family of radios, vastly superior to the older US Army equipment used by the Argentine Army. These included a half mile-range radio-telephone carried by section leaders in an ammunition pouch, a backpacked 2 mile-range set with a throat microphone, also used by section leaders and by platoon commanders, and 5 to 10 mile-range sets at company and battalion level. These could be connected by a 2-mile landline for secure communications or set up as automatic relay stations, extending range without weight penalty for the forward troops. There was a hand-cranked trickle-charger for the batteries, but a full charge realistically required a vehicle-mounted generator (as did the Argentine Army radios, which is why some jeeps were found at the top of the hills around Stanley). Battery life only became an acute problem during the long battle at Darwin/Goose Green, and in general the Clansman radios gave trouble-free service and worked well in atmospheric conditions that all but silenced the Argentines.

Good communications compatible across the three services produced overwhelming British superiority in fire support. The infantry battalions were accompanied by a Royal Artillery Battery Commander with two forward observers at the company level, Naval Gunfire Observers and Forward Air Controllers. In addition, infantry platoon and section leaders were trained

---

* Ironically the only victim of the terrain was the sole Samson recovery vehicle, which collapsed the Murrell Bridge on 13 June and capsized into the stream, from which it was itself recovered by a Chinook helicopter.

and equipped to call in fire support. However lack of adequate transport meant the artillery had to operate without the modern apparatus of fire direction, which to some extent denied the British the full benefit of the new 105mm light gun that outranged the Argentine Army's Italian Oto Melara pack howitzer by over 4 miles. The Argentine-built 155mm guns in turn outranged the British 105s by 3 miles, but they had limited ammunition and their primary mission was to return fire against Royal Navy ships.*

The Argentines did not, as the British did, use gridded maps and could only call in variations from fixed defensive fire points, which precluded close support. Both sides soon found the peat tended to swallow up the effects of 105mm high explosive (HE) shells, and extreme precision is required when firing air-bursting shrapnel shells (VT, from the variable timing fuses) in close proximity to one's own troops. **Diagram 3** shows how the limited range of their artillery conditioned the Argentine defence of Stanley. On neither side were the infantry expected to move forward without gunner support and, lacking the means to maintain more than a couple of batteries in forward positions, a static defence of a tightly circumscribed perimeter was really the only option open to the Argentines. Not the least of their errors was to fly in two artillery groups equipped with 105s, when half the number of 155s, with nearly three times the throw-weight of the British guns, would have been far more effective. Today, peat regeneration has reduced the craters dug by 105mm HE to dimples: but the excavations made by the 155s still bear witness to how fortunate the British were that their enemy chose quantity over quality.

Naval gunfire provided a unilateral British advantage, but the Royal Navy had forgotten (as it has obstinately refused to accept since) its historic function of bringing a crushing weight of ordnance in support of littoral operations. The rapid-firing 4.5-inch naval gun is smaller than the armament on a main battle tank and does not have the requisite earth-moving ability. Throughout May the gunships came inshore by night and day until the 12th (when *Glasgow* and *Brilliant* discovered the shortcomings of their air defence missile systems), thereafter only for a few hours per night, using the rest to travel from and to the distant Carrier Group. The ships carried Naval Gunfire Observers from 148 Battery, 29 Commando Regiment RA, who were inserted

---

* Two 155mm guns were flown in on 14–15 May, two more on 12–13 June.

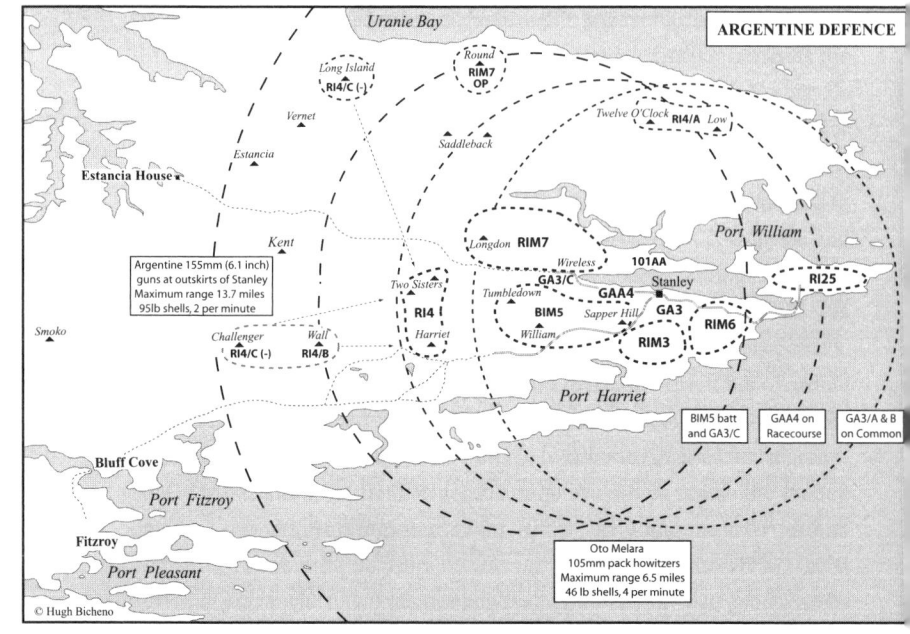

Diagram 3: LAND ARTILLERY

Within the ARGENTINE DEFENCE map:

Uranie Bay

Long Island
RI4/C (-)

Round
RIM7
OP

Vernet

Twelve O'Clock RI4/A Low

Saddleback

Estancia

Estancia House

Kent

Argentine 155mm (6.1 inch)
guns at outskirts of Stanley
Maximum range 13.7 miles
95lb shells, 2 per minute

Longdon RIM7

Wireless   101AA

Port William

Two Sisters

GA3/C

Tumbledown

GAA4

Stanley

RI25

Smoko

RI4

BIM5

Sapper Hill GA3

RIM6

Challenger

Wall

Harriet

William

RIM3

RI4/C (-) RI4/B

Port Harriet

BIM5 batt
and GA3/C

GAA4 on
Racecourse

GA3/A & B
on Common

Bluff Cove

Port Fitzroy

Fitzroy

Port Pleasant

Oto Melara
105mm pack howitzers
Maximum range 6.5 miles
46 lb shells, 4 per minute

© Hugh Bicheno

Within the BRITISH ASSAULT map:

Uranie Bay

BRITISH ASSAULT

Long Island

Round

Vernet

Saddleback Beagle Ridge Twelve O'Clock Low

Estancia

3 Para

2 Para

45 Cdo Kent

Longdon

Port William

Wireless Ridge

Airstrip

Two Sisters Tumbledown

Stanley

42 Cdo

Goat Ridge

Sapper Hill

Smoko

1/7 GR

Challenger

Harriet

William

2 SG

Wall

1 WG

Port Harriet

2 Para

Port Fitzroy

British 105mm light guns on
western slope of Kent & Challenger
Maximum range 10.7 miles
35 lb shells, 5 per minute

N

Port Pleasant

© Hugh Bicheno

0 1 2 3 4 5
miles

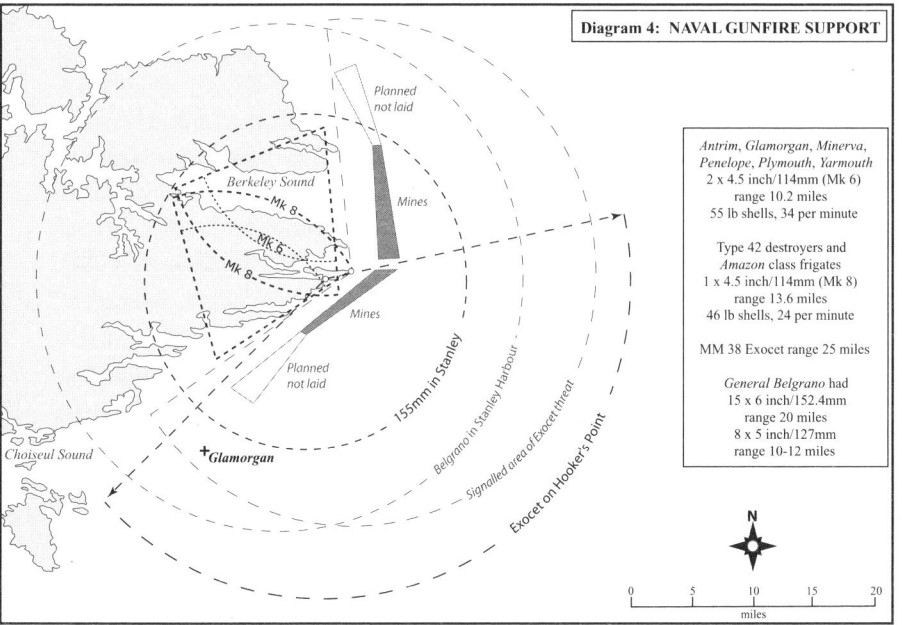

Planned not laid

Berkeley Sound

Mk 8

Mk 8

Mk 8

Mines

Mines

Planned not laid

155mm in Stanley

Belgrano in Stanley Harbour

Signalled area of Exocet threat

Exocet on Hooker's Point

Choiseul Sound

+*Glamorgan*

Antrim, Glamorgan, Minerva, Penelope, Plymouth, Yarmouth
2 x 4.5 inch/114mm (Mk 6)
range 10.2 miles
55 lb shells, 34 per minute

Type 42 destroyers and
Amazon class frigates
1 x 4.5 inch/114mm (Mk 8)
range 13.6 miles
46 lb shells, 24 per minute

MM 38 Exocet range 25 miles

General Belgrano had
15 x 6 inch/152.4mm
range 20 miles
8 x 5 inch/127mm
range 10-12 miles

N

0   5   10   15   20
miles

by helicopter to direct fire. This unit had been three months away from dissolution, along with the rest of the Royal Navy's amphibious capability, in response to cuts in budget allocation. After the war Thompson admitted he should have reserved naval gunfire for counter-battery work, because despite its accuracy it was not until the land-based artillery got in range that the axiom about green troops breaking under bombardment was finally confirmed. There is no substitute for throw-weight, and morale suffers far more from heavy area fire than from selective precision.

The Royal Navy gunships might have been neutralized if the Argentines had proceeded with an early proposal to repeat the sensible use of *Canopus* in 1914 and bring the cruiser *General Belgrano* into Stanley Harbour. As **Diagram 4** illustrates, this was probably the single act that could have tipped the scales against the British. The defence of Stanley would have been immeasurably strengthened by her 6-inch and 5-inch guns (plus two twin radar-directed 40mm AA guns and two Sea Cat missile batteries). As shown in the next chapter, despite heroic efforts Stanley airstrip was never disabled, and *Belgrano* was not only a much smaller target but also, of course, mobile. In the absence of any other explanation it is to be assumed the Argentine Army did not wish to give the Argentine Navy such a prominent role.

The British could have *lost* this war at sea or in the air. But the war could only be *won* by the infantry, and at the core of their struggle lie factors to be addressed with circumspection. After troop numbers and equipment are tabulated, the topography assessed and weapons ranges calculated, in the end it came down to one group of young men overthrowing another in savage contests where the greater will to dominate prevailed. An essential component of that dominance was the killer instinct. It cannot be sanitized and we should not avert our gaze, but to look too hard is to indulge in the pornography of violence. Graphic memoirs have credibly reported that British troops shot or bayoneted wounded men and others no longer trying to defend themselves: and – in a few cases – mutilated the dead. There is, however, a yawning moral gulf between acts committed in hot blood, when momentum must be maintained and when attacking troops cannot even stop to look after their own casualties, and the killing of men whose surrender has been accepted. There was at least one such incident and the perpetrator should perhaps have been punished as an example, even though there were extenuating circumstances. But two men who cut ears from the enemy dead were both later killed in action, an omen powerful enough to ensure it became a rare, non habit-forming vice in the British Army. For the rest, men whose own lives were in the balance cannot be said to have possessed *mens rea,* the state of mind required in law to indicate culpability. If the standards of normal jurisprudence are applied to the behaviour of men in battle, then the circumstances of close quarter combat are such as to justify unconditional acquittal on grounds of temporary insanity.

The British owed their victory to the ferocity of infantry who went into combat stressed beyond the point to which even the best-trained troops should be pushed. Fear of death or injury may be the last straw, but psychiatric casualties multiply under challenging non-combat conditions, including cold, poor nutrition, uncertainty, and prolonged fatigue. All of these conditions were gratuitously inflicted on the Paras and Marines in the period between the breakout from San Carlos, on 27 May, and the battles for the Stanley hills sixteen days later. After marching across East Falkland to arrive when the enemy was still scrambling to reform his defences, the Paras and Marines were held back on snow- and wind-swept hillsides, while the unfit Guards of the second wave were ferried forward. This was done at the expense of logistical support for an assault that military logic demanded should be made without delay. The folly of opening up a second front – when there were barely enough transport resources to support one – was compounded by the reasons for it, which were the Army's belated desire for the appearance of parity with the Navy, and concern the Guards should not be seen to follow in the footsteps of less august regiments. Meanwhile, the front line was eroded by non-combat casualties ('Other' in **Appendix B**), and for every man lost to exposure and illness there must have been several whose physical and mental resources were exhausted. It is not surprising that some of the men became feral when at last released to discharge their remaining energy on the enemy.

It is a cliché of military history that victory goes to the side that commits the fewest mistakes. It is more accurate to say that – since warfare is by nature uncertain – success goes to the one that wins the initiative, and is therefore able to force errors on the enemy. The Argentine effort was seriously undermined by strategic misconceptions, but they might still have won if they could have imposed even a temporary check on the British advance. That they were unable to do so speaks more of motivation than of weapons or tactics. For all the patriotic exhortation, many of them were shocked to discover they had not come to liberate fellow Argentines, but to impose alien rule on people who hated them. Nor could they fail to question the wisdom of their military-political leaders in looking for trouble abroad when there was more than enough at home. At no point were the conscripts told that all they had to do was hold on for the winter. On the contrary, when on 17 May their hot meals were cut to one a day – despite visibly ample food stockpiles in Stanley – they received an unequivocal message that they were in for a long siege. Thus they were not psychologically prepared to resist the furious assaults that came out of the night during the last days of the war. Consequently only a small minority even fired their weapons, the rest doing nothing to attract attention until they could safely surrender.

Contributing to the Argentine debacle was a further predicament. The troops best trained and equipped for the conditions were the Patagonia-based

Marines and Major General García's Army 5 Corps, but the still unresolved conflict with Chile meant that only one Marine battalion and part of one 5 Corps brigade could be released. Thus the crippling anomaly that the South Atlantic theatre commander, Vice Admiral Lombardo, and nominal overall land commander, García, were unfamiliar with the great majority of the units posted to the islands.* A further layer of confusion was added by appointing a civil administration specialist as governor and not replacing him when it became clear he would have to fight a war. Although not all the officers under his command were so restrained, the mild-mannered Brigadier General Menéndez and his staff behaved impeccably towards the islanders. but he was not a leader and never developed a coherent plan for the defence of the islands, consenting without demur to Galtieri's disastrous strategic conception of the land battle as a passive holding action, while attrition by the Argentine Navy and Air Force defeated the British.

Pursuant to his vision of the land war as a holding action, Galtieri insisted both the main islands should be defended. He also decreed a division of responsibility with about 10,000 men around Stanley forming *Agrupación* (Army Group) *Puerto Argentino*, under the command of Brigadier General Jofre, and a little over 3,000 men of *Agrupación Litoral*, under Brigadier General Parada, covering the rest of East Falkland, Lafonia and all of West Falkland. The conscripts of Jofre's own X Brigade were mainly a hardbitten crew drawn from the industrial slums of Buenos Aires, while those of Parada's III Brigade were the descendants of the warlike Guaraní, who under the tutelage of Jesuit warrior missionaries held out against the Spanish and Portuguese longer than any other Amerindian people. There was nothing wrong with the raw material, but neither brigade was acclimatized or trained to deal with the conditions. Incomprehensibly, one of Parada's regiments (RI 4) was allotted to Jofre and Brigadier General Daher's two IX Brigade regiments (RI 8 and RI 25) were divided between the Army Groups, the whole constituting a thoroughly confused command structure.

Deprived of his own troops, Daher became Menendez's Chief of Staff and was given responsibility for the Special Forces, which consisted of the sixty-four-strong Argentine Army Comando 601, the forty-man 'Scorpion'

---

* Neither officer made any significant contribution to the campaign. Their task became one of administering operational decisions made by their Commmanders in Chief in the Junta.

detachment from the Gendarmería (paramilitary federal police), and an Air Force Special Operations Group. They were later joined by Comando 602, an ad hoc group of fifty para-trained officers and NCOs put together by the charismatic Major Aldo Rico, which was thrown into battle within twenty-four hours of its arrival in the islands. The Argentine Army had not developed any doctrine for the employment of the Special Forces and in the weeks before the British landing of 21 May, while the SAS and SBS came ashore to acquire operational intelligence, Comando 601 wasted its time and a great deal of aviation fuel flying all over the islands to check on the local inhabitants. Once British air attacks began to bite, extra shoulder-mounted AA missiles were flown out to Stanley – at first mainly Blowpipe, but later Soviet SA 7s supplied by Libya – only to find that few soldiers knew how to use them. Several who did were members of Comando 601, and as a result the unit was tasked with setting up mobile AA ambushes. This came at the expense of the roles for which they were eminently qualified, which were to act as coast watchers to provide early warning of a British landing, to stay behind as air and artillery observers, and to strike behind enemy lines. In the end they were used as assault troops, winning a number of well-deserved medals for valour but contributing far less than they could have done.

One could go on itemizing the factors that contributed to British success, but in the end it all comes down to training, training, training. It not only permitted the British to get the most out of their men and equipment, but also led the Argentines to believe that because they could not perform certain tasks, the enemy would not be able to either. A representative example was 2nd Lieutenant Guillermo Anaya, son of Admiral Anaya. As an Army helicopter pilot serving with Combat Aviation 601, Anaya assured Menéndez that it was impossible to fly at night using passive night goggles. However the pilots of C Flight, 824 Squadron, flew SAS and SBS teams to night insertions all over the islands throughout the war, using an earlier generation of goggles. In one of the best Argentine accounts of the war, *Comandos en acción*, Isidoro Ruiz Moreno sadly summed up the disparity:

> A routine-bound and bureaucratic Army will always encounter
> the same problem – the possession of large stocks of weapons

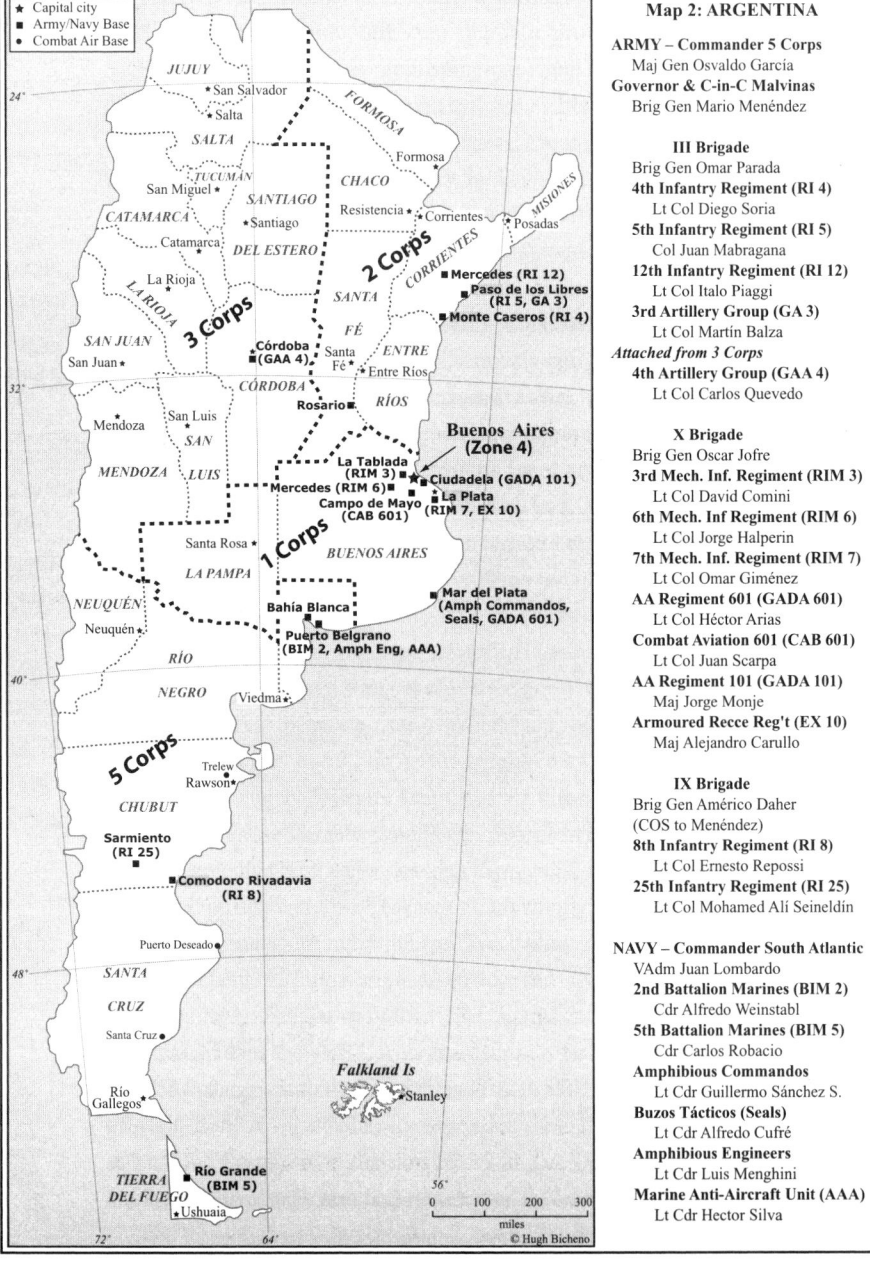

Map 2: ARGENTINA

ARMY – Commander 5 Corps
Maj Gen Osvaldo García
Governor & C-in-C Malvinas
Brig Gen Mario Menéndez

III Brigade
Brig Gen Omar Parada
4th Infantry Regiment (RI 4)
Lt Col Diego Soria
5th Infantry Regiment (RI 5)
Col Juan Mabragana
12th Infantry Regiment (RI 12)
Lt Col Italo Piaggi
3rd Artillery Group (GA 3)
Lt Col Martín Balza
Attached from 3 Corps
4th Artillery Group (GAA 4)
Lt Col Carlos Quevedo

X Brigade
Brig Gen Oscar Jofre
3rd Mech. Inf. Regiment (RIM 3)
Lt Col David Comini
6th Mech. Inf Regiment (RIM 6)
Lt Col Jorge Halperin
7th Mech. Inf. Regiment (RIM 7)
Lt Col Omar Giménez
AA Regiment 601 (GADA 601)
Lt Col Héctor Arias
Combat Aviation 601 (CAB 601)
Lt Col Juan Scarpa
AA Regiment 101 (GADA 101)
Maj Jorge Monje
Armoured Recce Reg't (EX 10)
Maj Alejandro Carullo

IX Brigade
Brig Gen Américo Daher
(COS to Menéndez)
8th Infantry Regiment (RI 8)
Lt Col Ernesto Repossi
25th Infantry Regiment (RI 25)
Lt Col Mohamed Alí Seineldín

NAVY – Commander South Atlantic
VAdm Juan Lombardo
2nd Battalion Marines (BIM 2)
Cdr Alfredo Weinstabl
5th Battalion Marines (BIM 5)
Cdr Carlos Robacio
Amphibious Commandos
Lt Cdr Guillermo Sánchez S.
Buzos Tácticos (Seals)
Lt Cdr Alfredo Cufré
Amphibious Engineers
Lt Cdr Luis Menghini
Marine Anti-Aircraft Unit (AAA)
Lt Cdr Hector Silva

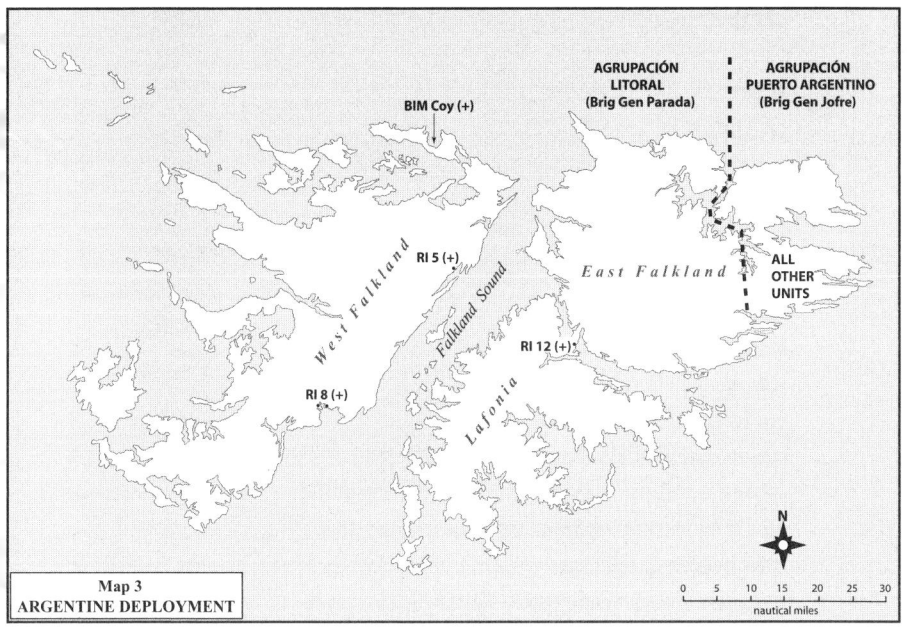

Map 3
ARGENTINE DEPLOYMENT

0   5   10   15   20   25   30
nautical miles

which nobody knows how to use because they have not been fired in practise. Thus the money spent on them was wasted and saving them [for use in combat] was a false economy.

Most accounts by Argentine veterans allege enormous British numerical and equipment superiority, indicating the half-defeated state of mind they brought to the battle. But it was also a convenient excuse, permitting some to carry away from the islands a belief that they had proved their manliness even in defeat. Thirty-five-year-old Lieutenant Carlos Domínguez of RI 25, a legend in his own mind for having made a rude gesture at the TV cameras after the surrender, was of the opinion that 'despite being outnumbered and outgunned, we were not *maricones* like they were. They never fought man to man but always ran away when the bullets flew. They only dared attack us when they had destroyed us with their artillery and knew they were stronger.' Aldo Rico, no less a fanatical Nationalist than any member of Seineldín's regiment of zealots, but who, unlike Domínguez, had fought and knew what he was talking about, dealt summarily with a leading question about the

British being mercenaries who fought for pay, not country. To fully appreciate his reply, it must be remembered how deeply significant the term 'dignity' is in Argentine Nationalist discourse:

> My experience with the English soldier is very positive – for them. I believe he is a good soldier. Above all because he has a moral awareness of what human dignity means. The English did not bring to battle any man who was not prepared to survive in combat. In an army, over and above any technological advances, the man remains the most important factor. And it shows no respect for human dignity to bring unprepared men to battle.

6 Preliminaries

RATHER THAN DUPLICATE the many chronological accounts of the war available on the net and in print, this chapter will seek to identify points early in the conflict where time's arrow might have been turned from the course it took. The diplomatic background has also been done to death and, anyway, I have nothing to add to the general observations made in earlier chapters. The current vogue for 'what if' history is entertaining and serves the purpose of reminding readers that 'historical inevitability' is nonsense: a seemingly obvious point that nonetheless meets sharply increasing sales resistance the higher up the intellectual ladder people consider themselves to be. As we have seen, issues dating back to the Reformation played an important role in creating the cultural momentum for the war: but in the final analysis all wars come about because of the impatient ambition of some and the determination of others to thwart them. How they then play out is no less contingent than any other aspect of human history, often on quite small decisions whose significance only becomes apparent in retrospect.

One can imagine the look of confident superiority on Admiral Anaya's face as he activated the long-postponed second phase of the occupation of the South Atlantic islands. Under the cover of a contract to clear scrap metal from South Georgia, awarded to the Buenos Aires businessman (and front man for the Argentine Navy) Constantine Davidoff, a party of Marines led by

Alfredo Astiz was landed at Leith and, being Argentines, felt compelled to blow their cover by raising the national flag and firing shots in the air. To the alarm of the Junta the British did not assume the position as expected – indeed there were unmistakable signs of a robust reaction. This panicked Buenos Aires into bringing forward the invasion of the Falklands, scheduled to take place two months later in late May, when winter would have imposed a six-month delay on any British counterstroke. Although the FCO wanted to treat the South Georgia provocation as it had the occupation of Southern Thule, unspinnable signals from Governor Rex Hunt in Stanley and Captain Barker of the ice patrol ship *Endurance* made it impossible. Meanwhile, the Argentines did not conceal their contempt for the pleas by the British ambassador in Buenos Aires to refrain from forcing themselves on the islanders, when London was so close to handing them over anyway. Viewed through Argentine eyes, it was just one last confirmation of chronic British bad faith and cowardice.

Although the Argentines feared the British might fly in reinforcements, the FCO opposed any such 'provocative' act. Nonetheless, an outright scuttle was stymied by the simultaneous presence in Stanley of the Royal Marines' Naval Party 8901 and its annual relief, which doubled the size of the garrison (to sixty-eight), and by Hunt and Barker's initiative in landing the Marines from *Endurance* at Grytviken on South Georgia. Fighting could not be avoided unless someone in London was prepared to order a preemptive surrender, and the historical obloquy of Prime Minister Neville Chamberlain for doing precisely that at Munich in 1938 made a repeat performance unthinkable. Some are born brave, some achieve bravery, but civil servants must have bravery forced upon them, and it is a tribute to the genius of Argentine diplomacy that it created a situation in which even the most frantic appeasers in Whitehall could find no wriggle room. I have already covered the several ways in which the performance of British officials fully lived down to Anaya's assessment of them and have no desire to gild the lily. I do not think it fair to blame some and praise other individuals according to whether their appointments demanded ignoble or robust behaviour: it was an institutional failure, in which the personality of the officials involved had little influence on developments.

Nor would I wish to give the impression that officials were unrepresentative of their political masters. The debate in the Commons that followed the Argentine invasion, barring the words of Michael Foot cited in Chapter 1, was such as to compel a charitable reassessment of the annually maligned Guy Fawkes. It was a snivelling, *sinvergüenza* collective performance that was to be echoed by the post-war Franks Committee, which included a minder for the reputation of every government that had contributed to the debacle. This to ensure the final report should conclude that 'if the British government had acted differently in the ways the Committee has indicated, it is impossible to judge what the impact on the Argentine Government or the implications for the course of events might have been.' If this was correct, there was a prima facie case for the abolition of all embassies and SIS stations, because if the behaviour of foreign governments is impossible to predict there is no point in studying them. Since this was very far from being the case of an Argentine regime that had advertised its intentions for years, the Franks Report stands as just one more of the many paper monuments to the web of mutually fondling associations that constitutes the British 'establishment'.

Although the more notably emetic performances were by Labour MPs, this was to be expected. Had the party roles been reversed, no doubt assorted Tories would have broken ranks to stake out a position in opposition to their own leader as well as the government, gambling on a British defeat. As it was, however, the prize for guessing wrong went to Tam Dalyell, who ended his sole spell on the front benches by defying Foot, something he was to spend the rest of his interminable career trying to justify. Anthony Wedgwood 'Tony' Benn chose attack as the best form of defence for his share of responsibility, as a Cabinet Minister, in the appeasement and arms sales to Argentina by the Wilson and Callaghan governments, and denounced the Tories for doing the same. But the most reprehensible performance was by Ted Rowlands, who when a Foreign Office Minister went to Buenos Aires to cringe and wriggle after the Southern Thule occupation, and who now chose to reveal that the British could read Argentine diplomatic ciphers.*Argentine embassies used the same, top of the line Swiss Crypto

---

* Seeking thereby to show that the Argentine invasion could not have been a surprise, something that still awaits explanation. But for a Privy Councillor to make such a revelation in public session was unpardonable.

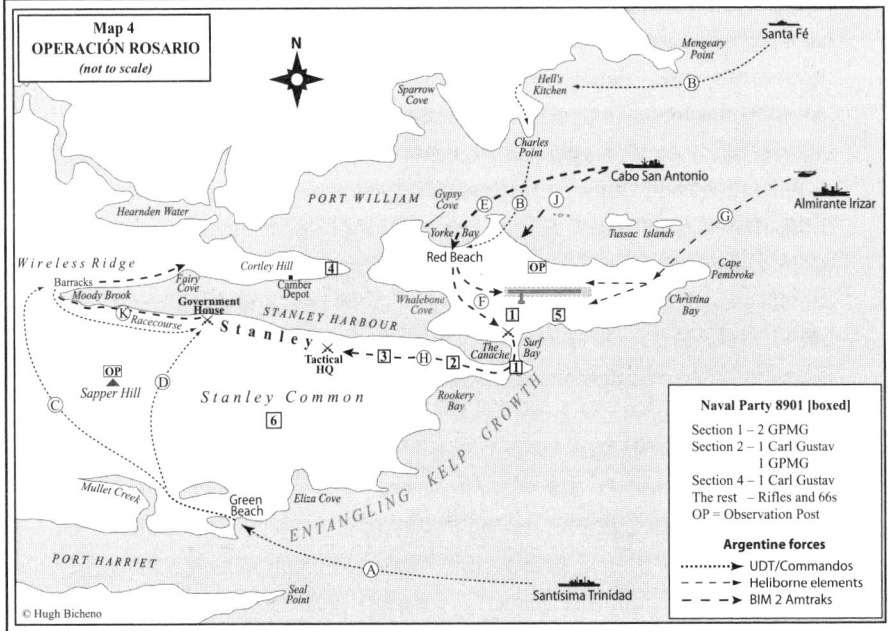

**Map 4
OPERACIÓN ROSARIO**
(not to scale)

N

Santa Fé

Mengeary
Point

Hell's
Kitchen

Sparrow
Cove

Charles
Point

Cabo San Antonio

PORT WILLIAM

Gypsy
Cove

Yorke Bay

Almirante Irizar

Hearnden Water

Red Beach

Tussac Islands

OP

Cape
Pembroke

Wireless Ridge

Cortley Hill

4

Christina
Bay

Barracks

Moody Brook

Fairy
Cove

Cambet
Depot

Government
House

Whalebone
Cove

Racecourse

STANLEY HARBOUR

F

1

5

Stanley

The
Canache

Surf
Bay

Tactical
HQ

3

H

2

Sapper Hill

OP

D

Stanley Common

Rookery
Bay

Naval Party 8901 [boxed]

Section 1 – 2 GPMG
Section 2 – 1 Carl Gustav
1 GPMG
Section 4 – 1 Carl Gustav
The rest – Rifles and 66s
OP = Observation Post

C

6

Argentine forces

••••••► UDT/Commandos
– – – ► Heliborne elements
— – –► BIM 2 Amtraks

Mullet Creek

Green
Beach

Eliza Cove

ENTANGLING KELP GROWTH

PORT HARRIET

Seal
Point

Santísima Trinidad

© Hugh Bicheno

Operational Sequence

A. 2100-2345 – Marine Commandos in inflatable rafts led by Captains Sánchez and Giachino land from the invasion flagship, the (British Type 42) destroyer *Santísima Trinidad*.

B. 0100 – Underwater Demolition Teams land from the (US *Guppy* class) submarine *Santa Fé* to seize Charles Point lighthouse, cross to Pembroke Peninsula and to secure Yorke Bay beachhead.

C. 0630 – main commando force under Sánchez attacks deserted Moody Brook barracks before returning to join siege of Government House.

D. 0630 – Giachino leads smaller commando force against Government House, killed during siege.

E. 0630 – Amtraks depart LST *Cabo San Antonio* to land BIM 2 and leading elements of RI 25 at Yorke Bay. C-130s with the main body of RI 25 begin to take off from Comodoro Rivadavia.

F. 0730 – RI 25 secures Stanley airport, BIM 2 loses an Amtrak in combat at the neck of Pembroke Peninsula.

G. 0800 – Additional RI 25 and FAA personnel to airport by helicopter from icebreaker *Almirante Irizar.*

H. 0830 – BIM 2 Amtraks advance on Stanley, lose another in short battle at White Rocks.

J. LCTs deliver artillery from *Cabo San Antonio*. First C-130 lands 0845

K. Surrender at 0915. Amtraks advance through Moody Brook towards Camber, bog down at Fairy Cove.

120

AG machine systems as their armed forces, so this was the precise equivalent of publicly announcing, during World War II, that the Allies had broken the Enigma system used by the Nazis. It is unlikely we shall ever know how much damage this betrayal of trust did to national security, but if anyone other than an MP had given the information to the Argentines they would have been prosecuted. One is compelled to wonder whether, after the usual early warning from Chilean Air Force radar failed, signals intelligence might have prevented the horrible deaths of so many of his fellow Welshmen on *Sir Galahad* if Rowlands, a representative New Labour peer since 2004, had not warned the Argentines that their most secret communications were an open book.

The Argentine plan for the occupation of the Falklands on 2 April 1982 combined overwhelming force with an effort by Marine commandos to capture Governor Hunt and to take out the Royal Marines at the Moody Brook barracks. The decapitation plan was dependant on surprise and it is a measure of the inflexibility of Argentine decision-making that it went ahead unchanged even after it was known the garrison was alert. The snatch squad that went to Government House failed: its commander Captain Giachino was mortally wounded in the back courtyard, two others captured after breaking into the empty maid's quarters, and two more wounded at the fence around the vegetable garden (see **Map 33**, p. 322). The main commando force under Captain Sánchez Sabarots blasted the barracks, but there was nobody there.

NP 8901 having done as much as could be expected, Hunt ordered them to surrender when the Argentine Amtraks rumbled through Stanley towards Government House. Rear Admiral Büsser, the overall invasion commander, was anxious to minimize British humiliation: but his efforts were undone by photographs flashed around the world of his men standing over prostrate Royal Marines, which had the predictable effect on British public opinion. The airfield had not been rigged with demolition charges and an advance party of RI 25 captured it intact, permitting the airlift of the rest of the regiment to proceed. Seineldín's men were intended to be the permanent garrison as part of 5 Corps, but in the chaotic scramble to pack the islands with troops after the leading elements of the British Task Force sailed on 5 April, RI 25's task became limited to the defence of the airport peninsula:

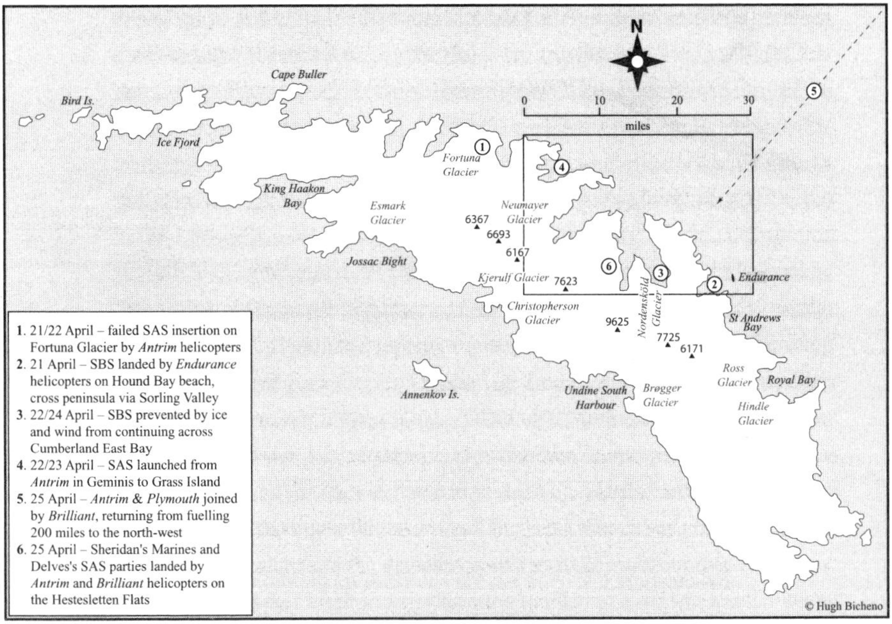
N
Cape Buller
Bird Is.
Ice Fjord
King Haakon Bay
Esmark Glacier
Fortuna Glacier
Neumayer Glacier
Jossac Bight
Kjerulf Glacier
Christopherson Glacier
Nordenskjöld Glacier
Endurance
St Andrews Bay
Annenkov Is.
Undine South Harbour
Brøgger Glacier
Ross Glacier
Royal Bay
Hindle Glacier
0 10 20 30
miles
6367
6693
6167
7623
9625
7725
6171
1. 21/22 April – failed SAS insertion on Fortuna Glacier by *Antrim* helicopters
2. 21 April – SBS landed by *Endurance* helicopters on Hound Bay beach, cross peninsula via Sorling Valley
3. 22/24 April – SBS prevented by ice and wind from continuing across Cumberland East Bay
4. 22/23 April – SAS launched from *Antrim* in Geminis to Grass Island
5. 25 April – *Antrim* & *Plymouth* joined by *Brilliant*, returning from fuelling 200 miles to the north-west
6. 25 April – Sheridan's Marines and Delves's SAS parties landed by *Antrim* and *Brilliant* helicopters on the Hestesletten Flats
© Hugh Bicheno

Map 5: SOUTH GEORGIA

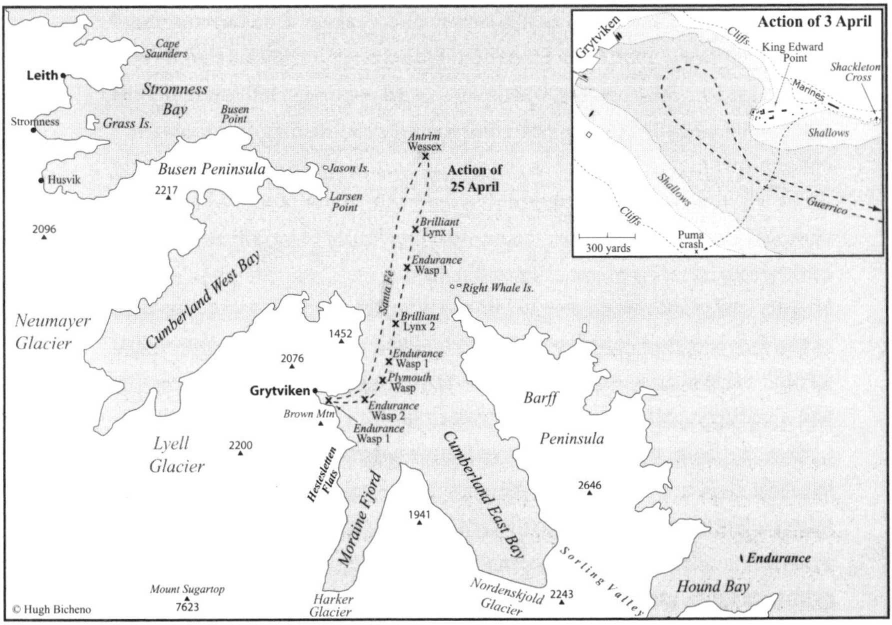
Cape Saunders
Leith
Stromness Bay
Busen Point
Stromness
Grass Is.
Busen Peninsula
Jason Is.
Larsen Point
Husvik
2217
2096
Antrim Wessex
Action of 25 April
Brilliant Lynx 1
Endurance Wasp 1
Right Whale Is.
Santa Fe
Brilliant Lynx 2
Endurance Wasp 1
Plymouth Wasp
Endurance Wasp 2
Endurance Wasp 1
Cumberland West Bay
Neumayer Glacier
1452
2076
Grytviken
Brown Mtn
Barff Peninsula
Lyell Glacier
2200
Hestesletten Flats
Moraine Fjord
Cumberland East Bay
2646
1941
Sorling Valley
Endurance
Hound Bay
Mount Sugartop
7623
Harker Glacier
Nordenskjold Glacier
2243
© Hugh Bicheno
Action of 3 April
Grytviken
Cliffs
King Edward Point
Shackleton Cross
Marines
Shallows
Shallows
Guerrico
Cliffs
300 yards
Puma crash

a waste of the only Argentine Army regiment on the island that could have gone out to meet the British Marines and Paras in their march across the island. But it was even more wasteful to have shipped back to the mainland the Marine commandos and BIM 2 who spearheaded the invasion, taking appropriately trained and equipped troops away from the islands even as less suitable substitutes were being recalled to the colours on the mainland.*

The action at Grytviken on 3 April was a purely Argentine Navy operation, where a display of overwhelming force once again failed to produce a bloodless victory. The small party of Royal Marines from the *Endurance* shot down a Puma helicopter full of Argentine Marines and put over 1,000 bullets and two 84mm rockets into the corvette *Guerrico* when it ventured into the bay with intent to overawe. Argentine casualties in the two incidents were three killed and seven wounded, and if the Carl Gustav had not twice misfired the *Guerrico* might well have been sunk. With one man painfully wounded the defenders surrendered and, in accordance with the rules of war, disarmed the mines and booby traps they had set around their position. When the boot was on the other foot, Astiz used the white flag to lure British troops over mines he had laid at Leith, only to discover that their trigger mechanisms were frozen solid. Thus it was that he and his fellow members of the 'Sworn to Die' detachment surrendered without firing a shot and without even managing to cheat a few enemy casualties in support of their claim to have fought valiantly against superior numbers. Rather than extradite him to France to answer for the murder of the nuns, which would have been an intelligent gambit in the propaganda war, the British government chose to 'play by the rules' and returned Astiz to a hero's welcome in Buenos Aires.

Roger Perkins's *Operation Paraquat* is a detailed and entirely satisfactory account of the fall of Stanley and South Georgia, and of the recovery of the latter just over three weeks later. It was not militarily significant, and the only casualties during the recovery were on board the World War II era submarine *Santa Fé,* caught on the surface and, although attacked eight times by Royal Navy helicopters, still able to moor at King Edward

---

* Conscripts were identified by their birth year, thus those whose military service had just begun were *Soldados Conscriptos* 63 (S/C 63). Those who had recently completed it and were recalled were S/C 62, etc.

Point under her own power. Politically it was another matter, and one of the abiding images of the war was Thatcher treating the tongue-tied Nott like an unsatisfactory dog outside 10 Downing Street, while calling on the media to 'Rejoice, rejoice.' The BBC sucked its teeth at such demeaning triumphalism and, while continuing to broadcast at best irresponsible revelations about British ship and troop movements, began to rebroadcast tendentious Argentine propaganda to 'balance' the official bulletins from the MoD, which if they did not tell all the truth at least did not strain credulity.

By 1 May the strike element of the Task Force reached the Falklands area of operations and the aero-naval phase of the war began. Given that they knew there were Royal Navy nuclear attack submarines off their coast, it was bold of the Argentine Navy to mount a pincer attack with a Battle Group including its aircraft carrier *25 de Mayo* approaching from the northwest, while the old cruiser *General Belgrano* and her Exocet-equipped WWII-era destroyer escorts acted as decoys to the south-west. Light winds prevented the *25 de Mayo* launching her Skyhawks and the whole fleet returned to port for the duration after *Conqueror* sank *Belgrano* the next day. In Britain the usual suspects have yapped ever since that the excision of a major threat to British sailors was a war crime – unechoed by the Argentine Navy, which was in no doubt that warships could be attacked anywhere and has never claimed the sinking of the *Belgrano* was anything other than a legitimate act of war. *Spartan* could have sunk the *25 de Mayo* a week earlier in Argentine territorial waters, but permission was denied for diplomatic reasons and contact was lost, leaving her free to attack the Task Force.* The potentially appalling military consequences of the earlier decision gave added force to the demand by Rear Admiral Woodward, commanding the British Carrier Group, that *Belgrano* should be sunk.

With regard to the heavy death toll, after the war Woodward rebuked *Belgrano*'s captain for failing to have his ship at battle stations: 'if you are in the process of invading another country's islands, and they are, in turn, not pleased with you, it is probably best to remain in a fairly efficient defensive position.' He felt much the same about the *Sheffield,* sunk two days later by the first Argentine Naval Air Arm Exocet attack when on picket duty with her

★ In his depressing memoir *Here Today Gone Tomorrow* Nott claims the credit (*sic*) for this.

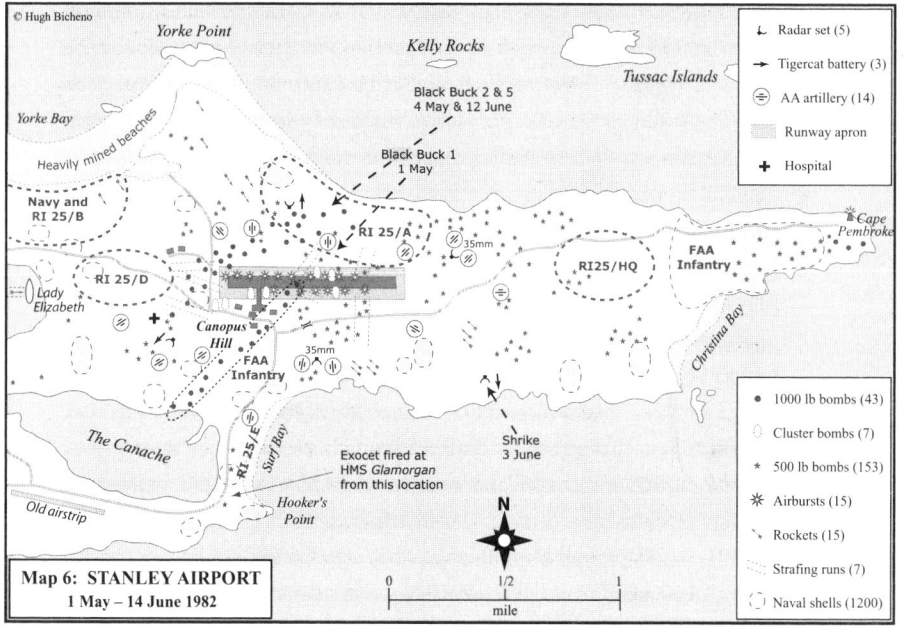

© Hugh Bicheno

Map 6: STANLEY AIRPORT
1 May – 14 June 1982

Yorke Point

Kelly Rocks

Tussac Islands

Black Buck 2 & 5
4 May & 12 June

Yorke Bay

Black Buck 1
1 May

Heavily mined beaches

Navy and
RI 25/B

Cape
Pembroke

RI 25/A

35mm

FAA
Infantry

RI25/HQ

RI 25/D

Lady
Elizabeth

Canopus
Hill

35mm

FAA
Infantry

Christina Bay

The Canache

RI 25/E

Surf Bay

Exocet fired at
HMS *Glamorgan*
from this location

Shrike
3 June

Old airstrip

Hooker's
Point

N

Radar set (5)

Tigercat battery (3)

AA artillery (14)

Runway apron

Hospital

1000 lb bombs (43)

Cluster bombs (7)

500 lb bombs (153)

Airbursts (15)

Rockets (15)

Strafing runs (7)

Naval shells (1200)

0   1/2   1
mile

N.B. Total casualties 3 KIA, 18 WIA. It seems the Argentines only counted the Black Buck bombs as thousand pounders –
the Harriers lobbed many more, but presumably they made less of a psychological impact.

radar and electronic countermeasures systems shut down and her galley
deep-frying potatoes. Her captain recalled Woodward's greeting when he
arrived dripping wet on the flagship *Hermes*: 'Sounds as though you've
been pretty careless, Sam.' Both sides suffered from an initial feeling of
unreality, but whereas the Argentines expected negotiations to follow the
'first blood', for the British it was a head-clearing blow that initiated an
overdue shift from an exercise to war-fighting mode.

Arguably more dislocating to Argentine expectations than the loss of the
Belgrano was the 1 May attack on Stanley airfield mounted from Ascension
Island by the RAF, which had re-equipped its due-for-the-scrapheap Vulcan
bombers for mid-air refuelling from no less geriatric Victor tankers. Two of
the former and eleven of the latter were involved in the first of the Black
Buck raids, at the time the longest range bombing missions ever undertaken,
to enable one Vulcan to drop twenty-one 1,000lb bombs diagonally across the
airfield at 0438 local time. Only the first one hit the paved strip, the closest

the British ever came to denying the airfield to the enemy. A second attack on 4 May missed the runway completely and the last Black Buck, on 12 June – given the impossible task of bombing airfield facilities *without* hitting the runway – put most of its bombs in the water. Two other Black Buck raids tried to take out the long-range radars on the outskirts of Stanley using US-supplied Shrike anti-radiation missiles, which caused minor damage to the Air Force's powerful Westinghouse radar near Stanley on 31 May, and destroyed one of GADA 601's Skyguard fire control radars near the airfield on 3 June, killing the crew.

Stanley airfield was the main battlefield of the logistics war. Menéndez estimated the garrison's daily requirement to be 17 tonnes of food and 9.5 tonnes of fuel – 2,000 litres for vehicles and 7,500 for aircraft, the latter enough to have them all in the air for just one hour. Forty-five air transport sorties between 1 May and 13 June delivered 470 tonnes of stores (41 per cent of the requirement) and 514 men, taking back 568 sick and wounded, while by the Argentine count the airfield peninsula was hit by 218 bombs, 1,200 naval shells and was strafed twenty-two times: an enormous investment to no permanent effect.

The battle for the airfield was only saved from being a serious British defeat by the unconscionable Argentine failure to include materials and engineers for the extension of the Stanley runway in their invasion plan, or to give it top priority once the British Task Force sailed. Like the decision not to moor *Belgrano* in the harbour, this smells of inter-service rivalry: if the Air Force had been able to stage its Skyhawks, Mirages and Daggers through Stanley it might have been seen to win the war single-handed, to the detriment of the other two services' prestige. If this was the reason, it was as politically misjudged as it was militarily indefensible, for the Air Force emerged from the war crowned with the laurels won by the brave efforts of its pilots, and consequently escaped much of the opprobrium that enveloped the armed forces after the war.

If Black Buck 1 and the follow-up raids by the Task Force Sea Harriers did not close the airfield, the rude awakening they gave the Argentine garrison was to have far-reaching secondary effects in the logistics war. Two large civilian freighters now fled Stanley harbour without unloading all of their cargo. One of them, the 20,000-ton *Formosa,* was attacked in error by the Argentine Air Force later that day and sailed back to the mainland with a UXB in her hull, along with the 3,737 railway sleepers and 200 rails that were to have been used to build bunkers on the Stanley hills. The second, the 10,000-ton *Carcaraña,* had barely begun to unload and sailed with 50 tons of aviation fuel, all the ammunition and vehicles for B Battery, GADA 10, large quantities of food, and the launcher and ammunition for an Argentine-built multiple rocket launcher with a range of 12.5 miles, which would have made a priceless addition to the Argentine arsenal. *Carcaraña* took refuge in Port King (see **Map 8**, p. 133) and transhipped the ammunition to the coaster *Monsunen,* which returned safely to Stanley on 3 May. The bulk of her cargo, however, was loaded on the 3,900-ton *Isla de los Estados,* which was destroyed with the loss of all save two of her crew by the frigate *Alacrity* in Falkland Sound during the night of 10–11 May.

These losses were all the more painful because *Formosa*'s sistership *Córdoba* had earlier run aground in Mar del Plata, after which her crew refused to make the crossing. Some of her cargo was flown out, but fork-lift trucks, materials to extend the runway and a large amount of barbed wire were lost to the garrison. The 5,300-ton *Bahía Buen Suceso* sailed into Stanley on 11 April with most of the anti-aircraft artillery and missile batteries that won the battle for the airport. She departed Stanley on 29 April to supply the garrisons on West Falkland, but on 16 May when docked at Fox Bay was abandoned by her crew after witnessing air attacks on *Carcaraña* across Falkland Sound, neither ship playing any further part in the war except to attract further air attacks. Remaining were the FIC coasters *Monsunen, Forrest* and the tiny wooden *Penelope,* and the lightly armed 90-ton Argentine Coast Guard cutters *Río Iguazú* and *Islas Malvinas.* The World War II vintage tug *Alférez Sobral* and the spy trawler *Narwal,* respectively disabled and sunk at sea by air attacks on 3 and 9 May, were mainland-based. *Río Iguazú* was attacked by Harriers and *Monsunen* by frigates on 22 May. Both were beached but *Forrest* towed *Monsunen* to Goose Green, where she was recaptured on 29 May. Apart from a valiant weeklong odyssey by the crew of *Penelope* in early June, carrying thirty drums of aviation fuel to Stanley from the *Buen Suceso,* the rest remained within sight of Stanley for the duration.

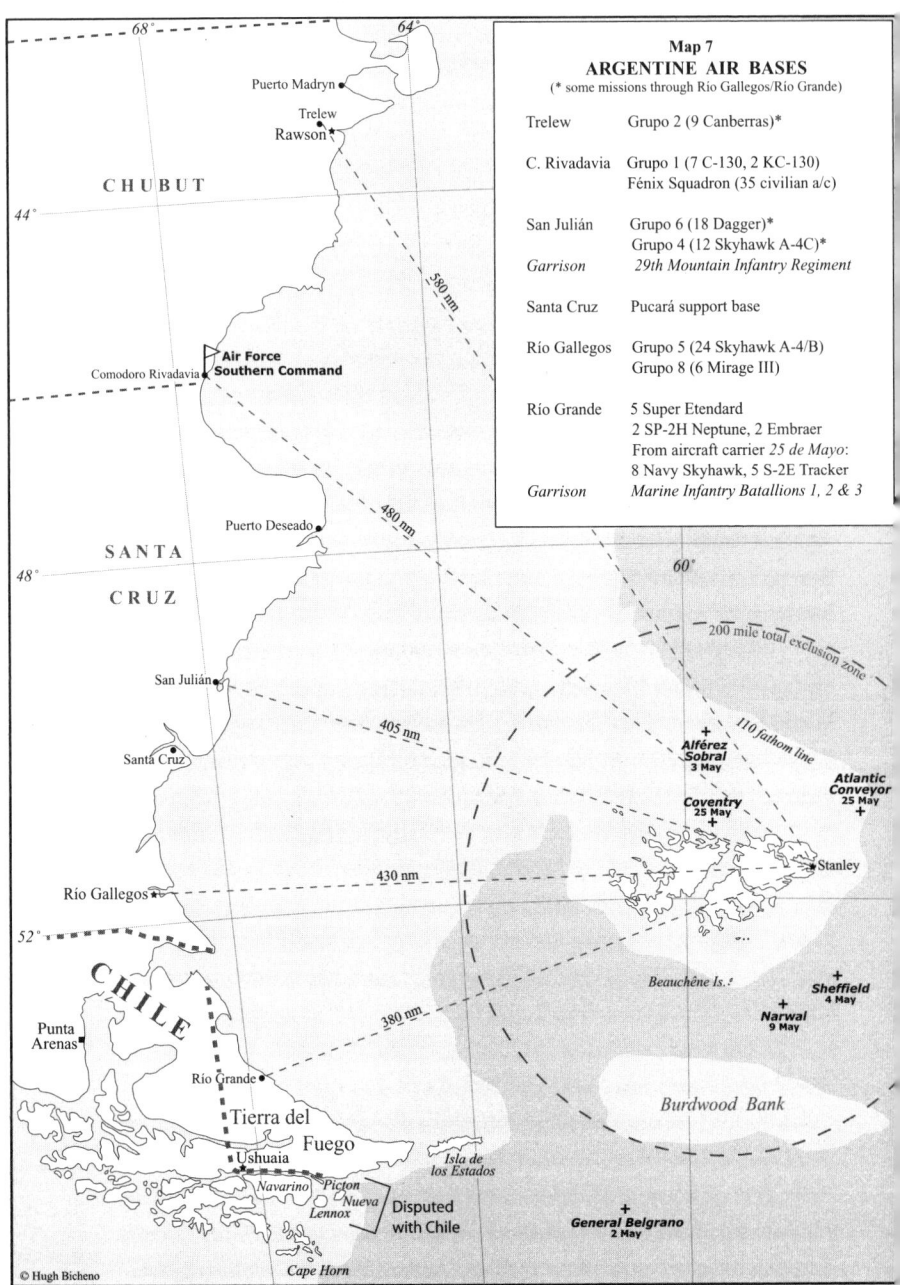

Map 7
ARGENTINE AIR BASES
(* some missions through Río Gallegos/Río Grande)

Trelew	Grupo 2 (9 Canberras)*
C. Rivadavia	Grupo 1 (7 C-130, 2 KC-130)
	Fénix Squadron (35 civilian a/c)
San Julián	Grupo 6 (18 Dagger)*
	Grupo 4 (12 Skyhawk A-4C)*
Garrison	*29th Mountain Infantry Regiment*
Santa Cruz	Pucará support base
Río Gallegos	Grupo 5 (24 Skyhawk A-4/B)
	Grupo 8 (6 Mirage III)
Río Grande	5 Super Etendard
	2 SP-2H Neptune, 2 Embraer
	From aircraft carrier *25 de Mayo*:
	8 Navy Skyhawk, 5 S-2E Tracker
Garrison	*Marine Infantry Batallions 1, 2 & 3*

Puerto Madryn

Trelew
Rawson

CHUBUT

44°

68°

64°

580 nm

Comodoro Rivadavia · **Air Force
Southern Command**

Puerto Deseado

480 nm

SANTA

48°

CRUZ

60°

San Julián

405 nm

Santa Cruz

200 mile total exclusion zone

110 fathom line

Alférez
Sobral
3 May

Atlantic
Conveyor
25 May

Coventry
25 May

Stanley

430 nm

Río Gallegos

52°

CHILE

Punta
Arenas

380 nm

Río Grande

Tierra del
Fuego

Ushuaia

Navarino Picton
Nueva
Lennox   Disputed
with Chile

Isla de
los Estados

Cape Horn

Beauchêne Is.

Sheffield
4 May

Narwal
9 May

Burdwood Bank

General Belgrano
2 May

© Hugh Bicheno

The attacks of 1 May also initiated the battle for air superiority. The Harriers destroyed a ground-attack Pucará at Goose Green with a cluster bomb and killed the pilot along with seven ground crew. Another two Pucarás were disabled and seventeen men wounded, a blow from which the morale of the local Air Force contingent never recovered. Panicky reports of British landings led to the premature launching of a major effort by the mainland-based units, which searched in vain for enemy ships near the islands (finding only the *Formosa*) and lost two Mirage fighters, a Dagger fighter-bomber, and a Canberra medium bomber to the latest model of Sidewinder missile, mounted on the Sea Harriers – courtesy of Caspar Weinberger – with an assist from the Stanley anti-aircraft artillery, which shot down the already battle-damaged aircraft of the luckless Flight Lieutenant García Cuerva, who was killed.

Apart from the Exocet attack by Naval Air Super Étendards on 4 May that destroyed *Sheffield,* the next major attack did not take place until 12 May, to the dismay of the British who hoped to win a battle of attrition in open water where the Sea Dart missile was most effective. The Argentine Air Force knew the system's capabilities from the Type 42 destroyers acquired from Britain by the Argentine Navy, and it shaped the battlefield. It did so because the islands were near the range limit of the Argentine fighter-bombers when fully laden, and only the Skyhawks could refuel from their two KC-130 tankers (see **Appendix D**). Sea Dart forced them to fly very low within the Falklands area of operations, greatly increasing fuel burn and limiting their time on target. It also obliged them to attack too low for their British 1,000lb bombs to arm before hitting the target. Para-retarded bombs offered a solution, but either there were not many stockpiled or else few were trained to use them. Despite an irresponsible BBC broadcast on 23 May (of an appallingly indiscreet MoD background briefing), which confirmed the failure of the bigger bombs, the Argentine Air Force continued to use them instead of switching to 500lb bombs, whose reduced mass and momentum made it possible for them to arm crucial milliseconds earlier. Overall, the biggest unforced error committed by the Argentine Air Force was to be so obsessed with ship killing that they failed to appreciate how easily they could have disabled the thin-skinned British warships with cannon and rockets.

The Argentine Air Force was introduced to the short-range Sea Wolf missile when they finally responded to desperate pleas from Stanley to do something about the Royal Navy ships that were shelling Argentine positions around the clock. The British ships were vulnerable because of procurement decisions conditioned by the essentially political misconception that smaller ships were cheaper: hence aircraft carriers designated 'through-deck cruisers'. Thus, for a saving of only one per cent of the total cost, the first ten Type 42 air defence destroyers were built so short and narrow that they had the worst sea-keeping qualities and least functional operations area of any post-war Royal Navy warship. Weight had been shaved to the point where they could not even mount a close-in air defence system without sacrificing the ship's boats or a major rebuild.* 'Something' is never better than nothing in modern warfare: the loss of *Sheffield* and *Coventry* was the direct result of 'thinking small', and it was only by sheer good fortune that a third ship of the class did not join the list on 12 May.

The shore bombardment group that day was composed of the Type 42 *Glasgow*, escorted by the gunless but Sea Wolf-equipped Type 22 frigate *Brilliant*. In a hectic ten minutes starting at 1345 they were attacked south of Stanley by two flights of Grupo 5 Skyhawks out of Río Gallegos. The first flight was detected 30 miles out and although *Glasgow*'s gun and Sea Dart systems were down, luckily three of the four aircraft attacked *Brilliant*. Sea Wolf downed two and caused the third to crash into the water. Acting Pilot Officer Vázquez, in the fourth, bored in on *Glasgow* but dropped too early, his bombs skipping off the water and over the stern of the destroyer. It was when seeking to engage the second flight, which sent three against *Glasgow* and only one against *Brilliant,* that the limitations of Sea Wolf were revealed. Designed to defend its own ship, the system crashed when required to engage *Glasgow*'s attackers and all four aircraft made terrifyingly accurate attacks. *Brilliant* was spared when the bombs dropped by Pilot Officer Arraras also bounced over her, but one of the six 1,000lb bombs aimed at *Glasgow* passed right through her before exploding in the sea on the other side. Nonetheless, she was beyond local repair and limped back to Britain. The successful pilot, Pilot Officer Gavazzi, committed the tragic error of flying low over Goose Green after the attack and was killed

---

* The last four, laid down in 1978–80, were 'stretched' to correct the more egregious flaws in the class.

by the radar-directed Oerlikon 35mm guns that had shot down a Sea Harrier on 4 May, killing Lieutenant Taylor, and was to shoot down Squadron Leader Iveson's Harrier GR 3 on 27 May. There can be no doubt the Royal Navy ships would have been far better able to defend themselves if the obsolete Sea Cat system had been ripped out and replaced with the Oerlikon or a similar system.

Astonishingly, a navy liberally equipped with the sea-skimming Exocet, and which would have been deluged with similar missiles in the event of a war with the Warsaw Pact, did not have a close-in defence system fitted as standard throughout the fleet. The Swedes had a 'fire and forget' sea-skimmer in service as early as 1958 and the Norwegians developed an air-launched equivalent (adopted by the US Navy) in the 1960s. The navies of the world were put on notice when the Israeli *Eilat* was sunk by a Soviet Styx missile fired from an Egyptian patrol boat in 1967, and by 1982 there were eight or nine far superior anti-ship missiles in service. Sea Wolf could intercept a shell in flight but, as noted, was a point and not an area defence system, installed only on the two Type 22 frigates and on the older *Andromeda*. The rest could only manoeuvre, fire chaff (radar-reflective foil) and pray their electronic countermeasures could spoof enemy missiles. Fortunately the Argentines only had five air-launched Exocets and were prevented from acquiring more, but even those few had the Royal Navy in a blue funk throughout the campaign, and almost caused a squadron of the SAS to be sent on a suicide mission to destroy the missile-carrying Super Étendards at their mainland base.

The Royal Navy rapidly improvised a helicopter-borne Airborne Early Warning system, ready by the end of the war, and immediately afterwards embarked on a crash programme to equip the fleet with the US Phalanx close-in weapons system, which if installed opportunely would have neutralized Exocet and dealt summarily with low-flying aircraft as well. Why the fleet went into battle almost defenceless against the most likely surface threat it would face, in any war, was among the many issues unaddressed in post-war analysis. However, the most serious was that although anti-submarine warfare was the principal mission of the Royal Navy, to which all other functions had been sacrificed, it was unable to

131

THE BATTLE FOR AIR SUPERIORITY

(non-combat accidents and ships' helicopters not listed)

	DATE	TIME	AIRCRAFT/PILOTS LOST	DOWNED BY
1	1 May	0825	3 Pucarás (PO Jukic killed)	Sea Harrier (SHAR) bomb
2	1 May	1628	Mirage (FO Perona ejected)	SHAR Sidewinder
3	1 May	1630	Mirage (FLt García Cuerva killed)	Sidewinder/own AAA
4	1 May	1641	Dagger (FO Ardiles killed)	SHAR Sidewinder
5	1 May	1747	Canberra (FO González, PO de Ibáñez killed)	SHAR Sidewinder
6	4 May	1320	*Sea Harrier (Lt Taylor killed)*	AAA (Goose Green)
7	6 May	0900	*2 Sea Harriers (LCdr Eyton-Jones, Lt Curtis killed)*	Collision
8	9 May	AM	2 Grupo 4 Skyhawks (PO Casco, PO Farías killed)	Hit South Jason Island
9	9 May	1607	Puma (3 crewmen killed)	*Coventry* Sea Dart
10	12 May	1345	3 Grupo 5 Skyhawks (FO Bustos, PO Ibarlucea, PO Nivoli killed)	*Brilliant* Seawolf
11	12 May	1430	Grupo 5 Skyhawk (FO Gavazzi killed)	Own AAA (Goose Green)
12	15 May	0440	6 Pucarás, 4 Turbo Mentors, 1 Skyvan	SAS raid (Pebble Island)
13	21 May	0815	Chinook, 2 Puma on the ground	Harrier GR3 cannon
14	21 May	0840	Pucará (FLt Benitez ejected)	SAS Stinger
15	21 May	0841	*2 Gazelles (Lt Francis, Sgt Evans, LCpl Giffin killed)*	Small arms
16	21 May	0950	*GR3 (RAF FLt Glover ejected)*	Blowpipe
17	21 May	1030	Grupo 6 Dagger (PO Bean killed)	*Broadsword* Seawolf
18	21 May	1210	Pucará (Sq Ldr Tomba ejected)	SHAR cannon
19	21 May	1310	2 Grupo 4 Skyhawks (FO Manzotti, PO López killed)	SHAR Sidewinder
20	21 May	1435	Grupo 6 Dagger (FO Luna ejected)	SHAR Sidewinder
21	21 May	1453	2 Grupo 6 Daggers (FLt Donadille, Sq Ldr Piuma ejected)	SHAR Sidewinder
22	21 May	1455	Grupo 6 Dagger (FO Senn ejected)	SHAR cannon
23	21 May	1511	2 Naval Skyhawks (Cdr Philippi ejected, Lt Marquez killed)	SHAR Sidewinder
24	21 May	1521	Naval Skyhawk (Sub Lt Arca ejected)	SHAR cannon/own AAA

(continued after maps)

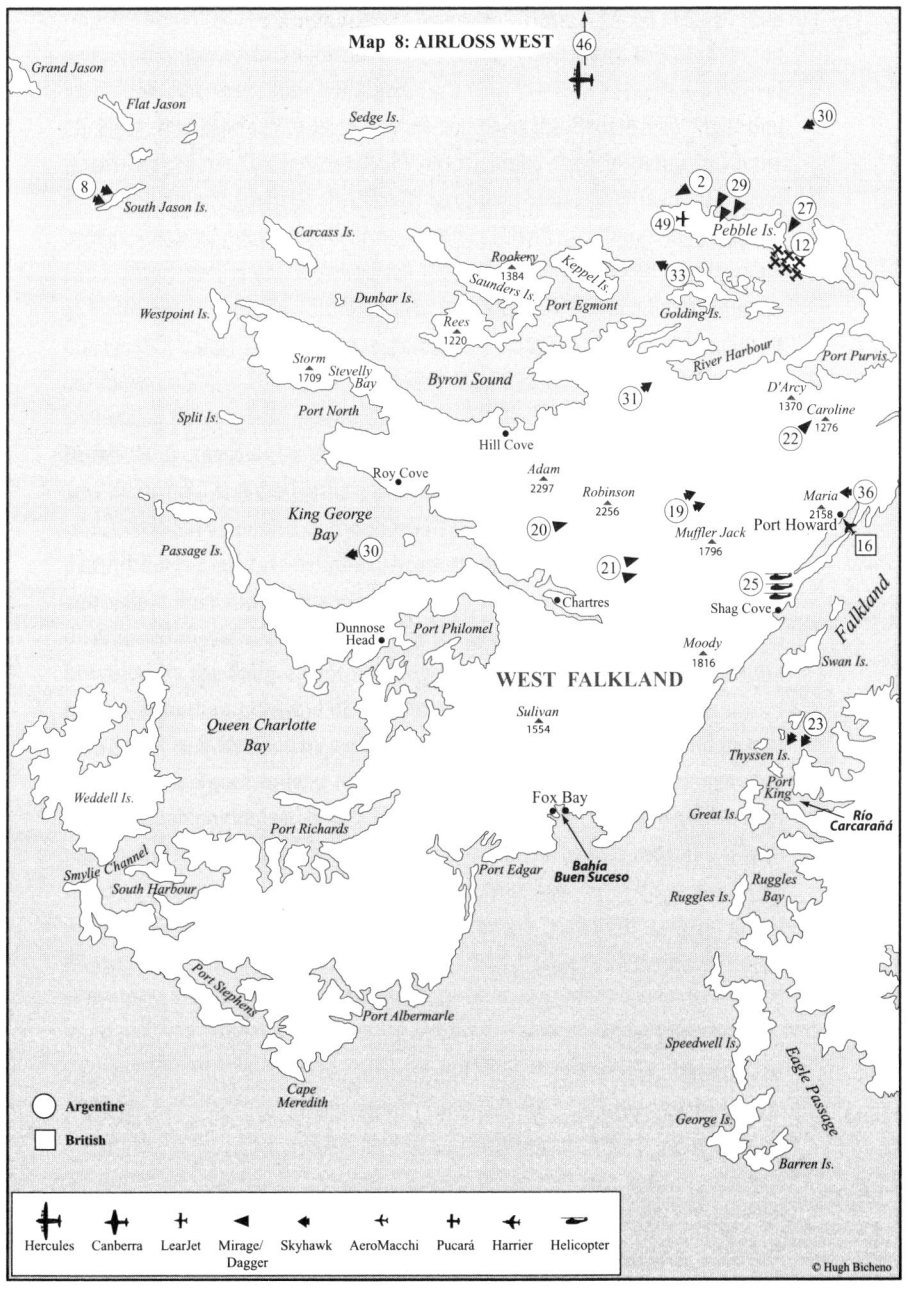

Map 8: AIRLOSS WEST

Grand Jason

Flat Jason

Sedge Is.

30

8

South Jason Is.

2

29

49

27

Pebble Is.

12

Carcass Is.

Rookery
1384

Keppel Is.

33

Dunbar Is.

Saunders Is.

Westpoint Is.

Rees
1220

Port Egmont

Golding Is.

River Harbour

Port Purvis

Storm
1709

Stevelly
Bay

Byron Sound

31

D'Arcy
1370

Caroline
1276

Split Is.

Port North

Hill Cove

22

Roy Cove

Adam
2297

Robinson
2256

Maria
2158

36

King George
Bay

20

19

Muffler Jack
1796

Port Howard

16

Passage Is.

30

21

25

Shag Cove

Chartres

Falkland

Dunnose
Head

Port Philomel

Moody
1816

Swan Is.

WEST FALKLAND

Sulivan
1554

23

Queen Charlotte
Bay

Thyssen Is.

Port
King

Weddell Is.

Fox Bay

Great Is.

Río
Carcaraña

Port Richards

Smylie Channel

South Harbour

Port Edgar

Bahía
Buen Suceso

Ruggles Is.

Ruggles
Bay

Port Stephens

Port Albermarle

Speedwell Is.

Eagle Passage

Cape
Meredith

George Is.

Barren Is.

○ **Argentine**

□ **British**

| Hercules | Canberra | LearJet | Mirage/ Dagger | Skyhawk | AeroMacchi | Pucará | Harrier | Helicopter |

© Hugh Bicheno

133

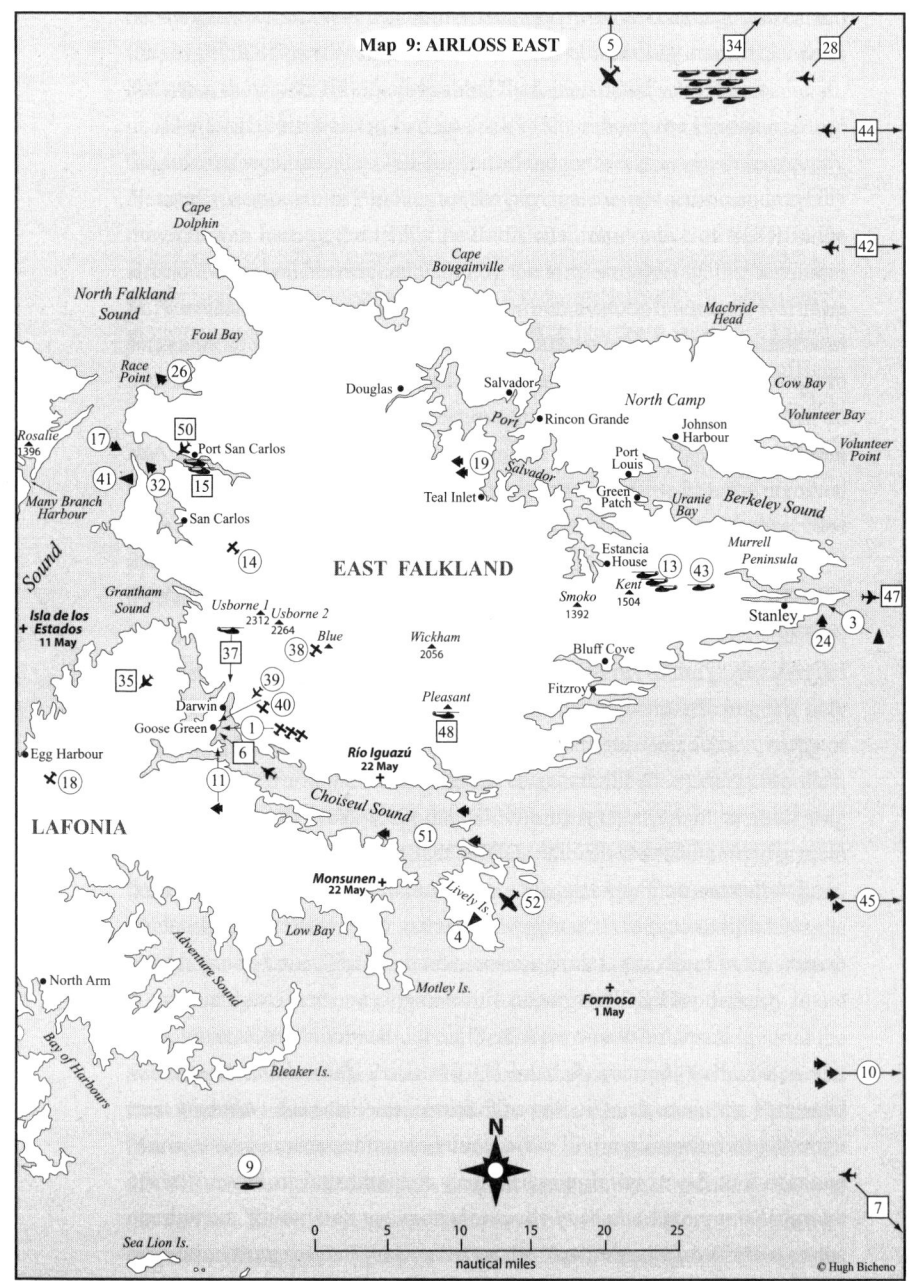

Map 9: AIRLOSS EAST

Cape Dolphin

Cape Bougainville

North Falkland Sound

Foul Bay

Race Point ㉖

Douglas •

Salvador •

North Camp

Cow Bay

Volunteer Bay

Rosalie 1396

⑰

㊿ Port San Carlos

Rincon Grande

Johnson Harbour

Volunteer Point

㊀ ㉜ ⑮

⑲

Port Louis

Green Patch

Berkeley Sound

Many Branch Harbour

• San Carlos

Teal Inlet •

Uranie Bay

Murrell Peninsula

Sound

⑭

EAST FALKLAND

Estancia House •

⑬ ㊸

47

Grantham Sound

Usborne 1 2372

Usborne 2 2264

Smoko 1392

Kent 1504

Stanley •

③

Isla de los Estados 11 May

㊲

㊳ Blue

Wickham 2056

Bluff Cove

㉔ ▲

㉟

⑨ ⑩

Darwin •

Pleasant ㊽

Fitzroy •

Goose Green ①

⑥

Río Iguazú 22 May

⑪

Egg Harbour •

⑱

Choiseul Sound

㊶

LAFONIA

Monsunen 22 May

Lively Is.

㊱

④

• North Arm

Low Bay

Motley Is.

Formosa 1 May

㊺

Adventure Sound

Bleaker Is.

⑩

Bay of Harbours

⑨

N

⑦

Sea Lion Is.

0   5   10   15   20   25

nautical miles

© Hugh Bicheno

134

DATE	TIME	AIRCRAFT/PILOTS LOST	DOWNED BY
25 23 May 1020		2 Puma, 1 Augusta on the ground	SHAR cannon
26 23 May 1350		Grupo 5 Skyhawk (FO Guadagnini killed)	Multiple weapons
27 23 May 1600		Grupo 6 Dagger (PO Volponi killed)	SHAR Sidewinder
28 23 May 2000		*Sea Harrier (RN Lt Cdr Batt killed)*	Exploded on take off
29 24 May 1115		3 Grupo 6 Daggers (Sq Ldr Puga, FLt Díaz ejected, PO Castillo killed)	SHAR Sidewinder
30 24 May 1215		Grupo 4 Skyhawk (PO Bono killed)	Multiple weapons
31 25 May 0830		Grupo 4 Skyhawk (FLt Palaver killed)	*Coventry* Sea Dart
32 25 May 1230		Grupo 4 Skyhawk (PO Lucero ejected)	Rapier
33 25 May 1240		Grupo 5 Skyhawk (FLt García died of exposure)	*Coventry* Sea Dart
34 25 May 1636		*3 Chinook, 1 Lynx, 6 Wessex*	Exocet (*Atlantic Conveyor*)
35 27 May 1330		*Harrier GR 3 (Sq Ldr Iveson ejected)*	AAA (Goose Green)
36 27 May 1700		Grupo 5 Skyhawk (FO Velasco ejected)	Multiple weapons
37 28 May 1200		*Scout (Lt Nunn killed)*	Pucará cannon
38 28 May 1220		Pucará (PO Giménez killed)	Flew into Blue Mountain
39 28 May 1650		Naval Air Aermacchi (Lt Miguel killed)	Blowpipe
40 28 May 1709		Pucará (PO Cruzado ejected)	Small arms
41 29 May 1200		Grupo 6 Dagger (PO Bernhardt killed)	Rapier
42 29 May 1547		*Sea Harrier (RN Lt Cdr Broadwater ejected)*	Slid off flight deck
43 30 May 0930		Puma (6 Gendarmes killed)	SAS Stinger
44 30 May 1215		*Harrier GR 3 (Sq Ldr Pook ejected)*	Small arms
45 30 May 1450		2 Grupo 4 Skyhawks (FO Vazquez, FO Castillo killed)	*Exeter* Sea Dart
46 1 June 1050		Hercules (WCdr Meisner and 7 crew killed)	SHAR Sidewinder and cannon
47 1 June 1450		*Sea Harrier (FLt Mortimer ejected)*	Roland
48 6 June 0408		*Gazelle (Maj Forge and 3 crew killed)*	*Cardiff* Sea Dart
49 7 June 0905		Learjet (WCdr de la Colina and 4 crew killed)	*Exeter* Sea Dart
50 8 June 1200		*Harrier GR3 (WCdr Squire unhurt)*	Crashed on landing
51 8 June 1647		3 Grupo 5 Skyhawks (PO Arraras, Acting PO Vázquez, FO Bolzán killed)	SHAR Sidewinder
52 13 June 2255		Canberra (FLt Pastrana ejected, FLt Casado killed)	*Exeter* Sea Dart

locate and destroy the 1,300-ton German-built diesel-electric submarine *San Luis,* despite knowing its location off the north coast of East Falkland from signals intelligence, and even though it had serious problems with its diesel engines, bilge pump, snorkel equipment and fire control computer. *San Luis* remained on station from 28 April to 11 May and on the last day fired torpedoes, admittedly beyond realistic range, at the frigates *Arrow* and *Alacrity* without being detected. Not so the 'biologicals' of the South Atlantic, which took a multi-million pound hammering from hundreds of anti-submarine torpedoes and depth charges, giving rise to a sardonic joke among the troops on *Canberra*: 'The war's over, lads: the whales have surrendered.'

The air war could have altered the outcome of the ground campaign only if the Argentine Air Force and Naval Air defeated the British landing. The next chapter deals with the battle of San Carlos, but to anticipate the main point it was unprecedented to mount an amphibious operation without having local air supremacy, declared an essential prerequisite by Commander-in-Chief Admiral Fieldhouse at Ascension on 17 April, during the only meeting of all the senior commanders to take place during the campaign. As a result, the Landing Force took several severe logistics hits, the first when *Canberra* and *Norland* fled San Carlos during the night of 21 May taking with them the unit stores of four regiments, including vital replacement radio batteries, the Wombat rocket launchers, all ammunition not carried ashore by the men and enough rations to feed the whole brigade for eighteen days. The loss put the Commando Logistics Regiment on a hand-to-mouth basis of sending stores forward as soon as they were unloaded. Ironically, it proved to be the first of many blessings in disguise, because on 27 May four Grupo 5 Skyhawks attacked the beachhead and Flight Officer Velasco put two of his four para-retarded bombs, which fortunately did not explode, into the roof of the abandoned Ajax Bay refrigeration plant, which was in use as a hospital. Two more bombs, which *did* explode, went into the painfully built up ammunition dump nearby. Any larger stockpile would simply have made a bigger bang and killed more men.

Velasco also played a leading role in a well conceived and executed combined attack by Grupo 5 Skyhawks and the Naval Air Super Étendards on 25 May, Argentina's National Day, which sank the Type 42 destroyer *Coventry* and the 15,000-ton freighter *Atlantic Conveyor*. The *Conveyor* was carrying Brigadier Thompson's hopes for salvation in the form of four heavy-lift Chinooks, a Lynx and six Wessex helicopters, of which only one Chinook had flown off before the attack. *Conveyor* was also carrying a team from the Navy's Mobile Air Transport and Salvage Unit, engineering equipment and materials to build an airstrip ashore, and tents for 4,500 men. As Thompson laconically observed in *Sinews of War*, the simultaneous loss of both the means to make a rapid advance and to shelter the troops from the elements, 'while removing the means to speed up the operation, made an early termination even more imperative.'

Coventry was lost trying to cover the northern approach to San Carlos, setting up a Type 42/22 picket off Pebble Island with *Broadsword*. *Coventry*'s Sea Dart brought down two Skyhawks earlier on the 25th thanks in part to a data link with *Broadsword*'s superior radar equipment. As in the case of *Glasgow* and *Brilliant* on 12 May, however, the combination could not cope with a determined low-level attack, this time using the hills of West Falkland and Pebble Island to close the range without being detected. Even after the Skyhawks broke cover, *Coventry*'s radar could not pick them up against the background clutter. *Broadsword*'s could, and the Sea Harrier Combat Air Patrol, in hot pursuit, was warned off to permit Sea Wolf to engage. Unfortunately the system crashed and the frigate was hit by a 1,000lb bomb, which bounced off the water up through her flight deck, destroying a Lynx and sending her out of the area of operations for repairs until 1 June. During the second attack, Sea Wolf had rebooted and was ready to fire when *Coventry* passed between *Broadsword* and the Skyhawks, breaking the radar lock. In a perfectly executed attack Velasco put three 1,000lb bombs deep into the destroyer's hull, where they exploded and caused her to capsize in fifteen minutes.

With British attention firmly fixed on the battle off Pebble Island, the Super Étendards completed a wide sweep to the north of the Carrier Battle Group, only 60 miles north-east of Stanley, accurately tracked because of the to and fro of the Harriers by the long-range Argentine radar near Stanley. The luckless *Conveyor* was not, as some have alleged, being

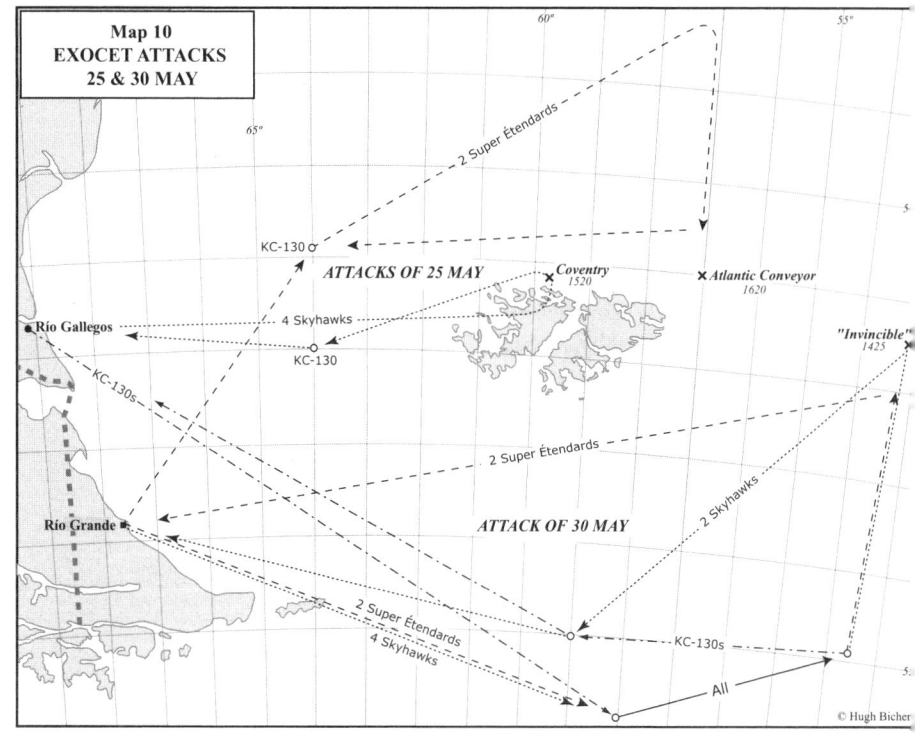

Map 10
EXOCET ATTACKS
25 & 30 MAY

ATTACKS OF 25 MAY

2 Super Étendards

KC-130

KC-130

Río Gallegos

4 Skyhawks

KC-130

Coventry
1520

✕ *Atlantic Conveyor*
1620

"Invincible"
1425

KC-130s

2 Super Étendards

ATTACK OF 30 MAY

Río Grande

2 Skyhawks

2 Super Étendards
4 Skyhawks

KC-130s

All

© Hugh Bicheno

used as a decoy, but had in fact been placed furthest away from the expected line of enemy attack. It seems likely the onboard radar on one of the two Exocets picked up *Conveyor* after emerging from a cloud of chaff fired by either *Exeter* or *Ambuscade,* which formed the outer northern defence of the Battle Group. The other missile may have been the target at which *Invincible* fired six Sea Darts, but if so they, as well as the second Exocet, were terminally confused by chaff. The 25 May attacks drove the carriers back to their pre-landing station 100 miles further out to sea, with a corresponding reduction in the time the Sea Harriers could spend on Combat Air Patrol. However the Argentines could not exploit this because they had suffered such severe attrition, not only from combat losses but also from mechanical failures in poorly maintained aircraft repeatedly pushed to their limits. By contrast the Harrier deck crews maintained near-perfect serviceability in often appalling conditions.

On 30 May another combined Naval Air/Argentine Air Force operation employed their last remaining Exocet against the Carrier Task Force. The Argentines' desire to strike a vital blow was so great that some of those involved still insist they hit the *Invincible*. It was another well planned, well executed attack, but it hit nothing for the same reason their first four Exocets failed to find the highest value targets: the Super Étendards were judged too valuable to risk within Sea Dart range and fired their missiles at the first targets on which they could get a radar lock. On 30 May this was the frigate *Avenger,* with the Type 42 destroyers *Exeter* and *Cardiff* 10 miles to her north. *Invincible* was a further 10 miles to the north-east, 40 miles away and not even detected by the Super Étendards when the Exocet was launched. The destroyers, the second generation of the class with superior electronics to the *Sheffield* and *Coventry,* detected the attack early and deployed chaff, decoys and electronic countermeasures helicopters, sending the missile into the sea between them. Four Skyhawks charged behind the missile and two were blasted out of the sky by *Exeter* Sea Darts. The remaining two attacked *Avenger* and came away convinced that her landing pad was a carrier flight deck and that the smoke pouring from her stack and the flash of her weapons were proof the Exocet had hit.

The list of air losses accompanying **Maps 8** and **9** (pp. 133–134) are drawn from Chris Hobson and Andrew Noble's *Falklands Air War,* probably the definitive account of this over-written aspect of the conflict. The destruction of a Chinook and two Pumas on the ground near Mount Kent on 21 May came close to destroying Argentine tactical mobility at a stroke, because the other Argentine Army Chinook, two more (of five) Pumas and six (of nine) Hueys – almost the whole of Combat Aviation 601 – were also under camouflage nets in the area. As it was, after two Pumas and one of the three Augusta Hirundo gunships were destroyed on West Falkland two days later, the Argentine helicopter force was driven back to the cover of the SAMs and anti-aircraft artillery around Stanley. Barring a brave but forlorn attempt to reinforce the beleaguered garrison at Goose Green on 28 May, Parada's hopes of conducting airmobile warfare with his widely dispersed command went with them. With regard to fixed wing aircraft, the Argentines looked to their Air Force to win the war for them and the bare facts of attrition show that the British won air superiority over the mainland fighter-bombers. But they never won air supremacy, nor could a small force of Harriers hope to do so once the enemy chose not to dash himself to death on Sea Dart. The Argentines won a few rounds, notably in keeping the air bridge operating and in stopping daytime shelling by the Royal Navy: but although they did all that brave men could, they were technologically outmatched and unable to deliver a knockout punch.

7 San Carlos

WHEN LAND AND SEA battles overlap both elements are at their most vulnerable: the soldiers because they are tightly packed and without the means to strike back, the sailors because they are obliged to provide a fixed target. No day of World War II has been more studied than 6 June 1944, D-Day in Normandy, because even those with little interest in military history know it was the moment of truth, when the Allied neck was put on the block in the presence of an enemy still capable of swinging an axe. So it was thirty-eight years later, when British forces landed in San Carlos Bay without having first won air supremacy. It was the boldest decision in a campaign studded with them and, like the rest, depended for success on a *necessary* under-estimation of the enemy: which is only to say that major Argentine strategic and operational errors had to be assumed for the entire enterprise to have any hope of success. To force those errors, the fleet HQ planners at Northwood confounded the national stereotype and went for it without hesitation, in the knowledge that only delay made defeat certain.

Both sides knew the best opportunity for the Argentines to impose their will would come at the moment of disembarkation. The Argentines reasoned that time pressure would force the British to mount a direct assault on Stanley, but that if they came in through a back door, it would be the one the Argentines themselves would have used. Their strategy from the first was to occupy the islands with intent to negotiate from strength, and they thought the British might do the same in the limited campaigning time open to them by seizing West Falkland as a forward base. Such a move would tighten the blockade of the Argentine forces at Stanley, provide shelter for British troops through the winter, and permit a methodical build-up for a spring offensive. Intriguingly, London did entertain the option, as one of several possibilities, and the embarked planning staff were requested to identify a 'stone aircraft carrier' upon which to build an airfield from which to operate the Harriers and, in time, the more capable Phantom and Buccaneer aircraft inherited by the RAF after the fleet carrier *Ark Royal* was decommissioned in late 1978.

In retrospect the scheme was always a strategic imbecility. From the British point of view, domestic and international pressure for a negotiated settlement would have become intolerable long before a siege could become effective, and the civilian population held hostage by the Argentines made the full rigours of blockade unthinkable. However the Argentines, having incorrectly calculated that international pressure would prevent a British military response, now panicked into the opposite error of discounting it altogether and decided they must defend West Falkland. After the war the Army blamed its failure to guard San Carlos on a Navy assessment that the British would not land there, because they would never commit to a landlocked environment where Sea Dart was neutralized. But whether or not San Carlos was judged a likely landing site, the logic of defending West Falkland made it imperative to establish a strong presence at Fanning Head, the narrowest point between the islands. The vulnerability of the detached garrisons became obvious after *Alacrity* blew up *Isla de los Estados* in Falkland Sound on 11 May, and in the ten days before the landing some of the men and equipment left to rot on West Falkland should have been shuttled to San Carlos with what were still, at that stage, adequate air transport resources. I have found no explanation for this baffling lapse in any of the Argentine literature, beyond a blistering verdict that Brigadier General Parada was totally unfit for command.

The post-war memoirs of the Woodward, Thompson and Amphibious Force Commodore Clapp highlighted a cultural divide between the sea/land and blue water schools, aggravated by a poorly defined command structure. Much of the ill-feeling the memoirs revealed can be attributed to poor communications, but the principal irritant was that Fieldhouse did not, and arguably could not for lack of suitable candidate, appoint a three-star Theatre Commander. At their first meeting on 16 April, Thompson and Clapp found Woodward personally jarring, but more damagingly believed he was trying to preempt the issue of who should exercise overall authority. They complained to Fieldhouse, but even when all four met the next day the air was not cleared and relations among the theatre commanders never recovered. Clapp and Thompson were lucky to count on the extensive local knowledge acquired by Marine Major Southby-Tailyour as commander of NP 8901 in 1977–79. Southby-Tailyour had travelled the islands extensively and could inform debate on the most promising landing sites, in particular with details such as the peat 'lips' jutting over what might otherwise seem to be ideal landing beaches. He did falsely portray Volunteer Bay as unsuitable in order to protect the resident colony of King Penguins, but the embarked planners good-naturedly ignored him. Luckily for the penguins the site was rejected because any landing in the North Camp led to the operational bottleneck at Green Patch (see **Map 11**, p. 144). The Goose Green isthmus ruled out Lafonia for the same reason and, barring the 'stone aircraft carrier' concept (discarded soon afterwards, once it had become apparent that the only realistic air defence solution was to seize Stanley airport), options rapidly reduced to a choice between a direct assault on Stanley or a more distant landing elsewhere on East Falkland.

The choice fell on San Carlos once it became apparent the precondition of air supremacy could not be met. It was the only site sheltered from wave action and protected by hills, but in the narrow waters of Falkland Sound even the Sea Wolf frigates would have difficulty picking up targets approaching over West Falkland. The lack was to be made up by the Rapier missile units of T Battery, 12 Air Defence Regiment RA, to be installed quickly on the hills around the bay. It proved a potentially fatal mistake: the Rapier units had been inaccessible during the journey south and were badly in need of maintenance, and in the frenzy of restowing equipment at Ascension the repair facilities were left behind. Even if the units had arrived in pristine condition, the system was not designed to fire downwards and, because the Identification Friend/Foe of the Royal Navy helicopters was not programmed into the radar tracking system, the missiles could only be fired visually.

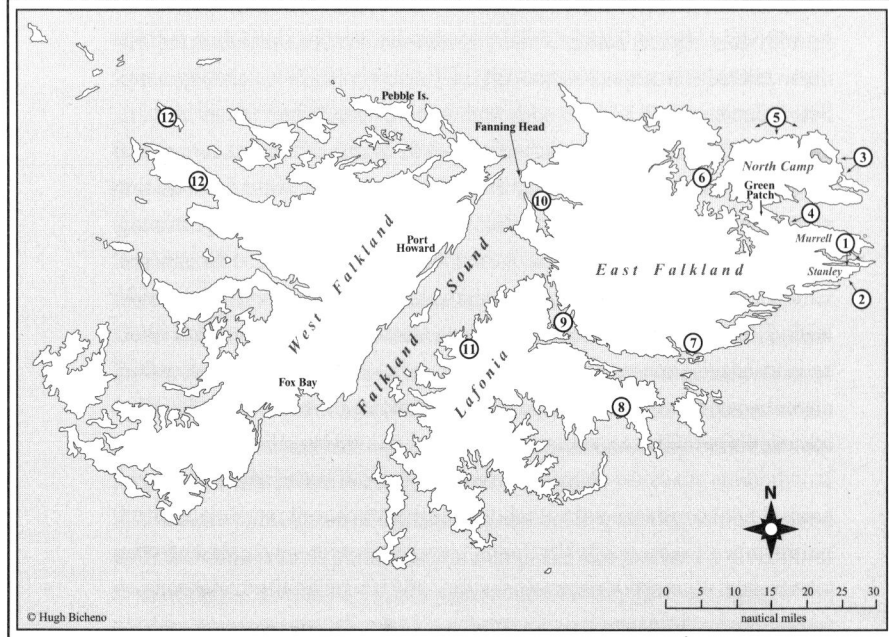

Map 11: LANDING SITES STUDIED BY BOTH SIDES

1. Direct assault on Stanley – along with 2 believed by the Argentines to be the most likely options for a primary or a secondary assault, freezing a preponderance of their garrison around the airport and town until the end

2. Beaches south of Stanley – never seriously considered by the British, heavily defended by the Argentines

3. Cow and Volunteer Bays – early favourite of embarked staff because furthest from Argentine mainland air bases, discarded because not sheltered from wave action and because of bottleneck at Green Patch

4. Uranie Bay – considered the best direct assault site by the British, covered by Argentine outposts

5. North Camp beaches – same disadvantages as 3 and SBS found landing sites unsuitable

6. Salvador Water – favoured by Brig Thompson but inaccesible for larger ships, which would need to unload outside

7. Mare Harbour/Bertha's Beach – best site for an amphibious assault but highly vulnerable to air attack

8. Low Bay – sheltered site considered possible by both, discarded because of bottleneck at Goose Green

9. Goose Green/Darwin – believed to be a strong possibility by the Argentines, not by the British

10. San Carlos Water – site finally selected, considered extremely unlikely by the Argentines

11. Egg Harbour – compromise site safest from air attack but same disadvantage as 8

12. Carcass Island & Stevelly Bay – sites considered for the 'stone aircraft carrier' concept

Through no fault of the crews or of what was, and remains, an excellent system, Rapier could not provide the prompt air defence cover that Clapp and his team, without consulting the Battery Commander, blithely assumed it would.

On the plus side, San Carlos enjoyed the invisible protection of an Argentine belief, maintained practically to the end of the war, that the only thing that could bring about a result before winter would be a British landing near Stanley, and that any other would be a feint designed to draw them out of position. This view was held for so long in the face of so much seemingly indisputable proof to the contrary as to constitute compelling circumstantial evidence that they were tricked. Aldo Rico warned his superiors not to believe the British would act in a straightforward manner (*como la gente*), and it would be extremely surprising if Operation Corporate was not enveloped in a 'bodyguard of lies'.* The best deceptions reinforce what the enemy is inclined to believe, but when that belief is maintained beyond all reason the familiar smell of an old and crafty rat wafts to the nostrils of military historians. The landings at San Carlos achieved complete operational surprise, and if deception was not involved then the Argentine commanders must be counted among the most self-deluded in history.

Belatedly realizing that Fanning Head was a neural point following the devastating SAS raid on Pebble Island on 15 May, Parada weakened the garrison at Darwin/Goose Green by ordering C Company, RI 25, detached from its parent regiment on the Stanley airfield peninsula, to move to Port San Carlos on 15 May. The company, commanded by Lieutenant Esteban, had been at Darwin since early April and was to prove the hardest nut to crack in the battle fought there on 28 May. How much harder it might have been if Esteban and sixty-three men had not been detached (as Combat Team Güemes – *gweh-mehz*) to Port San Carlos deserves a prominent place in the 'what if' file. Esteban's group downed two Gazelles and damaged a Lynx on 21 May, but he could not communicate with Stanley directly and made only one brief report to Lieutenant Colonel Piaggi, his field commander at Goose Green. Two days later Daher sent patrols into the area to acquire operational intelligence, which would not have been necessary if Esteban had been told his primary mission was to observe and report.

* Winston Churchill's description of the deception operations which protected the date and place of D-Day 1944.

It was not, however, hence the designation 'Combat Team'. Although not adequate to the task of defending the entrance to the Sound, Güemes was equipped with two 105mm rocket launchers and two 81mm mortars, each with a two-man crew. Esteban sent them to Fanning Head along with eleven riflemen under the command of Sub-Lieutenant Reyes, an infantry, not a support arms specialist.* Reyes took up a position on the western side of Fanning Head, overlooking the Sound but out of radio contact with Port San Carlos, and failed to dig in or even to emplace his weapons properly. According to his own testimony, in the early hours of 21 May he heard the noise of British landing operations, which were indeed proceeding within a mile of his location, but in the night mist could not tell where it was coming from. He fired two illumination rounds, both of which failed to ignite, and then fired all his rocket and mortar ammunition blindly into the Sound before sending his radioman to the top of Fanning Head to make contact with Esteban. The signaller had barely set up when the crest was swept by a violent bombardment from *Antrim*. Reyes concluded the British had some ultra-fast means of zeroing in on radio transmissions and did not try again, deciding instead to march his men back to Port San Carlos along the coast. They were immediately brought under machine-gun fire Reyes thought 'as accurate as if by day'.

The machine-gun fire, and the fire control for the bombardment that so disconcerted Reyes, came from an SBS party delivered by *Antrim*'s Wessex along with Spanish-speaking Marine Captain Rod Bell. He set up a loud-speaker, which failed to work, and then shouted what Hugh McManners, one of the SBS team, thought was something about 'Royal Marine desper-adoes'. Bell and the SBS were loath to kill anyone and initially fired to warn: a mistake soon underlined by counter-fire from a MAG. The man respon-sible was Platoon Sergeant Colque, among the four unwounded of the eight later captured, who was wearing a Royal Marine sweater and belt 'razzed' during the 2 April invasion. Reyes says he took his 'best men' and ventured around the southern end of the peak, where he observed the landings, and was still there when the air attacks took place later in the day. Even if true, having abandoned his radio he could contribute nothing to the battle. More

---

* When Seineldín formed C Company in March, Reyes was put in charge of 'Gato', one of three rifle platoons. The Support Platoon was 'Aguila'; both were subsumed in the ad hoc organization of Combat Team Güemes.

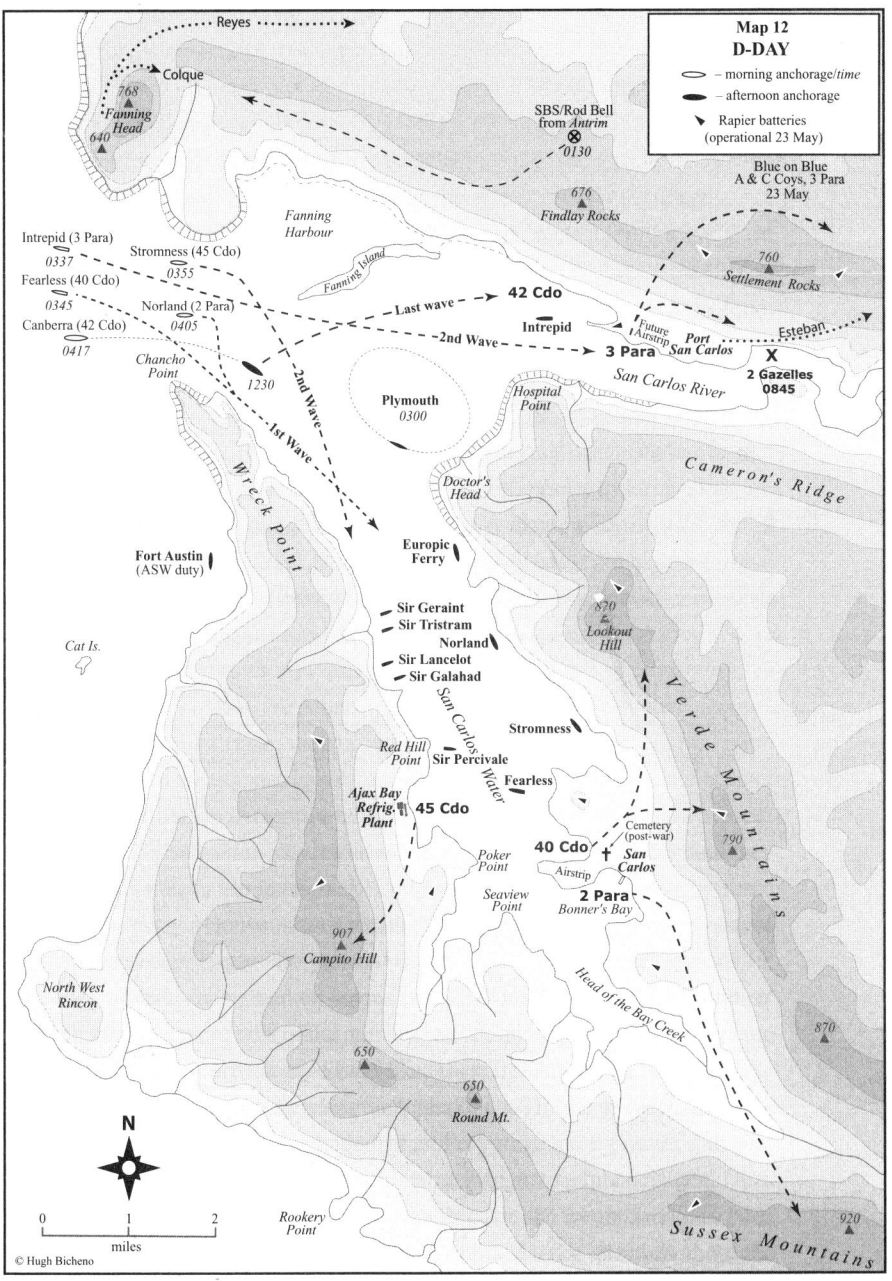

Map 12
D-DAY

- morning anchorage/*time*
- afternoon anchorage
▼ Rapier batteries (operational 23 May)

Reyes

Colque

768
Fanning Head

640

SBS/Rod Bell from *Antrim*
⊗ *0130*

Blue on Blue A & C Coys, 3 Para 23 May

676
Findlay Rocks

760
Settlement Rocks

Fanning Harbour

Fanning Island

Intrepid (3 Para)
0337

Stromness (45 Cdo)
0355

Fearless (40 Cdo)
0345

Norland (2 Para)
0405

Canberra (42 Cdo)
0417

Last wave → **42 Cdo**

2nd Wave → **Intrepid**

3 Para
Future Airstrip
Port San Carlos
Esteban

Chancho Point

1230

2nd Wave

1st Wave

Plymouth
0300

Hospital Point

San Carlos River

X
2 Gazelles
0845

C a m e r o n ' s   R i d g e

Doctor's Head

Fort Austin (ASW duty)

Europic Ferry

870
Lookout Hill

Cat Is.

Sir Geraint
Sir Tristram
Norland
Sir Lancelot
Sir Galahad

V e r d e   M o u n t a i n s

Stromness

790

Red Hill Point
Sir Percivale

Ajax Bay Refrig. Plant
45 Cdo

Cemetery (post-war)

Fearless

40 Cdo
San Carlos

Poker Point

Airstrip

Seaview Point

2 Para
Bonner's Bay

907
Campito Hill

North West Rincon

650

Head of the Bay Creek

870

650
Round Mt.

N

0   1   2
miles
© Hugh Bicheno

Rookery Point

S u s s e x   M o u n t a i n s

920

Wreck Point

San Carlos Water

likely is that he escaped to the north, covered by Colque's rearguard action. The rest is a pathetic story of a group of soldiers who had faith in an officer who did not know what he was doing and kept them pointlessly in the field. One died and the remaining NCO lost both feet to gangrene. Reyes was awarded the MVC, for no reason identifiable from his own account.

Esteban, meanwhile, beat a fighting retreat, in the course of which he disabused the British of the belief that mounting a GPMG and rockets on fragile Gazelles turned them into gunships. He brought away his forty-four remaining men to Douglas Settlement on the north coast, where he contacted Stanley through the islanders' short-wave radio network and was retrieved by helicopter. He was much given to 'controlling' the civilian population – the one thing all Argentine officers knew how to do well – and at Port San Carlos he left behind booby traps (one of them rigged to a British helmet captured on 2 April) in a settlement containing seven children. He was a competent and inspirational officer, though: he did not lose a man to trench foot or other injury during the long retreat and insisted on being flown back into battle at Goose Green on 27 May. His three other sub-lieutenants also proved to be effective officers, but although the British would have had a harder time had there been more like them, there can be little doubt that they were indirectly responsible for a number of extra Argentine deaths. The two men in the first Gazelle were killed outright, but Esteban's men continued to fire on the crew of the second as they swam away from their ditched helicopter, and at Goose Green on 28 May one of his sub-lieutenants shot Lieutenant Barry in the back during what came to be known as 'the white flag' incident. Those episodes made British troops less inclined to give quarter to those seeking to surrender in later battles.

The downing of the Gazelles was the sole contribution of the Argentine Army to the events of 21 May, but knowledge that there was an aggressive enemy patrol 'out there' – and that some of them might be wearing British kit – led to a potentially fratricidal clash on 23 May between A and C Companies of 3 Para involving GPMG and mortar fire: a major breakdown of command and control, for which the Operations Officer was temporarily suspended from duty. Two lance corporals and five privates from A Company were disabled as well as an attached lance corporal from 9 Parachute Squadron RE. Sergeant Colbeck of Support Company commented that such incidents

'are unfortunately not uncommon – Northern Ireland had seen many such
. . . fatigue, poor visibility, bad planning and an over-eagerness to engage the
enemy are some of the factors that make them more likely.' Like all operational accidents they have a far more serious effect on morale than combat
casualties, in this case creating bad blood between the two companies and
shattering the confidence of Major Osbourne, C Company commander.

The edginess of the troops paradoxically owed much to the absence of
enemy ground activity, and they relieved their feelings with every weapon to
hand when the Argentine Air Force attacked targets in the bay itself. When
you are occupying the sides of a valley and fire at aircraft flying low through
it, those on the other side are by far the most likely to be hit. The grace of
God factor worked to prevent further casualties, but there is a stone memorial
at San Carlos Settlement to the sole fatal casualty suffered by 40 Commando
during the campaign, just as surely a victim of poor fire control as the eight
men lost to 3 Para on 23 May. It is not hard to imagine what a disproportionate effect the Argentines might have achieved had they sent their Special
Forces to probe the beachhead, but the division of responsibilities agreed
by service chiefs more concerned with relative prestige than with military
effectiveness turned the Battle of San Carlos into an exclusively aero-naval
contest.

At 0830 Piaggi at Goose Green received Esteban's report of 'a large ship
with many landing craft and seven warships' and retransmitted the message
to Stanley. Wing Commander Pedroza, the CO of the Goose Green airbase,
immediately ordered a Pucará strike, which was interrupted by shells from
Ardent in Grantham Sound. Flight Lieutenant Benitez took off alone, but
as he loitered over the Sussex Mountains he was shot down by a US-supplied
Stinger missile fired by an SAS patrol returning from an early morning
spoof raid on Darwin. Two more Pucarás followed a little later, but the Stinger
operator was unable to repeat his first success and the two aircraft turned
away to nose around *Ardent*. Deterred from attacking by gunfire and a
hopeful Sea Cat launch, they fired rockets at an abandoned house from
which they believed *Ardent*'s fire was being directed – and then three Harriers
pounced on them. Flight Officer Micheloud escaped while the Harriers
concentrated on Squadron Leader Tomba's aircraft, which finally fell to
the guns of Lieutenant Commander 'Sharkey' Ward, CO of 801 Naval Air

Squadron, after surviving five earlier attacks, all at extremely low level. Tomba ejected at the last moment and walked back to Goose Green, his report of being the mouse to Ward's cat ensuring that the Pucarás did not fly again in the presence of a Harrier Combat Air Patrol.

At Stanley a flight of two naval Aermacchis was ordered to reconnoitre San Carlos but one of them suffered a mechanical failure, leaving the other, piloted by Lieutenant Crippa, to fly out alone along the north coast of East Falkland. Rounding Race Point he first encountered a Lynx and was about to engage it when he saw *Argonaut,* the stopper in the bottle off Fanning Head. He attacked with cannon and rockets, wounding three men and putting a hole in the ship's radar antenna. He then flew on along the Wreck Point peninsula, attracting a Sea Cat from *Intrepid,* a Blowpipe from a soldier on *Canberra*, and small arms fire from everyone. Untouched and undeterred, he circled back to get an accurate count of the ships in San Carlos Water and radioed the information back to Stanley.

But by then the British had enjoyed six priceless hours of unharassed activity and the two assault ships (LPD) *Fearless* and *Intrepid,* six RFA landing ships (LSL) and two civilian transports were now close inshore within the bay. *Canberra,* the 'white whale', was in the safest deep water location between the cliffs of Fanning Head and Chancho Point, covered to the east by *Plymouth* and to the west by *Argonaut* and *Broadsword.* Some commentators have alleged the Argentine pilots had orders to attack the warships in the Sound, but in fact they were the only targets on display. Had the air attacks been directed by properly equipped forward observers, the attacking aircraft would have gone for the higher value targets within San Carlos Bay, and the day might well have been a disaster for British arms.

The choice of landing site was vindicated and the high ground around the bay effectively sheltered the amphibious force, but there was a second part to the gamble, which was to force the Argentine Air Force to do battle in a place of British choosing, in the hopes of winning, on the day, the air supremacy that in theory should have been obtained beforehand. On either the 20th or the 22nd the landings would have enjoyed overcast conditions, in which the Argentine Air Force could not have attacked. However the British planners could only be sure of overcast conditions to cover the vulnerable approach of the Landing Force – the probability that 21 May might be clear was accepted because any delay ate into the limited time available for the land forces to complete their mission. The setting consideration was that the fleet could not remain on station in the open ocean much beyond mid-June. The limitations of the Royal Navy's air- and ship-borne radar equipment meant it was forced to use Battle of Britain vintage tactics of surface controllers directing aircraft against incoming 'bandits', and the Mark I eyeballs of theHarrier pilots and the operators of the visually aimed Sea Cat and Blowpipe would have to make a virtue of necessity. Having given up its own airborne early warning capability, the Royal Navy was compelled to trade multi-million pound warships for second-hand jets dropping bargain-basement bombs.

The gamble had to be made good by raw physical valour in the field. In terms of future funding, the Royal Navy was objectively in a win-win situation: but those put at risk by over-commitment to anti-submarine over air defence, and missiles over guns, were unlikely to take such a detached view. A tall cross stands today on Campito Hill, overlooking the last resting places of *Ardent* off the North West Islands and *Antelope* off Ajax Bay. Previous *Antelopes* were luckier, but only one man survived when an earlier *Ardent* was sunk fighting overwhelming odds in 1940, and her predecessor was lost with all hands doing the same at Jutland in 1916. Modern technology shaped the battlefield by forcing the Argentine pilots to fly too low to identify the optimum targets and below the height necessary to permit their bombs to arm: but they were also drawn away by men who honoured the traditions of their service by putting themselves in harm's way, knowing that neither their ships nor their weapons were adequate to the task at hand. It is reassuring that the First Sea Lord, as I write, is Admiral Sir Alan West DSC, skipper of *Ardent* in 1982.

At about the time Crippa attacked, Grupo 6 launched a flight of Daggers from Río Grande and another two from San Julián. After the massacre of Grupo 5 Skyhawks on 12 May they were relieved to learn the British had chosen a landing site that permitted an overland approach. Eight of the nine aircraft made it to the target and burst over Falkland Sound through the gap between Goat Hill and Mount Rosalie, directly opposite the entrance to San Carlos Bay. Flight Lieutenant Dimeglio and Pilot Officer Castillo arrived

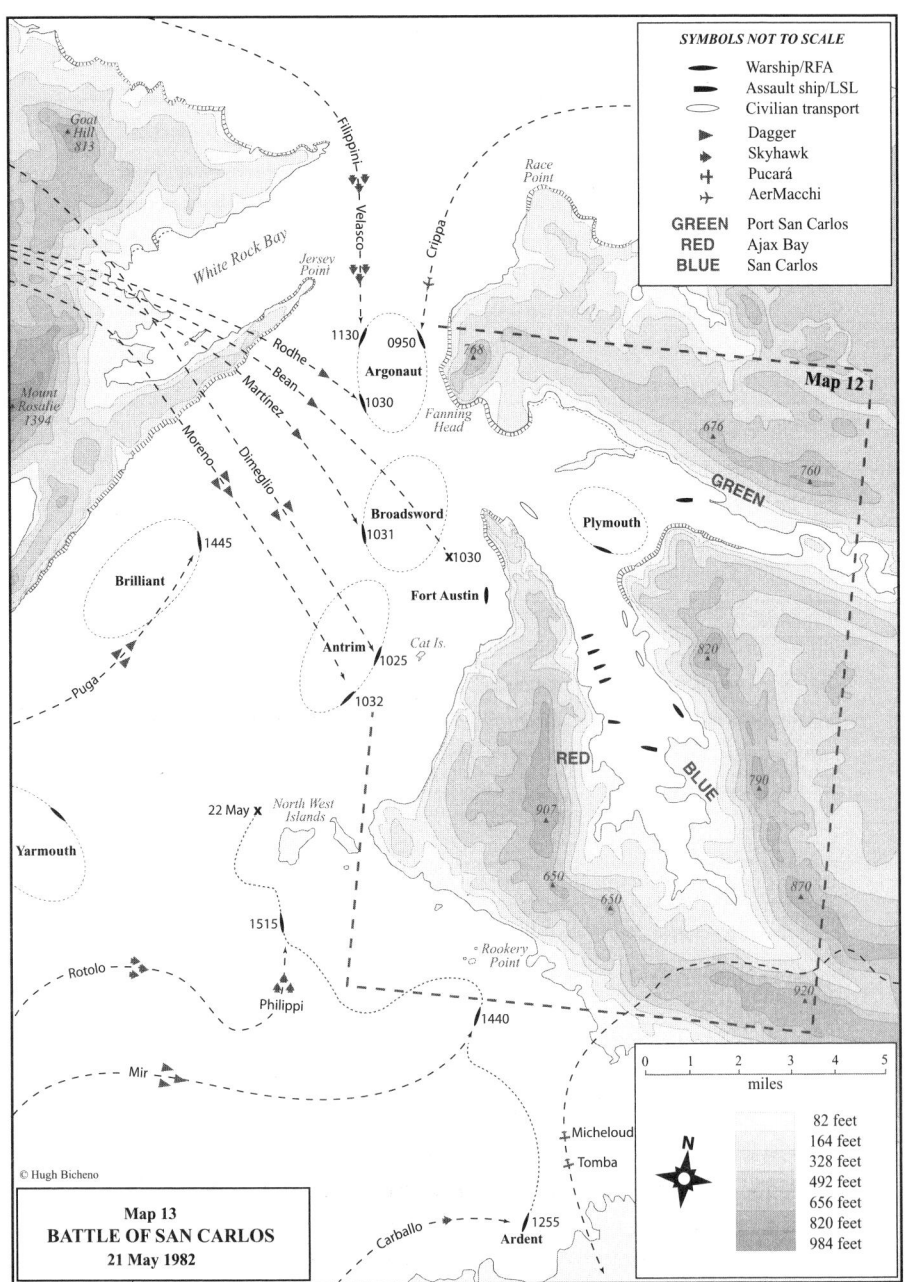

SYMBOLS NOT TO SCALE

Warship/RFA
Assault ship/LSL
Civilian transport
Dagger
Skyhawk
Pucará
AerMacchi

GREEN Port San Carlos
RED Ajax Bay
BLUE San Carlos

Goat Hill 813

Filippini

Velasco

Crippa

Race Point

White Rock Bay

Jersey Point

Map 12

768

1130 / 0950

Argonaut

676

Rodhe

Bean

Martinez

1030

Fanning Head

GREEN

760

Mount Rosalie 1394

Moreno

Dimeglio

Broadsword

1031

Plymouth

Plymouth

x 1030

Fort Austin

820

1445

Brilliant

Antrim

Cat Is.

1025

RED

BLUE

790

Puga

1032

907

22 May x

North West Islands

Yarmouth

650

650

870

1515

Rookery Point

920

Rotolo

Philippi

1440

Mir

0   1   2   3   4   5
miles

Micheloud

Tomba

N

82 feet
164 feet
328 feet
492 feet
656 feet
820 feet
984 feet

© Hugh Bicheno

Carballo

1255

Ardent

Map 13
BATTLE OF SAN CARLOS
21 May 1982

first from Río Grande and attacked *Antrim,* hitting her with cannon but missing with their bombs. Minutes later the six Daggers from San Julián attacked together. The first, led by Flight Lieutenant Rohde, split up to attack *Argonaut, Broadsword* and the RFA *Fort Austin,* the last posted outside Wreck Point on anti-submarine duty. Again they hit the warships with cannon but missed with their bombs, while Pilot Officer Bean's run against *Fort Austin* was fatally interrupted by a *Broadsword* Sea Wolf. The second flight of three led by Flight Lieutenant Moreno concentrated on *Antrim,* which fired a Seaslug in the vain hope of distracting them. She was hammered by forty cannon shells and a 1,000lb bomb from dead astern that careered across her flight deck and smashed through several compartments, including the Seaslug magazine, causing several fires and crippling her radar. *Brilliant* took over as Air Defence Controller. *Antrim*'s bomb was defused and reverently lowered over the side that night, but she was out of action for the day and, barring largely symbolic escort duty in the fleet repair and replenishment area, out of the war.

Overclaiming for the single kill led the British to believe they had not done too badly, although it was not firepower that blunted the effect of what might have been a devastating first attack, rather the unrehearsed overland approach chosen by Grupo 6, which made too many last minute demands on the pilots. Grupo 5 made better use of the terrain when they attacked an hour later. Two flights of Skyhawks led by Pilot Officers Velasco and Filippini swept around White Rock Point at wave-top level and put two 1,000lb bombs into *Argonaut* below the waterline. Neither detonated, but one penetrated her boiler room and left her without power or steering, while the other hit the Sea Cat magazine and started a major fire. Two men were killed. The ship nearly ran aground on Fanning Head and was saved only by the manual release of her anchor. Towed into San Carlos Water that evening by *Plymouth,* the tough old frigate remained there for eight days having the bombs removed and her machinery repaired. Although in theory able to function as a static air defence asset after repairs to her Sea Cat system, in practise *Argonaut* had become a decoy target and, like *Antrim,* was effectively out of the war.

The screen was now down to the two newest (*Brilliant* and *Broadsword*) and oldest (*Plymouth* and *Yarmouth*) escorts in the Task Force, with *Ardent* still committed to harassing the Argentine garrison and air base at Goose

Green. For clarity of presentation **Map 13** (p. 152) shows the afternoon attack on *Brilliant* at her morning station off the coast of West Falkland, but in reality by that time she had moved into the mouth of San Carlos Bay and *Yarmouth* had taken her place, leaving *Ardent* dangerously isolated off the southern shore of Grantham Sound. In the early afternoon she received a reprieve when two of four Grupo 5 Skyhawks from Río Gallegos fell out because of refuelling problems and a third bombed the abandoned *Carcaraña* in Port King. The last, flown by Flight Lieutenant Carballo, flew around the headland and attacked so low that one of his wing tanks hit the radar antenna, bending it thirty degrees out of true. His bomb missed, but *Ardent* was not to be so lucky when the second strike by Grupo 6 approached from the south two hours later. Two Daggers of six from Río Grande dropped out with mechanical problems and another fell to a Harrier Sidewinder over West Falkland, but the remaining three, led by Flight Lieutenant Mir, made a textbook attack on *Ardent,* attacking her from astern on convergent axes and putting two 1,000lb bombs into her hull. One detonated, destroying her hangar and helicopter, blowing her Sea Cat launcher overboard, cutting power to her main gun and starting a large fire. Most of the twenty-two men who died with *Ardent* were killed in this attack.

Three San Julián Daggers, led by Squadron Leader Puga, attacked *Brilliant* about the same time, missing with their bombs but hitting her heavily with cannon, which temporarily disabled Sea Wolf as well as riddling her loaded Exocet launcher. They also wounded, among others, Lieutenant Commander Hulme, the officer in charge of air defence, who had just directed the Harrier Combat Air Patrol to a successful interception of three more San Julián Daggers over West Falkland. Ward, who shot down two of them, recalled calling up Hulme to ask for more 'trade' and being told to wait. 'I said: "What do you mean wait?" He said: "Well, we've just had our ops room strafed with gunfire, with 30mm cannon. The man across the desk from me has lost the top of his head and I've been hit in the arm and I'm just collecting myself." I felt awful. I said: "Okay – sorry about that," and within seven seconds he was back on line saying "Right, we think we've got trade for you, up to the north." It happened just like that, quite amazing.'

Tragically for the men struggling to save the stricken *Ardent* she now drew a last attack by six of the eight Naval Air Skyhawks, normally carried by the aircraft carrier *25 de Mayo* but now based in Río Grande. Expert in naval attack and each carrying four 500lb Snakeye bombs designed for low-level delivery, the first three, led by Commander Philippi, put several into the frigate's already devastated stern.* The second three, led by Lieutenant Commander Rotolo, may have added to the destruction, and the previously unexploded 1,000lb bomb probably cooked off in the fire. *Ardent* still took another day to sink and her builders, Vosper Thorneycroft, had reason to be proud of their handiwork. The departing naval aircraft paid a high price for their gleaming white colour scheme, with Philippi forced to eject and one of his wingmen killed by Harriers as they fled south down Falkland Sound, and the third so damaged that Sub-Lieutenant Arca was unable to land at Stanley and forced to eject. The abandoned Skyhawk flew in circles until shot down by the airfield anti-aircraft artillery.

That night *Fort Austin* was brought into the bay, and *Canberra, Norland* and *Europic Ferry* left San Carlos without unloading most of their stores. The score for the day was two Gazelles downed, one frigate sinking, a destroyer and another frigate disabled and both the irreplaceable Type 22s with varying degrees of battle damage, against five Daggers, five Skyhawks and a Pucará destroyed. In ground attacks away from San Carlos the Argentines lost a Chinook and two Puma heavy lift helicopters near Mount Kent, but Flight Lieutenant Glover's Harrier GR3 was shot down at Port Howard after imprudently returning to make a second attack on a fully alerted target. Five battalions had been landed without loss, but until the logistics were made good the operation could only be accounted a partial success. Woodward had lost the use of three more escorts, which added to the sunken *Sheffield* and the disabled *Glasgow,* and followed shortly by the loss of *Antelope* and *Coventry,* was an unsustainable rate of loss. On the other side, sixty strike sorties were launched from the mainland, forty-four reached the islands and thirteen aircraft were lost. There were more where they came from, however, and only four pilots were killed, the rest returning to their squadrons to share their hard-won experience, some to fly combat missions again.

Bad weather spared the beachhead on the 22nd, but on the 23rd four

---

* Snakeyes deploy retarding fins, causing them to drop more sharply, thus permitting the low-flying parent aircraft to escape damage from the explosion of its own bombs.

Grupo 5 Skyhawks, led by Carballo, flew inland before attacking from the east to put two 1,000lb bombs into newly arrived *Antelope,* which did not detonate, and to near-miss *Broadsword* with two more, which exploded in the water just beyond her. *Antelope* moved to Ajax Bay and was mortally damaged that night when one of the bombs exploded, killing Staff Sergeant Prescott RE who had been trying to defuse it.* The ship's long death agony provided some of the most haunting images of the war. On the 24th the Argentines at last concentrated on the logistics ships. Seven Grupo 6 Daggers attacked at midday, providing some spectacular video footage as they missed *Fort Austin, Stromness* and the returned *Norland* with their bombs. Five Grupo 5 Skyhawks attacked an hour later without success but this was closely followed by a potentially war-winning strike by Grupo 4 Skyhawks. Three aircraft led by Vázquez – he of the 12 May near-miss on *Glasgow* – put two 1,000lb bombs in *Sir Lancelot* and another in *Sir Galahad.* None exploded: if they had, the Commando Logistics Regiment and the Royal Corps of Transport's Port Regiment detachment, with 300 men and indispensable stores still embarked on the two LSLs, would have been crippled, and with them the land campaign.

That such crucial elements were still vulnerably afloat speaks of operational inexperience and more faith in the Rapier batteries than the system was able to justify. Nobody could know as night fell on the 21st that the Argentines would not mount another attack of such intensity, although this was in part because the Royal Navy did not again offer them so many easy targets. What tipped the balance on that first crucial day was the lack of Argentine forward observers and the resulting tunnel vision that caused the pilots to concentrate on the warships, most egregiously in the *Ardent* overkill. Nothing succeeds like success and the inspired choice of landing site saved the amphibious force from destruction. Ironically, it nearly went wrong because of a reversal of the usual charge that armed forces prepare to fight the last war. the Royal Navy was, albeit inadequately, prepared to fight World War III – it simply was not equipped for the World War II-style, low-level bombing attacks it faced around San Carlos.

---

* He was awarded a posthumous DSC.

8 Darwin/Goose Green

PART ONE

FOR THOSE RESISTANT TO the idea that grand strategy is the political dimension of war, the attack by 2 Para on the Darwin/Goose Green isthmus was a pointless battle. Political pressure, so goes this theory, caused Northwood to override Thompson's objections and to insist on a strategically irrelevant operation. This is a misconception. Even if there had been no other justification, after the loss of *Coventry* and *Atlantic Conveyor* it was vital to register a British success in order to win back the headlines, puncture Argentine self-confidence and persuade neutral countries to remain on the fence. But there were also two compelling 'pure' military reasons to take out the Argentine presence at the narrow neck of land between East Falkland and Lafonia: it completed the isolation of the garrisons on West Falkland, and while it remained in Argentine hands it posed a deadly threat to the beachhead. On 25 May Menéndez requested the dispatch of a battle group from the air-transportable brigade in Córdoba, to be dropped in Lafonia – which is one big Drop Zone – to join the garrison at Goose Green and to attack the beachhead. The Argentine High Command denied the request, but not until the last days of the war did it finally rule out the possibility of making an airborne drop on northern Lafonia supported by attacks across the Sound from the troops in West Falkland.

Thompson believed the garrison at Goose Green – as it was – could have been masked cheaply, but would not have been so sanguine had he been told it might be reinforced without warning by a battle group of the best infantry in the Argentine Army. His ruffled feathers were still on display five years later when interviewed by Yorkshire TV for *The Untold Story,* when he confessed to having thought 'right, I'll win this war for the buggers and then I'll resign.' One may deduce the real untold story, which is that he was not told why he must capture (as opposed to merely raiding) Goose Green because the information came from the US National Security Agency. After Rowlands sportingly informed the Argentines that their encrypted radio traffic was an open book, one might have supposed there was no need to be coy about it and that Northwood could have shared signals intelligence product with the Amphibious and Landing Force Commanders. However there was a fourth party involved – the Soviet electronic intelligence ships that maintained constant surveillance of the Task Force. US goodwill did not extend to giving the Soviets insight into NSA eavesdropping capability, or a windfall mass of encrypted traffic for their super-computers to play with.*

Considerations of signals security probably also lay behind the otherwise bizarre British decision not to appoint an overall, in-theatre, operational commander. Only Northwood possessed the facilities to handle and evaluate signals intelligence correctly. Woodward's flagship *Hermes* had the equipment but not the staff, and the Landing Force had neither. Once Clapp and Thompson set off for San Carlos, they were out of the loop.

FOR A NUMBER OF REASONS – not least a personality clash between Thompson and Lieutenant Colonel Jones, the CO of 2 Para – the attack was launched with half the usual artillery support. Thompson allotted Jones only three guns from 8 Battery, 29 Commando Regiment RA, and barely enough helicopter support to fly them and a limited supply of ammunition to Camilla Creek House in the Sussex Mountains. At the time, Thompson could call on only six Sea King and five Wessex helicopters: four other Sea Kings, their pilots recently equipped with passive night goggles, were permanently allocated to the Special Forces for their night insertions, and another was fully committed to fuelling the ravenous generators of the Rapier batteries around the beachhead. Thompson was justifiably angry about his superiors'

---

* Ironically all US and NATO cryptographic secrets had been fatally compromised by the Walker family and friends, active agents of the KGB within the US Navy from 1967–85.

obliviousness to the logistical realities and believed the raid Northwood wanted him to make on Goose Green was a distraction from the serious business of accumulating stores and helicopters for the advance across East Falkland. He called the raid off, therefore, when bad weather prevented the guns being flown to Camilla Creek during the night of the 24th, giving rise to Jones's furious comment: 'I've been waiting twenty years for this and now some fucking Marine has cancelled it.'

Had he not already done so, Thompson would certainly have cancelled the raid on the 25th after *Atlantic Conveyor* went down, taking with it his hopes for early amelioration of the transport bottleneck. Instead, he received a blunt 'or else' order from Northwood to capture, not raid the isthmus, and *at the same time* to break out of the beachhead towards Stanley and in general to be more aggressive. Jones had aggression to spare, some of it overflowing in Thompson's direction, and their last exchange was terse: 'Do you think you can do it?', Thompson asked after telling the bristling Jones he could count on no additional artillery or transport. 'Yes,' Jones replied. 'Well, get on with it then.' In 1995, in a manly break with British officialdom's most sacred tradition, Thompson took personal responsibility:

> I should have acquiesced with Jones's request for a troop of [tanks] –
> two Scimitars and two Scorpions. I should have given 2 Para more
> support. Indeed it would have been better . . . to have taken my
> Tactical HQ and a second commando or battalion down to Goose
> Green, and done the job in a few hours.

Bless, but he went too far in his desire to shield the memory of a fallen hero. Jones always intended to launch a full-scale assault and believed the fire support, which would include (weather permitting) Harrier strikes by day and naval gunfire from *Arrow* in Grantham Sound by night, was adequate. His appreciation, quite rightly, was not based on numbers. The Brigade intelligence assessment on the component units and ration strength of the Argentine Battle Group (in the British Army normally 1,000+ men) holding the isthmus was accurate, but so was the SAS eyeball report that it was poorly deployed.[*] Jones conveyed the second, but not the first, to his subordinates at the pre-battle 'O' Group, interrupting his intelligence officer when he began to

---

[*] Both assessments ignored the numerically significant FAA presence around the Airfield (see next chapter).

tell them more than Jones wanted them to know. It was not political pressure but Jones's personality that led to the attack being rushed beyond reason, without even allowing the company commanders time to recce their initial objectives. Had he known that Thompson's job was on the line he might have obtained the tanks and more guns, but everything points to a furious unwillingness to tolerate any delay whatever. In his defence, the historic function of the Paras is to seize objectives and wait for support to catch up, counting on speed and audacity to compensate for lack of firepower. Added to which Jones could be sure the Argentine conscripts would find a night assault terrifying, and confidently expected the enemy to fold if hit hard from the dark.

Although this was a reasonable assumption when facing troops the SAS reported to be slovenly and seemingly aimless, it is extraordinary that Jones – recently an instructor at the Infantry Training Centre – drew up a scheme that made no allowance for 'friction': the things that always go wrong in combat, compounded by the unavoidable delays and mishaps that affect any body of men crossing unfamiliar terrain in the dark. It was over 2 miles from Camilla Creek House to the Start Line and 4 miles further to Goose Green, and Jones believed 2 Para could cover the distance and defeat the enemy in one night. Since they had to man-pack their close support weapons and all the ammunition for the whole assault, they left six 81mm mortars behind because they could only carry enough bombs to provide a minimum reserve for two. They did take all their 66, 84 and Milan anti-tank weapons, and they had twice the normal number of machine-guns – 2 Para had been issued with new GPMGs just before the war began and Jones did not return the old ones. However, their enormous combat loads limited the number of radio batteries they could carry, and they also left sleeping bags and personal gear behind. Neither would have mattered if the battle were short and sharp, but it lasted through two bitterly cold nights. As a result, by the end of the battle command and control had dissolved and the battalion had hit the wall.

The principal complication was that the guns and mortars ran out of ammunition as a result of the attack on Ajax Bay mentioned in Chapter 6, which destroyed all the ammunition netted and ready to be choppered forward to support the 2 Para attack: 200 mortar bombs and 300 shells for the three 105mm guns. Compounding this, cannon fire holed the only 10,000-litre rubber pillow-tank available, plus the Mexeflote raft transporting it ashore.

The loss of scarce cargo nets and of the hoped-for improvement in refuelling capacity came at a moment when Thompson's helicopters were almost fully committed to the vital SAS insertion on Mount Kent (see **Chapter 10**), which meant that 2 Para drew the short straw and it was not until the 29th that the shortfall in batteries, ammunition and, belatedly, some creature comforts were made good.

It is impossible to make a dispassionate examination of the battle without offending against the 'of the dead speak kindly or not at all' stricture: in this case of a very brave man who died trying to make his over-ambitious battle plan work by personal example. The fault lies in the citation for Jones's posthumous Victoria Cross, which invested an act born of enraged frustration with excessive significance. One ventures warily into this minefield, as there may be some left unflailed by Spencer Fitz-Gibbon's *Not Mentioned in Despatches,* which I suspect would have been better received if the author had balanced his criticism of Jones's command style with greater appreciation of the contribution he made to the mental and physical preparation of the battalion. Jones had the highest opinion of his men, and they of him, but both his plan and his behaviour during the battle reveal little confidence in his company commanders. We may eventually learn more from the confidential reports he wrote about them, but for our purposes it suffices to know that he believed them deficient in dash, the combination of rapid situational appreciation and initiative historically most prized in the cavalry.* Behind it all lay a pre-modern belief in heroic leadership and a deep faith that friction could be abolished by the unmediated force of his personality acting on the wellsprings of violence in his men.

I have reluctantly entered the numbers game in the key to **Maps 14** and **15** (pp. 163–164) only because of the lasting echoes of contemporary reports that 2 Para overcame odds of three to one and killed 200 men in so doing. The three-to-one ratio requires counting Argentine troops that were never engaged plus administrative staff who played little or no part in the battle, while omitting 2 Para's own rear echelon – as well as the rest of 8 Battery and J Company, 42 Commando, which were hastily choppered forward by Thompson and ready for action on the 29th. The exaggerated figure for

---

* His scheme looks more like one for mechanised infantry than for heavily burdened men on foot. It is as though Jones planned it around the tanks and did not rethink it properly after he was denied them.

ARGENTINE
(approx. 1,100 all personnel)
Task Force Mercedes
12th Infantry Regiment (RI 12)
CO – Lt Col Piaggi,   2 i/c – Maj Frontera
Chaplain – Fr. Mor
Q Coy (132 + 1 x 120mm)
  Sub-Lt Peluffo (41 + 3 MAG to Darwin Hill)
A Coy (175 + 6 MAG)
  Lt Manresa/CSM Cohelo
  2 Platoon – Sub-Lt Malacalza
  Support Platoon – 2Lt Muñoz
  (2 x 81mm mortars, 105mm RCL)
  Recce Platoon – 2Lt Morales/Sub-Lt Garra
  (Landrover-mounted HMG)
C Coy (150 + 1 MAG, 1 x 81mm mortar)
  Lt Duazo
8th Infantry Regiment (37 + 3 MAG)
  Sub Lt Aliaga
C Coy, 25th Infantry Regiment (RI 25)
  Bote detachment (45)
  2Lt Estévez
  Romeo detachment (33)
  Sub-Lt Gómez Centurión
Combat Engineer 601 Section (11)

Combat Group Güemes (64)
  Lt Esteban, 2i/c 2Lt Vásquez

Combat Group Solari
  Capt Corsiglia
  B Coy, RI 12 (132 + 81mm, 105 RCL)
  Lt Gorriti (stayed behind)

Artillery support
GAA 4 half battery (45 + 3 x 105mm howitzers)
  Lt Chanampa
GADA 601 battery (33 + Skyguard, 2 x twin 35mm)
  Sub-Lt Braghini

Air Base Condor
WCdr Pedrozo
  Infantry (57) – *Acting OC Lt Esteban*
  (2 x 81mm mortars, 1 HMG, 4 MAG,
  Pucará rocket pod)
  AAA (45 + Elta radar, 6 x twin 20mm)

  Air Operations Personnel (100)

BRITISH
(approx 575 combat personnel)
2nd Battalion, The Parachute Regiment
CO – Lt Col Jones,   2 i/c – Maj Keeble
Adj – Capt Wood*   Psyops – Capt Bell RM*
Chaplain – Capt Cooper*
HQ Coy (55)
  Maj Ryan/RSM Simpson
A Coy (90 + 8 GPMG, 3 x 84, 66s)
  Maj Farrar-Hockley/CSM Price
  Forward Observer – Capt Watson
  1 Platoon – Sgt Barrett/Cpl Abols
  2 Platoon – 2Lt Coe/Sgt Hastings
  3 Platoon – 2Lt Wallis/Sgt Beattie
B Coy (90 + 9 GPMG, 3 x 84, 66s)
  Maj Crosland/CSM Richens
  Forward Observer – Capt Ash
  4 Platoon – Lt Hocking
  5 Platoon – Lt Weighell/Sgt Aird
  6 Platoon – Lt Chapman/Sgt McCulloch
C (Patrols) Coy (55 + 9 GPMG, 4 x 84, 66s)
  Maj R Jenner/CSM Geddis
  Patrols – Capt Farrar
  Recce – Lt Connor
D Coy (90 + 9 GPMG, 3 x 84, 66s)
  Maj Neame/CSM Greenhalgh
  FSC – Lt Page Forward Observer – Sgt Bullock
  10 Platoon – Lt Webster/Sgt O'Rawe
  11 Platoon – 2Lt Waddington
  12 Platoon – Lt Barry/Sgt Meredith
Support Coy (128)
  Maj H Jenner/CSM Cotton/CQMS Pye
  2 Mortars – Capt Worsley-Tonks*
  6 Milan – Capt Ketley
  6 SFMG – Lt Lister
  Assault Pioneers – Sgt Bell
  Snipers – Sgt Head
59 Ind. Commando Squadron RE (20)
  Recce Troop – Lt Livingstone*

Artillery Support
8 Battery, 29 Commando Regiment RA (43)
  Troop (3 x 105mm light guns)
  Battery Commander – Maj Rice*
Air Defence Troop RM
Section, 42 Battery, 32 Guided Wpns Regt RA

HMS *Arrow* (1 x 4.5-inch)
  Naval Gunfire Observer – Capt Arnold
  * with Tactical HQ

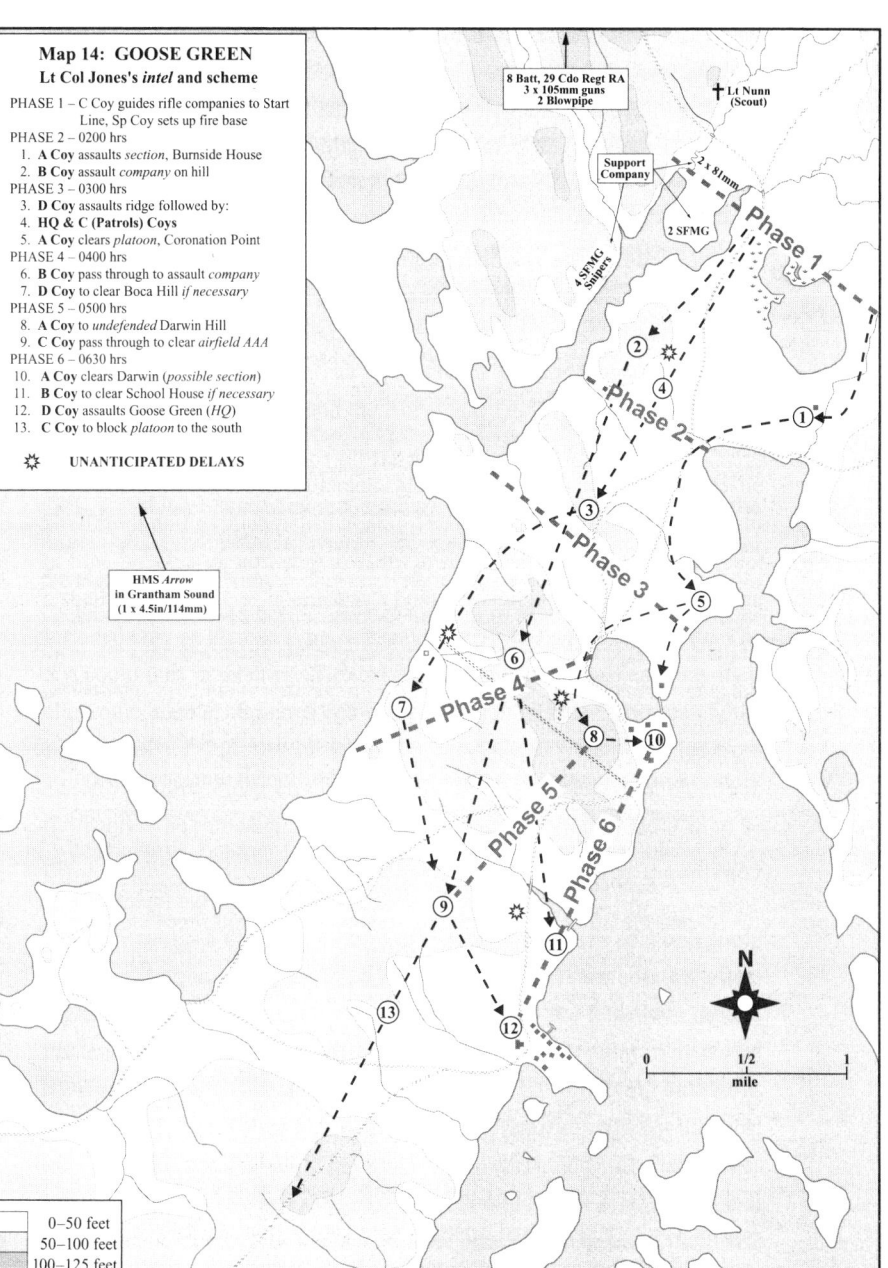

Map 14: GOOSE GREEN

Lt Col Jones's *intel* and scheme

PHASE 1 – C Coy guides rifle companies to Start
         Line, Sp Coy sets up fire base
PHASE 2 – 0200 hrs
  1. **A Coy** assaults *section*, Burnside House
  2. **B Coy** assault *company* on hill
PHASE 3 – 0300 hrs
  3. **D Coy** assaults ridge followed by:
  4. **HQ & C (Patrols) Coys**
  5. **A Coy** clears *platoon*, Coronation Point
PHASE 4 – 0400 hrs
  6. **B Coy** pass through to assault *company*
  7. **D Coy** to clear Boca Hill *if necessary*
PHASE 5 – 0500 hrs
  8. **A Coy** to *undefended* Darwin Hill
  9. **C Coy** pass through to clear airfield *AAA*
PHASE 6 – 0630 hrs
 10. **A Coy** clears Darwin (*possible section*)
 11. **B Coy** to clear School House *if necessary*
 12. **D Coy** assaults Goose Green (*HQ*)
 13. **C Coy** to block *platoon* to the south

  ☼   **UNANTICIPATED DELAYS**

8 Batt, 29 Cdo Regt RA
3 x 105mm guns
2 Blowpipe

✝ Lt Nunn
(Scout)

Support
Company

2 x 81mm

Phase 1

2 SFMG

4 SFMG;
Snipers

Phase 2

HMS *Arrow*
in Grantham Sound
(1 x 4.5in/114mm)

Phase 3

Phase 4

Phase 5

Phase 6

N

0   1/2   1
mile

0–50 feet
50–100 feet
100–125 feet

© Hugh Bicheno

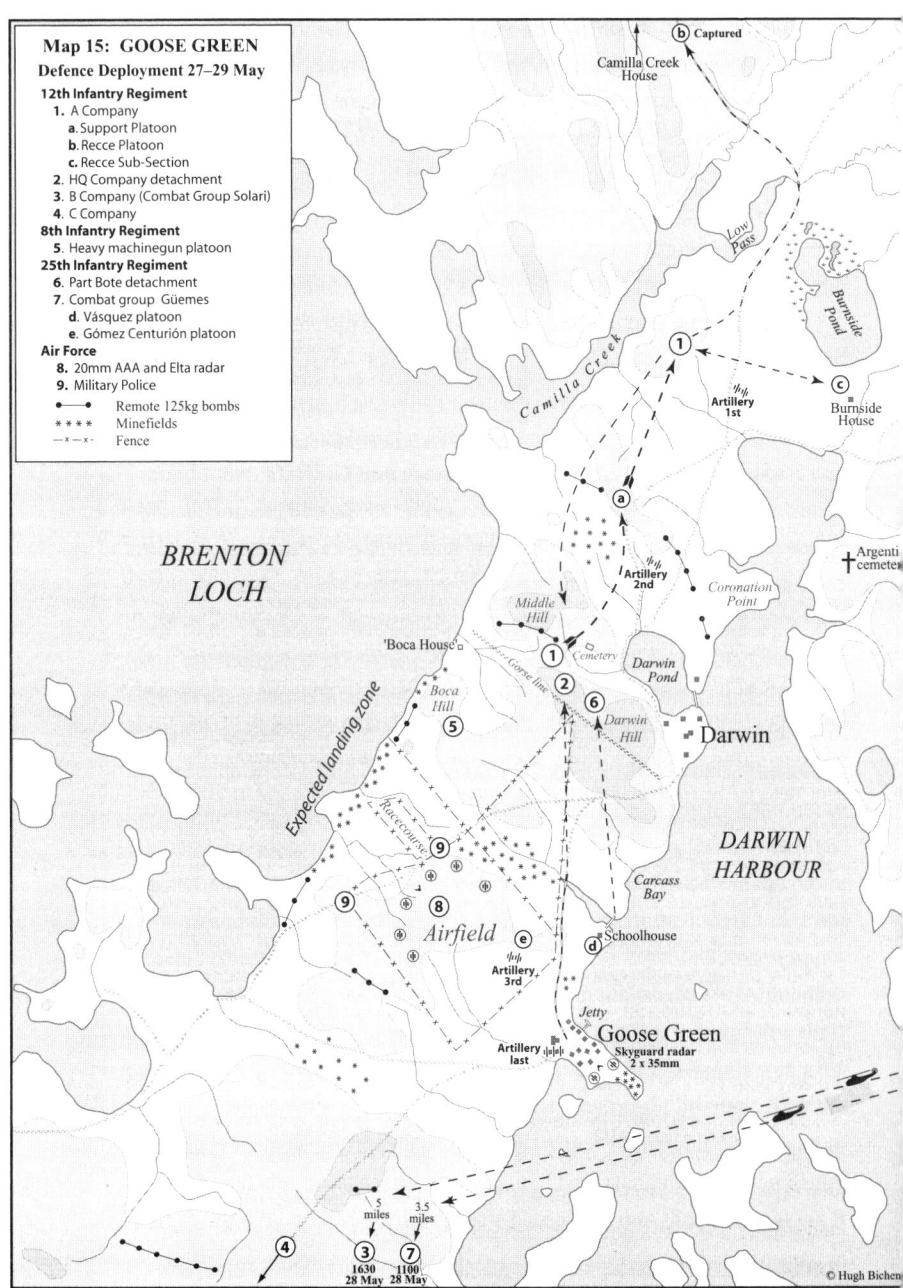

Map 15: GOOSE GREEN

Defence Deployment 27–29 May

12th Infantry Regiment
1. A Company
   a. Support Platoon
   b. Recce Platoon
   c. Recce Sub-Section
2. HQ Company detachment
3. B Company (Combat Group Solari)
4. C Company

8th Infantry Regiment
5. Heavy machinegun platoon

25th Infantry Regiment
6. Part Bote detachment
7. Combat group Güemes
   d. Vásquez platoon
   e. Gómez Centurión platoon

Air Force
8. 20mm AAA and Elta radar
9. Military Police

●—●　　　Remote 125kg bombs
＊＊＊＊　Minefields
—x—x—　Fence

Camilla Creek House

(b) Captured

Low Pass

Burnside Pond

(1)

⁴⁄ℓ⁄ Artillery 1st

(c) Burnside House

Camilla Creek

BRENTON LOCH

(a)

⁴⁄ℓ⁄ Artillery 2nd

Argenti cemeter✝

Coronation Point

Middle Hill

'Boca House' ▫

Gorse line

(1) Cemetery

(2)

(6)

Darwin Pond

Darwin Hill

Darwin

Boca Hill

(5)

Expected landing zone

Racecourse

(9)

(9)

(8)

Airfield

(e)

⁴⁄ℓ⁄ Artillery 3rd

(d) Schoolhouse

Carcass Bay

DARWIN HARBOUR

Jetty

Artillery last ⁴⁄ℓ⁄

Goose Green

Skyguard radar 2 x 35mm

5 miles

3.5 miles

(4)

(3)
1630
28 May

(7)
1100
28 May

© Hugh Bichen

164

enemy killed started as a mistranslation of Piaggi's first estimate of all casualties (in Spanish *bajas* or 'downs'), including those missing, but it was broadcast to persuade other Argentine units that resistance was lethally futile. It then acquired a life of its own, as propaganda so frequently does. 2 Para ran into tougher resistance than Jones anticipated, but numbers had little to do with it. Knots of determined defenders had to be blasted out of their positions, the Argentine artillery was brilliantly handled, and if they had not been thoroughly mucked about by their high command it is possible the defenders would have forced Thompson to commit another battalion, with knock-on effects right across the operational spectrum.

THE SENIOR ARGENTINE officer was Pedrozo, CO of Air Base Condor, whose men and guns were deployed around the north-western perimeter of the Airfield to cover likely landing sites. Piaggi commanded the mixed bag of Army Task Force Mercedes, consisting of elements from three infantry regiments that arrived in dribs and drabs over the preceding month. Logistical support had been chaotic, with Piaggi's own regiment (RI 12) still lacking its full equipment of radios, support weapons and even entrenching tools. He had also lost B Company, which went to form Combat Group Solari, Parada's operational reserve on Mount Kent. Piaggi assigned the bulk of his newly-joined S/C 63s to Lieutenant Duazo's C Company and posted it to the southern flank, where he thought it less likely to be engaged by the enemy. The northern flank was covered by the S/C 62s of Lieutenant Manresa's A Company, posted along a substantial peat wall overgrown with gorse that had once marked the boundary of the lands sold to the infamous Samuel Lafone in 1846. An asset-stripper who never visited the islands, Lafone imported Patagonian gauchos to wipe out the wild cattle in the area that bears his name. His interest became the principal asset of the Falkland Islands Company formed in 1850, which dominated the economy of the islands until 1982. Thus the first land battle of the war was fought over a feature paradigmatic of all that made it possible for the Argentines to portray the sovereignty dispute as a matter of decolonization rather than self-determination.

Piaggi deployed his force to counter a seaborne assault, a possibility considered by Jones but rejected after consultation with Southby-Tailyour, who could not guarantee to navigate the landing craft through the kelp and uncharted rocks in Brenton Loch. It was fortunate he could not, because practicable landing sites were heavily mined, overlooked by some of the 20mm anti-aircraft artillery around the airfield and covered by Argentine Air Force infantry and a machine-gun platoon detached from RI 8 (the regiment at Fox Bay in West Falkland). These troops were dug in on reverse slopes and sited to have inter-locking fields of fire along the waterfront, but poorly placed to counter an overland attack from the north. Whatever adjustments Piaggi and Manresa might have made following the landings at San Carlos were rendered moot by orders from Parada to advance up the isthmus to bring an alleged British observation post on Mount Usborne under artillery fire. The move was a sadly inadequate substitute for the original plan to fly in a 155mm gun to bombard the beachhead, cancelled in mid-deployment after the ammunition had already been choppered in. Manresa's company left Darwin Hill on the 25th and took up a position on a hill at the northern entrance to the isthmus, with the Support Platoon on a ridge a mile further south. Also sent forward were two GAA 4 howitzers under Lieutenant Chanampa, who was to use a pair of commandeered civilian Landrovers to handle his guns with the panache of a horse artilleryman on a Napoleonic battlefield.

A road now runs through Manresa's original position, a line of trenches halfway down the northern slope of Darwin Hill that seems to have been dug mainly for shelter from naval gunfire and the prevailing westerly wind. Presumably his intention was to fight any amphibious assault from the Gorse Line. One can still see the outline of a mortar pit, (hence there must also have been infantry trenches), between Darwin Hill proper and its north-western continuation ('Middle Hill' for ease of reference), where the Combat Engineers installed a line of remote-detonated 125kg aerial bombs. Manresa does not appear to have positioned men to cover another minefield laid north of Middle Hill, a basic error, and although the isthmus is one of the better drained places on the islands, the trenches on the hills and around the airfield were built with overhead cover well above the lie of the land. Being able to see without being seen until you open fire is surely topic number one, day one, in any infantry tactics course.

The position was, nonetheless, immeasurably stronger than the one Manresa's men now occupied on a hill overlooking Camilla Creek, Low Pass and Burnside Pond, where the foxholes were once again sited well above the military crest and dug in a half-moon, to provide all-round defence of the feature from the land side. Active moves were confined to sending the Recce Platoon to provide advance warning of an enemy advance either from Camilla Creek House or across the neck of land between Burnside Pond and Darwin Harbour. Second Lieutenant Morales's patrol, ascending the Sussex Mountains with one of the two jeep-mounted radios RI 12 possessed, was captured by 2 Para's Forward Air Control party. Sub-Lieutenant Garra's patrol, sent on foot to Burnside House, wisely dug in a little distance behind the farm buildings, which were shot up and grenaded a little before 0300 by A Company, opening 2 Para's attack nearly an hour late. Inside the farmhouse, Kelper Gerald Morrison, his wife, mother and a visiting friend hugged the floor, saved from certain death by the inaccuracy of the preliminary artillery bombardment and no less than three misfires by A Company's Carl Gustav.

Under fire from *Arrow* in Brenton Loch, and with the westerly wind carrying sound away from them, Manresa's main force was not alerted by the attack on Burnside House.* They still did not stand-to when 2 Para's Support Company SFMGs and mortars opened fire on them fifteen minutes later, possibly because most of it landed on the unmanned western side of the hill. Finally the pickets hesitated, uncertain whether the men advancing towards them might be their own recce patrols, and were killed as Major Crosland's B Company advanced 'two up one back' through the heart of the position, taking a few prisoners but finding mainly abandoned trenches (presumably Manresa's command post). Crosland's men were supposed to halt on the hill while Major Neame's D Company advanced on the left to assault the unnamed ridge where Manresa's Support Platoon was located. Unfortunately there is no obvious topographical break between the hill (actually several successive small hummocks) and the ridge, and B Company overran its objective. During the advance only the left-hand platoon came under fire, in fact from D Company on its flank, which it returned. Nonetheless B Company became scattered, and with no point of reference did not finally regroup until Crosland resorted to the desperate expedient of firing flares and using a strobe to reunite them at a point somewhere between the hill

---

* The following may require frequent looks back at **Maps 14** and **15**, pp. 163–164. They are much clearer than the actual battlefield, which is a series of gently rolling grass hills indistinguishable one from the other.

and the ridge. Anxious to get out of D Company's way and aware that any counter-march would greatly increase the probability of a friendly fire encounter, Crosland decided to veer right and occupied the north-western end of no-name ridge.

D Company's advance was delayed by the unanticipated need to clear the trenches on the eastern side of the hill, and by the exchange of fire with B Company. The delay displeased Jones, who scouted forward and came under fire, returning to goad Neame. Neither officer had a clear idea where they were, so Neame adopted an arrowhead formation and made an advance to contact towards what he hoped was his Phase 3 objective. The ridge was held by 2nd Lieutenant Muñoz with about fifty men, two mortars and a 105mm rocket launcher. The main trench line formed an unforgivably tidy line along a fence on the upper slope of the ridge, although the dead ground was covered by several trenches placed at a right angle further west to fire across the front of the ridge. D Company fortuitously made an oblique approach that hit the crossfire trenches first. Three Paras were killed clearing the trenches, including Lance Corporal Bingley, who was awarded a posthumous MM, and two others wounded. The company then rolled up the main position, finding conscripts curled up in their foxholes or even their tents, asleep in the psychiatric phenomenon of combat denial. In the engagements on the hill and ridge Manresa's company lost twenty killed, thirty-seven wounded and forty unwounded prisoners (many of whom wisely waited until daylight to make their surrender), and played no further part in the battle as a coherent unit.

Despite poor leadership not all the Argentine conscripts folded, which in conjunction with non-combat friction dislocated Jones's plan and prevented the next phase, B Company's attack on the main Argentine position on Darwin Hill, from taking place under cover of darkness. The actual and potential exchanges of fire (known as 'blue-on-blue' incidents) between B and D Coys underlines why Jones wanted his companies to attack in an ordered sequence and to stop once each objective was taken. But with the coming of dawn and the running down of the radio batteries, restrictive control not only ceased to have that justification but also rapidly became impractical, not least because Jones dashed off again, this time to the eastern side of the isthmus. Learning that Major Farrar-Hockley (son of the legendary Colonel-Commandant of the Parachute Regiment) had halted the advance of

A Company after breezing through the first two objectives, Jones angrily radioed him to advance at once, then left his 2 i/c Major Keeble on the ridge and went forward with his Tactical HQ to take personal control of the left flank advance. His anger was unjustified: Farrar-Hockley's orders were to remain in reserve while B Company made its Phase 4 attack, and it made no sense to advance until the trenches on Darwin Hill were cleared. As it was, only the last of the darkness saved A Company when it advanced into what two junior Argentine officers had turned into a killing ground.

AFTER ORDERING MANRESA forward, Piaggi put together a platoon from HQ Company and sent it to Darwin Hill under newly graduated Sub-Lieutenant Peluffo and Staff Sergeant Jumilla with the three reserve MAGs. With forty-one men to Manresa's 175, Peluffo could only hold the central section of the trenches on the hill, leaving unmanned the trenches in the saddle between Darwin and Middle Hills and on a Spur covering the right flank of the position (see **Map 16**, p. 172). Peluffo posted his MAGs on either flank and at a position near the Cemetery to cover the valley of dead ground on his northern front. In the evening of the 27th Piaggi ordered 2nd Lieutenant Estévez, the senior RI 25 officer in the absence of Esteban, to take a platoon forward to reinforce Peluffo. Although his forty-five men were mainly S/C 63s, Estévez was intent on advancing to meet the enemy until persuaded by Peluffo to stay and cover his flank. Estévez also had an artillery net radio to direct the guns, which Chanampa skilfully retrieved from the debacle at the north of the isthmus and brought back to the lee of the airfield anti-aircraft artillery in the expectation of a dawn air attack – although in the event sea mist kept the Harriers decked for most of the day. After the battle started, part of the Recce Platoon led by Corporal Ríos fell back from Burnside House and joined the men on Darwin Ridge. Peluffo entrusted Ríos with the MAG on his right flank.

Estévez died winning the CHVC not far from where Jones died winning the VC, on a feature so topographically insignificant that it barely featured on the Ordnance Survey map both were using.* Seineldín had imbued RI 25 with his own religious fervour and Estévez, who had a strong premonition that he would die, left a letter for his father with the Chaplain, which reads in

---

* For British and Argentine decorations see **Appendix F**.

part: 'God, who is a generous Father, has wished that this, his son, totally without merit, should live this unique experience and give up his life as an offering to our Fatherland.' The Chaplain, Dominican Fr Santiago Mora, was quite a character and both he and his opposite number in 2 Para, Captain the Rev. David Cooper, were old-style fighting padres, who shared the dangers of the front line with their men. The resemblance goes further, because Mora spoke to his men about remembering their moment of closeness to God for the rest of their lives in terms almost identical to the homily Cooper gave in Christ Church Cathedral at the end of the war. Mora was impatient with Seineldín's ostentatious religiosity but had a high opinion of the fighting spirit of RI 25, which he contrasted with the generally low morale of others in Task Force Mercedes. After the war he was blunt about the anxious young men who came to him hoping he could arrange for divine intervention to spare them the horrors of combat:

> I told them so many times that neither God nor the Virgin perform miracles for those not in a condition to receive them. As the saying goes, to God imploring but with the war club scoring [*a Diós rogando pero con el mazo dando* – equivalent of 'Praise God and pass the ammunition']; unfortunately there were few ready to swing the club.

IT WAS FARRAR-HOCKLEY'S misfortune to run into two groups as ready to swing the club as any on the Falklands. Estévez had deployed half his riflemen at the military crest, the rest and his support weapons (two MAGs and at least one 90mm rocket launcher) in the trenches on the Spur. He himself remained in the open, moving among the men while trying to direct the artillery. His plan appears to have been to bracket any enemy attack, using artillery fire to prevent them escaping the fire of his riflemen, and then to counter-attack. Completely unsuspecting, Farrar-Hockley detached Lieutenant Wallis and 3 Platoon to the peninsula opposite Darwin settlement, his Phase 6 objective, and came around Darwin Pond with 2nd Lieutenant Coe's platoon in the lead. The first contact was a challenge by Acting Lance Corporal Miño and S/C 62 Moschen, members of the Recce Platoon on picket duty, who may have thought the Paras were more of their own men retreating from Burnside House. They died in a hail of bullets, but after that a storm of fire fell on the Paras.

Far from recoiling, 2 Platoon charged with Corporal Adams's section breaking right and Corporal Camp's section left, driving Estévez's men back up the Spur. Adams and his GPMG man, Private Tuffin, were wounded – probably by the MAG at the Cemetery, which also drove back a later attempt by Barrett to flank right. Additional fire from Peluffo's men west of the Spur drove the Paras to a line of cover provided by gorse bushes, leading to thicker cover in a gully on the eastern side of the feature. The leading Paras attempted to get behind the Argentine positions on the Spur but were driven back, leaving painfully wounded Private Worrall behind. Some ten men, including Coe and his platoon sergeant, were involved in a successful effort to rescue Worral, during which Corporal Prior was killed. Amazingly, the only other fatal British casualty was the unfortunate Sapper Corporal Melia, a mine clearance specialist killed at the edge of Darwin Pond when Chanampa's defensive fire barrage landed close behind A Company. Bad light and the speed of the Paras' response caused Estévez's ambush to misfire: but only just.

On the other side of the isthmus, B Company could not now recover the line of advance envisaged in Jones's plan. Crosland made the best of the situation by taking the company along the coast, with the intention of attacking his Phase 3 objective – the enemy company supposed to be in the saddle between Darwin and Middle Hills – from the flank and from behind. Detaching his 2 i/c with Lieutenant Weighell's platoon to advance over Middle Hill, he went around it with the other two. As he approached the Gorse Line he came under heavy fire from the RI 8 platoon on the eastern slope of Boca Hill, commanded by Sub-Lieutenant Aliaga, another new graduate. Meanwhile, Weighell's platoon came under fire from Darwin Hill, a bullet passing through his helmet. Two men were wounded and the rest were lucky to survive when one of the string of remote controlled 125kg aerial bombs planted against just such an approach was detonated.* After helping to recover the wounded, Private Illingworth went back to retrieve their ammunition and was killed, for which he was awarded a posthumous DCM. B Company was now pinned down even more effectively than A Company in the Gorse Gully, because the enemy positions were beyond the range of the company rocket launchers. The flank march would probably

---

* Mike Curtis, one of the men knocked down by the bomb, describes the episode grippingly in *CQB*.

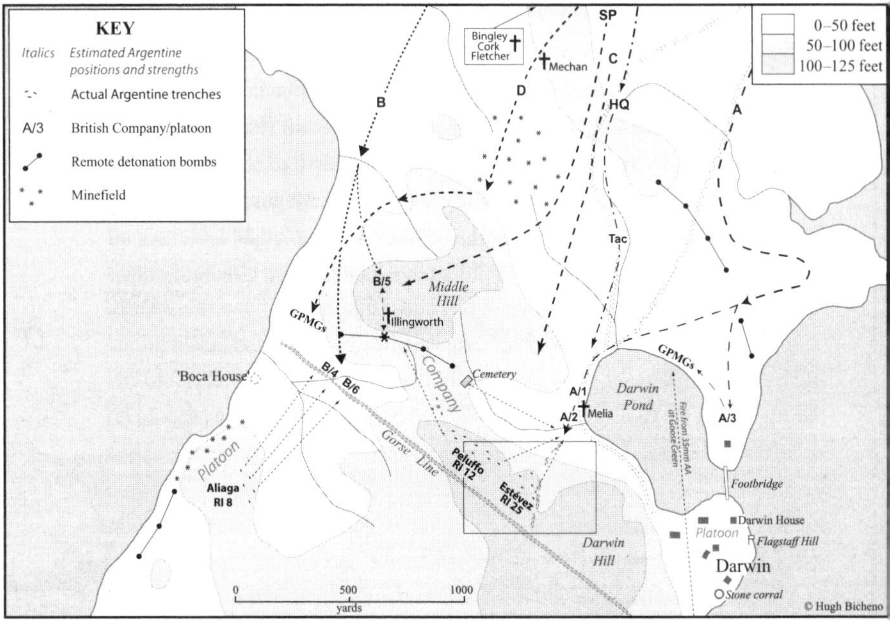

KEY

Italics — *Estimated Argentine positions and strengths*

⌒ — Actual Argentine trenches

A/3 — British Company/platoon

•—• — Remote detonation bombs

✳ — Minefield

0–50 feet
50–100 feet
100–125 feet

Bingley
Cork
Fletcher
✝Mechan
SP
C
D
HQ
B
A
Tac
B/5
Middle Hill
GPMGs
✝Tillingworth
B/4 B/6
'Boca House'
Company
⌂Cemetery
GPMGs
A/1
A/2 ✝Melia
Darwin Pond
A/3
Platoon
Gorse Line
Peluffo
RI 12
Estévez
RI 25
Fire from 35mm AA at Goose Green
Footbridge
Aliaga
RI 8
Darwin Hill
■Darwin House
Platoon ✝Flagstaff Hill
Darwin
○Stone corral

0   500   1000
yards

© Hugh Bicheno

Map 16: MIDDLE HILL – DARWIN HILL

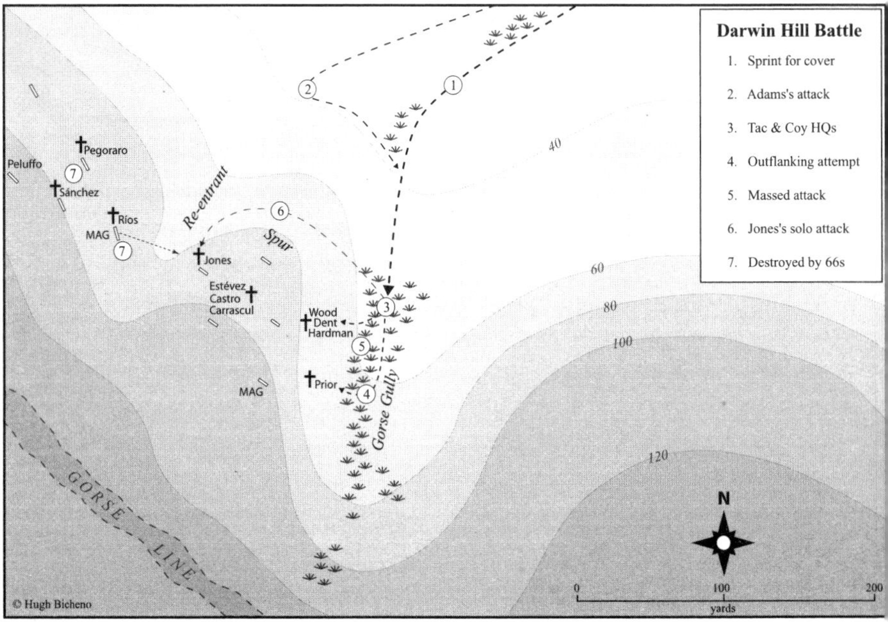

Darwin Hill Battle

1. Sprint for cover
2. Adams's attack
3. Tac & Coy HQs
4. Outflanking attempt
5. Massed attack
6. Jones's solo attack
7. Destroyed by 66s

40

②
①

✝Pegoraro
Peluffo
⑦
✝Sánchez
Re-entrant
⑥
✝Ríos
MAG
⑦
Spur
✝Jones
Estévez
Castro
Carrascul
60
Wood
Dent
Hardman
③
⑤
80
100
MAG
✝Prior
④
Gorse Gully
120

GORSE LINE

N

© Hugh Bicheno

0   100   200
yards

172

Gorse Gully
(facing north-east from Cpl Prior marker)

Mount Usborne

Jones

A/1 & A/2 Platoons — — — — GPMG line ← — — — — — — → A/3 Platoon

† Melia

Darwin Pond

Line held by A Coy now densely overgrown

† Wood
Dent
Hardman

Photo Diagram 16: DARWIN HILL

Re-Entrant
(facing east from Cpl Ríos trench)

Blue Mountain
(Giménez crash site)

Trenches

† Estevez?

Darwin Pond

† Jones

have worked if dawn had held off for another hour, but now the only silver lining was that daylight also revealed the enemy positions, which would not long survive once Support Company came forward with the Milans.

A thousand yards to the north, in the middle of the isthmus, D Company advanced over the top of no-name ridge, which it had captured during the night, and walked into an artillery barrage, probably defensive fire called in by Estévez on Darwin Hill. Private Mechan was killed but the rest of Neame's men were miraculously unharmed when they ran through the unmarked and fortunately unguarded minefield in the valley to lie up on the northern slope of Middle Hill. There they thankfully brewed up and sorted themselves out while Neame attempted to get his orders changed now that B Company had usurped his planned line of advance. Jones refused, and as a result Neame could not support A Company's unplanned and uncoordinated assault on Darwin Hill.

To summarize: Piaggi had lost Manresa's company, one of two jeep-mounted radios along with a 50-calibre, and half the MAGs, 81mm mortars and 105mm rocket launchers with which he began the battle. Against this a hard core of Manresa's men under Company Sergeant-Major Cohelo joined Peluffo on Darwin Ridge, occupying the empty trenches on the western flank. Muñoz's shattered Support Platoon had lost its heavy weapons at the ridge and retreated past the Gorse Line, but when the survivors reached the airfield they found two 81mm mortars pointing out to sea and a large stock of ammunition, abandoned by the Air Force infantry. Muñoz's men put them to good use: among the casualties they inflicted was Captain Young, 2 i/c B Company, who survived a wound to the liver despite remaining on Middle Hill for ten hours before being evacuated. On the British side, 2 Para's mortars were almost out of ammunition, the limited remaining supply of shells for the guns was being husbanded for counter-battery fire, there would be no further support from *Arrow* (which withdrew at dawn), there was no immediate prospect of air support, the radio batteries were running down, the leading rifle companies were pinned down, Support Company had not caught up, and the cover of night was gone. To put it mildly, things had not gone according to plan.

9 Darwin/Goose Green

PART TWO

JONES SNARLED 'Don't tell me how to run my battle' when Neame proposed taking D Company along the shoreline to relieve the pressure on Crosland's men at Middle Hill: the phrase says it all and there is no need to labour the point. The stalemate along the Gorse Line did not finally break until after his death and the charitable view, expressed in the VC citation, is that his example inspired the battalion to new endeavours. Less charitably, the man who restored momentum to the 2 Para attack was Lance Corporal José Luis Ríos, manning the MAG at the right of the RI 12 line, who shot a British soldier who had eyes only for the RI 25 trench he was attacking on the other side of the re-entrant. That soldier was Jones, courting death no less fearlessly than Estévez, who died nearby. Released from the constraints of Jones's plan, only now could Major Roger Jenner's C Company go forward to support the attack on Darwin Hill, and Major Hugh Jenner's Support Company advance to support B Company from Middle Hill.

I doubt if another skirmish in any war has been written about as much as the one in which Jones, his Adjutant Captain Wood, A Company 2 i/c Captain Dent and Corporal Hardman died. Fitz-Gibbon's account is as accurate as any intellectual reconstruction of an affair of the spirit – enveloped in deafening noise, blinding smoke and violent emotion – is likely to be, but unfortunately nothing similar has been published from the Argentine side. Many of the men on the Spur were newly-conscripted S/C 63s and yet they not only stuck with it long after honour was satisfied but even came out in the open to contest the ground with the Paras, taking their lead from Estévez. He was shot in the leg early, then wounded by shrapnel and finally killed by a bullet to the head while trying to direct artillery fire into the Gully. According to their MVC citations, first Lance Corporal Mario Castro and then S/C 63 Carrascull continued to radio corrections back to Chanampa until they were killed in their turn. Directing artillery is a skilled task, however, and the target-rich Gully was not shelled.

I believe the positions still identifiable on the Spur were occupied by the support weapons, and that the riflemen were in hastily dug foxholes erased by time.* The defence only became static after 2 Para's mortars began to fire white phosphorus: nasty stuff banned for anti-personnel use by the Geneva Convention, but permitted to lay down smoke, as though such a fine distinction were possible in battle. The smoke was whipped away by the strong wind but the phosphorus drove the defenders to cover: Castro did not make it and died screaming for his men to shoot him. Horrified by this, bereft of their officer and now isolated, it is also likely that the men on the Spur were running out of ammunition, since they were neither reinforced nor resupplied. My photo-diagram (p.173) shows the heavily overgrown Gully today, but contemporary photos show much less cover. If Piaggi had sent the rest of the RI 25s to support their comrades on the Spur, they might have enfiladed the Paras to deadly effect.

I am indebted to Ken Greenland of Darwin House for the information that shells from Sub-Lieutenant Braghini's 35mm anti-aircraft artillery, on the Goose Green promontory, hit the main house in Darwin. According to Greenland, this happened while it was firing at A Company's 3 Platoon on the far side of Darwin Pond, where they were trying to set up their GPMGs to support the attack on the Spur. Greenland's information contradicts 2nd Lieutenant Wallis's recollection that he proposed setting up the firebase and Farrar-Hockley vetoed it. 3 Platoon had six of the company's eight GPMGs precisely for that purpose, albeit intended to support the eventual Phase 6 attack on Darwin. Possibly Farrar-Hockley was concerned about the danger of blue-on-blue, but it is more likely that Braghini's fire drove Wallis back to the cover provided by Flagstaff Hill (where the 'D' of Darwin is on

---

* Of the six RI 25s killed on the Spur only LCpl Oviedo was 'bunker busted' – the others died in the open.

Map 15, page 164: the flagstaff is one of the spars from the *Great Britain*) and Farrar-Hockley agreed he should abandon the enterprise. Wallis also came under fire from RI 12's sole 120mm mortar, sited among the houses in Goose Green: fortunately for the Paras it was a patched-up weapon welded to its baseplate, which required the crew to use wooden quoins to vary the elevation like gunners in the black powder era.

The fact that Major Rice, the Battery Commander, and Captain Worsley-Tonks, the battalion Mortar Fire Controller, took part as infantry in the charge in which Wood, Dent and Hardman were killed, suggests the assault came on the heels of the last substantial barrage from their distant weapons, before the guns and mortars were compelled to conserve ammunition. Jones sensed the enemy was weakening and with the words 'Come on A Company, get your skirts off,' urged about twenty of the eighty men in the Gully 'over the top'. They were enfiladed and the charge driven back by a MAG, fifty yards to their left, manned by Lance Corporal Olmos, who had wounded Worrall and killed Prior three hours earlier. On the right, Jones ran around the front of the Spur in dead ground, followed by his bodyguard, Sergeant Norman, and radio operator, Sergeant Blackburn. The MAG position at the Cemetery must have been abandoned by this time, or else they could not have got as far as they did. But once in the re-entrant they were in the sights of Lance Corporal Ríos on the right of Peluffo's line, who fired at Norman before turning the gun on Jones as he scrambled up the side of the Spur, cutting him down within a few yards of the trench he was attacking.

Other Paras now followed the route taken by Jones, bringing 66s with them. Company Sergeant-Major Price missed but then Corporal Abols scored a direct hit on Ríos, and the other men in the trench were too shocked to continue fighting. At the same time Jones's instinct belatedly proved correct and the men on the Spur – many of them burned by phosphorus – began to emerge with their hands up. With his flank guard gone, Peluffo's position became indefensible. He saw the rocket attack on Ríos's trench and thanks to his testimony two of his men, S/C 62s Pegoraro and Sánchez, were awarded posthumous MVCs for refusing to surrender when called on to do so in Spanish (by the omnipresent Captain Bell, RM), and dying at their posts. That Peluffo could see these actions, plus the fact that he was directing Chanampa's guns, makes it likely his command post was the second and highest of the rear element of what seems to have been a saw-toothed line: the next to be attacked after the trenches held by Ríos, Pegoraro and Sánchez had fallen. Peluffo was knocked down by a bullet that went through his helmet, grazing his skull, and being unable to stand felt that further resistance was useless. He ordered one of his men to tie a cloth to his rifle and stand up to wave it. A bullet hit the rifle but Peluffo prevailed on the shaken man to try again. If, as seems likely, his command post was visible from the other trenches, it explains why the whole position now sprouted white cloths. Peluffo recalls that the Paras stood up, which they would not have done unless quite certain the fighting was over.[*]

When news of Jones's mortal wounding came over a radio net that had become steadily less informative as batteries were husbanded, the rump of Tactical HQ and the battalion 2 i/c Major Keeble were back at the ridge, with Support Company nearby. Keeble promptly gave Crosland command of the right wing and sent Support Company across to reinforce him. C Company had already moved forward to the rise in front of Darwin Hill and this was probably the reason why the Cemetery MAG position was abandoned. Peluffo recalls machine-gun fire coming from his front, so the collapse of his position was not solely due to A Company pepper-potting and 66s. Keeble himself set off towards Darwin to join the key command personnel who had gone forward with Jones. It might have been better to commit all the reserves to the right, because the swinging door envisaged by Jones would have forced the enemy to abandon Darwin Hill anyway; but without knowing the details Keeble had to assume the death of his CO signalled an incipient disaster on the left.

Support Company set up its Milans and SFMGs on Middle Hill, from which it blasted the RI 8 position on Boca Hill. D Company did not, as reported at the time, cunningly advance in the lee of a bank along the shore to outflank Boca Hill, because to do so it would first have had to cross a wide-open gap, where a nameless stream drains into Brenton Loch. Nor did it 'storm' Boca House, since only the foundations remained of the building that stood there long ago. Instead, Neame set up six of his GPMGs at the western base of Middle Hill and poured suppressive fire onto the hapless

---

[*] The RI 12s on Darwin Hill had 9 killed and 17 wounded, including Peluffo. RI 12 lost thirty-five killed in the whole campaign, including two on Harriet.

RI 8s, which in combination with the hellishly accurate Milans silenced them. Aliaga was seriously wounded and with five men killed and fifteen more wounded, the remainder either fled or ceased firing to wave bits of cloth. Only now did Neame take his men along the foreshore to hook around the hill, picking their way through the tripwire-rigged 125kg aerial bombs planted to cover this stretch of the shore. One of them detonated and knocked down four men, including the wrathful Sergeant Meredith of 12 Platoon, who thought it had been tripped by a clumsy private. Possibly so, but the bombs also had remote triggers and one of the RI 8s on Boca Hill may not have been entirely cowed. Believing the explosion signalled further resistance, Support Company opened up from Middle Hill until Neame screamed at them to stop over the radio. Only then was he able to move forward to secure the objective Jones had thought he might take, 'if necessary', some seven hours earlier.

LEAVING THE RIFLE companies to process prisoners, to tend to their own and enemy wounded and to 'regroup' – a term encompassing every aspect of personal and unit maintenance – let us go back to the rear echelon, which had been fighting a battle of its own. About an hour before Jones was killed, a flight of three Pucarás from Stanley attacked the logistical tail of 2 Para at Camilla Creek House with rockets, causing no damage. When two of them flew on towards the 105mm guns, they were warmly received by the Blowpipe Troop guarding the battery. Pilot Officer Cimbaro was lucky to survive a near miss and Pilot Officer Argañaraz was flipped over when a missile exploded in the ground immediately under his very low-flying aircraft. The Blowpipe operator had every reason to believe he had made a kill, but in fact Argañaraz, who had ferried his Pucará from the mainland only the previous evening, regained control. Although the Pucarás did no physical damage, they did ground the British helicopters and interrupt much-needed resupply of the guns and mortars.

Meanwhile the San Carlos beachhead dodged a bullet at about this time, when a flight of six Grupo 5 Skyhawks came in from the mainland led by no less than the CO of their Air Brigade, Wing Commander Dubourg. Anxious to repeat the previous day's success, they arrived to find the target area covered in low cloud. One cannot overstate the importance of luck in warfare. The Pucarás from Stanley returned two hours later, with Cimbaro leading a new wingman, Pilot Officer Giménez, and they pounced on two Scouts flying forward from Camilla Creek House on a casualty evacuation mission to Darwin Hill. One of the Scouts, piloted by Captain Niblett, managed to evade Cimbaro, but Giménez shot down the other, killing the pilot, Lieutenant Nunn (who was awarded a posthumous DFC), and maiming his observer. On the way back to Stanley, in atrocious visibility, Giménez flew into Blue Mountain, his disappearance a mystery until the crash site was discovered in 1986.

While the Pucarás kept British attention on the Sussex Mountains, six Hueys and a Puma, escorted by two Hirundo gunships, transported Lieutenant Esteban's re-equipped and reinforced Güemes detachment along Choiseul Sound to a landing site 4.5 miles south of Goose Green. The weather began to clear later in the day and a second mission could not be flown until dusk, when almost the whole of Combat Aviation 601 plus an Argentine Air Force Chinook brought most of RI 12's B Company (Combat Group Solari) back from Mount Kent and delivered it 6 miles south of Goose Green.

However, the attrition suffered by Argentine fixed and rotary wing aircraft in the weeks preceding the battle meant they could not mount persistent interdiction of 2 Para's logistical support, nor deliver the timely support that the no less limited British helicopter resources – operating over a much shorter distance – brought to the battlefield. The hiatus in helicopter movements following Nunn's death did not last long and stockpiles of ammunition for the guns and mortars were flown in.* The Scouts also supplied the troops at Darwin Hill with the batteries and the creature comforts left behind the night before, and began morale-boosting casualty evacuation operations. Unfortunately this support was limited to A Company, because the helicopters could not risk crossing the hill until the manoeuvre elements on the right cleared the anti-aircraft artillery from the Airfield. Overall, although Combat Aviation 601 and the island-based Argentine Air Force and Naval Air units made a Herculean effort and pushed their luck to the limit, the garrison at Goose Green felt hemmed in and increasingly isolated in the face of opponents who had now regained momentum.

---

* A hardy perennial in every war is that field commanders re-learn that combat ammunition expenditure bears no relation whatever to peacetime estimates based on the actuarial costs of storage and obsolescence.

Most maps of the battlefield reproduce the reversed 'P' of runways marked on the Ordnance Survey map. Actually the Airfield is just that – a large rectangle of flat grassland marked with a boundary fence and very little else except a windsock and a shed for fire-fighting equipment at the north-eastern corner. To the north-west there is another relatively flat fenced area with a small grandstand to one side – site of horse races during an annual farmers' jamboree (see **Map 15**, p. 164). The crest of Darwin Hill is visible from practically any point in this area, which was occupied by some forty-five men manning six twin 20mm anti-aircraft artillery guns, supported by fifty-seven Air Force Military Police. When Esteban arrived he was ordered to take command of these men, while 2nd Lieutenant Vásquez took the RI 25 reinforcements to join Sub-Lieutenant Gómez Centurión's platoon covering the northern flank. Given the matter of the abandoned mortars it is fair to assume the Air Force MPs had begun to abandon the Airfield during the night, and if Pedrozo agreed to the appointment of an army officer to command them, it suggests a lack of organic leadership. The anti-aircraft gunners stuck with it longer, until three of the guns and their Elta radar set were destroyed by missile fire. This can only have been Milans from Support Company on Darwin Hill. But before abandoning the last of the guns, on the northern perimeter, the Air Force gunners contributed to the largest number of casualties suffered by 2 Para in a single incident.

They were able to do so because of an extraordinary tactical blunder. Keeble and Roger Jenner decided that C Company's Recce and Patrols Platoons, joined by Wallis's 3 Platoon from A Company and some of HQ Company, should go over the top of Darwin Hill. It was supposed to be a standard two up one back advance to contact, but in fact went forward as a rather ragged extended line: Captain Farrar of Patrols even had his men fix bayonets. Either uncertainty about the identity of the men advancing over the hill or disbelief at a sight not seen since the first day on the Somme caused the Argentines to hold their fire until all three platoons were descending the forward slope: and then every cannon, mortar and gun from Goose Green to the Racecourse cut loose. Private Holman-Smith was killed, Jenner and ten others wounded – many horribly – in a few minutes. The men of Recce and Patrols must have set a new record for running fully laden to reach the dead ground along the stream without losing even more men,

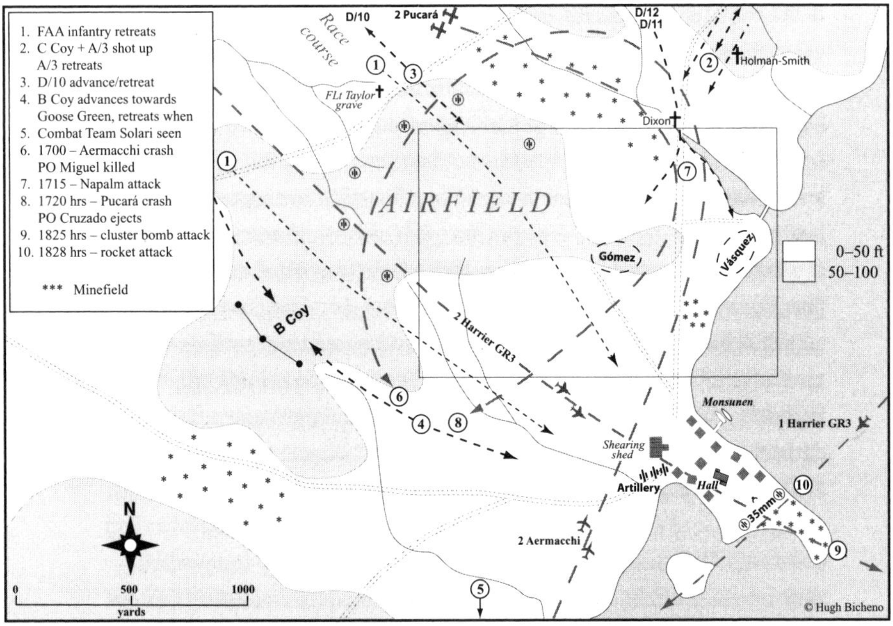

Map 17: **GOOSE GREEN AIRFIELD – SCHOOLHOUSE**

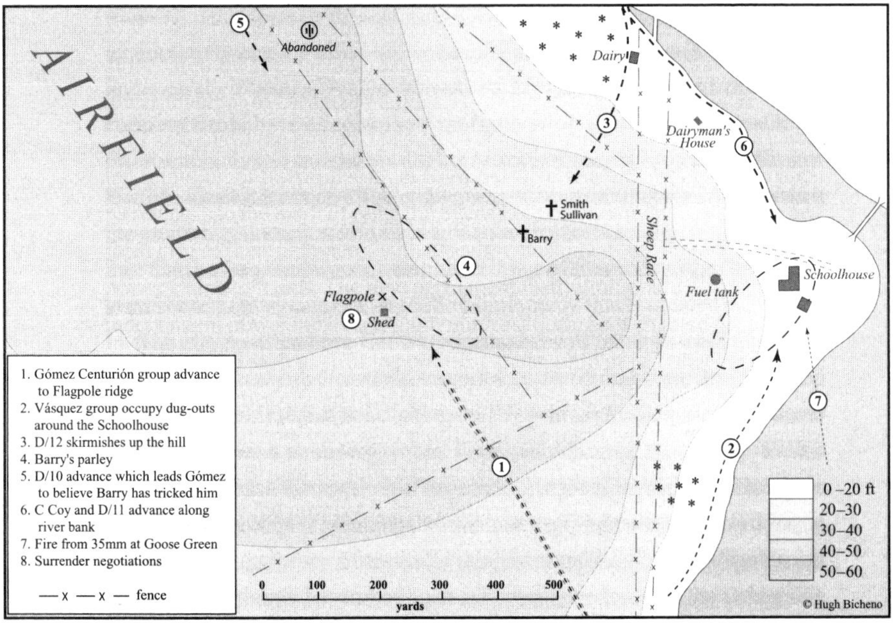

Map 17 (top) legend:

1. FAA infantry retreats
2. C Coy + A/3 shot up
   A/3 retreats
3. D/10 advance/retreat
4. B Coy advances towards
   Goose Green, retreats when
5. Combat Team Solari seen
6. 1700 – Aermacchi crash
   PO Miguel killed
7. 1715 – Napalm attack
8. 1720 hrs – Pucará crash
   PO Cruzado ejects
9. 1825 hrs – cluster bomb attack
10. 1828 – rocket attack

*** Minefield

0–50 ft
50–100

Labels (top map): D/10, 2 Pucará, D/12 D/11, Holman-Smith, Race course, FLt Taylor grave, Dixon, AIRFIELD, Gómez, Vásquez, B Coy, 2 Harrier GR3, Monsunen, 1 Harrier GR3, Shearing shed, Artillery, Hall, 35mm, 2 Aermacchi, N, © Hugh Bicheno

0 500 1000
yards

Map 17 (bottom) legend:

1. Gómez Centurión group advance
   to Flagpole ridge
2. Vásquez group occupy dug-outs
   around the Schoolhouse
3. D/12 skirmishes up the hill
4. Barry's parley
5. D/10 advance which leads Gómez
   to believe Barry has tricked him
6. C Coy and D/11 advance along
   river bank
7. Fire from 35mm at Goose Green
8. Surrender negotiations

— x — x — fence

Labels (bottom map): AIRFIELD, Abandoned, Dairy, Dairyman's House, Smith Sullivan, Barry, Flagpole, Shed, Fuel tank, Schoolhouse, Sheep Race, 0–20 ft, 20–30, 30–40, 40–50, 50–60, © Hugh Bicheno

0 100 200 300 400 500
yards

182

because there is not a wrinkle of cover on the slope they descended. Having lost three men wounded, 3 Platoon withdrew over the Gorse Line and, like the rest of A Company, played no further part in the battle. Farrar-Hockley flatly refused to vary any further from his original orders, and Keeble did not force the issue.

On the western side of the isthmus, Crosland decided to break completely with Jones's scheme and took B Company on a long hook south, around the Airfield, while the Milans and SFMGs went to join the rest of Support Company on Darwin Hill. D Company set off across the front of the hill in the direction of Goose Green, with 10 Platoon advancing wide to the right, to clear what was believed to be an enemy command post near the racecourse grandstand. D/10 found the position recently abandoned and continued across the Airfield perimeter until driven back by another blue-on-blue, with SFMG fire from Support Company on Darwin Hill making any further advance impossible.

British accounts tend to concentrate on the struggle at the north-eastern corner of the Airfield, but the whole feature is best seen through Piaggi's eyes, as the outer perimeter he had to hold. There was scant chance of that once the British guns and mortars were resupplied and their forward observers set up alongside Support Company on Darwin Hill. There appears to have been little overall command and control on the British side, but that was not how it looked to Piaggi. As he saw it, the Airfield came under a coordinated attack from three sides and by the time he ordered it abandoned the defenders had already voted with their feet to escape the hellish bombardment.

Artillery dominates the battlefield, but one should not discount the significance of men who make a stand without regard for the consequences. The power of one such individual is well illustrated in *A Soldier's Song,* in which Ken Lukowiak of Support Company recalls an episode when he and some others on Darwin Hill came under fire from a sniper at the southern end of the Airfield. Lukowiak's group must have been sheltering behind a break in the peat bank under the Gorse Line, because one of the men with him was hit in the leg despite being, as he thought, under cover. They observed a bush moving towards them and were relieved to discover it was a member of Support Company's Sniper Platoon. To the fury of the men behind the hedge, the sniper stood on top of the bank to spot with binoculars, attracting further small arms and mortar fire, and then killed the enemy marksman, estimated after the battle to have been over 1000 yards away, with a single shot.

B Company's bold advance south of the Airfield was perceived by Piaggi as the last nail in his coffin. Crosland had an easy relationship with his men and wore a black wool hat instead of a helmet, an act of showmanship much admired across a regiment that prized contempt for danger. Charisma is desirable in an officer but luck is essential, and happily he had it to spare. The line he took ran through an area not covered by the anti-aircraft artillery on the Airfield, therefore mined with remote detonated aerial bombs. B Company spent the night among them and although they would probably have done little damage, they were not triggered. But Crosland's greatest stroke of luck came when Piaggi chose not to counter-attack from Goose Green, and that he did not believe the newly-conscripted S/C 63s of Duazo's C Company, posted at the south of the isthmus, were capable of offensive action.

The same could not be said of Combat Team Solari, which as we have seen was brought back from Mount Kent by Combat Aviation 601 to a place from which it might easily have attacked Crosland's men. B Company pulled back rapidly from a promising advance to within small arms range of Goose Green, calling in artillery fire on the new arrivals. Lieutenant Chapman of 6 Platoon recalled being very frightened by the arrival of the enemy helicopters. 'What the fuck do we do now?' he asked Crosland. The reply was not reassuring: 'It looks like Arnhem – day three.'*

Fortunately Crosland's evocation of Arnhem was premature. The officer commanding Combat Team Solari, Lieutenant Gorriti, did not fly in with the first wave, staying behind to change into dry clothing. The second wave was cancelled by Parada, leaving Gorriti and forty men, mainly Sub-Lieutenant Mosterín's Rifle Platoon, stranded on Mount Kent. We will meet them again on Mount Harriet. Solari was therefore under the nominal command of Captain Corsiglia of HQ Company, a logistics specialist. With one platoon dropped half a mile from the other two, the insertion south of Goose Green was a shambles even before the artillery fire called in by B Company arrived, driving them to cover on the foreshore and extinguishing any aggressive intentions they might have had.

* 2 Para was virtually destroyed by SS Panzergrenadiers at the battle for the bridges at Arnhem in 1944.

Not knowing this as they dug in with bayonets, cups and even spoons, the men of B Company could be excused for doubting how fortunate they were through the long cold night that followed. They probably felt they had used up their luck shortly before the arrival of Solari, when two enemy aircraft crashed very close to them. Lance Corporal Dunbar had ammunition belts torn from his hands by debris from the first, while the second, still fully bombed up, cartwheeled through the company showering it with aviation fuel, which miraculously did not ignite. It would be remarkable if these incidents did not create an acute sense of foreboding among Crosland and his men, who might have pulled back if night had not intervened, and with it a heightened probability that any such move, in the absence of proper communications, would precipitate a major blue-on-blue with their comrades holding Darwin Hill.

THE TWO CRASHED AIRCRAFT had attacked Neame's D Company, whose luck was not nearly so good, suffering more than half of 2 Para's fatal casualties during the war. As D/11 and D/12 crossed the isthmus they were sheltered from view of the Airfield, but not from a pair of Naval Air Aermacchis that swept in from the south and attacked them with cannon and rockets. Pilot Officer Miguel's aircraft was hit by a Blowpipe fired from Darwin Hill and dived into the ground, killing the pilot and making a believer of B Company's Dunbar. On emerging into sight of Goose Green the two platoons came under artillery fire from Chanampa's guns, now firing at full elevation, and Private Dixon was killed by shrapnel. They became intermingled with Recce and Patrols Platoons in the dead ground along the stream, under small arms fire from enemy infantry around the buildings of the Darwin boarding school establishment to the east, and from the topographical crest of a hill overlooking them immediately to the south.

These were RI 25 platoons led by, respectively, 2nd Lieutenant Vásquez (Esteban's 2 i/c at San Carlos) and Sub-Lieutenant Gómez Centurión, the son of a lieutenant general who played a leading role in the PNR regime. The son is still celebrated in Argentine military folklore as the man who killed Lieutenant Colonel Jones. In fairness, the citation for his CHVC says only that he caused the enemy 'important losses' and he was certainly a very brave young man, who risked his life on a number of occasions, including an excursion during the night of 28–29 May to rescue one of his wounded men from a position overlooked by the British on Darwin Hill. But it cannot be discounted that his parentage and the attribution of Jones's death, not to mention being one of Seineldín's blue-eyed boys, are the real reasons why he received the nation's top award over more obviously deserving candidates. Alternatively, as some Argentines still allege, Jones's VC citation and the witnesses to his death are all part of a diabolically conceived and supernaturally sustained British disinformation campaign.

Training once again took over and the Paras sorted themselves out quickly to suppress the two enemy positions. Patrols, D/11 and Recce Platoons worked their way down the stream towards the Schoolhouse, while Lieutenant Barry's D/12 skirmished up what became known as 'Flagpole Hill' from the windsock mast at the summit. Not long afterwards, and only about fifteen minutes after the Aermacchis, two Pucarás came in from the northwest cutting grass with their propellers. Flight Officer Micheloud, leading, dropped napalm bombs that sent up an imposing fireball no great distance beyond D/12, but Pilot Officer Cruzado's aircraft was riddled with small arms fire before he could deliver his rockets and phosphorus bombs. He ejected seconds before his aircraft impacted near B Company, survived being shot at as he hung from his parachute and was taken prisoner by men who changed their mind about the fate he deserved once he was on the ground. The morale effect of these air strikes was mixed. The men directly involved in the fighting only saw the attacks, which cheered the RI 25s and made their assailants more cautious, whereas those on Darwin Hill and in Goose Green saw the two aircraft go down, boosting the Paras' confidence and disheartening the Argentines.

There followed the infamous 'white flag' incident, which was to cost D Company three more killed. As reported at the time, a Para officer was treacherously killed after going forward to accept the surrender of the Argentines at the Schoolhouse, who were displaying a white flag, after which the Paras destroyed the building, killing fifty defenders. In fact, the incident took place on Flagpole Hill, the white flag was probably just paper caught on a fence, only three Argentines died, not in but near the Schoolhouse, which was set on fire by Braghini's 35mm anti-aircraft cannon after the defenders had cleared the area, and the Argentines only suffered fifty-five killed in the whole battle, including Pilot Officers Giménez and Miguel. There is no better illustration of the unreliability of eyewitness testimony. This version was put together from interviews with the participants conducted immediately after the event by Robert Fox, a BBC radio reporter. There is no doubt he accurately reported what he observed and was told, but unfortunately it was not only wrong in substance but in almost every detail.

The dead officer was Barry, who exposed not only himself but other members of his platoon by going forward without authorization to take what he hoped would be the surrender of the men on Flagpole Hill. He encountered Gómez Centurión, who thought the man approaching him with his rifle over his head was himself trying to surrender. Gómez spoke fluent English and after he discovered Barry's real mission said 'Get back down the hill, you son-of-a-bitch.' As Barry was crossing a fence, his rifle resting against the wire, Gómez heard firing to his left (presumably D/10 being shot up by Support Company), concluded that the parley had been a deliberate distraction for an outflanking manoeuvre, and shot Barry in the back. This is Gómez's own version of events, published in 1983, and the story that the shooting was in retaliation for machine-gun fire from Darwin Hill is a concoction by British historians. Almost everything 2 Para did in this corner of the battlefield was suicidally ill-considered, which must be attributed to the cumulative effects of intense physical exertion, sleeplessness, and battle shock.

Corporal Sullivan and Lance Corporal Nigel Smith were also killed by rifle fire at around this time, as were two of Gómez's conscripts and his platoon sergeant, Sergio García, the latter probably by his opposite number Meredith. Gómez retreated, possibly unnerved by the loss of García but also because the hill was, at last, brought under effective artillery and mortar fire, which detonated a large fuel and bomb dump to his rear. He sent a runner to warn Vásquez, who pulled his men out of the Schoolhouse area just as C Company and D/11 got within 66 range. Even so, Vásquez lost a lance corporal and two conscripts killed and several wounded during the rapid retreat. The last act of the day was the arrival of three Harrier GR3s to deliver long-requested close air support. Understandably, given that Braghini's guns had shot down two Harriers already, the GR3s struck at his position on the promontory, two of them sweeping in from the north-west over the settlement to miss long with cluster bombs, the third near-missing short with rockets from the north-east – although shrapnel from this attack in fact disabled the guns. Crosland's men, overflown by the first two, were shocked by the experience, and one can well imagine its effect on the 100 Kelpers and 600 Argentines in Goose Green.*

BATTLE IS AN AFFAIR of the human spirit. 2 Para, with fifteen dead and thirty-three wounded, was tired, more cautious but no less determined than it had been in the early hours of the 28th. With 200 missing (none of the dead and few of the ninety-odd wounded had been brought back to Goose Green), Task Force Mercedes was beaten. During the night Keeble sent forward two prisoners bearing the blunt message that if Piaggi did not surrender, the settlement would be shelled and he, Piaggi, would be responsible for any civilian deaths that occurred. Unstated was the rule, almost as old as warfare itself, that a garrison which refuses to surrender opportunely may expect no quarter in the assault that follows. Although he had used the civilian hostages to win immunity from artillery and air attack for his HQ and guns, when the time came Piaggi chose not to precipitate a blood bath. More questionably, he chose not to break out to the south, from where some of his command might have been retrieved. He and his 2 i/c were cashiered after the war, whereas despite being – rightly – judged the main culprit by the Army's post-war enquiry, Parada was permitted to retire with rank and pension unaffected.

Keeble was shocked at the number of men who surrendered, which confirms how little Jones thought his subordinates needed to know. There is a contradiction between this and the extremely high level of competence his tightly choreographed scheme demanded of them. Given limited artillery support and the timescale he envisaged, he should have devised the simplest possible fire plan with maximum force concentration. As it was, energy was dispersed all over the battlefield and 2 Para scrambled to overcome one unforeseen setback after another. Superior training and small unit aggression prevailed, but it would probably have done so more quickly and almost certainly more cheaply in a sequential attack along a single, more easily controlled line of advance. However the most serious flaw in the whole

---

* Solari came in during the night, raising the number to 750, but Duazo's company stayed out until the next day.

operation was revealed at the end. If the battle had ended with Goose Green levelled and dozens of civilians killed, it would have been a political disaster. The most startling thing about Darwin/Goose Green is that Northwood ordered a full-scale assault without considering the lethal effect it might have on a sizeable number of the people in whose name the war was being fought.

In a spiteful postscript, a booby-trapped napalm container caused the death of an Argentine conscript a few days later. Enveloped in flames he was shot by RAMC Staff Sergeant Fowler, an act of mercy for which his career was to be blighted by the MoD's cowardly overreaction to an Argentine protest made through the Red Cross, even after the protest was withdrawn when the full facts were known. On 25 June a grenade booby-trap (one of many, including at least one in a soft drink can, scattered around a settlement containing many children) killed Lance Corporal Limbu, the sole fatality suffered by the Gurkha Rifles. Esteban's RI 25s had already shown their penchant for this sort of thing at Port San Carlos and must be presumed responsible.

10 Deadly Lull

BETWEEN THE LAST DAY of fighting at Goose Green on 28 May and the loss of two ships with fifty-four men killed and fifty-seven wounded off Fitzroy and in Choiseul Sound on 8 June, the British expedition gained a second infantry brigade and a new overall land commander – and came close to losing the war. Although time pressure was the underlying cause, the injection of Brigadier Wilson's unbalanced and unprepared Army 5 Brigade greatly increased it by stalling the momentum built up by 3 Commando Brigade. Of Goose Green, Keeble later mused that 'the Argentines lost the battle rather than the Paras winning it – in fact I suspect that is how most conflicts are resolved.' Indeed; and during the following ten days the Argentines came closer to winning thanks to unforced British errors than they ever did by their own efforts. The losses on 8 June were the price for an unplanned and unnecessary advance along the southern coast of East Falkland, which two days earlier came within a hair's breadth of bringing about the annihilation, by friendly fire, of 2nd Battalion, Scots Guards.

Before that, however, things went very well for the British. The 'tab' by 3 Para and the 'yomp' by 45 Commando across East Falkland are the signature exploits of the war. Thompson ordered them to set out before he released Jones to attack the Darwin isthmus, while at the same time committing most of his meagre helicopter resources to exploit an opportunity identified by an SAS patrol to seize Mount Kent, the highest of the peaks forming the outer line of hills around Stanley peninsula. Thompson's plan, which he began developing during discussions about the landing site, was to establish a brigade Forward Maintenance Area at Port Salvador, the large and complex fjord that bisects the northern coast of East Falkland, with a further Distribution Point at the end of the eastern finger reaching out towards Stanley. A prerequisite was to capture the high ground that overlooked it.

The task was made easier by the withdrawal of Combat Team Solari from the eastern slope of Mount Kent to reinforce the garrison at Goose Green, as we saw in the last chapter. By the time Daher sent his Special Forces to plug the gap, the SAS had consolidated its hold on the mountain. Since this was the only attempt made to disrupt the British advance and is well reported from the Argentine side, it is worth examining in some detail.

When the British landed at San Carlos, two of the three Assault Sections of Comando 601 were on AA ambush duty on West Falkland, where they brought down Flight Lieutenant Glover's GR 3 with Blowpipe. After the landing, they were desperately needed to scout the beachhead and an attempt to extract them came to grief on 23 May when two Pumas and a Hirundo gunship were destroyed by Harriers at Shag Cove. The surviving Puma was able to recover the First Assault Section the next day. The Second remained on West Falkland, where it acted as a force multiplier by giving the impression of a far more aggressive Argentine presence than the two regiments gloomily dug in around Fox Bay and Port Howard in fact represented. The Special Forces had excellent backpacks and combat webbing, and their constant patrolling kept the British nervous about possible raids across the Sound until the end of hostilities. On 10 June a Second Assault Section patrol discovered an SAS observation post overlooking Port Howard and in the ensuing firefight Captain Hamilton was killed and his Goanese signaller Sergeant Fonseca captured.*

In the absence of the Comando 601's First and Second Assault Sections, on 23 May Daher sent the Third to Mount Simon, an Air Force detachment to Mount Wickham and a group of ten Marines under Lieutenant Commander Camiletti to Chata Hill (see **Map 18**, p.192). Both the Air Force and, more surprisingly, the Comando 601 section called for extraction within

* Like FLt Taylor, killed at Goose Green on 4 May, the Argentines buried Hamilton with military honours. Both tombs remain. Twelve others are buried in the official cemetery at San Carlos, the rest were repatriated.

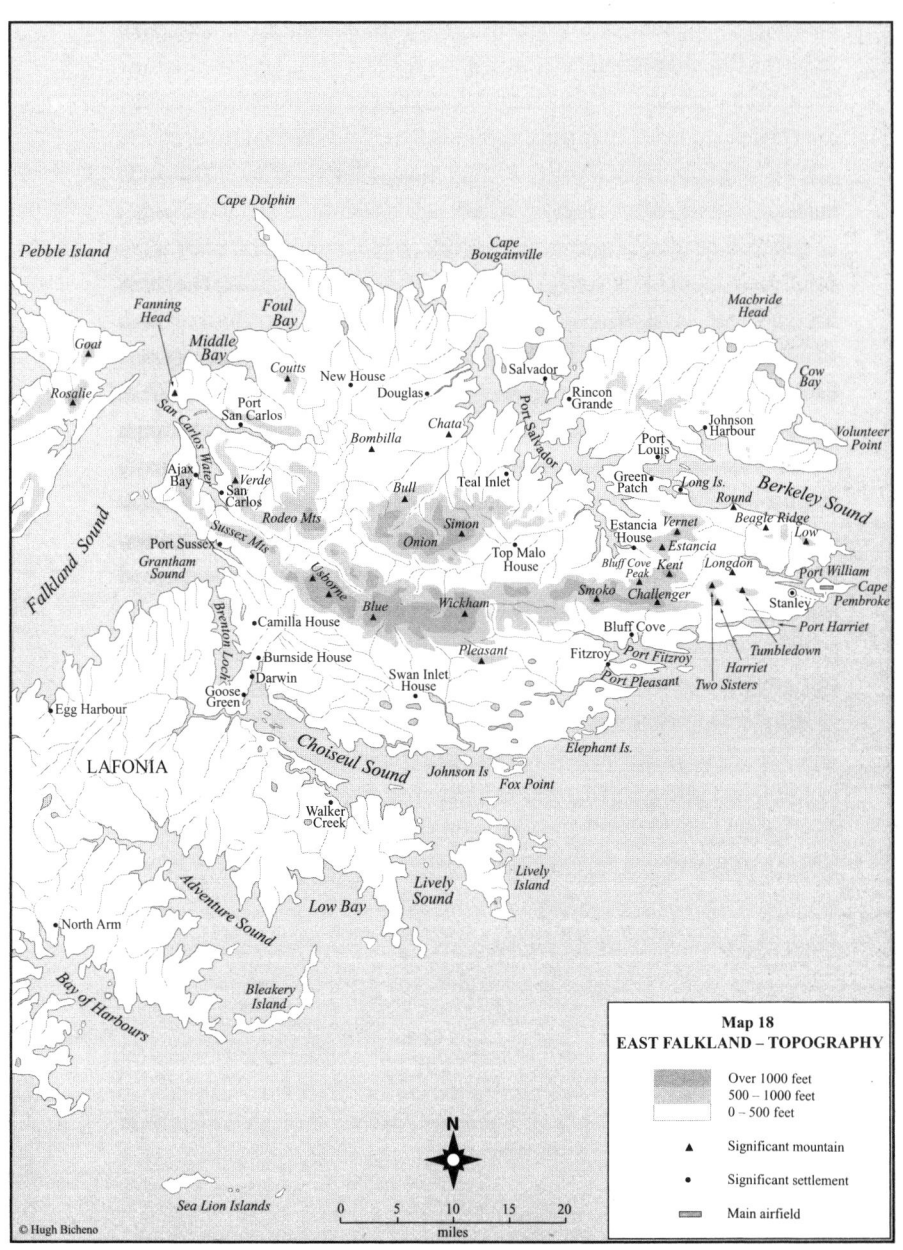

Map 18
EAST FALKLAND – TOPOGRAPHY

Over 1000 feet
500 – 1000 feet
0 – 500 feet

▲ Significant mountain

• Significant settlement

Main airfield

© Hugh Bicheno

N

0   5   10   15   20
miles

192

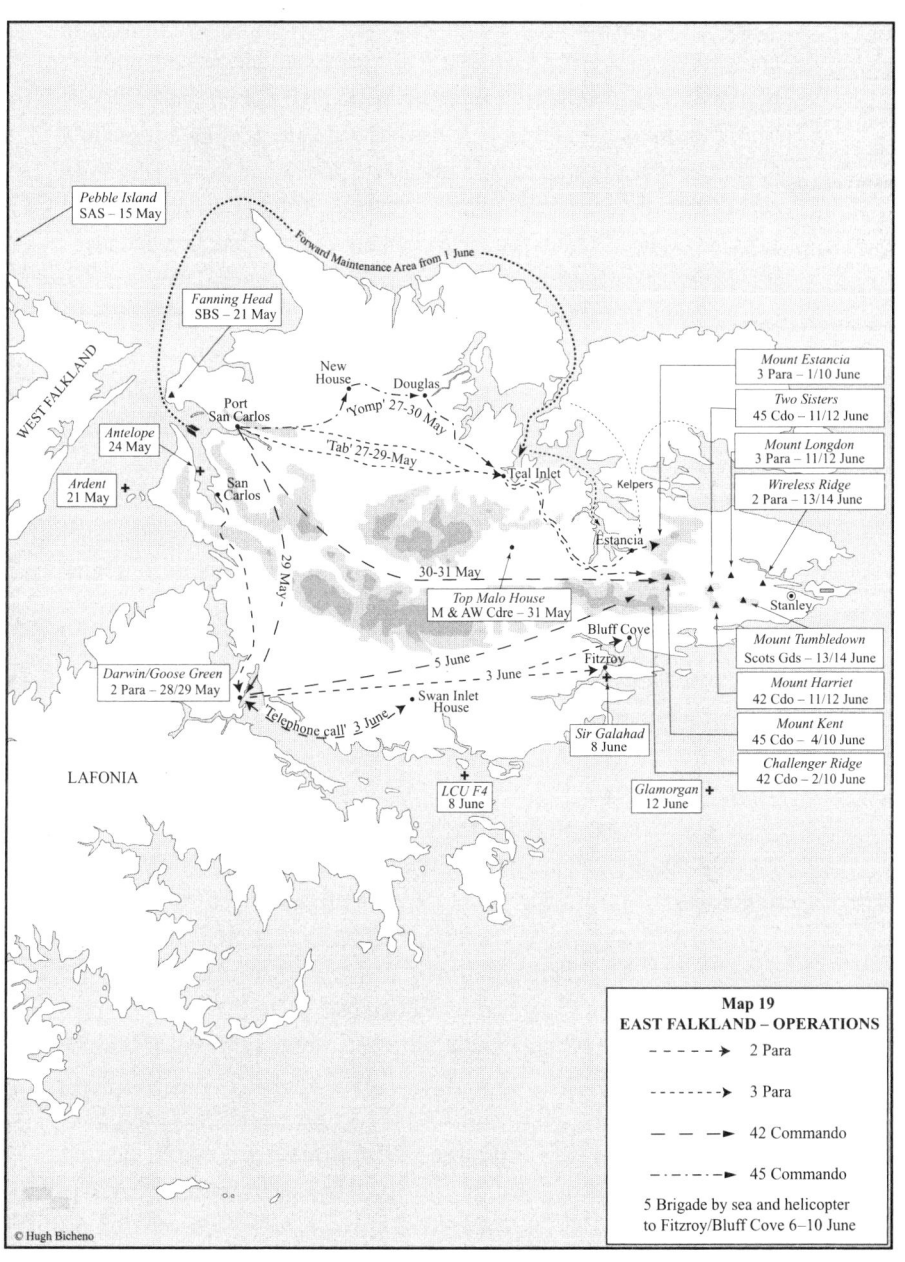

Pebble Island
SAS – 15 May

Forward Maintenance Area from 1 June

WEST FALKLAND

Fanning Head
SBS – 21 May

New
House   Douglas

Port
San Carlos   'Yomp' 27-30 May

Antelope
24 May   San
Carlos   'Tab' 27-29 May   Teal Inlet

Ardent
21 May   Kelpers

Mount Estancia
3 Para – 1/10 June

Two Sisters
45 Cdo – 11/12 June

Mount Longdon
3 Para – 11/12 June

Wireless Ridge
2 Para – 13/14 June

Estancia

29 May   30-31 May

Top Malo House
M & AW Cdre – 31 May   Bluff Cove
Fitzroy

Stanley

5 June   3 June

Darwin/Goose Green
2 Para – 28/29 May   'Telephone call' 3 June   Swan Inlet
House

LAFONIA   Sir Galahad
8 June

Mount Tumbledown
Scots Gds – 13/14 June

Mount Harriet
42 Cdo – 11/12 June

Mount Kent
45 Cdo – 4/10 June

Challenger Ridge
42 Cdo – 2/10 June

LCU F4
8 June   Glamorgan
12 June

© Hugh Bicheno

Map 19
EAST FALKLAND – OPERATIONS

- – – – → 2 Para

- – – – – → 3 Para

— — — → 42 Commando

–·—·—·→ 45 Commando

5 Brigade by sea and helicopter
to Fitzroy/Bluff Cove 6–10 June

twenty-four hours, having found it impossible to make progress. The Marines proved of sterner stuff and Camiletti set up a base camp at Bombilla Hill before going forward himself during the night of 24–25 May to Verde Mountain, overlooking Ajax Bay, where he was promptly discovered by a 40 Commando Marine seeking a sheltered place to commune with nature. Camiletti's radio operator got back to Bombilla and the group was extracted to Stanley, but all Daher learned from them was that there were 'a lot of helicopters'. This was the closest any of the Argentine Special Forces groups came to the sort of reconnaissance missions routinely performed by the SAS and SBS: their training and their radio equipment was simply not up to the job. They were instead employed as shock troops, and although their forays did little to disrupt the enemy, the sight and sound of their own men riding out to meet the enemy (literally: a patriotic Kawasaki dealer in Buenos Aires donated twenty-five scrambler bikes) was a morale booster for the conscripts in their dismal defensive positions on the hills around Stanley.

On 25 May Menéndez signalled the mainland requesting the immediate dispatch of a second Army Special Forces group, Comando 602, recently formed under the command of Major Rico. Presaging his future political career, Rico resolved pending equipment requests by taking what he wanted by force from whey-faced 'bureaucratic shits' manning the armouries. This included all the passive night goggles he could lay his hands on and several Weatherby Magnum 300 rifles with telescopic sights, with which he hoped to snipe helicopters. Although they had only just begun to train as a unit, the fifty-man group flew out to Stanley on the 27th and was sent into battle almost immediately. They were tasked with forming a screen across the British line of advance, to cover the redeployment of RI 4 from a south-facing line based on Harriet, Wall and Challenger, to a new axis facing west, across Harriet, Goat Ridge and Two Sisters.

The Special Forces operation was supposed to be completed in the evening of the 29th, but after the three Comando 602 sections were flown out a band of snow showers caused the CO of Combat Aviation 601 to postpone the follow-up until the next morning. On the British side, the same weather front defeated the helicopters flying in HQ and K Coys, 42 Commando, which had to return to San Carlos in short hops, as the pilots repeatedly landed to feel their way home in a swirling white-out. Unaware that

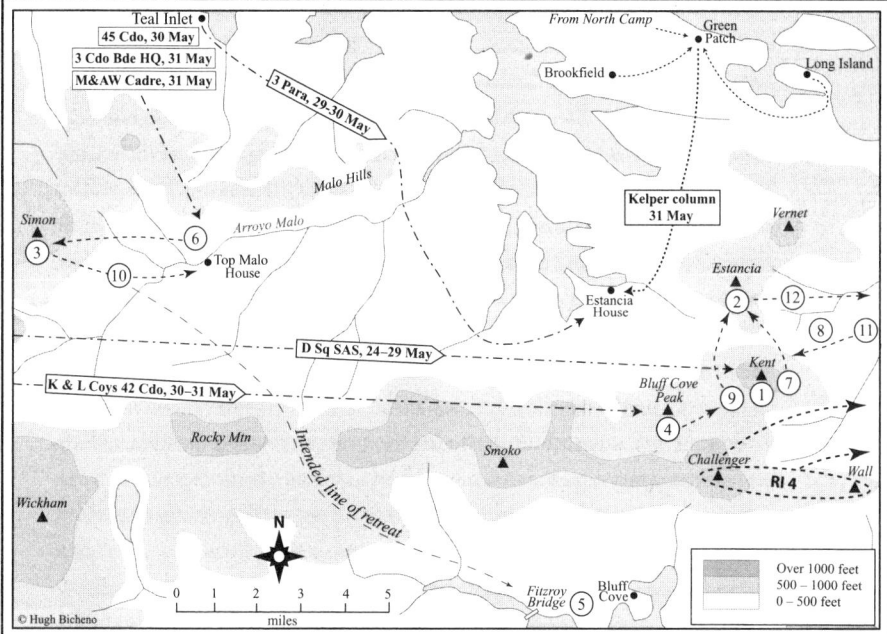

Map 20: SPECIAL FORCES CLASH

1. Abandoned by Combat Group Solari 28 May, occupied by SAS (Maj Delves)
   Objective of HQ Section (Capt Villaruel) & 3rd Assault Section (Capt Ferrero), Comando 602
   To be followed by Gendarmería SF 'Scorpions' (Maj Spadaro) and B Coy, RI 6 (Maj Jaimet)

2. Objective of Comando 601 Group (Maj Castagneto) – cancelled

3. Objective of 1st Assault Section, Comando 602 (Capt Verseci)

4. Objective of 2nd Assault Section, Comando 602 (Capt Fernández)

5. Combat Engineers 601 Coy – blow bridge before retreating

6. Insertion of Verseci's section morning 29 May, reaches Mount Simon by 1300 hrs

7. Combat between SAS and Ferrero's section night of 29–30 May. Ferrero & Villaruel withdraw to Mount Estancia

8. Puma transporting leading Gendarmería platoon (Capt Emetrio) shot down 1100 hrs 30 May

9. Combat between SAS and Fernández's section morning and evening 30 May. Fernández withdraws to Mount Estancia

10. Retreat of Verseci's section 30 May, overnight shelter in Top Malo House where assaulted by the Mountain & Arctic
    Warfare Cadre, RM, morning 31 May

11. Castagneto's Comando 601 Group driven back by mortar fire morning 31 May

12. Villaruel, Fernández and Ferrero retreat towards Stanley midday 31 May

the second wave had been postponed, the 602s went ahead with the operation to recover Mount Kent. Captain Ferrero's twelve men used their superior passive night goggles to penetrate the British defensive screen and forced the SAS, with two men badly wounded, to retreat. Captain Villaruel's HQ section landed on the northern side of the mountain in what proved to be a radio black hole, and pulled back across the valley towards Mount Estancia in an unsuccessful attempt to regain contact with the other sections and with Daher in Stanley. Ferrero was in the lee of the mountain but Captain Fernández's twelve men, landed on Bluff Cove Peak, were exposed to the full force of the weather. They immediately went to ground, but their insertion was reported and added to the concerns of the SAS on Mount Kent who, unlike their opponents, now knew they were on their own.

During the night Daher ceded operational control to Rico, while Thompson gave local command to Major Delves, the commander of the SAS detachment, with orders to hold Mount Kent at all costs. Delves might have found the job impossible if Rico had been able to talk to his section commanders, or even if Ferrero, Fernández and Villaruel had been able to talk among themselves. In a desperate effort to achieve some coordination Ferrero sent two men across Mount Kent to make contact with Fernández, which they succeeded in doing. Unfortunately when Fernández's section tried to join up with Ferrero next morning, they were ambushed and lost two men killed. Returning to Bluff Cove Peak, Fernández managed to attract the attention of one of the helicopters engaged in moving RI 4, and gave the pilot a written message for Rico. By the time Rico received it, he knew that the Puma carrying the first section of the Scorpions had been shot down, with all on board killed or wounded. At the time the Argentines thought the Puma had fallen to two Harriers that made a slashing attack along the valley at about this time, but it was actually brought down by a Stinger fired by the SAS on Mount Kent. Fernández's note was the last straw, and Rico cancelled the planned insertion of Comando 601 to Mount Estancia, instead ordering its commander, Major Castagneta, to mount an overland rescue mission for the surviving Scorpions and for the trapped 602s.

Fernández tried again to join up with Ferrero in the evening, but was ambushed once more. One of his men was captured but Fernández managed to fight his way out and left two SAS men requiring urgent casualty evacuation. Into the middle of this came helicopters carrying the leading elements of 42 Commando with four 81mm mortars, and a lively time was had by all until the landing site between Mount Kent and Bluff Cove Peak was finally declared safe for the fly-in of three 105mm guns in the early morning of the 31st. Fernández extracted his men with great skill and withdrew to Mount Estancia, where he somehow managed to join Ferrero and Villaruel without precipitating a blue-on-blue. Meanwhile, Castagneto's group roared into action on their Kawasakis and in commandeered Landrovers and were greeted by a barrage from 42 Commando's mortars as they approached the Murrell Bridge (see **Map 22**, p. 208). They abandoned the Landrovers and advanced on the bikes, but the mortars followed them and they finally fell back, leaving one of their number wounded. Castagneto was awarded the CHVC for this action and for general service, although probably the Argentine cause would have been better served if the dynamic Rico had been in charge of 601 from the beginning.

If the Scorpions had come forward on the heels of the 602s, Mount Kent would have fallen to them and then it would have been down to how quickly K Company, 42 Commando or Major Jaimet's para-trained B Company, RI 6, could be brought into action. This was the only encounter battle of the war, fought at night in weather conditions so bad that any normal human being would have dug a hole and pulled it in after him, and the newly-arrived 602s performed well against the best troops in the British Army. If they did not regain a feature that should never have been left unguarded – and which they would have been compelled to abandon in a day or two anyway – they did at least prevent the SAS interfering with the redeployment of RI 4.

The remaining Comando 602 section under Captain Verseci was flown to a landing site east of Mount Simon, where the 601 insertion of 23 May had set up an observation post and left a cache of supplies. Verseci had good radio reception but found he could not transmit. Although he had two Blowpipes and two Magnum 300s with him, his orders were to observe and report, not to engage the enemy. Therefore, while trying to get his radio to work, he reluctantly refrained from attacking the helicopters flying in front of his observation post, including the sole British heavy-lift Chinook with an underslung 105mm gun during the failed attempt to reinforce the SAS on Mount Kent in the evening of 29 May. When he finally gave up on the radio and decided to attack the helicopters, he and his men were assaulted by snow-laden katabatic winds, which made it impossible for them to stay on Mount Simon and even put their survival in doubt. Verseci led his men down from the mountain to take refuge in an abandoned farmhouse called Top Malo House, intending to cross the Wickham Heights to Fitzroy the next day.

They were spotted by a patrol of the Mountain and Arctic Warfare Cadre, RM (M&AW), the only troops on the islands trained and equipped to operate in such appalling conditions, who were posted on the Malo Hills to provide a flank guard for the march of 3 Para and 45 Commando along the coastal plain. The next morning nineteen M&AW men under their CO, Captain Boswell, came to call. In a desperate fifteen-minute action two of the 602s were killed and six wounded, but four of the Marines were also badly hurt in the shoot-out. When interviewed after the war, Rico said the episode that most impressed him in the entire campaign was that although the wounded 2nd Lieutenant Losito shot one Marine in the stomach and tried to shoot another before passing out, the one he had tried to kill knelt down, used Losito's neckerchief to tourniquet his leg, injected him with morphine, put an M on his forehead and said 'No problem, it's war' – before returning to the battle. He also admired the professionalism of Boswell's austere comment to Verseci: 'Never in the house'. It was at the end of this interview that he made the savage contrast between Argentine and British respect for human dignity quoted at the end of Chapter Five.

RICO MIGHT PERHAPS have qualified his comment if he had known more about Wilson's 5 Brigade and a deployment that pitilessly revealed the limitations of 'muddling through'. The taproot of the disaster at Fitzroy on 8 June was initial Army reluctance to deepen its involvement (beyond the two Para battalions) in a Navy-run operation that seemed likely to be cancelled before any serious fighting took place. Once called on to provide a second brigade, however, the Army demanded an equal chance to gain renown, which meant that a second, southern front had to be opened so that the Army brigade could be seen to fight shoulder to shoulder with 3 Commando Brigade. 5 Brigade brought no organic logistical support with it and the Guards – fresh from ceremonial duties – were simply not fit enough: the Welsh could not even manage to cross the Sussex Mountains when ordered to march from San Carlos to Goose Green. The Gurkhas managed the same march with no difficulty but could not be given the leading role, in part because the Argentines were making much of the 'mercenary' issue, but mainly because the contrast with the Guards would have been so professionally and culturally embarrassing.

The least disruptive, shortest and safest way forward was to use the northern route opened up by Thompson, fully secured by the time 5 Brigade disembarked on 1 June. This alternative was rejected because it would be seen as the Army following the Marines. Although the Service Chiefs were responsible for setting the tone, operational responsibility rests with the newly arrived Land Forces Commander, Marine Major General Jeremy Moore, who sailed down with Wilson from Ascension to South Georgia on the *QE 2,* cut off for ten crucial days (20–30 May) because the liner was not equipped with secure communications. During the voyage, Moore made promises he did not feel able to revoke after he arrived, and found how far Thompson had advanced the enterprise in the interim. Given the brilliant success of the northern advance, the proper use of 5 Brigade was to free 40 Commando from guarding San Carlos and 2 Para from Goose Green so they could join the attack under Thompson's operational command. That is almost what happened in the end, and a stronger divisional commander would have ignored inter-service politics to insist on it from the start.*

In addition to the reasons in favour of reinforcing success to the north, there were compelling reasons not to open up a southern front. First and most significant, it was the direction from which the Argentines expected an attack to come: a belief assiduously fostered by a carefully orchestrated pattern of naval bombardment, electronic spoofing and disinformation. The southern route was also two and half times longer than the northern because ships had to sail down Falkland Sound and around Lafonia. If they set out in daylight, the Argentines at Port Howard or Fox Bay would report it to the mainland and the Argentine Air Force would certainly launch a strike against them, so operations were limited to the (fortunately) long nights. Not long enough, however, for a ship to navigate the difficult entrances to Port Pleasant

---

* A 40 Commando company was attached to the Welsh Guards to make up for their losses at Fitzroy and 2 Para was returned to 3 Commando Brigade for the final battle.

or Port Fitzroy, unload, and return to the relative safety of San Carlos before dawn. In addition, the threat from the mobile Exocet battery on the Stanley peninsula made it necessary for ships to sail close to the coastline, which was infested with propeller-tangling kelp, not merely in the places marked in **Map 21** (p. 201) but also adorning a number of offshore seamounts. Strong wave action added to the hazard by breaking loose rafts of the stuff to trap the unwary. Not least, and unlike Port Salvador after Mounts Kent and Estancia were secured, the two coves were plainly in sight of the Argentines on Harriet.

Despite all this, Wilson initiated a spontaneous advance and was permitted to persist in it, exposing his leading battalion to the mauling that would have been forthcoming from a more mobile enemy, and forcing the Royal Navy to incur great and unnecessary risks to support it. There is a very simple rule about risk-taking in war: if it succeeds you will be crowned with laurels and have palms laid at your feet; if it fails you become a goat to be driven into the desert bearing the sins of everyone else who contributed to the debacle. The goat in question was carrying plenty of his own, although what did for him almost as much as committing the Task Force to a reckless operation was the suspicion that he was headline-grabbing and, oddly, his bilious green Wellington boots. The Royal Navy and RM view of journalists was that, as far as possible, they should be told nothing until after the war, and then only who had won. Wilson chose to make himself stand out by actively courting the press, with the result that when his gamble failed and the Argentine Air Force found the LSLs *Sir Galahad* and *Sir Tristram* sitting in Port Pleasant on one of the clearest days during the campaign, the TV cameras had all the light they needed to immortalize the moment when his career came to an end.

It could have been much, much worse. The Task Force was unaware that the Argentines had dismounted an Exocet launcher from the damaged *Guerrico* and flown it to Stanley until the night of 28 May. A misfire spared *Glamorgan,* sailing parallel to the coast and believing all she had to fear were the 155mm guns: but a few hours later *Avenger* experienced a very near miss indeed, when a missile flew close over her stern. Reasoning that the Argentines would wish to give the weapon the best possible arc of fire, Naval Intelligence deduced it must be located at the eastern end of the airport peninsula, which was ferociously shelled. In fact it was mounted on a mobile

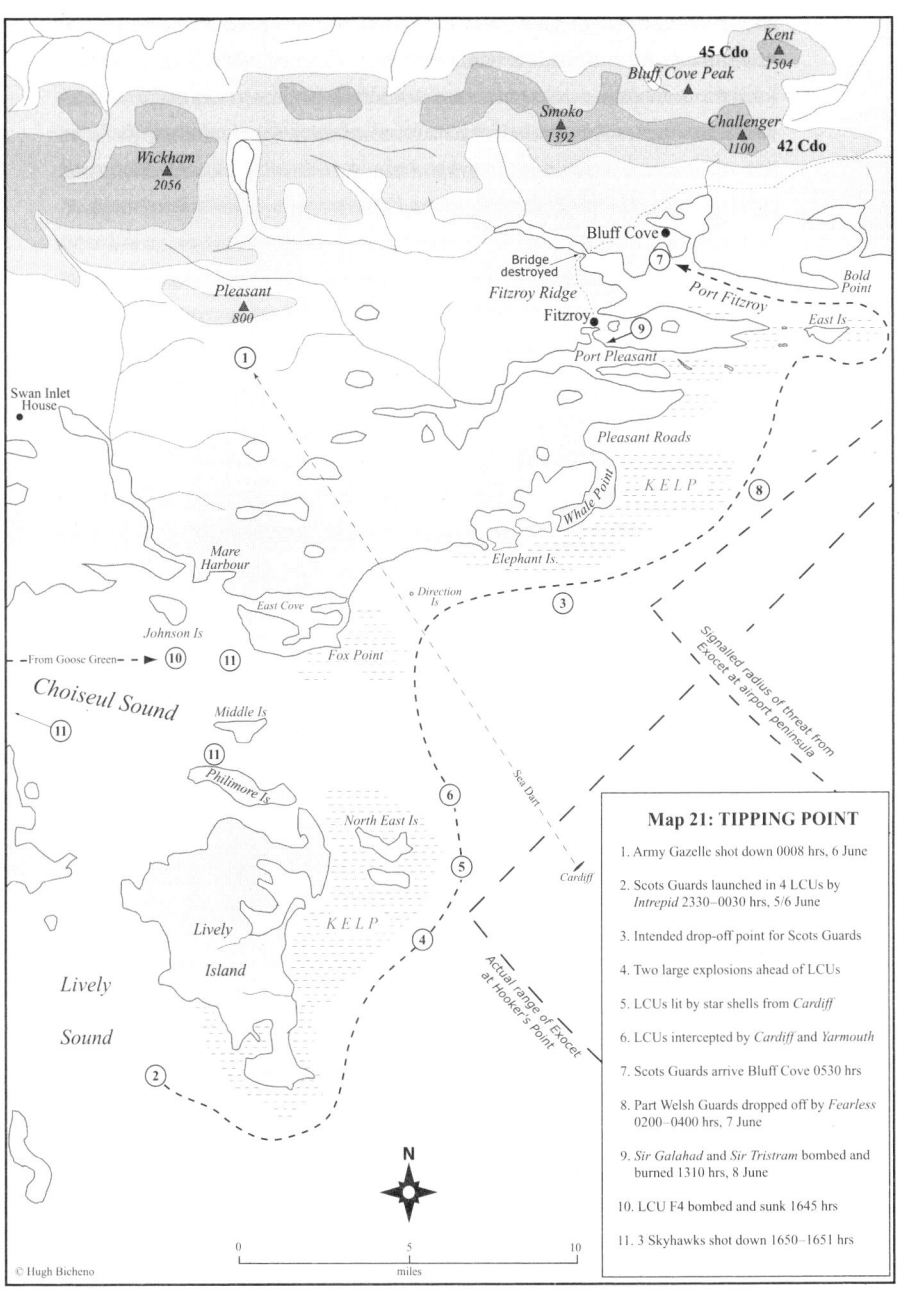

Map 21: TIPPING POINT

1. Army Gazelle shot down 0008 hrs, 6 June

2. Scots Guards launched in 4 LCUs by *Intrepid* 2330–0030 hrs, 5/6 June

3. Intended drop-off point for Scots Guards

4. Two large explosions ahead of LCUs

5. LCUs lit by star shells from *Cardiff*

6. LCUs intercepted by *Cardiff* and *Yarmouth*

7. Scots Guards arrive Bluff Cove 0530 hrs

8. Part Welsh Guards dropped off by *Fearless* 0200–0400 hrs, 7 June

9. *Sir Galahad* and *Sir Tristram* bombed and burned 1310 hrs, 8 June

10. LCU F4 bombed and sunk 1645 hrs

11. 3 Skyhawks shot down 1650–1651 hrs

© Hugh Bicheno

0   5   10
miles

platform that spent the day amid the houses of Stanley and rolled out at night to Hooker's Point, its arc of fire restricted by headlands on either side but 5 miles south-west of the reported location. Furthermore, the signalled area of danger was a 20-mile arc, whereas the specified maximum range of the missile was 25 miles. This discrepancy may account for one of the episodes that made the night of 5–6 June the narrowest point in the hourglass, when it could all have gone terminally wrong for the British.

For the full story of what would have gone straight into any anthology of great British military disasters, I refer the reader to Ewen Southby-Tailyour's fascinating *Reasons in Writing*. On 3 June Wilson flew to Goose Green and learned from a local resident that there was a telephone link between Swan Inlet House and Fitzroy. Keeble, on the eve of being superseded by 2 Para's new CO, Lieutenant Colonel Chaundler, was keen to exploit the opportunity and Wilson authorized him to take a small party forward to make a call in the five light Scouts available. Keeble learned that the Argentines had abandoned Fitzroy and nearby Bluff Cove. When he returned, Wilson commandeered the priceless Chinook, packed Farrar-Hockley's A Company into the six helicopters, and sent them forward to secure the settlement. British observers on the heights above Bluff Cove presumed, in the absence of notification of own troop movements, that the helicopters were Argentine and reported their arrival to the full battery of British 105mm guns now installed behind Mount Kent. A barrage was only checked at the last moment when the spotters fortunately had second thoughts.

The hair sustaining the Sword of Damocles held for a few days longer. Moore chose to support Wilson's initiative and two Sea Kings were made available to take the rest of 2 Para forward the next day. They were out of radio range of Goose Green, something to which Wilson did not turn his attention for two days. During the night of 5–6 June the Scots Guards sailed around Lafonia in the Assault Ship (LPD) *Intrepid,* whose captain belied the ship's name by refusing to risk her further than Lively Island. Nor was this the only lapse from the Senior Service norm. Woodward's staff failed to warn *Cardiff* and *Yarmouth,* which were 5 miles east of Lively Island that night in the hope of shooting down one of the nightly Argentine transport flights. Unaware of any British presence, they therefore assumed any activity in their area would be hostile.

Woodward, meanwhile, informed Clapp that there would be no warships in the area, while complaining that the whole operation was unnecessary, that the Navy was taking all the risks, and why couldn't the Guards just march across the island, etc. Woodward's overarching duty was to preserve the carriers, not merely for the duration of hostilities but also for indefinite guard duty afterwards, and so at this time he also yielded to the increasingly agitated requests of her captain to take *Hermes* out of the line for long overdue maintenance. The flagship's Harriers could still stage through *Invincible*, but Woodward would surely not have agreed to move 50 miles further out to sea had he appreciated that the land forces were about to be more exposed to air attack than at any time since 21 May: therefore the factor most responsible for what followed was the failure of the staff at Northwood to remain abreast of events.

Clapp expected the captain of *Intrepid* to embark the Scots Guards in his four landing craft (LCU) and launch them off Elephant Island, no more than two hours away from Bluff Cove, under the direction of Southby-Tailyour. Instead the captain dropped them in the lee of Lively Island, more than three times as far away. Echoing the doomsday mood of Woodward and Northwood, the captain argued that the loss of one of the LPDs would be as grave as losing a carrier and would force the government to sue for peace. He had no desire to go down in history as the (possibly dead) man most associated with defeat, so while *Intrepid* fled, 600 Scots – crammed like sardines into the LCUs – had to endure seven hours of battering by the heavy waves, drenched with spray and nearly frozen by the gale-force wind.

About an hour into the journey, Southby-Tailyour saw two large explosions ahead, which remain officially unexplained. The Argentine accounts do not mention firing any Exocets that night, but the explosions occurred precisely on the western end of the arc of fire from Hooker's Point, if at least a mile beyond the theoretical maximum range. If there was an Exocet fired that night the target was probably *Cardiff,* to the east of the LCUs and outside the signalled Exocet threat area, but well within range of Hooker's Point. She had a busy and blamelessly disastrous night. A little after midnight an aircraft showed up on radar moving overland precisely along the corridor believed to be used by Argentine transport aircraft. *Cardiff* fired a Sea Dart at maximum range and there was exultation when a hit was confirmed.

Captain Harris had no reason to doubt it was a legitimate kill: yet he did, and that sixth sense saved the Scots Guards. The target in fact was an Army Air Corps Gazelle carrying Royal Signals personnel belatedly sent by Wilson to set up a radio relay to enable him to communicate with 2 Para at Bluff Cove.*

That nagging feeling caused Harris to check first when a number of sea craft showed up on radar against the low outline of Lively Island. Instead of firing on what, according to his information, could only be enemy patrol craft, he sent up starshells that lit up the labouring LCUs. Southby-Tailyour, likewise informed that the only ships he might encounter would be hostile, considered running for land before continuing on his way. A little later *Cardiff* loomed out of the darkness and flashed him an order to heave-to, which he did, and then flashed the single word 'Friend'. 'To which side?' answered Southby-Tailyour. Instead of staying to clarify the situation, Harris raced off into the night, his doubts about the aircraft he had shot down now hardening into angry certainty. To round off the night, *Cardiff*'s own Lynx helicopter developed gearbox trouble while spotting for shore bombardment and diverted to *Arrow,* which came within a whisker of shooting it down.

During the next night (6–7 June) Captain Larken of *Fearless* proved more robust than his *Intrepid* colleague and, when the four *Intrepid* LCUs failed to meet him off Elephant Island, brought the Welsh Guards nearly 5 miles nearer Bluff Cove than he was required to. The US Marines have the *mot juste* for most occasions, and the situation prevailing at Bluff Cove/Fitzroy was what they would call a 'clusterfuck'. Wilson, now installed at Fitzroy, not only failed to resolve the situation but made it worse. The proximate cause was that the Argentine Combat Engineers, before departing, blew up a section of the bridge over the inlet between Bluff Cove and Fitzroy, increasing the walking distance between the two settlements from four to nearly fifteen miles. Once the Scots Guards had thawed out and were able to relieve 2 Para at the perimeter around Bluff Cove, the Paras' new CO Chaundler decided to hijack the LCUs to carry his men across the inlet. He sent Keeble, with Wilson's blessing and in his personal helicopter, to get them.

---

* Three of the four men killed are buried at San Carlos. Oddly, half the men buried there were victims of fratricide.

Southby-Tailyour was not present to argue, having flown to San Carlos to coordinate the night's operation because radio communications were still haphazard. He had left orders with the LCU coxwains to await his return, so they were reluctant to yield to Keeble's demands. Eventually three of them succumbed to Keeble's forceful argument (some accounts mention a casually waved pistol) that they could deliver his men to Fitzroy and be back in time for the night's activities. Loading Chaundler's men they set out, only to be driven back by worsening weather conditions. Goaded by Chaundler they tried again as night fell and inched their way to Fitzroy, where they were stormbound and unable to return to Bluff Cove. When Southby-Tailyour returned from San Carlos he found them gone, but expected them to return in time to be guided by him to meet *Fearless* and unload the Welsh Guards and the other units on board.* His hopes were dashed and *Fearless* could only unload half its human cargo on the two LCUs she carried – the other two were at the Teal Inlet Forward Maintenance Area.

The list of aggravating factors for the disaster that unfolded next is long, but high among them must be the decision of Wilson and Lieutenant Colonel Rickett of the Welsh Guards to take their HQ and communications Landrovers forward during the first wave. The Guards' HQ, Recce and Support companies went ashore with the bridge repair detail, while two rifle companies, another Sapper detachment and the Signals Group returned to San Carlos. They transhipped to the LSL *Sir Galahad* during 7 June but were held up by the slow boarding of 16 Field Ambulance, RAMC, which delayed departure until 2030, too late to make the return trip under cover of the night. *Sir Galahad*'s captain petitioned for permission to delay departure until the following evening but Clapp, woken from an exhausted sleep and mindful of promises made to Wilson and Rickett, rejected the request. The final nail was that when *Sir Galahad* arrived off Fitzroy, the embarked Guards officers demanded that their men be delivered to Bluff Cove, despite assurances the bridge had been repaired, and when Southby-Tailyour tried to order them to do so they quibbled over rank and refused to budge. All this within a few hundred yards of Wilson and his staff.

Informed of a landing exactly where it was expected, the Argentine Air

---

* These included engineers from 9 Parachute Squadron, whose task was to repair the bridge, and a 3 Commando Brigade Royal Signals rear link detachment to bring some order into the communications chaos.

Force launched a coordinated strike, which first drew away the Combat Air Patrol by attacking and seriously damaging *Plymouth* in Falkland Sound. The diversion left five Skyhawks with a clear run at *Sir Galahad* and her sister ship *Sir Tristram*, fellow lucky survivor of the 24 May attack in San Carlos, which had arrived earlier and was now almost fully unloaded. Untroubled by any meaningful ground fire, the Skyhawks put two 500lb bombs, which failed to explode, into *Sir Lancelot,* and three more that did into *Sir Galahad.* Forty-six men died in the fireball that swept through the crowded tank deck of the *Galahad,* two in a smaller fire on the *Lancelot.*

A follow-up raid that afternoon was driven off by ground fire, including Blowpipe and Rapier missiles. The four Skyhawks withdrew along Choiseul Sound, where three of them were shot down by two Harriers. Unfortunately the interception did not take place in time to prevent an attack on one of the *Fearless* LCUs in Choiseul Sound, coming back from Goose Green where Southby-Tailyour had sent it, at Wilson's insistence, to collect more of his vehicles. Colour Sergeant Johnston and five others died and the vessel was wrecked, to sink that night while under tow. Johnston, already recommended for decoration following his heroism during the evacuation of *Antelope* on 23 June, was awarded a posthumous QGM.

Inter-service rivalry among the Argentines certainly did much to make their defence of the islands less effective than it might have been. However, apart from the airfield extension and the matter of mooring the *Belgrano* in Stanley harbour, there was not among them a decision solely attributable to inter-service rivalry that put the fate of their cause so needlessly at risk as the British insertion of 5 Brigade in a delicately balanced operational plan that would have achieved success without it. The northern flanking move by the Paras to Longdon and Wireless Ridge eventually went ahead as planned, and there is no reason to doubt that the Marine Commandos could have gone on to take Tumbledown after their capture of Harriet and Two Sisters. Nothing the Guards achieved compensated for the near-fatal delay their advent inflicted on the campaign, and responsibility rests predominantly with the most senior officers and officials in London. Blame for Argentine errors and omissions is mitigated by the inexperience of armed forces that had not fought a war for over a century. During that time the British fought two major and countless minor wars, yet despite this wealth of experience they showed themselves unable to dispense with the trivial, to define objectives and to pursue them coherently.

As to detailed responsibility, Nott was a weak Minister, particularly discredited in the eyes of the Royal Navy – the service that ran the war. It was his job to keep inter-service rivalry in check and he failed to do so. But, although it is possible he may have said something to the effect that the loss of an LPD would force the government to sue for peace, there was only one voice that counted and she would not have been so 'wet'. The judgement bears the signature of officials second-guessing their political masters, and suspicion hardens into certainty when one considers for how long the truth was suppressed. It took MoD four years and two investigations, the first either incompetent or a deliberate cover-up, even to admit the Gazelle blue-on-blue. By the time participants' memoirs revealed the full extent of the potential disaster surrounding the advance of 5 Brigade, the heat had gone out of the issue and it could be glossed over, as failures of British officialdom invariably are. The goat Wilson was duly driven into the wilderness, joined by Clapp, but the Defence establishment, the senior commanders in London and their staffs, basked in the glow of a victory they nearly threw away by, in my opinion, a gross collective lapse from the sustained good judgement their rank demanded, their men deserved, and their nation had a right to expect.

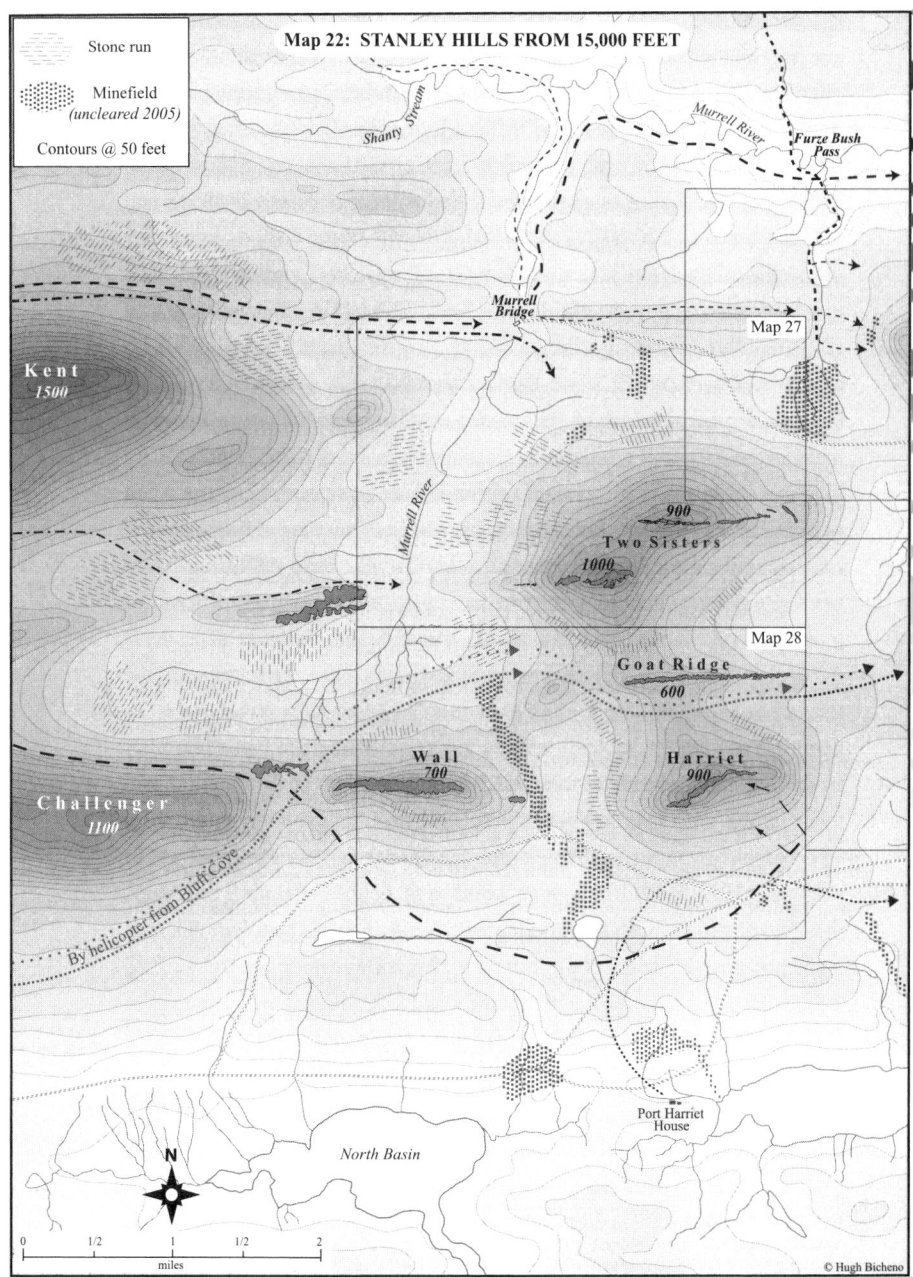

Map 22: STANLEY HILLS FROM 15,000 FEET

Stone run

Minefield
(uncleared 2005)

Contours @ 50 feet

Shanty Stream

Murrell River

Furze Bush Pass

Murrell Bridge

Map 27

Kent
1500

Murrell River

900

Two Sisters
1000

Map 28

Goat Ridge
600

Wall
700

Harriet
900

Challenger
1100

By helicopter from Bluff Cove

Port Harriet House

North Basin

N

0   1/2   1   1/2   2
miles

© Hugh Bicheno

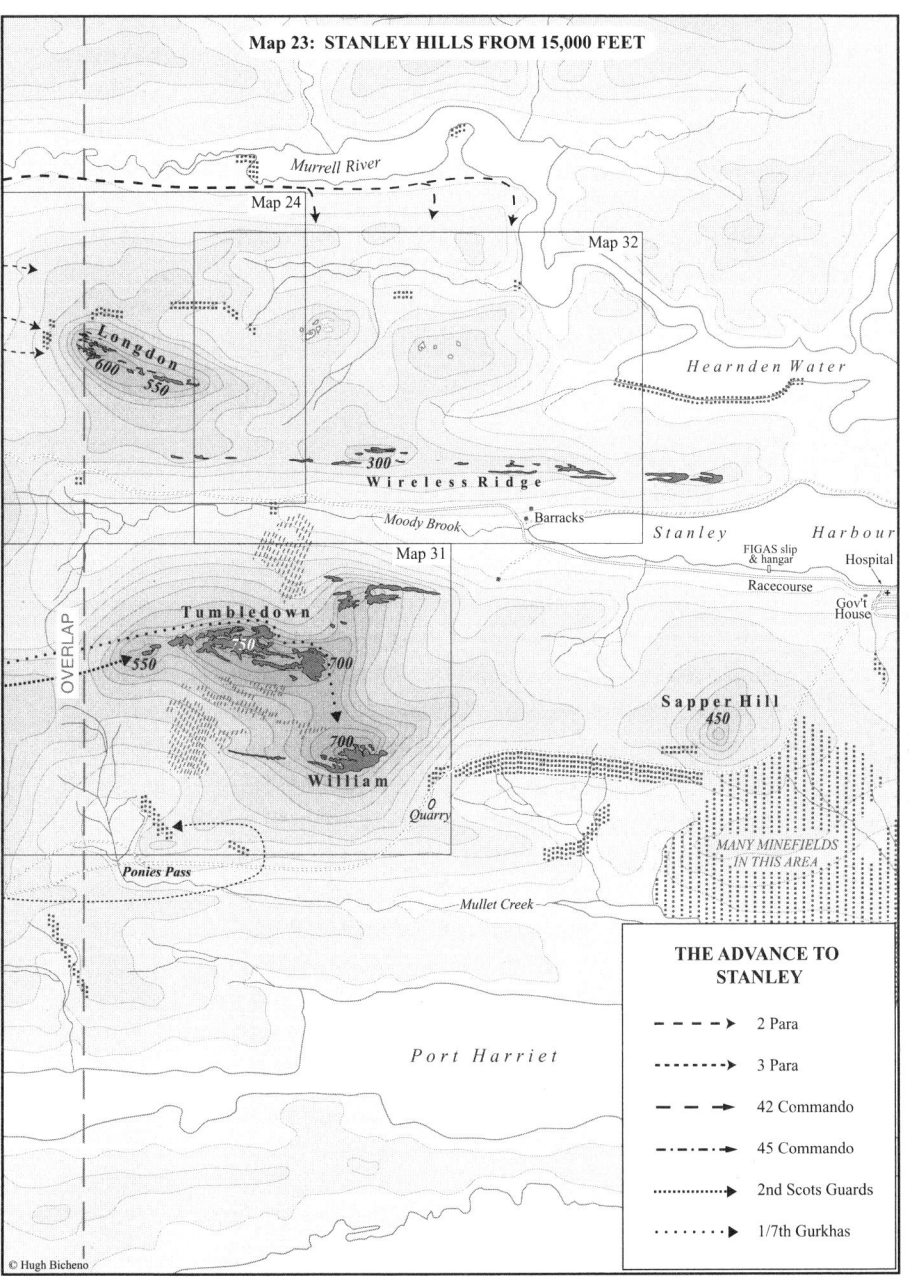

Map 23: STANLEY HILLS FROM 15,000 FEET

Murrell River

Map 24

Map 32

Hearnden Water

L o n g d o n
600 550

300

W i r e l e s s   R i d g e

Moody Brook

Barracks

S t a n l e y   *H a r b o u r*

FIGAS slip & hangar

Hospital

Racecourse

Gov't House

Map 31

T u m b l e d o w n
750 700

550

O V E R L A P

S a p p e r   H i l l
450

700

W i l l i a m

0 Quarry

MANY MINEFIELDS IN THIS AREA

Ponies Pass

Mullet Creek

P o r t   H a r r i e t

THE ADVANCE TO STANLEY	
– – – ▸	2 Para
·········▸	3 Para
– – ▸	42 Commando
–·–·–◂	45 Commando
············▸	2nd Scots Guards
········▸	1/7th Gurkhas

© Hugh Bicheno

209

11 Longdon

PART ONE

ALTHOUGH LONGDON COULD have been made almost impregnable to infantry with barbed wire, napalm would have made short work of a clearly defined, highly concentrated target area. Neither was employed in what became the toughest land battle of the war because the wire was in Mar del Plata on board the prudent *Córdoba,* and the British could not incinerate the hill because of political fastidiousness. Labour leader Michael Foot, whose support was essential to prevent the war becoming a partisan issue, once said his principal objection to the US war in Vietnam was the use of napalm. Why he considered it so much worse than all the other means men have devised to maim and kill each other is a mystery, but the emblematic photograph of a naked, screaming Vietnamese child fleeing a village bombed in error, her back scored by the hellish stuff, probably had much to do with it. As it was, none of the Labour heavyweights broke ranks, although the gadfly Wedgwood Benn tried to reprise the 1956 anti-Suez rally, when he appeared on the podium in Trafalgar Square with Foot and Aneurin Bevan. At Wedgwood Benn's side in 1982 was Neil Kinnock, two men taken seriously by party activists and the media but emphatically and repeatedly rejected in elections over the following decade.

Longdon was the lynchpin of the defence. Had the British landed in the north-east (as well they might, for the embarked planners considered Uranie Bay the best direct landing site) the hill would have stood squarely across their shortest line to Stanley. Even in the face of the British advance from the west, it covered the northern flanks of Two Sisters and Tumbledown, and protected the forward firebase for the GA 3 battery located at Moody Brook. Had the Argentines advanced their 155mm guns to this position they could have interdicted Thompson's logistics lifeline by bringing Salvador Water under fire. They could also have made their heavier metal tell in counter-battery fire against the British artillery behind Mount Kent, which they could only reach from Stanley using supercharge, to the detriment of the equipment. Longdon was also a strong firebase in its own right, with two 120mm mortars on the summit and two 105mm rocket launchers on its southern flank covering the valley leading west towards the Murrel Bridge. Reciprocally, the hill was itself covered by heavy weapons at the back of North Sister, on Tumbledown and on Wireless Ridge (see **Diagram 5**, p. 212).

Jofre allotted the sector north of Moody Brook to RIM 7 from his own X Brigade, a regiment with a high reputation within the Argentine Army. The CO, Lieutenant Colonel Giménez, posted his strongest company under Captain López to hold Longdon, with the regiment's 2 i/c, Major Carrizo Salvadores, as sector commander. B Company was an all-reservist (S/C 62) outfit, selected from the rest of the regiment to receive special training with an emphasis on marksmanship during the recently completed military service cycle, with a ration strength of 216 on the eve of battle. In addition to the rocket launchers and 120mm mortars, B Company had five 81mm mortars, a wire-guided Cobra anti-tank missile system, a Blowpipe anti-aircraft missile system, two .50-calibre heavy machine-guns (HMG) and at least six MAGs and older .30-calibre machine-guns (MMG). It was reinforced by forty-six men from the brigade combat engineers (Eng 10) under Lieutenant Quiroga, and by Lieutenant Dachary's twenty-four-man Marine Platoon with six more .50-calibre machine-guns, which were distributed to cover an arc from south-west to north-east around the perimeter.* Sub-Lieutenant Baldini's 1 Platoon held the western summit, where the hill reared up over a steep, boulder-strewn slope. Dead ground immediately beyond this was mined, then a gentle slope led to a rivulet running diagonally across the front of the feature. To the north Staff Sergeant González's 2 Platoon slanted away from the line of the hill to cover a gentle slope with minefields in three areas

---

* Dachary's brother Alejandro was the GADA 601 officer killed by the Shrike missile attack of 3 June.

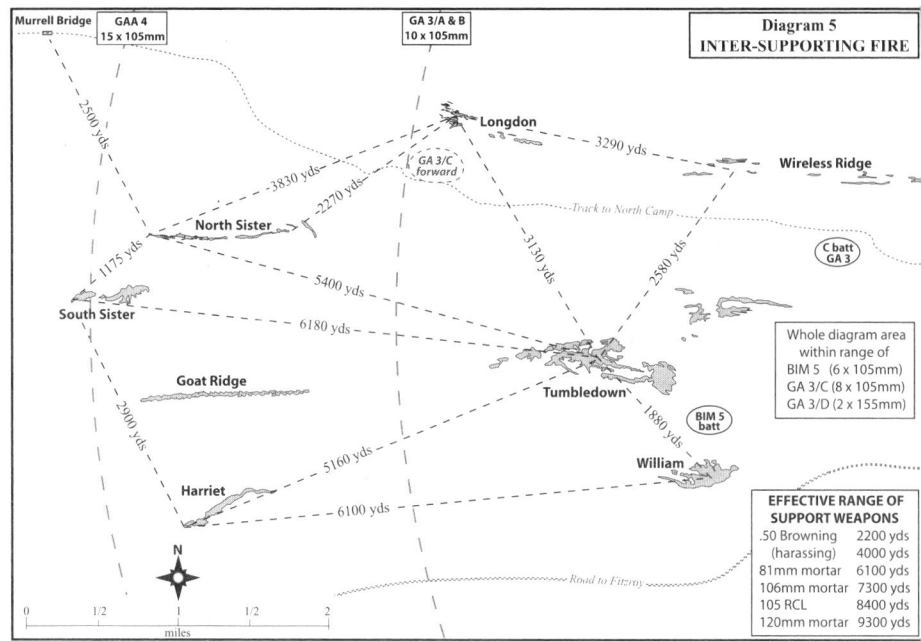

Diagram 5
INTER-SUPPORTING FIRE

Murrell Bridge

GAA 4
15 x 105mm

GA 3/A & B
10 x 105mm

2500 yds

Longdon

3290 yds

Wireless Ridge

GA 3/C forward

-3830 yds-

-2270 yds-

Track to North Camp

North Sister

C batt
GA 3

1175 yds

3130 yds

2580 yds

South Sister

5400 yds

6180 yds

Whole diagram area
within range of
BIM 5 (6 x 105mm)
GA 3/C (8 x 105mm)
GA 3/D (2 x 155mm)

Goat Ridge

2500 yds

Tumbledown

1880 yds

BIM 5
batt

5160 yds

William

Harriet

6100 yds

N

EFFECTIVE RANGE OF
SUPPORT WEAPONS

.50 Browning	2200 yds
(harassing)	4000 yds
81mm mortar	6100 yds
106mm mortar	7300 yds
105 RCL	8400 yds
120mm mortar	9300 yds

Road to Fitzroy

0   1/2   1   1/2   2
miles

of dead ground. To the south, Lieutenant Neirotti's 3 Platoon followed the contour lines to cover another gentle slope into the valley between Longdon and North Sister, and a large minefield in dead ground at the headwaters of the rivulet. The HQ Group occupied the secondary peak at the eastern end of the hill, with a platoon from Eng 10 in reserve beyond (see **Map 24**, p. 216).

It was a naturally strong position and during fifty-eight days of occupation the defenders made it more so. Firing positions were constructed by the Sappers, who improved existing formations within the rocks or blasted new ones to create sangars along the ridge, and used rocks from the ridge to line semi-buried bunkers on the flanks. All were roofed with fencing materials and plastic sheets before covering them and filling gaps in the rocks with blocks of peat, which doubled as camouflage. Duplicate, buried telephone cables linked the principal positions, and Carrizo Salvadores had dedicated radio links with Giménez on Wireless Ridge and Jofre in Stanley. The only notable departure from orthodoxy was at the western end where, seduced by the greater ease of building sangars in the extensive area of rock fall, Eng 10 built 1 Platoon's positions high on the slope, when they should have been 100 yards further out to obtain the flattest line of sight. To remedy this deficiency a Rasit (French ground surveillance radar that can detect a walking man at 14 miles) was co-located with one of the Marine .50-calibre machine-guns at the north-west corner, slightly forward of the main infantry positions and covering two unmarked minefields.

It is no coincidence that the area immediately in front of the Rasit/HMG posts became the British first aid and casualty clearing area (RAP) – it offered the best cover not only from enemy artillery but from the rest of Longdon as well. But what made it the Achilles heel of the position was that the flat, north-facing quartzite slabs in this quadrant form a number of corridors leading to the summit, protected from flanking fire. Some had MMG placed to fire along them, but the northern rocks were not adequately covered. During the night of 5–6 June a patrol consisting of Corporal Phillips and Privates Absolon and Hayward approached from the north through these rocks to penetrate as far as Corporal Carrizo's two 81mm mortars at the base of the steepest part of the western slope. At that moment the mortars were discharged to see if they drew counter-fire: the product of a disagreement between Carrizo and Baldini on their proper location.* Their answer came swiftly when an artillery strike, actually called in earlier by Phillips against the Rasit, landed on the slope below them, under cover of which specialist sniper Absolon shot at Baldini while Hayward fired a 66 at one of the mortar pits.

The ramifications of this incident were extraordinary. On the British side, Phillips believed the officer, the Rasit and one of the mortars had been taken out. Lieutenant Colonel Pike, CO of 3 Para, and through him Brigadier Thompson, were convinced by the success of this and other infiltrations that the hill could be taken by silent attack (without a preliminary artillery bombardment), which coincided with Thompson's desire to husband his limited stocks of artillery ammunition to support a further advance to Wireless Ridge if Longdon fell quickly. For the Argentines, Baldini did not realize he had been attacked by infiltrators and reported the speed and accuracy of the enemy response as an indication of the effectiveness of the British Cymbeline mortar-locating radar. Adding to the confusion was the sad fate

---

* Carrizo dates this to the evening of 11 June, but there was no British artillery fire at that time.

of a white horse the Argentines had been using to bring up supplies, which the recce patrol encountered during its approach. Phillips reported being fired on by the whole hill as he withdrew following the sniper and 66 attack, and he was not mistaken. The retreating patrol was detected by Sergeant Nista, the Rasit operator, and Carrizo Salvadores ordered defensive fire across his whole northern flank. When dawn revealed the unfortunate horse shot to pieces in front of 2 Platoon, Baldini not unnaturally concluded that Nista had got it wrong. But he was also convinced the British were spoofing the radar with electronic countermeasures and could detect its emissions, and that even if the Rasit contacts on this and earlier nights were British patrols, they were most probably feints to provoke defensive fire for Cymbeline to track. Any attack, he decided, would be preceded by a violent artillery bombardment: so there was no reason for his men to stand-to whenever Rasit picked up a contact, and good reason to use it sparingly.

So it was that when, in the early evening of 11 June, Nista reported a column of vehicles north of the Murrell river at Furze Bush Pass, and then a large body of men closing from the north-west who later went off the screen, Carrizo Salvadores did not call in artillery or fire his mortars at the targets. He also sent his orderly, S/C 62 Massad, to order Nista to turn off the Rasit, which he did about an hour before the assault, in which Massad was among the first to die. It was no spoof, however: the vehicles were the Landrovers and tractors driven by Green Patch Kelpers led by Trudi McPhee, continuing the invaluable assistance they had given the battalion ever since meeting it at Estancia House during its epic tab across East Falkland (see **Map 20**, p. 195). The large body of men thus granted the gift of operational surprise dropped off the Rasit plot because, guided by Kelpers Vernon Steen and Terry Peck, they had advanced to assault positions along 'Free Kick', the code name Pike gave to the rivulet and shallow ravine whose tactical significance the defenders had fatally overlooked.

I spent more time on Longdon than all the other Stanley battle hills put together in order to knit together an abundance of vivid personal accounts, much the most useful being Support Company veteran Vincent Bramley's interviews with ex-combatants from both sides in *Two Sides of Hell*. The Ordnance Survey map does not show the quartzite spine along the hill, but once an outline of the rock ridges is married to the contours – and to the

ARGENTINE

7th Mechanised Infantry Regiment (RIM 7)
CO – Lt Col Giménez (on Wireless Ridge)
OC Sector – Maj Carrizo Salvadores (2i/c RIM 7)
B Coy – Capt López
   HQ Group (2 x 81mm) mortars, 1 x Army HMG)
   1 Platoon – Sub-Lt Baldini/Sgt Spizuocco
   (Rasit radar, 1 x 105mm RCL, 1 x Cobra AT,
   2 x 120mm/2 x 81mm mortars, 2 Marine HMG)
   2 Platoon – SSgt González
   (3 x Marine HMG)
   3 Platoon – Lt Neirotti/Capt López
   (1 x 105mm RCL, 2 x 81mm mortar,
   1 x Marine/1 x Army HMG)
10th Combat Engineers
   Platoon – Lt Quiroga
Marine Infantry
   Platoon – Lt Dachary
   (6 x HMG distributed as above)
C Coy, RIM 7 (from 'Rum Punch')
   Platoon – 2Lt Castañeda

Artillery Support
GA 3/A and B (10 x 105mm howitzers)
   Forward Observer – 2Lt Ramos
From North Sister (RIM 6/B)
4 x 81mm mortars
From Tumbledown (BIM 5)
6 x 106mm mortars

BRITISH

3rd Battalion, The Parachute Regiment (3 Para)
CO – Lt Col Pike, RSM Ashbridge
2i/c Maj Paton, Intelligence – Capt Orpen-Smellie
A Coy – Maj Collet/CSM Munro
   Forward Observer – Lt Lee
   1 Platoon – 2Lt Moore/Sgt Dougherty
   2 Platoon – 2Lt Kearton/Sgt Phelan?
   3 Platoon – Lt Osborne/Sgt McCullum?
B Coy – Maj Argue/CSM Weeks
   Naval Gunfire Observer – Capt McCracken
   4 Platoon – Lt Bickerdike/Sgt McKay/Sgt Fuller
   5 Platoon – Lt Cox/Sgt Ross
   6   Platoon – Lt Shaw/Sgt Grey
C Coy – Maj Osbourne (not engaged)
D Coy – Maj Butler/CSM Rustill *
   Patrols – Sgt Pettinger
Support Coy – Maj Dennison/CSM Caithness
   Drums (SFMG) – Lt Oliver/Sgt Deaney
   Mortars – Capt James/Sgt Robson/Sgt Hallas
   Anti-Tank – Capt Mason/Sgt Knights/Sgt Colbeck
9 Para Squadron RE
   2 Troop – Capt Burns

Artillery Support
79 Battery, 29 Commando Regt RA (6 x 105mm)
   Battery Commander – Maj Patrick *
HMS *Avenger* (1 x 4.5-inch)
   Naval Gunfire Observer – Capt McCracken
(with B Company)
* With Pike's Tactical HQ

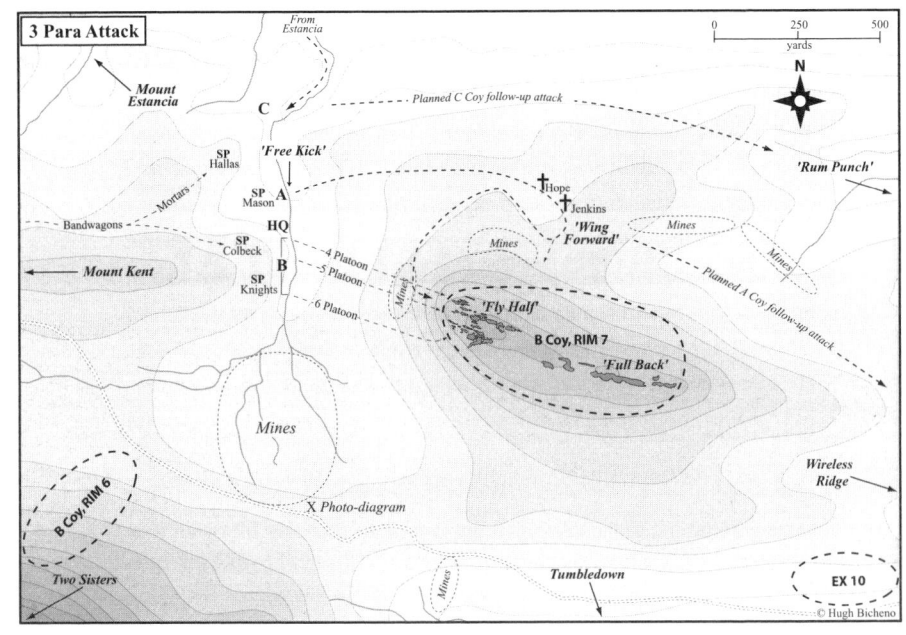

Map 24: LONGDON

From the South-West

Tents   Baldini   120   *The Bowl*

50

5 Platoon (over)

30   50

105

50

6 Platoon

Photo Diagram 24: LONGDON

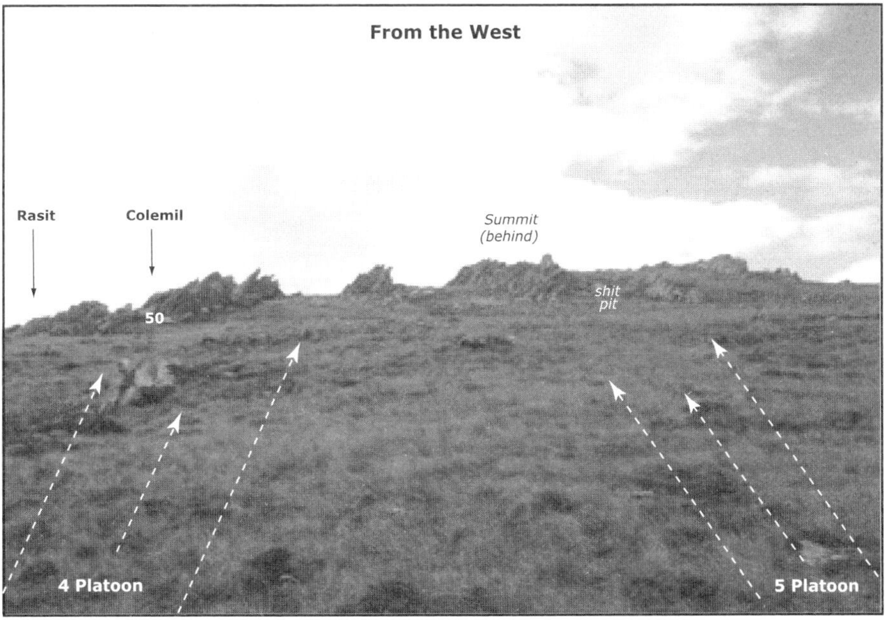

From the West

Rasit   Colemil   *Summit (behind)*

shit pit

50

4 Platoon

5 Platoon

Argentine Army map of the defensive scheme – it becomes clear how the micro-terrain conditioned the fighting. The tuning fork HMG bunkers and the round mortar pits are readily identifiable, as is the command post complex at the eastern end of the ridge. However, this is the hill most visited by tourists and picked over by souvenir hunters and, in the absence of the piles of shell cases that identify them elsewhere, I have selected the ruined sangars with the best line of sight as the most probable locations for MMG.* The infamous 'shitpit' is practically the only place within the western rock fall out of line of sight from the rest of the hill and also sheltered from the wind: important considerations in the location of a latrine but also dead ground where attackers could take cover, as many did before continuing noisesomely towards the summit. Finally, without the memorials placed by returning veterans to honour their fallen comrades it would have been impossible to identify the high water mark of successive attacks.

Pike shared his late 2 Para colleague's belief that the enemy would melt away in the face of the focused aggression of his battalion. His views on how sharp that focus should be were no doubt influenced by word on the grapevine that momentum was lost at Darwin–Goose Green when D Company stopped to sort out prisoners at the first objective, as well as by the report he relayed to his men of Argentine treachery in the white flag incident. Following the cross-island tab he wanted to assault Longdon on 3 June, in a daylight advance to contact with maximum artillery and air support. Given the resistance put up by the well dug-in defenders a week later it is fair to assume an attack on 3 June would have failed; but as it was, the logistics drag created by the arrival of the Guards made it impossible. Although some of Pike's officers breathed heartfelt sighs of relief, the men 'all felt bad for the CO, who was hard and strong and would always talk to the lads.' Ironically, this encomium comes from Vincent Bramley's warts and all memoir *Excursion to Hell,* which nearly curtailed Pike's career amid investigation by the Metropolitan Police of the shock-horror revelation that hideous things happen in battle, and that springs break when wound too tight, for too long.

Pike was a practitioner of directive control rather than order command, which is to say he gave his company commanders objectives but did not try

---

* Hard for the attackers to distinguish, given that the standard Argentine rifle (FAL) could fire on fully automatic.

to micro-manage how they were achieved. Collet, Argue and Dennison of A, B and Support Coys had served tours with the SAS, and the infiltration prowess of D Company was the result of Butler's insistence on training them in small patrols along SAS lines. It should not be thought that a three-year tour with the SAS conferred any great status in the eyes of the Paras – that was reserved for the permanent SAS cadre, who were known to regard their officers as a waste of rations. Company Sergeant-Major Weeks felt much the same about Argue, but did not let his feelings affect discipline within B Company. Not so C Company under Major Osbourne, a last-minute substitute for the popular Major Kernan, who was on attachment from the US Army and denied permission to go to war. Osbourne suffered the consequences and in an example of 'give a dog a bad name' they blamed him for the 23 May blue-on-blue at San Carlos, although responsibility lay as much with A Company's Collet and mainly with the battalion Ops Officer. C Company brought up the rear during the tab, suffered the highest dropout rate and played no part in the battle, although if the defenders had broken as expected, it was tasked with following through towards a hill in front of Wireless Ridge code-named 'Rum Punch'.*

I cannot refrain from mentioning – in the hope that Anaya *et al* may learn of it before they go to the billets reserved for them in hell – that many members of 3 Para's tough Mortar Platoon were devout homosexuals: a matter of absolutely no military significance (*vide* the deadly Spartans) but too rich in irony to be left uncontrasted with the swaggering *machismo* that contributed so greatly to bringing the war about.

The Milan and SFMG platoons were dispersed in support of A and B Coys with an eye to following up a rapid advance along the ridge and beyond to Wireless Ridge, and as a result they were fed into the battle in penny packets on a very restricted front. The perfect vision of hindsight sees that it would have been better to establish them as a strong firebase on 'Wing Forward', the low rise to the north of Longdon, from where they could have silenced the HMGs that prevented Longdon falling quickly. A firebase on Wing Forward would also have broken up the Argentine counter-attack (by a group of forty-five RIM 7/C men from Rum Punch led by Lieutenant Castañeda) that stopped B Company's last attempt to outflank the main

---

* Re-named 'Rough Diamond' by 2 Para when they moved up to attack Wireless Ridge.

ridge. Instead, A Company was sent to Wing Forward preparatory to exploiting forward to Wireless Ridge, from which it had to be brought back in order to take over the attack on Longdon. This said, fluidity had to be built into the scheme if both Longdon and Wireless Ridge were to be taken in one night. Pike undoubtedly would have made a radically different deployment, and Longdon would have fallen far more quickly and cheaply, if it had been his sole objective.

To complete the *mis en scène* it should be borne in mind that Longdon was only one of three assaults carried out by 3 Commando Brigade during the night of 11–12 June, and that each was designed to support the other. Harriet, which was where the Argentines anticipated the first attack to come and would therefore have the best developed defensive fire plan, was shelled heavily while the three British battalions stole forward to their start lines. 3 Para was to attack first in order to wrench enemy attention to their right flank, and to silence the heavy weapons on Longdon that could have enfiladed 45 Commando's assault up the north-western face of North Sister. Then 42 Commando was to stage a demonstration to the west of Harriet half an hour after 3 Para's assault began, so that the Argentines on Two Sisters would be looking south when 45 Commando attacked them from the north-west. 45 Commando's attack, in turn, would freeze RIM 6/B in place on the flank of North Sister, from where it might have attacked 3 Para from the rear (see **Map 24**, p. 216). When 45 Commando's attack was fully declared, 42 Commando would attack Harriet from the east, the opposite side to its earlier diversion. The overall plan was something of a three-card trick, designed to keep the Argentines guessing and to dislocate enemy expectations successively, and so facilitate operational surprise for all three attacks.

Pike assigned the ambitious first phase of the 3 Para attack to Argue's B Company, which was tasked with taking out key command and support weapons positions on the western slope before charging over the summit ('Fly Half') to silence the 120mm mortars. It was then to pursue the broken enemy along the ridge, forcing the Argentines to abandon their positions on the flanks, to seize the mortars and the enemy command post at the eastern peak ('Full Back'). Argue assigned the Rasit/HMG complex to Lieutenant Bickerdike's 4 Platoon, and the command post complex high in the centre of the slope to Lieutenant Cox's 5 Platoon. 4 and 5 Platoons would advance together from the north-east guided by a Patrols Company team under Sergeant Pettinger, who had been there before during several night infiltrations.* Lieutenant Shaw's 6 Platoon, guided by the intrepid Phillips, would set out first because it was tasked with taking out another command post on the south-western slope, which required a right hook to approach the slope at a forty-five degree angle to the others. There were known to be mines in the path of 4 and 5 Platoons and the men were firmly told there must be no stopping to look after casualties. To reduce the possibility that others might freeze in place if one of their number trod on a mine, Argue formed the two platoons in an extended line, while CSM Weeks cranked up the psychological tension and dramatised the need to preserve silence for as long as possible by ordering them to fix bayonets. The compelling logic of this was lost on Private Connery, a GPMG man who would normally have followed behind the rifle sections:

> I can't tell you how fucking shocked and surprised I was when we were at the base of Longdon waiting for the order to advance and they told us to get into an extended line. I couldn't help thinking some bastard was on drugs and that they had turned back the clock and we should be lined up in red tunics. And when I heard 'Fix bayonets' that was it. I knew we were in a lunatic asylum.

The first man to die during the assault was probably Lieutenant Ramos, the forward observer for the GA3/C battery at Moody Brook, doomed by the aerials above his observation post on the south-western side of Longdon. Ramos's bunker was the 'command post' Shaw's men were to take out first. They did so silently at about 2030, as timed by Carrizo Salvadores, who tried unsuccessfully to raise Ramos by landline at that time after being told by Giménez, his CO back at Wireless Ridge, that Ramos had sent a 'confused' radio report requesting identification of a body of troops near his position. Once again the Argentine pickets paid the penalty of uncertainty about the movements of their own troops, and Phillips and Shaw's men put out GA 3/C's eyes and also one of the Marine HMGs without a shot being fired. If the 105 rocket launcher on this front was where it is shown on the Argentine Army map, it was either not manned that night or else the

---

* Pettinger was awarded the DCM.

gun crew were asleep, because 6 Platoon advanced across their front without the alarm being raised. The Paras then split up as they passed through the ridge of rocks on their side of the slope. Lance Corporal Murdoch led the right-hand section towards the summit, while the left-hand section under Corporal Steggles, intent on attacking Carrizo's mortars with 66s, emerged from the rocks to find several pup tents pitched on the central slope. The first explosion was timed by Carrizo Salvadores at 2100, and most accounts say this was the detonation that blew a foot off Lance Corporal Milne, leading the left-hand section of 4 Platoon. Phillips, however, is adamant that the attack only went 'noisy' when Steggles threw a grenade at the tents (see **Map 25**, p. 224).

Corporal Carrizo – later shot twice in the head and thus perhaps not the most dependable of witnesses – affirms that 6 Platoon was deep within the Argentine position well before 4 and 5 Platoons. He was checking the sentries across the slope from his mortars when from the west he heard English voices and the sound of bayonets being fixed. This can only have been 4 and 5 Platoons getting ready at their start line. Carrizo says that he had barely begun to rouse his sleeping men when there was a loud bang followed by a scream, near at hand:

> Within seconds the whole place was alive with tracer bullets. Everyone was in a panic. I ran for cover and crawled into a bunker with a sergeant. It was impossible to fire my mortars now. Outside, the English were running past, screaming to each other and firing into tents and bunkers. I could hear my men being killed. They had only just woken up and now they were dying. I could hear muffled explosions followed by cries, helpless cries. The sergeant and I discussed surrendering, but decided to wait until it was over.

S/C 61 Chamorro of GA 3/C, manning one of 120mm mortars behind the summit, confirms that 6 Platoon's line of approach wrong-footed the defence: 'I couldn't fire because my mortar was facing the wrong way. The British were attacking from the very flank the military geniuses had told us they wouldn't come from.' They were also far too close for the 120s to engage and the gunners were forced to abandon them when the section led by Lance Corporal Murdoch burst over the crest. Speed was everything if B Company's plan was to work. Murdoch knew this and led the way around a steep bank between large boulders, which at one point seemed to mark a dead-end for 6 Platoon, before charging without hesitation into the 'bowl', a large oblong of clear ground beyond the summit. The plaque marking where he fell is 40 yards beyond the summit, near the edge of the hollow surrounded by boulders that marks the limit of B Company's advance along the ridge. He was mortally wounded by a sniper, his throat microphone on send and his death agony broadcast to his comrades. Unable to bear it, Private Laing ran forward to bring Murdoch back to cover – but the sniper was waiting for him and three bullets in the chest killed Laing outright.

Two of the Argentine survivors interviewed by Bramley confirm that Carrizo Salvadores radically altered his defensive scheme on 10 June to create a defence in depth, where D Company patrols had previously found none. S/C 62 Barreto was furious when ordered to move his .50-calibre machine-gun from a snug bunker on the southern flank to a new position, without overhead cover, on a rise in the middle of the ridge at the eastern end of the bowl. Thirty-six hours later he found himself at the core of a firing line that prevented B Company taking the ridge in one fell swoop. But before that Baldini's platoon on the forward slope put up stronger resistance than anyone could have predicted. Steggles's section was caught in the cross fire of Lance Corporal Díaz's by-passed MMG in the rocks on the south-western slope and a group of riflemen who came together under Corporal Pedemonte, who escaped death in the tents by fleeing in his socks, around another MMG on the western slope.* Private Greenwood was killed and Lance Corporal Scott mortally wounded, and the medic Private Dodsworth was killed while attending to Scott. Part of the section fell back to deal with Díaz, who did not stay to be dealt with, and Platoon Sergeant Grey was shot in the hand when trying to grenade Pedemonte's group. Seven other men were wounded at this time, several in the back, on the slope immediately below the summit.

Taking prisoners was out of the question and it was probably here that the much-hyped killing of three men trying to surrender – including one who begged for his life in American-accented English – took place. With fire coming from all sides, five men dead and eight disabled, Shaw requested and received permission from Argue to 'go firm' in the relatively sheltered

---

* Pte Connery later cut off his own and gratefully donned Pedemonte's excellent high-topped boots.

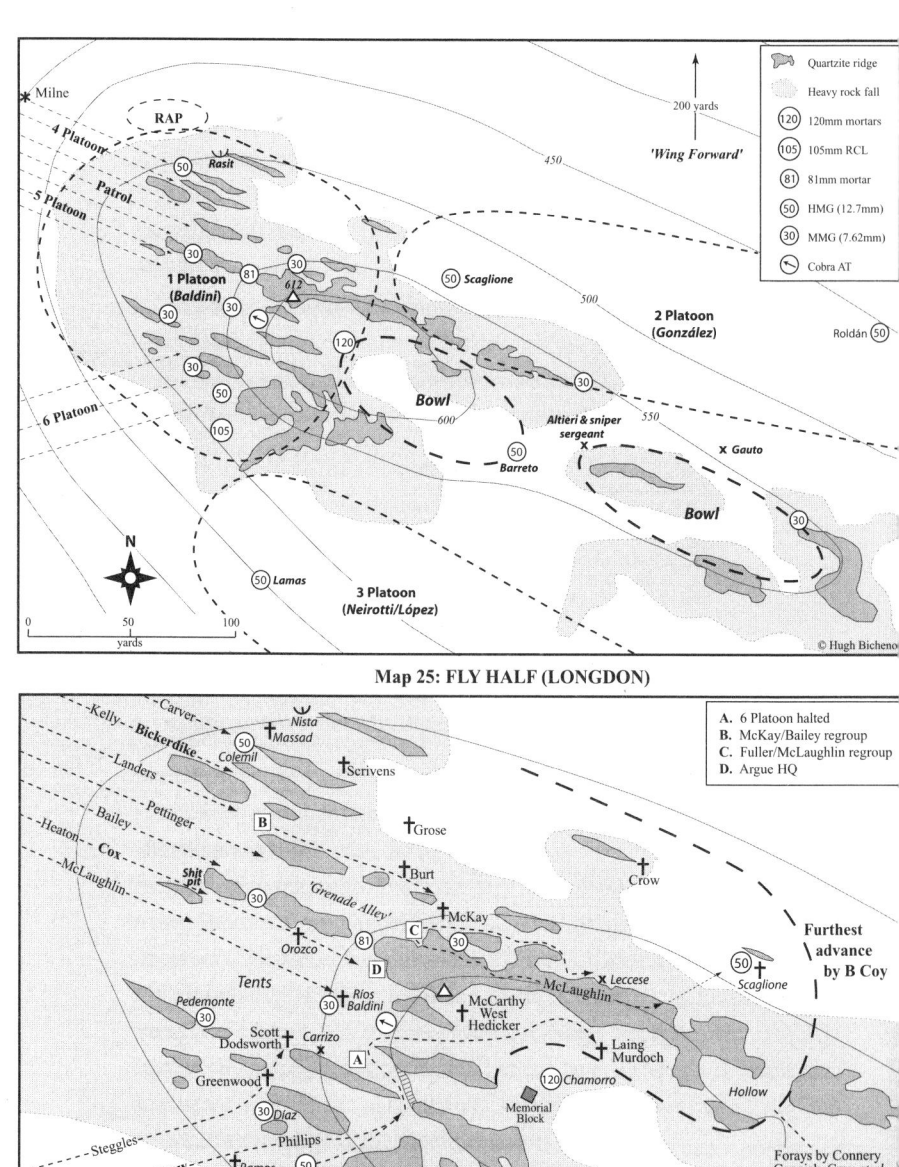

Map 25: FLY HALF (LONGDON)

A. 6 Platoon halted
B. McKay/Bailey regroup
C. Fuller/McLaughlin regroup
D. Argue HQ

© Hugh Bicheno

area next to the steep bank skirted by Murdoch during the first surge.

With 6 Platoon attracting much of the defensive fire and the rest going over their heads, the right-hand section of 5 Platoon under Corporal McLaughlin was able to rush to the summit over ground commanded by an MMG abandoned by its crew. McLaughlin's men killed Baldini and Lance Corporal Ríos as they tried to bring the gun into action, and then rushed the command post and control centre for the Cobra anti-tank system. Further left, Cox and Corporal Heaton's section were driven into the 'shitpit' by fire from a nearby MMG. The machine-gun was silenced with grenades and bayonets by Privates Gray and Gough who, after their 66s had both misfired, had to stand on their grenades to extract splayed split pins that should have been flattened with pliers before the off. Heaton's men then had to deal with a stand by a few men under Lance Corporal Orozco a little further up the slope, which ended in savage hand-to-hand fighting, before following McLaughlin to the summit. They were followed in turn by Argue, who set up his HQ in the rocks below the crest and got on the nerves of the section leaders by urging them to charge along the ridge. They ignored him and set about trying to dismantle the firing line at the eastern end of the bowl with GPMGs and 66s.* S/C 62 Altieri, one of Bramley's interviewees who was at the receiving end, said he was wounded by an explosion that killed a sergeant sniping with a night scope-equipped rifle. The sniper was wounded, not killed – there is no sergeant in the list of RIM 7 dead – but this may well have been the man who killed Murdoch and Laing earlier.

Pettinger's group and 5 Platoon's left-hand section under Corporal Bailey advanced into a corridor on the other side of the rocks from Cox and Heaton. They were stopped cold by a rain of grenades and by fire from an MMG mounted halfway up the northern face of the summit and from infantry trenches below it. The impasse created a no-go area about fifty horizontal feet and another fifty vertical below Argue's HQ, from which he was completely isolated by a wall of rock. Further north, 4 Platoon did not pause after Milne stepped on the mine and overran Marine Colemil's HMG before he could bring it into action. Correctly reasoning that surrender was not an option, he and his team fought on in the open and made their way across the slope towards the south, where he was knocked unconscious by a bullet,

---

* After adding enormously to the burdens carried across East Falkland, *all* of 3 Para's 84s misfired.

probably friendly fire, which left him with a permanent indentation along the top of his skull. Meanwhile, Bickerdike's platoon emerged into the open from the northern rocks into the night-sight of Marine Private 1st Class Scaglione's .50-calibre machine-gun at the western end of Staff Sergeant González's platoon. Either Scaglione or the MMG posted high in the rocks wounded Bickerdike, his radio operator and three others, and mortally wounded Private Grose, eighteen that day. Seventeen-year-old Private Scrivens was wounded trying to drag Bickerdike to cover and was later shot again and killed while being carried to the first aid post (RAP) over the shoulder of CSM Weeks.

B Company's situation was now desperate. 4 Platoon, Pettinger's group and Bailey's section of 5 Platoon were pinned down on the left. In the centre the rest of 5 Platoon could make no progress. On the right, 6 Platoon was out of it and even if it had not been, any attempt to attack around the southern flank would have run into the fire of the Marine HMG gun at the western end of Neirotti's platoon. Neirotti himself was wounded early, but company commander López took his place and at about midnight Carrizo Salvadores sent Quiroga's Sappers along the southern flank to launch a counter-attack on the summit. They got no further than Barreto's ridge but deployed to his left, closing off any prospect of a British advance on that side. On the north front 4 Platoon's Sergeant McKay – who took over command after Bickerdike was wounded – identified the only place where progress could be made. From where he regrouped with Bailey, he saw that a line of boulders offered cover from the elevated MMG, leading to the dug-outs below it. The route was also shielded from Scaglione's HMG by the curve of the hill. A rush close against the boulders was only likely to be spotted when crossing the gaps between them.

McKay called for fire support and Captain Mason, commanding the Support Group with A Company on Wing Forward, ordered Bramley's SFMG and Corporal McCarthy's Milan teams to fire on a bunker under a 'shark's fin' to the right of the peak. From Wing Forward this description corresponds to the location of the troublesome MMG high in the rocks. Bramley says it was attacked with 400 rounds and two Milans, which failed to silence it. We may, however, be confident that it moved the MMG team some distance towards the conclusion that they had done enough, the final step coming when they heard grenades exploding and screams from the firing positions below them. McKay led Bailey and three privates in a dash of about 35 yards to the end of the line of boulders, but in the crossing one private was wounded and young Private Burt was killed, bayonetting the ground as he fell to remain propped up by the rifle. As the three survivors attacked the first bunker beyond the boulder, Bailey was shot in the hip and the remaining private took cover, while McKay charged on alone. He took out another trench with grenades and his body was later found lying on top of it, within yards of the dead ground at the foot of the summit cliff face, from where he could have safely grenaded the MMG post above and to his left.

The machine-gun was silenced just the same, abandoned by the crew who decided to wait out the rest of the battle. Consequently, after Sergeant Fuller arrived from Company HQ to take command, the combined 4/5 Platoon group was able to move forward along 'grenade alley'. What followed was an impressive display of NCO power. Bickerdike was down and Cox lost control of himself until brutally snapped out of it by a punch in the face from CSM Weeks, who also shed any pretence of respect for Argue. 5 Platoon's Sergeant Ross was elsewhere on the hill and Weeks told Fuller to take charge. When a dazed Cox rejoined the group he was ignored. Fuller recalled McLaughlin from the summit and together they decided that Fuller's group would advance tight against the base of the long crag running south-east from the summit, while McLaughlin's section worked its way along the top. McLaughlin was in a state of exaltation that his wild Highland ancestors would have applauded, as recalled by an awed member of his section, not one of whom was killed or wounded during the battle:

> We were under very, very heavy fire . . . Suddenly, ahead of us, there was [McLaughlin], standing up on a rock, tracer everywhere, shouting: 'Come on lads. I'm fucking bullet-proof, follow me!' And we did. We followed him. On that mountain he was an inspiration to us all. He found his hour.

S/C 62 Leccese was in one of the sangars on the north face and recalls rolling grenades down on Fuller's group – until McLaughlin's men began to roll them down on him, at which point he and the rest of the defenders on the crag either retreated or reconsidered the advisability of drawing attention to themselves, leaving Scaglione's flank exposed. His sangar was covered to the north by a solid boulder, which shielded it from *Avenger* firing from beyond Volunteer Point, while the summit crag protected it from the British artillery behind Mount Kent. Throughout the campaign neither side dared fire their self-burying mortars at targets close to the front line, so by a process of elimination it seems most likely that Scaglione and his men were killed at their post by the 66s and grenades of McLaughlin's section.

We shall return after reviewing the battles for the Two Sisters and Harriet, which erupted at about this time. But before leaving, it is as well to emphasize the intensity of the first phase of the battle for Longdon. Within a mere 75 yards of each other three men performed deeds worthy of their nations' highest award for valour. Sergeant Ian McKay received a richly deserved posthumous Victoria Cross, but neither Marine Private 1st Class Claudio Scaglione nor Corporal Stewart McLaughlin received any recognition. Scaglione was overlooked because no surviving Argentine witnessed his tenacity. McLaughlin was killed several hours later by artillery on his way to the RAP, after having his back torn open by a rocket attack. Cox, with whom he had a violent altercation not long before, found severed ears in his ammunition pouches. Any chance that it might be handled discreetly blew away when someone tipped off the battalion padre, who made it the focus of his hand-wringing horror at the reeking havoc all around him.

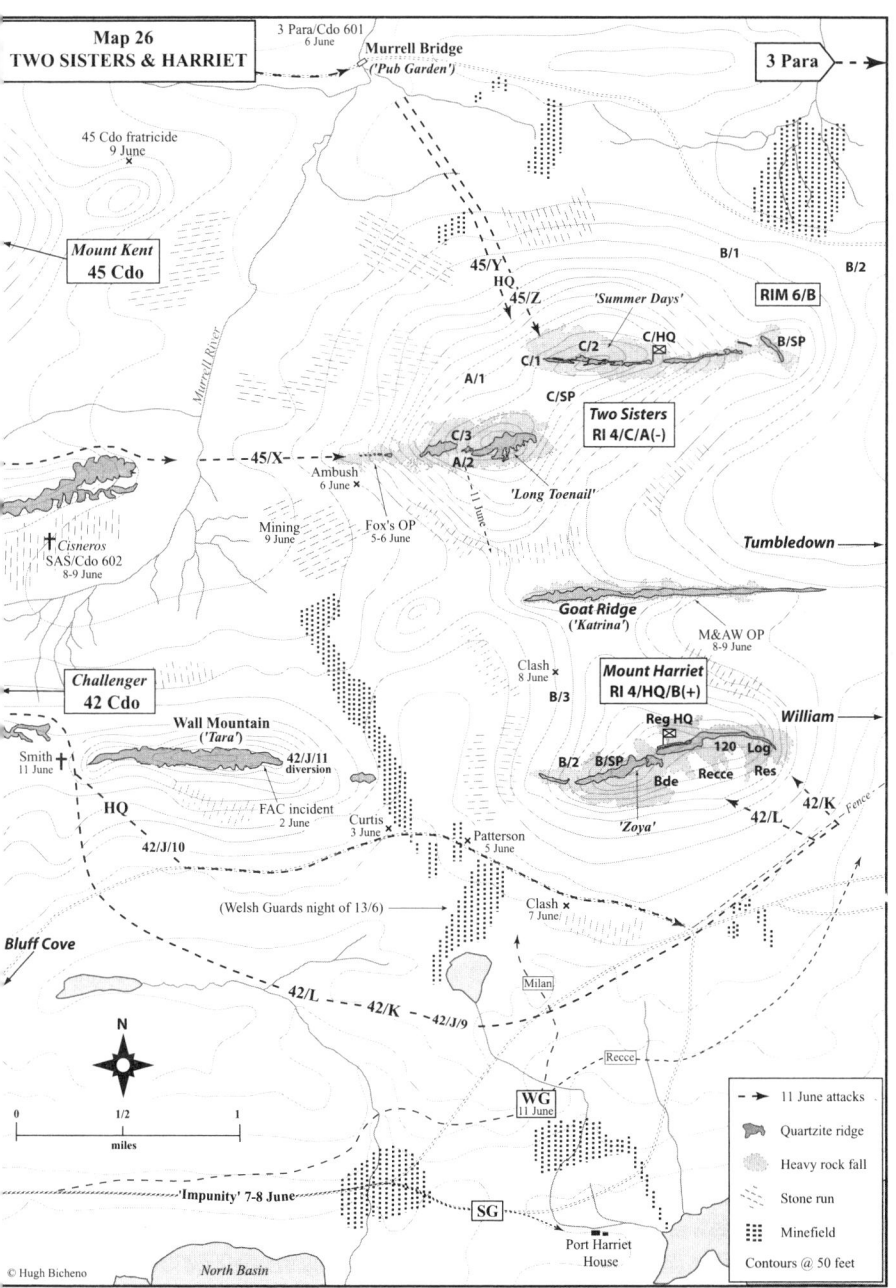

Map 26
TWO SISTERS & HARRIET

3 Para/Cdo 601
6 June

Murrell Bridge
('Pub Garden')

3 Para

45 Cdo fratricide
9 June

Mount Kent
45 Cdo

Murrell River

45/Y
HQ
45/Z

'Summer Days'

B/1

B/2

RIM 6/B

C/1   C/2   C/HQ   B/SP

A/1

C/SP

Two Sisters
RI 4/C/A(-)

45/X

C/3
A/2

Ambush
6 June ×

Mining
9 June

Fox's OP
5-6 June

'Long Toenail'

11 June

Cisneros
SAS/Cdo 602
8-9 June

Tumbledown

Goat Ridge
('Katrina')

M&AW OP
8-9 June

Clash
8 June ×

B/3

Mount Harriet
RI 4/HQ/B(+)

William

Challenger
42 Cdo

Wall Mountain
('Tara')

42/J/11
diversion

FAC incident
2 June

Smith
11 June

HQ

42/J/10

Curtis
3 June

Patterson
5 June

Reg HQ

B/2   B/SP

Bde
Recce

120 Log
     Res

'Zoya'

42/K

42/L

Fence

(Welsh Guards night of 13/6)

Clash ×
7 June

Bluff Cove

42/L   42/K   42/J/9

Milan

Recce

N

0   1/2   1
miles

WG
11 June

SG

'Impunity' 7-8 June

Port Harriet
House

© Hugh Bicheno

North Basin

➝	11 June attacks	
	Quartzite ridge	
	Heavy rock fall	
	Stone run	
	Minefield	
	Contours @ 50 feet	

12 Two Sisters

CONSIDERING HOW FEW of them could speak Spanish and the low priority the British have always given to their task, the work of 3 Commando Brigade's small Intelligence Group in producing accurate information about enemy dispositions and getting it to the front line cannot be praised too highly. Particularly since, inexcusably, it was not standard operating procedure for battalion intelligence officers to rush captured documents and significant prisoners back to Brigade. One would have thought that after a decade of intelligence-led operations in Northern Ireland things might have changed. The attack on Longdon–Wireless Ridge did not go wrong for lack of good intel: Thompson and Pike knew the two features were held by RIM 7 with about 800 men and that its strongest company was on Longdon, reinforced by a platoon of Sappers and another of Special Forces (actually Dachary's distinctively-uniformed Marines). When Pike decided to attack with a single company on a narrow front he knew it could only succeed if the enemy cut and ran: yet there were no deserters nor any prisoners taken to confirm this key assumption. There was strong evidence that it required a two-battalion attack for Longdon and Wireless Ridge to fall in one night – but the will that it should be otherwise proved stronger.

The opposite occurred at Two Sisters. Brigade intel knew from stragglers and documentation left behind when Parada's mobile reserve abandoned Mount Kent, and signals intelligence from the radio traffic accompanying the hasty abandonment of the outer enemy defences, that the Sisters had only been occupied since the end of May. Brigade also knew the twin peaks were held by a company that had spent the previous month exposed on Mount Challenger, at the western end of the original, south-facing Argentine deployment. Unlike Longdon, the Two Sisters (so called because from Stanley they look like pubescent breasts) would certainly have fallen to a *coup de main* in early June, which would probably have forced the defenders to abandon outflanked Mount Harriet as well. But it is not the Marines' way to rush into things and they carefully tested the enemy before attacking. RI 4, the regiment holding the Sisters and Harriet, was afforded the respect denied the larger, better-supported and well-established RIM 7 on Longdon, and was swiftly dismembered by a two-battalion attack with strong artillery support. One may fairly speculate that Para dash would have saved time and resources, but the reverse of that coin is that the Marines' approach would have taken Longdon more cheaply. In their separate ways both operations illustrate the most basic fact about military intelligence: no matter how compelling it may seem, it cannot persuade soldiers to act contrary to their training and inclinations.

After the fall of Two Sisters, a 45 Commando company commander commented that he would have died of old age holding the position, and it is indeed a naturally formidable feature, surrounded by long, gently uniform slopes offering little cover. But one wonders if anyone could have defended it significantly better with newly conscripted troops from the warm, lush Argentine north-east, led mainly by junior officers prematurely graduated from officer training school only two months earlier. Furthermore, although Piaggi's RI 12 won the blue ribbon in the buggered-about stakes, Lieutenant Colonel Soria's 671-man RI 4 came a close second, with a special mention for the unfortunates who ended up on Two Sisters. During May, Captain Maxpegán's C Company was divided between Challenger and Long Island Mount, far to the north overlooking Uranie Bay, locations entirely dependant on uncertain helicopter supply. Its logistics if anything got worse after the outposts were pulled back to the Sisters, the least accessible of the Stanley Hills overland. Soria also brought back two platoons from A Company, outposted on Mount Low–Beagle Ridge north of Stanley, and sent his 2 i/c, Major Cordón, to assume overall command of the Sisters. In all, Cordón

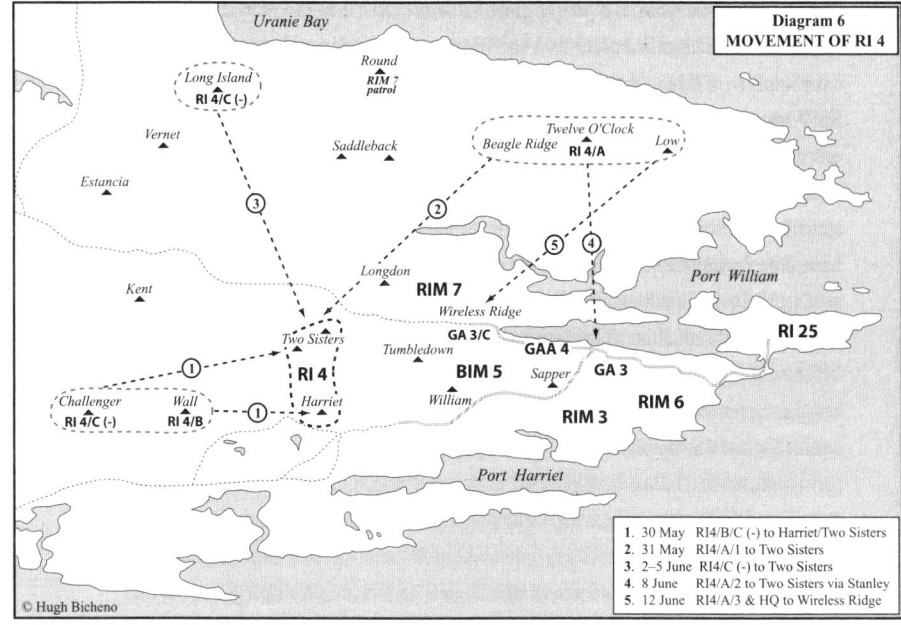

© Hugh Bicheno

Diagram 6
MOVEMENT OF RI 4

Uranie Bay

Long Island
RI 4/C (-)

Round
RIM 7
patrol

Vernet

Saddleback

Twelve O'Clock
Beagle Ridge   RI 4/A   Low

Estancia

Kent

Longdon
RIM 7

Port William

Wireless Ridge

Two Sisters
RI 4

GA 3/C

Tumbledown   BIM 5   Sapper   GA 3

Challenger   Wall   Harriet
RI 4/C (-)   RI 4/B

William

RIM 3

RI 25

GAA 4

RIM 6

Port Harriet

1. 30 May   RI4/B/C (-) to Harriet/Two Sisters
2. 31 May   RI4/A/1 to Two Sisters
3. 2–5 June RI4/C (-) to Two Sisters
4. 8 June   RI4/A/2 to Two Sisters via Stanley
5. 12 June RI4/A/3 & HQ to Wireless Ridge

had about 180 men under his command, indicating platoons half the size of RIM 7's on Longdon, each with two MAGs and a 90mm rocket launcher. In support, he had three .50-calibre HMGs distributed along the forward slope of the saddle between the two peaks and four 81mm mortars on the reverse. What he most notably lacked was the time to build proper sangars and bunkers, and the wit to bury his landlines.

RI 4 remained administratively part of Parada's brigade and dependent for supply on Daher's Logistics Group: but it was operationally under Jofre, who appears to have regarded it as little more than a breakwater for his own brigade. When he moved Major Jaimet's 120-man RIM 6/B into the area – with twenty sets of passive night goggles to RI 4/C's six – it was located at the rear of North Sister to cover the flank of his own men on Longdon, and did not cover the north-western slope up which 45 Commando later attacked. During Jofre's only visit to the sector, enlivened by the loss first of his own jeep and then a commandeered Landrover to water-filled shell-holes in the track running alongside Moody Brook, he did not go beyond RIM 6/B's positions, even though Cordón's command post was only a short extra distance away. It was ruinously small-minded of him to sacrifice RI 4 as he did, as it was to waste Seineldín's RI 25, also an orphan from its own brigade, on the airport peninsula. RI 25 should have been replaced by one of Jofre's own vehicle-bound regiments and entrusted with the Two Sisters, from where it could have contested the no man's land, including the crucial Murrell Bridge. Such a deployment would have had the added merit of permitting RI 4 to concentrate entirely around Harriet.

Instead, the only infantry support for RI 4 came from Daher's Comandos, who made several forays but could not exert the continuous pressure the task required. The Murrell Bridge itself is out of line of sight from the Two Sisters: but the terrain on either side of it is not, and when the men of D Company, 3 Para set up a forward patrol base in a position overlooking the bridge from the north, they were careful to move only in darkness or under the cover of a persistent mist, which cloaked the area for several days. On 5 June it cleared and Argentine observers on North Sister were astonished to see two Bandwagons setting up mortars near the bridge: presumably newly-arrived 45 Commando, venturing unknowingly into D Company's area of operations. Captain López Patterson, Cordón's 2 i/c, ordered his mortars and heavy machine-guns to fire at the Bandwagons, followed by an artillery barrage that landed long and stirred up 'an ants' nest' on the hill beyond, where the Paras were holed up. At dawn on 6 June Castagneta led a combined Comando 601/Gendarmería Special Forces fighting patrol into the area and two D Company patrols, relaxing after a night recce of Longdon, were forced to flee, leaving their rucksacks behind. Among the items that fell into Argentine hands, according to signals intelligence specialist Lieutenant Raúl Esteban, was a folder of communications procedures and code names that permitted them to track British units by their call signs and in some cases to predict their movements during the last days of the war.[*]

A more successful 45 Commando excursion brought the war to the doorstep of RI 4/C/3, a platoon of S/C 63s led by newly-hatched Sub-Lieutenant Llambías, under the wing of experienced Platoon Sergeant Valdéz (although with four newly-promoted lance corporals as section leaders). For a while, Llambías's platoon was the sole defence force on South Sister,

---

[*] Not as damaging as it might have been: Jofre's memoirs consistently fail to differentiate among casualty evacuation helicopters and those carrying troops or supplies, leading to a serious misreading of British intentions.

the foremost bastion of the Argentine line. During the night of 5–6 June an eight-man patrol of 59 Independent Commando Squadron Sappers under Sergeant Halkett, and Marines from 45 Commando Recce Troop led by Lieutenant Fox, set up an observation post in a string of boulders running downhill from South Sister towards the Murrell river. The next evening, Llambías and twelve of his men escorted a party of their own Marine Sappers to plant mines in a vulnerable area between two stone runs immediately in front of his position. They had the misfortune to pass close to Fox's men, who waited until the Argentines were well past them and out in the open before opening fire, killing five and wounding another six. S/C 62 Eduardo González was awarded the MVC for being the first to realize that it was not a blue-on-blue and returning fire, hitting Fox in the hand, after which both patrols called in artillery support and withdrew.

45 Commando continued to probe the Two Sisters, claiming kills that Argentine sources do not confirm, but building up an accurate picture of the defences and discouraging RI 4 from posting pickets. Unfortunately, during the night of 9 June the bill for the battalion's aggressive patrolling came due. A mortar section led by Sergeant Leeming, sent to identify a suitable firing position on a hill in front of the main slope of Kent, departed from its authorized area of operations without informing the Ops Officer and bivouacked near the base of the feature. An X Company patrol spotted them from above and radioed for clearance to attack, which being given they opened fire, killing Leeming, two corporals and a Marine, and wounding five others.* A week earlier Sergeant Hunt of the SBS was killed in a similar clash with an SAS patrol near Long Island and it seemed most improbable that two such highly experienced SNCOs could have made elementary errors of map reading and procedure. When the MoD refused to confirm the incidents even after they had become common knowledge, suspicion arose that the maps issued to Leeming and Hunt were incorrectly gridded. The pretence that the cover-up was 'to spare the relatives' feelings', when in fact it kept the wounds raw, lends credibility to the theory.

On 8 June Sub-Lieutenant Silva's RI 4/A/2 was withdrawn to Stanley by helicopter from Twelve O'Clock Mount, and Jofre was deeply impressed by Silva's evident fighting spirit and the proud state of the platoon after a

---

* Leeming, Cpl Uren and Marine Phillips are buried at San Carlos.

month on isolated outpost duty. Thanks to its long exposure on distant locations RI 4 suffered more non-combat casualties than any other regiment, but Silva did not lose a man. Although he was only one year senior, his arrival next day at South Sister was enormously heartening to Llambías, beset by prowling wolves. In addition to the ambush of 6 June there had been a clash with enemy forces on the far side of Goat Ridge on 8 June, and during the night of 8–9 June Comando 602 had fought an engagement directly across the valley (see next chapter). These incidents suggested the enemy might attack from the direction of the Murrell River headwaters, skirting the large minefield across the front of Harriet and Goat Ridge. Accordingly, within hours of Silva's arrival, the two young officers led out a combined patrol to plant mines and booby traps in a stone run that any such attack would cross. The excursion was a boost for morale and Silva was also careful to strengthen Llambías's confidence and authority by working through him to reconfigure the defensive layout for better line of sight and protection from artillery fire. The 'Silva effect' can be gauged by its lack in Sub-Lieutenant Nazer's RI 4/A/1, flown directly from Beagle Ridge on 31 May and posted on the forward slope of the saddle between the Two Sisters, which abandoned its exposed positions as soon as battle began.

The Two Sisters are almost surrounded by stone runs, ankle-twisting obstacles even by day and virtually impassable by night, and defensive positions on North Sister were set up to cover the gaps between them. RI 4/C/1 under Sub-Lieutenant Pérez Grandi was dug in around the western end and RI 4/C/2 under Sub-Lieutenant Mosquera was deployed along the northern face of the summit ridge, with Cordón's HQ in a gap between it and the secondary ridge running down to the positions held by RIM 6/B. Dead ground in a gap between two stone runs about 1,000 yards in front of Pérez Grandi's platoon was mined and the remaining corridor was a registered artillery defensive fire point. RI 4/C had a Rasit but it failed to pick up the assault. Llambías believed this was because of British electronic counter-measures, but a visit to the hill forcibly suggests another explanation: North Sister is the most wind-scoured of all the battle hills and the west–east run of the ridge seems to magnify it. I – no lightweight – was nearly knocked down several times when struggling along the north face. A parabolic antenna would have become airborne in short order, and the mind boggles to contemplate what it must be like up there when the katabatic gales blow down from Kent. I never felt more sorry for the Argentines than I did on that God-awful hill.

Things were not much better on the British side of the valley. The location of 45 Commando's bivouac between Kent and Bluff Cove Peak will always particularly spring to mind whenever I hear the term 'blasted heath', and the Marines got there after marching the longer route across East Falkland with less vehicular support than 3 Para. Despite this, 45 Commando had only twenty-three non-combat casualties, three more than 3 Para and only one more than 42 Commando, which came by helicopter. Captain Gardiner of X Company recalled that 'we refined our methods of living in this inhospitable place to such a degree that by the end, we were like wild animals and almost preferred it outdoors . . . We could have gone on forever.' Not really. They may have been the toughest men on earth, but bone-weariness and unrelenting, bitter cold took its toll. Slow reactions and errors of judgement were inevitable and affected how the battle was fought over the largest and tallest of all the battalion objectives.

The plan devised by Lieutenant Colonel Whitehead, CO of 45 Commando, began with a silent advance by X Company – which had done most of the patrolling in the days before – to take South Sister ('Long Toenail'), by now known to be aggressively defended. Accompanying X Company, the Milan and SFMG Troops would then set up a fire support base at the summit to rake lower-lying North Sister ('Summer Days'). The battalion had lost its Milan posts in the Ajax bombing of 27 May, and its Anti-Tank Troop was now equipped with GPMGs. To recover lost firepower, Whitehead borrowed 40 Commando's Milan Troop, which went forward with six posts and forty missiles. Once the fire support base was established and the enemy's attention firmly fixed on South Sister, Y and Z Companies would climb the northwestern slope from Murrell Bridge ('Pub Garden') to assault North Sister, against what was expected, by then, to be thoroughly disorganized opposition.

From Murrell bridge to the western end of Tumbledown, via North Sister, is a distance of over 4 miles, with the little matters of a thousandfoot hill and one of the soggier valleys on the Falklands to be negotiated on the way. I doubt if Thompson really believed it could all be done in one night: but Whitehead did, and his plan was designed to achieve a rapid

TWO SISTERS

ARGENTINE

4th Infantry Regiment (RI 4)

OC Sector – Maj Cordón (2i/c RI 4)

Sector 2i/c – Capt López Patterson (Ops RI 4)

Artillery Liaison – Lt Tagle

C Coy – Capt Maxpegán

  1 Platoon – Sub-Lt Mosquera

  2 Platoon – Sub-Lt Pérez Grandi

  3 Platoon – Sub-Lt Llambías/SSgt Valdéz

  Support Platoon – 2Lt Martella/SSgt Chiecher

  3 x HMG, 4 x 81mm/3.1-inch mortars)

A Coy (OC on Mount Low)

  1 Platoon – Sub-Lt Nazer

  2 Platoon – Sub-Lt Silva

10th Engineering Coy (Eng 10)

  Section – Cpl Pacheco

6th Mechanised Infantry Regiment (RIM 6)

OC Sector – Maj Jaimet (Ops RIM 6)

B Coy – Lt Abella

  2 Platoon – Sub-Lt Franco

  Support Platoon

  (105 RCL, 2 x HMG, 4 x 81mm/3.1-inch mortars)

Artillery support

C Battery, GA 3

(8 x 105mm at Moody Brook)

BRITISH

45 Commando Royal Marines (45 Cdo)

CO – Lt Col Whitehead, RSM Chapman

Intel – Capt Passmore, Ops – Capt Nichols

X Coy (+) – Capt Gardiner/CSM Bell (150 men)

Forward Observer – Capt Goodfellow

  1 Troop – Lt Kelly/Sgt Jolly

  2 Troop – Lt Caroe/Sgt Matthews

  3 Troop – Lt Stewart/Sgt McMillan

  40 Commando Anti-Tank Platoon (6 x Milan)

Y Coy – Maj Davis/CSM Meachin

  4 Troop – Lt Duck?

  5 Troop – Lt Dunning (W)/Sgt Davidson

  6 Troop – Lt Davies (W)/Sgt Gracie

Z Coy – Capt Cole

  Forward Observer – Lt Baxter

  7 Troop – 2Lt Mansell

  8 Troop – Lt Dytor

  9 Troop –

Support Coy –

  Recce Troop – Lt Fox

  Mortar Troop –

59 Ind. Commando Squadron RE

  Condor Troop –

Artillery support

8 Battery, 29 Commando Regt RA (6 x 105mm)

  Battery Commander – Maj Akhurst

HMS *Glamorgan* (2 x 4.5-inch)

  Naval Gunfire Observer - Capt Brown

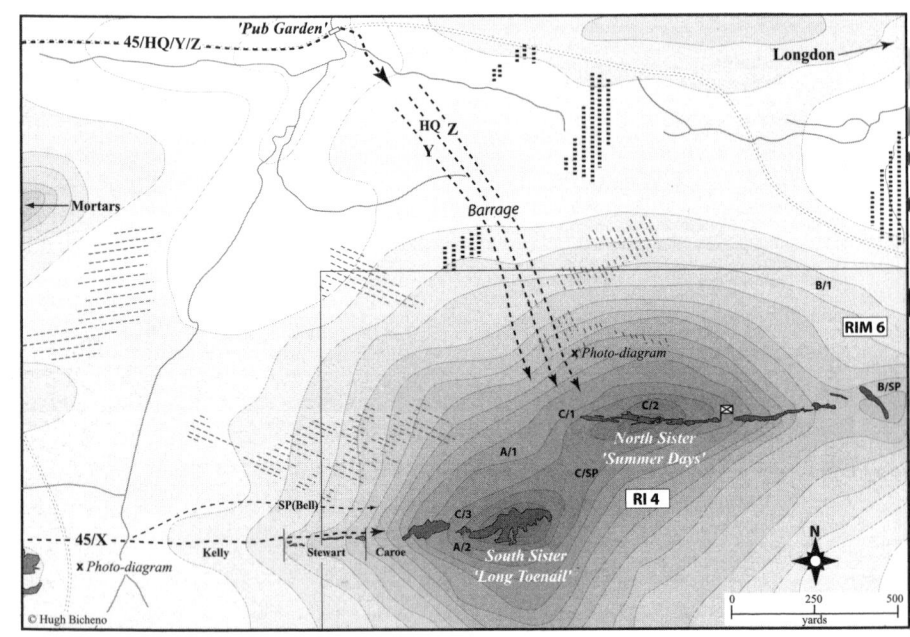

Map 27: TWO SISTERS

Legend:
- Quartzite ridge
- Scattered rocks
- Stone run
- Minefield

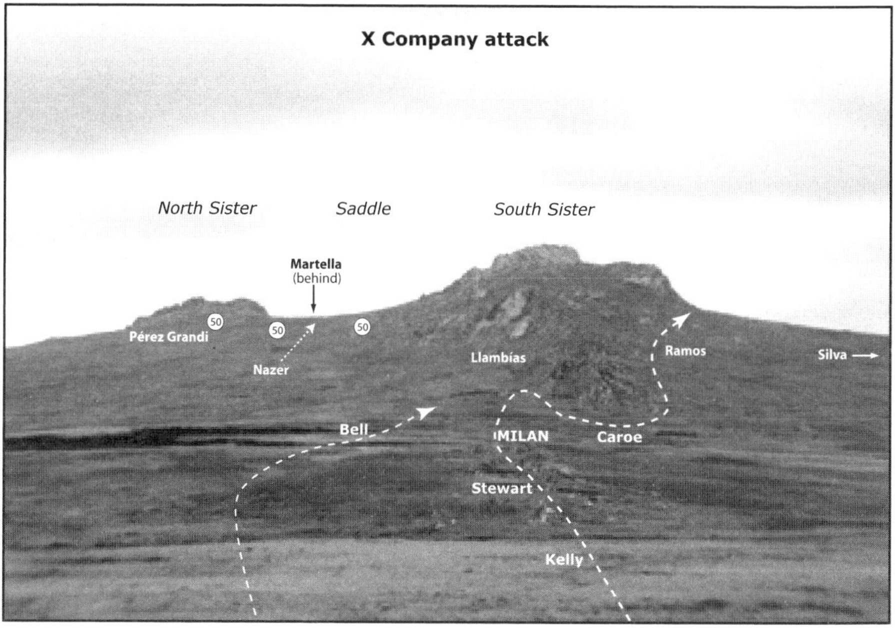

X Company attack

North Sister Saddle South Sister

Martella (behind)

Pérez Grandi 50 50 50

Nazer

Llambías

Ramos

Silva →

Bell

MILAN Caroe

Stewart

Kelly

Photo Diagram 27: TWO SISTERS

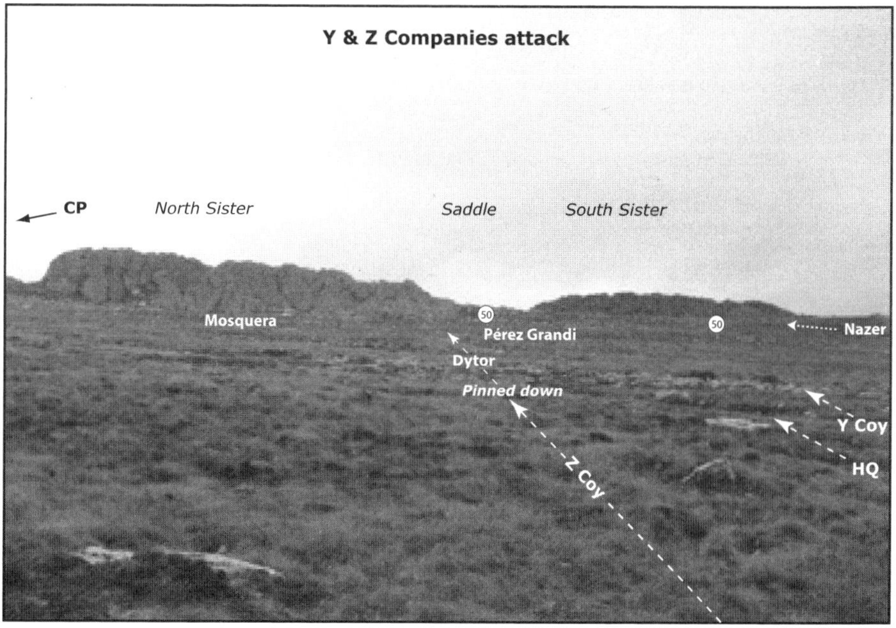

Y & Z Companies attack

← CP North Sister Saddle South Sister

Mosquera

50

Pérez Grandi

Dytor

Pinned down

Z Coy

50

Nazer

Y Coy

HQ

breakthrough at the Sisters so that Y and Z Companies would be relatively fresh and able to attack towards Tumbledown without delay.

Unfortunately friction intervened. X Company's Gardiner had not antici- pated how much the heavily burdened Milan Troop would slow him down, and although the route skirted the worst stone runs on the flanks of Kent, there was no way to avoid them all. The group was scheduled to reach the start point on the Murrell River at 2100 but arrived over two hours late after a six-hour march. Gardiner finally felt obliged to break radio silence to inform Whitehead of the delay, and was told: 'Carry on as planned. I will do nothing until I hear from you.' In fact he did a great deal, rethinking the attack scheme as he moved forward with Y and Z Companies to make it a simultaneous advance by all three companies. At the same time Whitehead worked out a new fire plan with Major Akhurst, the Battery Commander, and Captain Brown, the Naval Gunfire Observer, so that the attack could proceed with or without the fire support base on Long Toenail. Whitehead took the artillery observers with him, almost level with the leading sections of the rifle companies (Akhurst recalls treading in his footsteps like King Wenceslas' page for fear of mines), to provide rapid and accurate artillery suppression of any resistance they might encounter.

It will be recalled that 45 Commando's attack was supposed to prevent RIM 6/B attacking across the valley into the flank of 3 Para. The firing on North Sister did not start until after 2330, more than two and a half hours after things got noisy on Longdon, and throughout that time Jaimet acted as the forward observer for the Argentine artillery, requested to do so by Jofre after Ramos was killed. In addition, although RIM 6/B's 105mm rocket launcher malfunctioned, its well-bedded mortars at the eastern end of North Sister were in action against 3 Para from the start, possibly causing some of the casualties that brought Shaw's platoon to a halt. However RIM 6/B's two infantry platoons, perfectly placed to attack 3 Para from the flank, did not move. It cannot have been because of the unmarked minefields, for they were right among them and must have known exactly where they were. The finger points at Jofre for not giving Jaimet explicit orders to attack or at least to make a strong feint, perhaps reflecting his training in US infantry doctrine, which was highly 'positionist' for much of that nation's history.*

---

* The doctrine not formally buried until the 1982 Field Manual 100-5 set out the concept of AirLand battle.

Whatever the reasons, Jaimet failed to seize an opportunity to launch a counter-attack with a clear chance of inflicting a severe reverse on the British.

The second part of Thompson's operational three-card trick went forward as planned and was gratifyingly successful in drawing the defenders' attention. To anticipate the next chapter, 42 Commando's attack on Harriet kicked off with a noisy demonstration from the west that drew, to use the technical term, a shit-rain of defensive fire. As it affects the Two Sisters it caused 2nd Lieutenant Martella of Support Platoon to expend much of his ready-use ammunition on the long-awaited British attack, coming from the anticipated direction. Likewise convinced, Silva left South Sister with half his platoon to take up a position flanking the line of attack he had mined and booby-trapped two days earlier, leaving Llambías with about forty-five infantry and a small section of Sappers to face Gardiner's 150. With the Two Sisters defenders now looking south, X Company advanced across a gentle slope in the bright moonlight with Lieutenant Kelly's platoon leading until the pre-ridge line of boulders. Out to the left was a specially formed Support section under Company Sergeant-Major Bell with 66s and Bren guns (LMG) converted to fire 7.62mm ammunition. Lieutenant Stewart's platoon took over the advance until the end of the pre-ridge rocks, when it came under MAG fire from halfway up the hill now towering above them. Lieutenant Caroe's platoon therefore took over at the crucial moment and charged to cover in the lee of the quartzite arrowhead that forms the first substantial part of South Sister.

Caroe and his men had the great good fortune that Llambías's attention was drawn away by an outbreak of gunfire to his right rear, as Pérez Grandi's platoon and the .50-calibre machine-guns along the front of the saddle opened fire on Z Company, leading the main advance from the north-west. Generals as diverse as Napoleon and Montgomery have proclaimed the primacy of luck in battle, and by that token – were it not for the earlier blue-on-blue – MoD should have established a breeding programme for 45 Commando, because the fortuitous timing of their broken attack scheme could not have worked better. Whitehead, Y and Z Coys got across the Murrell Bridge just before a salvo from the Argentine 155mm guns bracketed it. Then, as they paused at the start line waiting to hear that X Company was in action, a 105mm artillery barrage crashed down 400 yards ahead of them at the point where, had they gone forward immediately, they would have been bunched together skirting a minefield between two stone runs. They advanced to the point where the defenders in the saddle were sky-lined and then went to ground because Whitehead now decided to revert to his original plan and wait for X Company to set up the fire support base. They were lying down, therefore, when Pérez Grandi sent forward a section under Acting Lance Corporal Gómez, who fired a flare that bounced through Z Company and was the first man to die. A sheet of gunfire from Pérez Grandi's platoon and the heavy machine-guns along the saddle ripped close over the heads of the recumbent Marines, and then Whitehead called in the artillery.

Although Wireless Ridge and the saddle between Tumbledown and William are also still heavily scarred, even after more than twenty years the beaten zone between the Two Sisters bears the most eloquent witness to the awesome power of the British artillery, which fired 1,500 shells at the Two Sisters that night.* The still-churned area occupied by Nazer's platoon in particular leaves one in no doubt why they decamped immediately, while the saddle itself is dimpled with craters, testimony to the tenacity of Martella's HMGs and mortars. They were also praised by Company Sergeant-Major Meachin of Y Company, irked by post-war reports that the battle was a walkover:

> We came under lots of effective fire from 50-calibre machine-guns . . . At the same time, mortars were coming down all over us, but the main threat was from those machine-gunners who could see us in the open because of the moonlight. There were three machine-guns and we brought down constant and effective salvoes of our own artillery fire on to them directly, fifteen rounds at a time. There would be a pause, and they'd come back at us again. So we had to do it a second time, all over their positions. There'd be a pause, then boom, boom, boom, they'd come back at us again. Conscripts don't do this, babies don't do this, men who are badly led and of low morale don't do this. They were good steadfast troops. I rate them.

One of the HMGs was placed to support Llambías on South Sister and in conjunction with his two MAGs drove Caroe's men back from the north

---

* Although the larger craters were made by defensive fire from the Argentine 155s after the hills were taken.

flank of the arrowhead. They eventually worked their way around the south side, held by the rump of Silva's platoon and one of Llambías's sections under Lance Corporal Ramos. The Milans were set up at the end of the pre-ridge boulders and in conjunction with Bell's group blasted Llambías himself out of his position on the northern side, where until the end he tried to support his comrades on North Sister. Several of his men suffered burst weapons from firing rifle grenades in support of Pérez Grandi's platoon but now, his helmet dented by rock debris from a Milan explosion, with two men killed and several wounded (including one who died after repatriation) Llambías fell back. Seven men followed him around the north face of the summit formation along a route that took them through the beaten zone, the rest dropped out to await an opportunity to surrender safely. Llambías had evidently paid close attention to his recent academy lessons on directing artillery fire: as he had when ambushed on 6 June, he was able to call in a timely and accurate barrage to cover his retreat. The forward Argentine batteries were by now committed to the battles on Longdon and Harriet, but South Sister was – just – within range of the two GAA 4 batteries on the Racecourse. 45 Commando's lucky star never shone brighter than when the GAA 4's first twelve-gun salvo landed on South Sister, where the Marines were already in good cover among the rocks, and not on the slope in front of North Sister, where Y and Z Coys were pinned down in the open.

Only one member of the half-platoon left by Silva to hold the southern flank of South Sister escaped: the survivor was S/C 63 Pérez, who brought with him a Marine beret and a British rifle and told a tale of being taken prisoner and then shooting his guard with a pistol Silva had given him. If true, the incident would have illustrated why it is not advisable to take prisoners during an assault. However, although the trophies did at least prove that Pérez made his way back from behind the British line, alas for his gilded lily the sole X Company casualty was wounded by shrapnel, not a bullet.

Silva himself stuck it out in his hastily-occupied flanking position between South Sister and Goat Ridge until he saw that the British had taken Harriet on his left, and South Sister on his right. He then led his men back towards the saddle between the Sisters, encountering Llambías on the way. Caught between the enemy and a large stone run, and knowing there were unmarked minefields in the valley beyond, there would have been no dishonour in surrendering. Instead Silva led the combined group east in single file, in effect mine-clearing with his feet. Four of his men were to be killed with him on Tumbledown two nights later. Llambías's group went to Sapper Hill and took part in the last fighting of the war.

South Sister fell at about 0120, and Major Cordón's command post on North Sister about half an hour later. His landlines did not survive the British bombardment and he played no role in the battle, for which he was cashiered after the war. What probably sank him was the contrast between his inaction and the dynamic performance of his 2 i/c, Captain López Patterson, who had been acting like the commanding officer ever since they moved to the Sisters. He continued to do so during the battle, joining Martella in the saddle and directing the mortars in support of Harriet until Pérez Grandi's platoon and the .50-calibres opened up on Z Company. He then ordered the mortars turned around and they inflicted most of the British casualties, killing Corporal Spencer and Marine MacPherson of Z Company, Sapper Jones of 59 Independent Commando Squadron and wounding, among others, two Y Company platoon commanders, Lieutenants Dunning and Davies. As we saw, most of the small arms fire from Pérez Grandi's platoon went over the heads of the attackers but one burst killed the popular Marine 'Blue' Nowak of Y Company, in whose memory the company flag bears a small blue square in the corner to this day.

Lieutenant Dytor's 8 Troop was in the lead and once again good fortune blessed 45 Commando, because their return fire seriously wounded Mosquera, whose platoon was sheltered from artillery and placed to fire into Z Company's flank. Carrying their officer with them, his men pulled out and retreated to Cordón's command post. Had they remained, Dytor's MC, Corporal Burdett's DCM and Corporal Hunt's MM might well have been posthumous.* Dytor stood up and, calling on his men to follow, charged up the slope into the flank of Pérez Grandi's position, shouting 'Zulu, Zulu!'. 'Get down you silly cunt!' and similar sentiments greeted the initiative, but the corporals and platoon sergeant literally kick-started the men up the hill and, faced with a horde of screaming demons firing from the hip, Pérez Grandi's platoon fled without inflicting a single further casualty.

---

* There are few clearly identifiable sangars on North Sister, but one of them is a machine-gun post at the base of the summit ridge, where it was ideally placed to enfilade 8 Troop's charge.

The saddle to which they retreated was no place to stay because now, in addition to the hellish bombardment, X Company had set up GPMGs on Long Toenail and 45 Commando's Mortar Platoon had overcome the problem of self-burying tubes that had so far kept it out of the battle. Martella, his mortars now silent for lack of ammunition, was killed as he tried to counter-attack towards South Sister, while a bomb that dropped among Nazer's platoon crippled him, wounded several others and completed the demoralization of the rest. López Patterson led four NCOs and forty-five conscripts (fifteen without weapons) away from the saddle. Looking back, he saw it swarming with what he estimated to be 400–500 enemy troops. He says he fired a Parthian burst at what he thought was an 'O' group of officers, but if so 45 Commando's luck held once more and he missed.

His target may have been Whitehead, ordering Dytor's platoon to continue along the ridge. The adrenalized men raced along the ridge, carrying a captured .50 calibre, to trap the hapless Cordón, his HQ section and Mosquera's men. The command post was the limit of Z Company's objective but when Y Company, moving below and parallel, came under fire from a MAG at the eastern end of the last section of the ridge, Dytor set up a fire base and was about to engage the new target until stopped by Whitehead, concerned that it had the makings of an epic blue-on-blue.

Lest my comments on the good luck enjoyed by 45 Commando be thought to detract from Whitehead's outstanding battle management, good luck comes to those who have made themselves worthy of it. One of his Italian subordinates said of another 'from the front' commander: 'Rommel is always calmness itself; with bullets and shrapnel flying all over the place and mowing people down all around him, he never gets hit. He just puts things right.' BBC reporter Robert Fox wrote much the same: 'Over the radio we could hear Colonel Whitehead's voice speaking to his company commanders in turn. It was a remarkable performance, cool, never ruffled, always giving the impression that he and his men had plenty of time for what they had to do.'

The eastern end of North Sister was held by RIM 6/B's Support Platoon with two MAGs, one of them manned by S/C 62 Poltronieri. He was the only conscript to be awarded the CHVC during the conflict for staying behind to fight a rearguard action while the rest of the company retreated down

Moody Brook valley. But why was it down to the heroism of a single angry conscript to perform this vital function? Some accounts allege that the mortars in this position caused 45 Commando's casualties, but Jofre's notes make it clear that Jaimet did not know what was going on until RIM 4/C refugees began streaming down the hill. As the intermediate sector commander he should have been in permanent contact with North Sister and Longdon, and once given permission to retreat he should have mounted a formal rearguard action. He did neither and would have lost his company if 45 Commando had pursued. Jaimet won a reputation for daring when fighting guerrillas in the wooded mountains of Tucumán, but as he was to show again on Tumbledown, he was not prepared to take the initiative on the bare hills of East Falkland. With a few exceptions like López Patterson, the contrast in the line regiments between those of middle and senior rank and young sub-lieutenants like Peluffo, Silva and Llambías damns the Argentine Army as a stultifying institution, no more capable of nurturing good quality in its ranks than it was in the country at large.

Jofre stated that he was not informed – by Jaimet – that Two Sisters had fallen until 0445, at which point he ordered GA 3 (presumably C Battery, the rest were out of range) to open fire on the north-western front of the feature. The British record heavy artillery fire on North Sister from about 0230, a quarter of an hour after 45 Commando radioed *Glamorgan* to report the capture of the eastern end of North Sister and to thank her for superbly accurate and timely naval gunfire. She was shortly to pay for remaining on the gun-line over an hour longer than scheduled, because in an effort to make up time and get back to the Task Force before dawn she cut the corner of the signalled Exocet 'box' (although in reality well within range of the missile battery on Hooker's Point – see **Diagram 4**, p. 109) and took a hit in her hangar. More stoutly built than the Type 42s she survived, but thirteen men died including Lieutenant Tinker, whose plaintive letters home became a banner for anti-Thatcherites when his parents published them in 1983. One wonders why they did – he was a volunteer, and whatever his private doubts he died doing the job he was trained to do, as did the unpublished thousands who wrote home expressing pride in their cause and their work.

There was one last minor skirmish on North Sister, when the leading elements of Y Company attacked an isolated four-man position held by men of Sub-Lieutenant Franco's RIM 6/B/2 (apparently unaware that the rest of their company had retreated), killing one man and capturing the others. RIM 4/C and RIM 4/A lost nine men killed and about 100 surrendered, half of them wounded, against British losses of four killed and ten wounded. 45 Commando was in fine fettle and at 0430 Whitehead radioed Thompson that he was ready to advance on Tumbledown. To his chagrin he was told to go firm on the Sisters.

I do not find the reasons Thompson gives for this in *No Picnic* convincing. The Argentines were on the run and all of military history supports the view that a hot pursuit will break an enemy more conclusively than any other act of war. I think it probable the rapid success of 45 Commando confronted Thompson with a political dilemma he had not thought through beforehand. The Marines had done well, but 3 Para was still hung up on the western slope of Longdon with its leading company shattered, and waiting in the wings were the Guards, whose contribution to the war had so far been redeemed from farce only by tragedy. If he ordered hot pursuit and the enemy collapsed without the Army being seen to play an equal role, inter-service vindictiveness would erupt. Any such confrontation might have led to the Marines being disowned by the blue water purists of the Navy, always looking for an opportunity to shed the ugly duckling amphibious capability. Better to play it safe and spare his beloved green berets not only further loss at the hands of the enemy, but also the risk of total destruction in an institutional crossfire.

13 Harriet

IF 45 COMMANDO's capture of the Two Sisters is an outstanding example of how a battalion commander can redeem a broken scheme on the hoof, the assault on Harriet by Lieutenant Colonel Vaux's 42 Commando illustrates the no less rare phenomenon of a battle plan that not only triumphantly survived contact with the enemy, but also overcame egregious political interference. Harriet will always bring to mind the musical creak of my prosthetic hips as I scaled the extremely steep slope up which K Company advanced. Also my growing surprise that even with the freedom to walk all around it in daylight, and able to view the feature from the other Stanley hills (albeit cursing my lack of an adequately wide-angle lens), I was still unable to capture the deceptive topography of a ridge where the helical, north-leaning quartzite spine in places barely shows above the soil and in others towers above it.*
Vaux's scheme took the fullest advantage of the terrain, an astonishing achievement when he only had the deeply misleading Ordnance Survey map and reports from night recce patrols to work with – because the aerial photographs Harrier pilots risked their lives to obtain never reached the hands of those who needed them most. I know of no battlefield where the intuitive element of great combat command is better illustrated.

Even with aerial photographs to hand, Harriet is difficult to decipher. The crest consists of two long rock commas divided by a narrow saddle of

---

* Thus **Photo Diagram** 28, the least bad of a dozen unsatisfactory efforts to capture the sweep of the hill.

248

peat. A large quartzite block descends from the saddle to the south-east, today crowned by the more accessible of two 42 Commando memorial crosses (see **Map 28**, p. 256). The other cross is on the prominent summit of the whole hill, which juts above the western ridge. The slopes are uniform and gentle in the quadrant from Goat Ridge to the valley between Harriet and Wall Mountain, but the entire southern front is steep, tending to concave and littered with boulders, particularly at the eastern end, where the rock fall is extremely dense. The southern face of the western comma consists of two sloping cliff faces separated by another peat saddle. These not only provided cover from naval bombardment but also seem to squeeze the soil on the other side, making it unusually well drained. The reverse occurs on the north-eastern face, where the ground at the foot of an unbroken, sheer drop – ideally the place where a defender would shelter his mortars and support elements – is uninhabitably boggy. The slope rises to abolish the precipice at the point where the eastern comma doglegs and divides to create three large sheltered bowls, undetectable from ground level and immune from anything except steeply plunging fire, with good line of sight in all directions save to the south-west, where the summit crag blocks the view.

Defending the hill was a heterogeneous force of about 400 men under the command of Lieutenant Colonel Soria, CO of RI 4. His HQ Company had occupied Harriet since mid-April, with B Company under Lieutenant Arroyo holding Wall. During the hurried redeployment at the end of May (see **Diagram 6**, p. 232), Soria was reinforced by Lieutenant Gorriti and the forty men of Sub-Lieutenant Mosterín's RI 12 platoon, left behind on Kent when Combat Group Solari made its ill-fated sortie to Goose Green. Parada also sent him the guard force from his own III Brigade HQ, about 100 men under Lieutenant García. RI 4's Recce Platoon under Sub-Lieutenant Passoli was reinforced by a section under Sub-Lieutenant Samyn from an RI 1 company that was fed into the Falklands a section at a time in early June. Soria assigned the western slope to Arroyo, who placed his two rifle companies under Sub-Lieutenants Giménez Corvalán and Bruny above stone runs and covering a large minefield on the far side of the valley. The Support Platoon under 2nd Lieutenant Monetti was placed behind Bruny and, like him, was sheltered from the sea by the ridge. The reinforced HQ Company under García covered the southern front, with a Rifle Platoon under 2nd Lieutenant Oliva placed to enfilade any advance up the south-western slope, and by Passoli's platoon 200 yards further east. Both were dug in about a third of the way down the hill, with good lines of grazing fire.

Arroyo's command post was in the saddle and García's just below it, both within 50 yards of Soria's own HQ and Communications sections in the summit bowls, which include a naturally formed mortar pit where I believe he had a couple of 60mm mortars to fire illumination rounds at his direct command. Multiple strands of telephone wire all over the hill testify to a mistaken choice, here as on the Sisters, of redundant over buried lines. To the rear, Gorriti's men covered the path and also provided porterage up from the road to Stanley used by Logistics Captain Farinella, a first-class scrounger, thanks to whom the men on Harriet never lacked. Next to Logistics were Sub-Lieutenant Juárez's four 120mm mortars set up to fire towards the isthmus between Port Harriet and North Basin (see **Map 26**, p. 229), two of which are still there rusting in unimpressive sangars (the emplacements abandoned on Wall were far superior).

42 COMMANDO WAS ALSO something of a mix-and-match battalion. At almost the last moment before embarkation M Company was taken away and flown to Ascension as the main component of the land force for the recovery of South Georgia, with Vaux's 2i/c Major Sheridan in overall command.* On *Canberra* it dawned on Vaux that his truncated battalion was likely to be assigned guard duty at the beachhead and he asked Captain Norman, the commander of the garrison that surrendered in Stanley on 2 April, to form a replacement company. Repatriated and now a reluctant Press Officer, Norman jumped at the opportunity to form J Company around a core of NP 8901 men, supplemented by cooks, clerks and mechanics. Within forty-eight hours he had nearly 100 men with the rank structure for a rifle company, subsequently supplemented by an artfully redesignated Milan Troop and equipped by semi-voluntary contributions from the replacement stores of shipmates 40 Commando and 3 Para.

Although 42 Commando was carried to the front line by helicopter and was spared the attrition experienced by 3 Para and 45 Commando in their march across East Falkland, the battalion went forward without its sleeping

---

* He rejoined Vaux in early June. M Company went on to recapture Southern Thule in the last operation of the war.

bags and other personal gear. As we have seen, K Company flew forward on 30 May to consolidate British control of Mount Kent, with Vaux's HQ and the Blowpipe Troop in the second wave. L Company followed on the 31st and marched straight to Mount Challenger from Bluff Cove Peak, followed in due course by K Company. They were joined on 2–3 June by J Company, flown in from Goose Green where it had earlier relieved 2 Para of prisoner-guarding duties. Vaux set up his new HQ mid-way between Kent and Challenger.

In the days following the capture of Kent, the arrival of 5 Army Brigade drained off helicopter assets and priority for the rest was to bring forward artillery and ammunition. It was not until a single Bandwagon struggled up from Teal Inlet on 2 June with the precious sleeping bags that the battalion was able to get proper rest. I did not visit 42 Commando's bivouac area because I was told it was a dire place, shunned even by sheep, and until the sleeping bags arrived most of the men were compelled to keep moving or huddle together for warmth in the bunkers abandoned by RI 4/C on Challenger. As the detachment of M Company to South Georgia showed, 42 Commando was regarded as the battalion best able to cope with extreme conditions: but even so it was pushed to the limit. As with 3 Para and 45 Commando, it was not so much physical exertion and exposure that wore them down, rather the morale-corroding knowledge that they were unnecessarily held back on the unforgiving heights.

In his vivid memoir *March to the South Atlantic,* Vaux comments that the Argentines committed a cardinal error in abandoning Wall, making him the gift of a vantage point from which to observe their deployment – and of a feature he was able to use to conceal his own movements from them. The Argentines did so because it was at the extreme range even of the closest battery, the BIM 5 howitzers behind Tumbledown (see **Diagram 3**, p. 108). The pattern of large minefields laid around Harriet before the San Carlos landing argues that they never intended to hold Wall, even if the British landed as expected on the southern coast of the Stanley peninsula. This was a strange decision, because the only stretch of surfaced road outside Stanley and immediate environs ran close to the southern face of Wall, making it an outpost they could have sustained relatively easily with wheeled transport. They could also have used the road to run two or three guns to a forward firing position, perhaps next to Harriet, as GA 3/C did to the north along the far less welcoming track to Longdon. The abandonment of Wall and with it the initiative on the southern flank is perhaps the most striking of the opportunities to delay the British that were wasted as a result of rigidly adhering to positionist doctrine.

An illustration of how it might have been otherwise came on 2 June, when two teams of forward artillery and forward air controllers, escorted by the 42 Commando Recce Troop led by Lieutenant Mawhood, got into serious trouble. After gratuitously drawing attention to themselves by shooting at an RI 4 patrol on the other side of the valley, Mawhood's men were shocked when Rico's Comando 602 rushed to Wall from Stanley in trucks, and began to climb the slope towards the saddle between Wall and Challenger. The Marines and the fire control teams retreated precipitately, leaving behind their rucksacks, sleeping bags and other equipment. Among the kit abandoned was one of two laser designators shipped to the islands to guide the 'smart bombs' that the Harriers began to drop – again, courtesy of Caspar Weinberger – towards the end of the conflict. The Forward Air Controller destroyed the laser designator before fleeing, but it was a major set-back. Worse was that Recce Troop was forced to leave the heights for Teal Inlet, because by now nobody could survive on Challenger without a sleeping bag. But worst of all was to have lost Wall, which caused Vaux great anxiety until the feature was re-occupied twenty-four hours later.

AFTER A SORTIE ON 5 June was aborted because he could not obtain a map of the minefields in the area, Rico kidnapped Sapper Lieutenant Eito, the officer responsible, and made him walk in front of a preliminary route recce on the 7th, before Comando 602 returned to the charge during the night of 8–9 June. Rico's plan was to attack enemy communications between Kent and Challenger,* but he was ambushed by an SAS patrol and Staff Sergeant Cisneros was killed in the first exchange (see **Map 26**, p. 229). During the skirmish that followed Rico recalled the combatants shouting increasingly colourful abuse at each other, in English: 'After each insult there were guffaws from one side or the other. We were about 40 or 50 metres apart.' His interdiction plan no longer viable, he called in artillery and retreated, but later regretted having done so: 'There is no next time. Every

* Although Rico did not know it, if the infiltration had succeeded he would have found Vaux's HQ.

battle is the last. And every soldier in combat should act as though it were the last. Because you never know if there will be another.'

Not surprisingly, Rico returned from the war with legendary status among his peers, putting him at the forefront of military unrest about the prosecution of junior officers for Dirty War offences. The process culminated in the *Carapintadas* ('painted faces' from their camouflage cream) barracks revolts of 1987 and 1988 and a blanket amnesty under a law of 'Due Obedience' that reinstated the 'just obeying orders' defence rejected by the Nuremberg War Crimes Tribunal after World War II.

EVEN AS RICO'S COMANDO 602 patrol was working its way around the large minefield in front of Wall, a party from the M&AW Cadre led by Lieutenant Haddow and 45 Commando K/1 led by Lieutenant Townsend crossed the valley in the opposite direction to set up an observation post on Goat Ridge. The mission was of crucial importance because the area between Harriet–Two Sisters and Tumbledown was *terra incognita* to the British planners. Townsend's task was to engage the enemy (Giménez Corvalan's platoon) in the saddle between Harriet and Goat Ridge, while Haddow's group slipped past to the eastern end. In the clash that followed two Argentines were killed, one of them cut in half by a 66. Llambías recalls finding the upper half the next day, noting the peaceful expression on the man's face. Townsend retreated without loss, but that was not how the incident was reported to Soria, who informed Jofre that a company-sized attack had been repulsed with thirty enemy killed. He also ordered Gorriti, commanding the reserve RI 12 platoon, to detach a section to cover the reverse slope of the saddle, which is why Mosterín and fifteen RI 12s were able to escape the debacle on 12–13 June. Meanwhile, Haddow's men set up on Goat Ridge and spent the whole of 9 June gathering operational intelligence, returning to their own lines that night. Thompson, Vaux and Whitehead could now plan in the knowledge that the enemy did not have any significant forces concealed on the reverse slopes of Harriet–Two Sisters.

For a week 42 Commando probed the heavily mined direct route to Harriet, finding a way along the Stanley–Fitzroy track at the expense of Marines Curtis and Patterson, who lost a foot each to anti-personnel mines on 3 and 5 June. On the 7th a four-man patrol led by Sergeant Collins, commanding K/2 Platoon, passed through the minefields and advanced well beyond them before spotting a section of RI 12s led by Corporal Baruzzo, approaching along the road. Collins led the way in a gallop into what proved to be a small pond, nearly drowning when the other members of the patrol piled in on top of him. There ensued an hour-long Mexican stand-off, with neither side anxious to initiate action, after which the Argentines withdrew to Harriet and the frozen Marines squelched back to Wall. Gorriti reported this to Soria as another enemy incursion repelled with heavy losses.

Moore flew to Kent from San Carlos on the 9th with a burden of political complications involving the need to find a role for the Guards in the offensive. Meanwhile the right hand of Wilson's 5 Brigade continued to show complete indifference for what the left hand of 3 Commando Brigade might be doing. The Scots Guards mounted Operation Impunity, a foray by their Recce Platoon to Port Harriet House in search of two howitzers and an Exocet battery that – had they existed – would by now have come to the notice of 42 Commando on Wall. A 'Boys Own Paper' spirit seems to have prevailed, as shown by an excursion in two Kelper-driven Landrovers along the track from Bluff Cove to Port Harriet by the Scots' Ops Officer, Captain Spicer, and HQ Company's Major Bethel, which took them into the middle of a minefield (anti-personnel mines, so they only lost a tyre), from which they gingerly retreated. Finally, when a helicopter went forward to Port Harriet in broad daylight, the defenders on Harriet woke up. 'Impunity' came to a hasty end as a Blowpipe exploded in the ground under the helicopter and then 120mm mortar bombs, followed by a barrage from the BIM 5 Battery, rained down around Port Harriet House. After an Argentine fighting patrol was spotted the Recce Platoon abandoned the observation post and all its kit. The platoon sergeant and two others were wounded during the retreat, which was reported by Soria as the destruction of a company-sized attack with sixty enemy bodies lying in the field. The area is clearly visible with binoculars from the top of Harriet, but the 'bodies' were either sheep, peat torn up by the bombardment, or wishful thinking.

Once again the gods of war showed extreme partiality to the British. The result of this initiative, following the Collins incident the day before and coinciding with the disaster at Fitzroy, convinced Soria and Jofre that they had shattered the long-awaited British attack from the south. The 155s shelled Wall sporadically and on the 11th scored a lucky hit on the Mortar Troop

HARRIET

ARGENTINE

4th Infantry Regiment (RI 4)

CO – Lt Col Soria,   OC Sector – Capt Pécora

Logs – Capt Farinella,   Comms – Capt Frizoli

Artillery Liaison – Capt Fox

III Brigade HQ Coy – Lt García

  Recce Platoon – Sub-Lt Passoli (RI 4)

    RI 1 Section – Sub-Lt Samyn

  120mm/4.7-inch mortars – Sub-Lt Juárez (GA 3)

  Brigade HQ Platoon – 2Lt Oliva

  Reserve Section 1 – Lt Gorriti (R 12)

  Reserve Section 2 – Sub-Lt Mosterín (RI 12)

B Coy – Lt Arroyo

  Forward Observer – Sub-Lt Tedesco

  2 Platoon – Sub-Lt Bruny

  3 Platoon – Sub-Lt Giménez Corvalán

  Support Platoon – 2Lt Monetti

Artillery Support

  BIM 5/Batt (6 x 105mm)

  GA 3/D (2 x 155mm)

  GAA 4 (15 x 105mm)

BRITISH

42 Commando Royal Marines (42 Cdo)

CO – Lt Col Vaux,   RSM Chisnall

2 i/c Maj Sheridan,   Intel – Capt de Jaeger

J Coy – Capt Norman/CSM Cummings

(*replacing M Company in South Georgia*)

  9 (Milan) Troop – Lt Beadon/Sgt Mitchell

  10 Troop – Lt Hornby

  11 (Milan) Troop – Lt Trollope

K Coy – Capt Babbington/CSM Millar ·

  2i/c – Lt Whiteley

  Forward Observer – Capt Romberg RA

  1 Troop – Lt Townsend

  2 Troop – Sgt Collins

  3 Troop – Lt Heathcote

L Coy – Capt Wheen/CSM March

  2i/c Lt Stafford

  Forward Observer – Capt D'Appice RA

  4 Troop – Lt McMillan

  5 Troop – Lt Burnell/Sgt Weston

  6 Troop – Lt Pusey/Sgt McIntyre

Support Coy – Capt Wilson (Adjutant)

  'Porter Troop' – Capt Sturman/Sgt Evans

  Recce Troop – Lt Mawhood

  Mortar Troop – Lt Rafferty/Sgt Rudland

59 Ind. Commando Squadron RE

  2 Troop – Capt Hicks

1st Battalion, Welsh Guards (WG)

  Recce and Milan sections

Artillery support

7 Battery, 29 Commando Regt RA (6 x 105mm)

  Battery Commander – Maj Brown RA

HMS *Yarmouth* (2 x 4.5-inch)

  Forward Observer – Capt Bedford RA

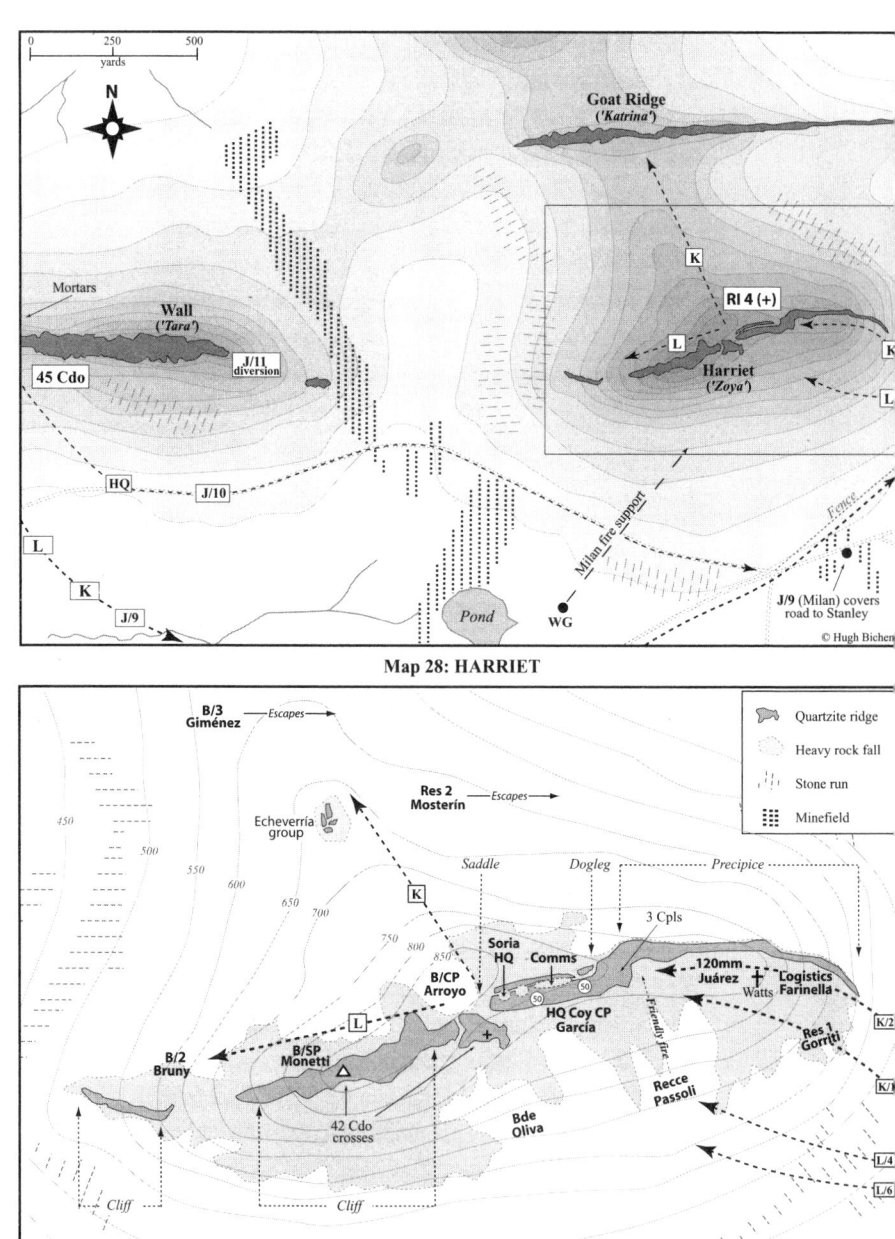

Map 28: HARRIET

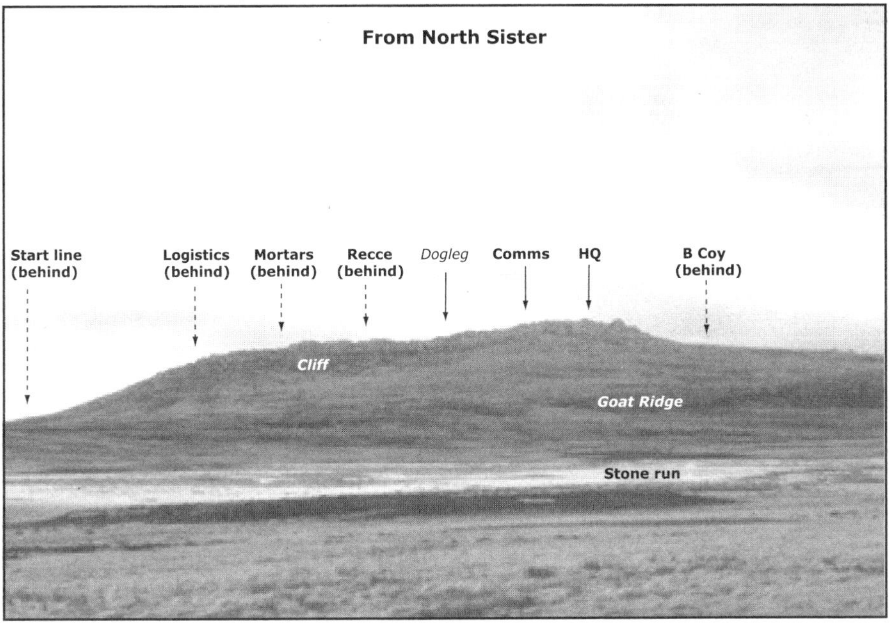

From North Sister

Start line (behind) — Logistics (behind) — Mortars (behind) — Recce (behind) — *Dogleg* — Comms — HQ — B Coy (behind)

Cliff

Goat Ridge

Stone run

Photo Diagram 28: HARRIET

From the South-West

Summit — *Saddle* HQ — Comms — *Dogleg*

Bde

Recce

120 — Log

Res K

L

start line

Modern causeway

257

behind it, killing Corporal Smith and almost disembowelling Marine Hagyard, who survived.* Oddly, when an enemy patrol was sighted coming from Bluff Cove that afternoon, BIM 5 battery only shelled it desultorily and Soria's 120s remained silent. It was, in fact, sections from the Welsh Guards' Recce and Milan Platoons, foisted on Vaux by Moore and moving forward in anticipation of a final night advance to set up a fire base opposite the western end of Harriet, and to secure the start line for 42 Commando's attack. Hard to believe, but they went ahead without coordinating their movements or communications procedures with the battalion they were supposed to be supporting, while drawing attention to the area through which Vaux planned to send his battalion in a wide night march to launch a surprise attack from the rear.

Fortunately, Soria believed that if the British were showing themselves in the south, they could not be planning offensive action from that direction. He was convinced they would require at least a week to regroup from their earlier defeat, and that in the interim the worst he could expect would be feints designed to draw fire and locate his heavy weapons. The ferocious British preliminary bombardment in the evening of the 11th, which killed two and wounded twenty-five, fed into this preconception – he assumed it was to punish RI 4 for the damage it had inflicted. Consequently he did not order his men to stand-to and, possibly also because his landlines were cut, reacted extremely slowly when 42 Commando attacked. At about 0100 on the 12th, two hours after small arms fire to his rear should have dispelled his illusions, he requested a creeping barrage up the eastern front of Harriet from the BIM 5 howitzers, only to be told that they were already firing at maximum range. We can see from **Diagram 3** (p. 108) that, unknown to Soria, BIM 5's guns must have been shelling the eastern end of Mount Wall: a final tribute to a highly successful diversion by J Company, 42 Commando, some two hours earlier, on which more below. In Soria's first sitrep to Jofre at about 0125, he reported only an enemy platoon of about forty men among his heavy mortars. Not long afterwards Jofre was stunned to receive a second, frantic call from Soria reporting 400–500 enemy attacking his HQ at the summit of Harriet, and desperately requesting additional artillery support.

---

* On the 12th a 155mm shell killed Welsh Guards Lance Corporal Thomas, who was running errands forward from Bluff Cove on a quad all-terrain scooter, a gift from the Prince of Wales.

BEFORE EXAMINING THE 42 Commando attack in detail it is as well to step back for a moment from battalion to brigade and see how it interlocked, as one battle, with the assaults on Longdon and the Sisters. The Marine Commandos went into action over two hours late, leaving 3 Para as the sole focus for the Argentine artillery and support fire from the neighbouring hills during that period. I broke my account of the battle for Longdon at the point when B Company's situation had become so desperate that only extreme heroism permitted it to advance at all, and when we return it will be to see how Pike brought A Company around to take over the assault. Just before Soria made his desperate appeal for help on Harriet, Carrizo Salvadores on Longdon told Jofre he had contained the enemy attack and did not need *any more* artillery support, a phrase as ambiguous in Spanish as in English. Presumably he meant *no additional* gunner support, but Jofre understood it otherwise and he ordered all guns in range to concentrate on Harriet. Although, as we saw in the last chapter, some guns fired at the Two Sisters, by that time they had fallen and RIM 6/B's support weapons, under threat, had ceased to fire at the Paras. Thus the western slope of Longdon briefly became a less lethal place just as A Company began to advance up it. Although the men of B Company felt they were the sacrificial lambs in the overall scheme, they had played a key role in forcing enemy errors at battalion and brigade level.

SECOND ONLY TO 3 Para's assault in drawing enemy attention away from the long, vulnerable approaches by the two Marine Commandos was the diversion mounted by 42 Commando J/11 from Wall ('Tara'). The timing was dictated by 45 Commando's Whitehead, who advised Vaux that action was imminent on Two Sisters at about 2300, at which in Vaux's words 'a spectacular *son et lumière* was enacted above Tara's eastern crags. Explosions, lights, small-arms fire and blood-curdling yells riveted attention in that direction.' As we saw this drew fire from the Support Platoon on Two Sisters as well as the BIM 5 battery, but 42 Commando's particular concern was with the enemy HMG and support weapons on the western slope of Harriet ('Zoya'), and these now obligingly revealed their locations by opening fire on J/11's diversion. They were illuminated by a dozen parachute flares fired by the Mortar Troop and fell silent after J/11 attacked them with Milans. The massive explosions completed the illusion of a major attack from the west.

45 Commando's delay in attacking the sisters may have prolonged the punishment of 3 Para but it coincided perfectly with 42 Commando's own careful deployment. The advance party of Lieutenant Beadon's J/9, with a team of mine-clearing Sappers from 59 Independent Commando Squadron and three Milan posts to cover the road from Stanley, had just reached the start line behind Harriet when the diversion erupted. Beadon was astonished to hear English spoken and laughter 100 yards up the slope, where he found the Welsh Guards, who were supposed to have secured the start line, sitting around and smoking. They were – one suspects with unkind words – told to remove themselves from the area of operations. They must have been seen by the defenders, but their very casualness probably salvaged tactical surprise: what soldier, seeing men smoking and relaxing behind his lines, would suspect they were the enemy? In fairness to the Welsh, while this was going on their Milan section set up precisely where it was supposed to and provided timely and accurate support for 42 Commando's attack.

After a further half-hour delay, while L Company caught up, Captain Babbington's K Company began the assault. Sergeant Collins's 2 Troop took the higher, more direct route towards the ridge, knifing two sentries on the way, while Lieutenant Townsend's 1 Troop advanced lower down the slope to attack the reduced RI 12 platoon, commanded by Gorriti, identified as a company in 42 Commando's plan. Babbington's forward observer, Captain Romberg, kept the guns of 7 Battery, 29 Commando Regiment and the turret on *Yarmouth* tracking 100 yards ahead during K Company's advance, but Townsend's men and Babbington's HQ had penetrated Gorriti's position before contact was made. It seems likely, therefore, that the first barrage crashed behind the RI 12s. It is to their credit that they fought at all after such a shattering awakening, wounding Lieutenant Whiteley, 2i/c of K Company, and two others. In Martin Middlebrook's *The Fight for the Malvinas*, Gorriti said he fought for about an hour, and it may have felt like it under heavy GPMG fire punctuated by 66s and 84s. It was more like fifteen minutes – but what is not in doubt is that as before, with Combat Team Solari, Gorriti did not share his men's fate.

Although too close to the ridge for artillery support, Collins' platoon did not need it as they swept through Farinella's Logistics Group and only met with light resistance when they attacked the heavy mortar position. In a bizarre twist of fate 42 Commando suffered its sole fatal casualty here, when Corporal Watts went to disarm three conscripts huddled in a trench and one of the terrified men shot him. Astonishingly, they were permitted to surrender. Vaux had emphasized that surrender should be encouraged and both 1 and 2 Troops now stopped to sort out prisoners and send them back to a holding area near the start line. They had also completed their first phase and set up to cover the flank of Captain Wheen's L Company, which left the start line at about midnight on a long diagonal up an undulating, almost rock-free slope towards the saddle at the centre of the ridge. Wheen's objective was the company position reported at the western end, on the other side of the hill, and he did not expect to encounter serious resistance until he approached the ridge. He was promptly disillusioned by a broadside of small arms fire from Oliva's platoon on the left, Passoli's Recce Platoon to the front, García's company command post above and behind Passoli, and two heavy machine-guns above García on the crest, none of which had featured in the intelligence briefing.

Two or three steady snipers with night sights could have inflicted heavy losses on Wheen's company, but RI 4's passive night goggles were all with B Company on the western slope and García's company had none. So it was that three platoons of Argentine riflemen with seven or eight machine-guns only wounded five men, among them the company 2i/c Lieutenant Stafford, on attachment from the Argyll and Sutherland Highlanders, and 6 Troop's Lieutenant Pusey. In battle, as elsewhere, you do not get a second chance to make a first impression. The enemy firing positions were pounded by artillery and naval gunfire talked in by Wheen's forward observer, Captain D'Appice, and mortar fire from beyond Wall. Worst of all, Milans snaked in from the Welsh on the defenders' right flank and – according to the painting by Peter Archer commissioned by 42 Commando – from Beadon's J/9 at its outpost covering the road to Stanley. Independent Radio News reporter Kim Sabido, who bravely accompanied the assault, recorded his awe that L Company was able to advance in the face of such heavy fire: but it must have been a close approximation of hell on the other side. A couple of large water-filled craters gouged by Milan still scar the area where Oliva's men were dug in, sufficient explanation why they kept their heads down for the rest of the battle.

There are no such pools in the area occupied by the Recce Platoon, presumably because L Company was too close to risk using Milan. Like

Gorriti, Passoli did not stay to share the fortunes of his men, but Samyn – another of the recently graduated dragon's teeth – conducted a spirited defence until wounded, after which his men lost heart. Their position was between the two attacking companies and L Company's suppressive fire on Samyn's men became 'friendly fire' for K Company as it renewed its drive towards the summit ridge. Everyone – down to the section leaders – was on the same radio net and rich profanity filled the airwaves until Babbington and Wheen established safe arcs of fire. Both now pushed on, each coming under fire from a separate heavy machine-gun on the ridge. The .50-calibres were set up in anti-aircraft mode, on high tripods, and the exposed gunners were brave to stick with it as long as they did. In Balza's *Relatos de soldados* Lieutenant Echeverría, RI 4's intelligence officer, who won the MVC for continuing to rally his men until badly wounded, refers to a 'soldier S' (S/C 62 Daniel Sánchez) who covered the retreat of Soria's HQ and fired his HMG until overrun. Happily Sánchez survived. He received no medal but won the admiration of his enemies, along with another, anonymous soldier among the rocks who sniped L Company until destroyed by an 84.*

The leading sections of K Company fought their way up onto the ridge at the dogleg, a natural choke-point defended by some of García's III Brigade HQ men. Corporals Eccles, Newland and Ward each won the MM for clearing this but Marines Bellingham and Pearson also deserved medals: the latter standing up to fire all his 84s in a crossfire from L Company and the Argentine defenders, despite vehement advice to get down from Newland, his section leader. Newland himself crawled around a huge boulder to find about ten Argentines and a MAG lined up on a flat rock. They were placed to massacre Eccles's and Ward's sections if they broke cover, and were coolly firing one at a time in order to conceal their strength. Newland made a solo attack with grenades and ran in after the explosions to shoot anyone still moving. He retreated to let Eccles and Ward attack with 66s and then circled around the back to cut off the Argentines' retreat. One man, badly wounded in the first attack, shot him through both legs before Newland emptied his rifle into him. Four S/C 62s from III Brigade HQ were killed here.

Once the dogleg had fallen, K Company spilled over to the slope on the

---

* Unlike the Paras, the Marines appear to have had few problems with the Carl Gustav, possibly because their foul weather training had taught them how to look after the system.

northern side and advanced in dead ground towards the ridge bowls, from which RI 4's HQ and Communications sections retreated to avoid encirclement. Jofre's last contact was with Soria's radio operator, who told him his chief had gone to join Arroyo's B Company and that he had remained behind to burn the code books. 'Tell me about the enemy,' Jofre said. 'They're everywhere. They're like ants,' the man replied. Gorriti says he and Captain Fox, the Artillery Liaison Officer, set fire to the communications centre tents and stores, which became the aiming point for a bombardment Jofre now called down on the crest of the ridge. Unless the Argentine gunners were uniquely precise on this occasion, some of their shells must have gone long, adding to the misery of Arroyo and Soria on the slope beyond. Vaux estimates that over 1,000 British shells and mortar bombs fell on Harriet and those exposed to it longest were the defenders on the summit saddle and the western slope, to prevent B Company from going to the assistance of García on the other side of the hill. To be hit by friendly fire after many hours of enemy bombardment was the last straw, and when L Company reached the saddle, they found it abandoned.

Echeverría and a group of soldiers, including the doughty Sánchez, retreated towards Goat Ridge and made a stand in a rocky outcrop, where they were flayed by 84s and 66s. Desperately wounded, Echeverría ordered the men to leave him but Corporal Roberto Baruzzo (of RI 12) stayed to take care of him, tending his wounds until he was loaded on a casualty evacuation helicopter and rushed to San Carlos for life-saving surgery. Baruzzo was awarded the CHVC for this and for exemplary leadership over the preceding week.[*] In the post-war literature the generally white, noisy and accessible members of Buenos Aires-based X Brigade got all the attention and the predominantly Amerindian/*mestizo* conscripts of distant III Brigade were ignored. They were uncomplaining and showed dog-like devotion to their officers, most of whom were paternally devoted to them: poor grist to the journalistic mill. For sheer grit none could rival the performance of III Brigade's ceaselessly shelled and bombed GA 3/C gunners at Moody Brook, and the relatively poor showing of their infantry comrades was the result of being hopelessly out-gunned and out-generalled. There is no reason to believe any of the other Argentine regiments, be they ever so white-skinned, would have done any better.

---

[*] A rather pointed comment on his officers, I suspect.

By the time Wheen advised that L Company was closing on the remaining enemy on the western slope, Vaux realized his HQ would not be able to reach Harriet before dawn if it took the cleared route to the south. Poor radio reception in the valley between the two hills forced him to remain on Wall during the battle, but he was now urgently needed at the front to coordinate the next phase. He decided to take the road, led by Norman and J/10, and the combined party raced along it as though hoping the mines would not notice if they walked over them quickly. Happily the mines in the road were anti-tank, hence tolerant of pedestrians. By the time Vaux arrived at Zoya the last large body of enemy soldiers, about sixty men with Soria and Arroyo, had been rounded up.

The hill was still dotted with groups waiting for daylight to surrender, one of which was encountered by Marine Timms, one of the NP 8901 members of J Company, when he went behind a large rock to commune with nature. Timms admitted that the ten men threw down their rifles a split second before he would have done so, sparing him the embarrassment of being the only British soldier to be taken prisoner twice during the war. With J Company taking over at the summit, K Company was released to clear towards Goat Ridge. Giménez Corvalán and Mosterín could see that both Harriet and the Two Sisters had fallen and retreated when the British artillery switched fire towards them. Giménez led his men back to Stanley, Mosterín fell back on Tumbledown and was then sent to William. His men, the last uncaptured remnant of RI 12, stayed with him. They were not called on to fight again, but considering all they had gone through I find it moving that they were prepared to do so.

It may seem churlish to question any aspect of 42 Commando's performance, but the battle did start over two hours late and then used up all the hours of darkness, making any further advance impossible. The contrast between 3 Para's accurate estimate of how long it would take to reach the start line and the delays experienced by both Marine Commandos is striking. Once battle began the main reason why Vaux's men advanced so slowly is that they stopped to deal with hosts of prisoners. Momentum was repeatedly lost and there could be no 'contagion' since the defenders further up the slope could not see their friends being treated with mercy. Even so, between 250 and 300 Argentines surrendered and only fourteen died.* In 42 Commando, K and L Coys each suffered only five more wounded (in addition to those already mentioned) while storming the hill – although seven more were injured by artillery the next day. It was as humane as any combat operation is likely to be – which tells us that Vaux never seriously considered a second phase attack onwards to Mount William.

Nor should he have been expected to. He knew Harriet was held by two companies and a battalion HQ, against single reinforced companies on Longdon and the Two Sisters. He also knew the Argentines regarded Harriet as the most important point on the outer defensive perimeter, and the tragically botched arrival of 5 Brigade at Fitzroy/Bluff Cove had focused enemy attention more than ever on the sector. To crown it, he was compelled to give the Guards a role in his attack, while they seemingly did everything possible to draw enemy attention to the area where he needed his men to advance unnoticed. He was fortunate that Soria had his Rasit radar mounted high on the ridge to spot for the 155s against the Royal Navy gunships, thus poorly located to pick up ground movements, and that the defenders had not unpacked two large passive night vision devices because they did not know how to use them. Like the whole campaign, Vaux's plan absolutely depended on enemy inexperience and errors to succeed, but to push his luck even further by advancing over mined, unscouted ground against Mount William was simply not on.

Accordingly, he used his infantry in classic style as beaters to 'drive' the enemy and, when they revealed their positions, shocked them into surrender with firepower, slowly but relentlessly. Soria later commented that without the artillery the British would have suffered many more casualties. As Bart Simpson would put it – duh! Guns have ruled the battlefield for centuries, and the reason his regiment was annihilated at so little human cost to the enemy was that British forward observers could call in pin-point fire on platoon objectives, while Soria could not even direct the nearest supporting battery to fire at the correct hill. His men deserved better.

* RI 4 recorded twenty-four killed in the whole campaign. Nine plus a RIM 6/B died on the Sisters, five with Silva on Tumbledown and two by the preliminary bombardment on Harriet. Killed during the assault were four III Brigade men at the dog-leg, two RI 12s in the first moments of the attack, an RI 1 and seven RI 4s.

14 Longdon

PART TWO

3 PARA BEGAN TO get a return on its early investment in the overall battle when RIM 6/B's mortars were silenced, when Jaimet could no longer spot for the artillery firing at Longdon, and when Jofre ordered the guns on the Racecourse to concentrate on Harriet and the Sisters. Although the western slope of Longdon became less lethal, the southern flank and the summit bowl were still areas where only crazily brave men ventured. Forays by Privates Connery, Connick and Gray* out of a steeply sloping hollow on the northern side of the bowl bear comparison with the heroism of McKay and McLaughlin (see **Map 25**, p. 224). One does not need to look too deeply to establish why they were not decorated. Connery told Bramley of bayonetting a man who screamed, in English: 'I want to see my grandmother . . . I want my grandmother.' Connery continued: 'All around there was killing and death. There was the acrid smell of battle and the awful smell of death. I was getting closer and closer to it. I was awash with adrenalin, floating, not the same guy at all. All the training was taking over, it was becoming instinctive. The smell of battle and death was being absorbed into my body.' Even the Vikings, not noted for their fastidiousness, were uneasy about the feral Berserkers in their midst. Good men to have on your side when things get ragged, but PR-conscious modern armies dare not make exemplars of them.

It was also the case that extraordinary courage was becoming almost

---

* Gray had a bullet pass through his helmet, very likely fired by Santiago Gauto on whom more below.

commonplace on Longdon. Pike himself came up with his Tactical HQ while the western slope was still under heavy bombardment, and nearly ventured into the bowl before heeding shouted warnings from Shaw's platoon. It was getting crowded around the summit as two groups of mixed Milans and SFMGs also came up, the first returning from Wing Forward led by Captain Mason and CSM Caithness, the second led by Sergeant Colbeck, who came to the battle along a different route to the rest of the battalion (see **Map 24**, p. 216). Only four Milans were fired on Longdon. Two were fired from Wing Forward at the machine-gun under the summit early in the battle. The third and fourth were fired by Colbeck and Sergeant Howard using top-of-the-range night binoculars Colbeck found in Baldini's command post. One missile misfired spectacularly into the night sky, but the second impacted among the rocks that block line of sight between Fly Half and Full Back, at the far (eastern) end of a second hill-top bowl. At the time, the defenders were making another stand along the nearer, western rim of this feature after falling back from the summit bowl, and it was their great good fortune to be inside Milan's 300-yard arming range. On Longdon the system was stymied by topography and the close range at which the battle was fought, which, coupled with the wholesale failure of the Carl Gustavs, made the Paras glad they had plenty of dependable 66s.

Pike gave Argue one more chance to capture the hill, in combination with Major Patrick, Battery Commander of 78 Battery, RA, who came forward with Tactical HQ. Argue's first scheme had been for the land artillery to isolate the western from the eastern summits (which Carrizo Salvadores confirms it did most effectively) and to use naval gunfire to take out individual obstacles. Consequently he went forward with the Naval Gunfire Observer, Captain McCracken, only to discover that precision did not have the expected effect. Targets McCracken could see from the summit were often sheltered behind sections of quartzite ridge from *Avenger*, firing from the north, and the curve of the hill made it impossible to observe the fall of shot against the heavy machine-guns on the northern slope. The main lesson of the first five hours of combat was that six light guns firing together are better than one firing sequentially: not, on the face of it, a startling discovery. It was only after Patrick brought 78 Battery to bear on the eastern end of the summit bowl that Barreto and the men fighting alongside his .50-calibre abandoned the gun and pulled back to the second bowl, Patrick then called in a rolling barrage to precede a hook along the northern flank by the combined 4 and 5 Platoons plus Mason's Support Team, followed by Argue and his HQ Group.

The outflanking move was led by Cox, who partially redeemed himself in the eyes of his men by taking point along a sheep track down the northern slope, passing Burt's body. The advance was into the area previously dominated by Scaglione's heavy machine-gun and cleared by the Fuller/McLaughlin attack, which had permitted Connery and others to reach the hollow from where they made their attacks into the bowl. Therefore it came as a brutal surprise when Cox and the leading element came under fire from the supposedly cleared area, which killed Private Crow and wounded two others. Argue assumed it was the same enemy, undeterred by previous attacks, or possibly men who had leaked from the ridge to escape Patrick's barrage. Instead it was the leading element of a spirited counter-attack by forty-six men of RIM 7/C platoon, well-equipped with passive night goggles, led by 2nd Lieutenant Castañeda from Rum Punch. Castañeda arrived at Carrizo Salvadores' command post at about 0215, and was ordered to take command of Staff Sergeant González's 2 Platoon to mount a counter-attack along the northern side of the hill.*

Carrizo Salvadores lost contact with González early in the battle, at roughly the same time Neirotti of 3 Platoon was wounded on the other side of the hill, and it was not until Bramley interviewed the RIM 7/B veterans that the mystery of the staff sergeant's whereabouts was resolved. González had, it seems, mortally offended S/C 62 Santiago Gauto, a product of Monte Chingolo, by common acclaim the hardest *barrio* of Buenos Aires. Gauto told Bramley of his satisfaction that during the battle the SNCO was more worried about where he was than by the enemy. 'I heard, too, that after the war he was still suffering so badly from shock that he lost all his teeth and hair. Good. It is also possible that he has since died. If that is the case the human race has lost nothing.' Bramley countered with his own *bête noire,* a platoon sergeant in 9 Parachute Squadron RE, attached to 3 Para. 'He was nasty and vicious in his orders. He picked on the lads throughout the whole campaign.

---

* Among the reasons why Carrizo Salvadores said he needed 'no more' artillery at this time was to avoid hitting Castañeda's men with friendly fire.

His name is known and so is his back. He turned out to be one of the small group who spent the night . . . hiding from a group of lads who had sworn to kill him in battle.' Bramley's second book was published after a June 1993 reunion in Buenos Aires among survivors of the two B Coys, sponsored by the Argentine *Gente* and TV Channel 11, and the British magazine *Today*. They discovered much in common . . .

Cox radioed Argue's HQ that he could not see where the fire was coming from and McCracken, who could, fired a 66 at the enemy position. Castañeda's men may have been in the rocks around Scaglione's ruined bunker, and when Cox ordered his rear section to shower the position with grenades one of them bounced back and exploded uncomfortably close to him. He went forward with Connery and after a struggle with the uncrimped pin posted a grenade over the rock that concealed their approach, then ran around it to find three semi-conscious Argentines. Connery finished them off with a FAL brought back from one of his forays into the bowl.* Unaware that he was dealing with fresh troops, Argue was elated to have cracked the position that had held up his company for so long, only to have his hopes dashed when the outflanking attempt ran into heavy machine-gun fire from further along the hill, and rifle fire from the slope above. Three men were wounded, including Gray who was hit in the helmet for a second time, the bullet creasing his skull before exiting the other side. With blood pouring down his face, even after B Company pulled back it took a direct order from CSM Weeks to make Gray leave the line for treatment. It was about 0300 and Argue's men could go no further. They had suffered over 50 per cent casualties and now it was A Company's turn.

At some point prior to B Company's last attack, Pike ordered Collett to assault Longdon from his position on Wing Forward. A Company had been pinned down for several hours by accurate sniper and machine-gun fire and Collett replied that the attack was simply not on. In the article Pike wrote for *Elite* magazine, regrettably his only substantial contribution to the extensive literature about the battle, he recalled reporting to Thompson his intention to bring A Company around to resume the drive along the ridge: 'leaving him in no doubt that we would succeed in the end'. Possibly Thompson may have suggested abandoning the attack. Pike himself admits

---

* It may have been Connery's discarded SLR that was later presented to Carrizo Salvadores by one of his men.

there were 'moments when I wondered, almost desperately, what more we had to do to force the Argentines to give up the fight: positions thought to have been suppressed burst into life again with fire as heavy as ever. There was only one thing to do, of course – to battle on until the will of the enemy was totally broken.'

Possibly Pike knew that 45 Commando's delay left RIM 6/B free to attack across the valley, an opportunity still open at this time but fortunately for 3 Para untaken. However he did not know that another large and well-equipped Argentine company could have intervened: 170 men with two 81mm mortars and seven MAGs from Armoured Reconnaissance Regiment 10 (EX 10) under Captain Soloaga, which left Stanley at 2330 with orders to advance to contact up Moody Brook valley. By 0300 Saloaga's command had reached a position about a thousand yards south-east of Longdon, closer over easier terrain than either RIM 6/B or Castañeda's company on Rum Punch (see **Map 29**, p.271).

Jofre intended to throw the EX 10 infantry into the battle for Longdon, but his hand was stayed by a breakdown in radio communications that left Carrizo Salvadores unable to speak directly with his CO Giménez back at Wireless Ridge. Jofre was put in the awkward position of acting as a relay between the two senior officers of RIM 7: the equivalent would have been if Argue could only speak with Pike through Thompson, and Jofre felt no less inhibited than Thompson would have been from intervening in the battalion commander's conduct of the battle. At much the same time that Pike was assuring Thompson that he could dominate the situation with A Company, Giménez told Jofre that the arrival of Castañeda's men had given Carrizo Salvadores the means to regain the initiative. By the time this was revealed to be a false hope, Jofre knew that the Sisters and Harriet were lost and that Longdon had become an exposed salient he would have to abandon anyway. Accordingly he left EX 10 in place to fight a rearguard action, covering the retreat of RIM 6/B and serving as a rallying point for the men falling back from Longdon.*

Pike recalled a renewal of accurate enemy artillery fire on the western slope at about 0300, but this was probably BIM 5's six heavy 106mm mortars

---

* López Patterson was recalled to Stanley, but the group of RI 4s he led from North Sister plus seven RIM 7s from Longdon swelled EX 10 to about 220 men.

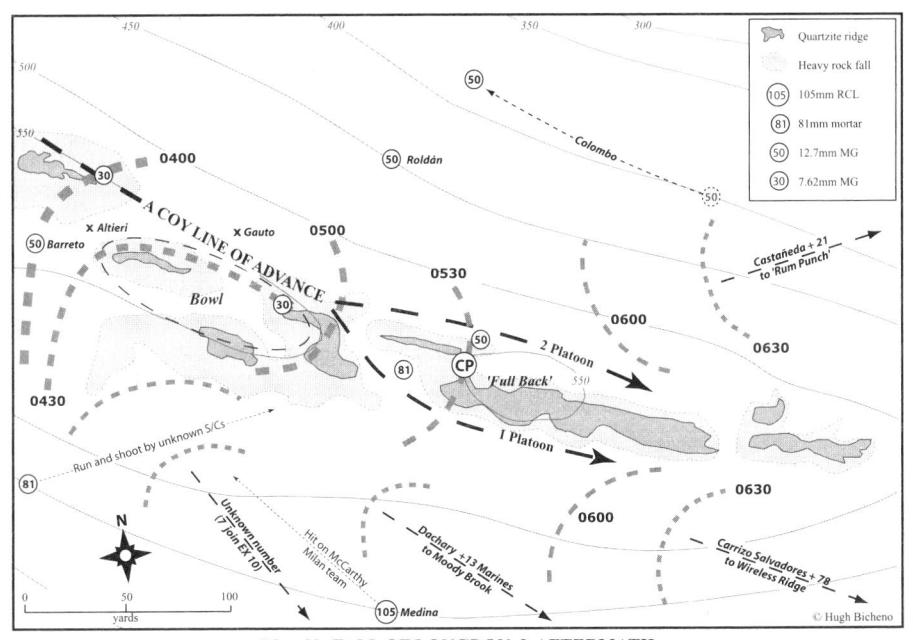

Map 29: FALL OF LONGDON & AFTERMATH

REDEPLOYMENT 12 JUNE

Retreat
Reinforcement

Longdon

RIM 7/C (-)

RIM 7/A

RI 4/A (-) from Low

RIM 7
Recce

RI 2/MG from mainland

RIM 6/B

EX 10

Wireless Ridge

RIM 7/HQ

North Sister

Moody Brook

GA 3/C
withdrawn to
Racecourse

RIM 3/A

BIM 5/Log

Amph Eng

Tumbledown

BIM 5/HQ

Felton Stream

Goat Ridge

BIM 5/N

BIM/Batt

RIM 3/C

BIM 5/M

BIM 5/N

William

BIM 5/O

Harriet

N

0   1/2
mile

© Hugh Bicheno

Quartzite ridge
Heavy rock fall
105   105mm RCL
81   81mm mortar
50   12.7mm MG
30   7.62mm MG

0400

A COY LINE OF ADVANCE

x Altieri   x Gauto

50 Barreto

Bowl

0500

0530

0600

0630

Castañeda + 21
to 'Rum Punch'

0430

81   CP
81   'Full Back'

2 Platoon

I Platoon

Roldán

Colombo

50

50

30

30

Run and shoot by unknown S/Cs

Unknown number
(? join EX 10)

Hit on McCarthy
Milan team

Dachary +13 Marines
to Moody Brook

0600

0630

Carrizo Salvadores + 78
to Wireless Ridge

105 Medina

N

0   50   100
yards

© Hugh Bicheno

271

on Tumbledown (see **Diagram 5**, p. 212). 3 Para was lucky there was nobody on Longdon to direct their fire, as otherwise the summit would have become untenable. They were also fortunate that long cohabitation had bred hatred for Dachary's Marines among the RIM 7s, chiefly because of their élite arrogance but also because they had their own logistics support and enjoyed abundantly better food, which they did not share. As a result, the Marines fought their own separate battle, expecting no support from the RIM 7s and, as we saw in the case of Scaglione's gun team, not getting it. The contrast with the stand made at the bowl alongside Barreto's heavy machine-gun was striking. Even so, Marine Sergeant Lamas's gun effectively closed off the southern flank of the hill, while Marine Lance Corporal Roldán did the same on the northern side, bringing forward S/C 62 Colombo's gun team to flank his own. It was their fire that stopped B Company's last attack and so disheartened Argue and Pike. It seems likely that Colombo's team, in the open, was killed or wounded by shell fire, but Roldán's dug-in HMG, despite the best efforts of McCracken and Patrick, did not fall silent until Dachary pulled his men back. Dachary must have buried his landlines extremely well, because he remained in contact with his gun teams until the end. Six of his twenty-three men were killed, and eight of the thirteen he brought away were wounded.* Even without infantry support the Marine heavy machine-guns shaped the battlefield: had they been less obnoxious to their Army peers they might have dominated it.

On their way to the summit Collett's men passed through the survivors of B Company and witnessed a violent altercation between Cox and McLaughlin over disputed authority. Corporal Sturge, a section leader in Australian 2nd Lieutenant Moore's 1 Platoon, took Cox aside: 'Come on sir, we don't want to see our young officers not keeping it together.' The episode made such a bad impression on Collett that he ordered his men to stay away from B Company to avoid contagion. I am in no doubt that similar scenes have occurred in every battle since warfare began, but one must wonder what moved Cox to be so frank about it to Christopher Jennings and Adrian Weale, authors of the tell-all *Green-Eyed Boys*.

At the other end of the hill, Carrizo Salvadores recalled thinking it was all

---

* Colombo made his own way back with the help of a wounded RIM 7. The remaining three in their distinctive combat kit may have been the 'special forces' 3 Para reported among the prisoners.

over when Barreto and twenty men who had stood with him fell back on his command post, only to have them urge him to lead them in a counter-attack to recover the heavy machine-gun and to rescue the comrades they had left behind. These were not yet beaten men: some of them recovered the 81mm mortar from the southern flank, firing and moving with it until they ran out of bombs. It was a brave effort, but the counter-attack ran into Patrick's barrage and the fire of six GPMGs massed by Support Company near the summit. Barreto used up another of his nine lives when the body of a comrade was hurled on top of him and shredded by bullets as he lay stunned.

Criticism of 3 Para's attack plan has focused on the decision to mount a silent attack, yet B Company only lost one man – to an anti-personnel mine – in the first rush. In return the enemy's artillery was blinded, the support weapons set up to cover North Sister were silenced, and Baldini's company-sized command was destroyed as a coherent force. It was the next phase, which was as noisy as anyone could wish, that went badly wrong when by-passed enemy positions brought 6 Platoon to a halt. By attacking with all three platoons simultaneously, Argue left himself without a tactical reserve when the enemy did not, as his plan required, cut and run. His inflexible artillery fire plan, compounded by the failure of the 84s, was the icing on the cake. The effect of Argue's miscalculation was compounded because Pike had left himself without an operational reserve by committing A and C Companies to objectives beyond Longdon, and by dividing up Support and D Companies in penny packets among the rifle companies. The original sin may have been Thompson's in ordering Pike to try for too much in one night: but the underlying offence at brigade, battalion and company level was an unwarranted underestimation of the enemy.

NOT LONG AFTER B COMPANY pulled back, McLaughlin's previously charmed section was struck by two rockets, identified as Strelas (Russian anti-aircraft missiles supplied by Libya). These must have been fired by RIM 6/B's support platoon as it pulled back from North Sister – no other unit with SAMs was in line of sight of the western slope of Longdon. Both McLaughlin and his deputy Private Gringham were severely wounded by the first, while the second killed the medic Lance Corporal Lovett instantly. Two stretcher bearers arrived and the wounded men hobbled separately towards the RAP with their assistance, but on the way McLaughlin and Lance Corporal Higgs were killed by a mortar bomb. Since it robbed his posthumous memory of the honour it otherwise deserved, one must wonder what possessed McLaughlin to take his grisly trophies. If the idea was to strike terror into the hearts of the enemy, it was superfluous. Thanks to some singularly ill-considered propaganda from their own side, the Argentine conscripts were already terrified – of the Gurkhas, whom many RIM 7s still believe were the fierce little men (Paras are not tall) who attacked them. Some returned home with tales of dope-crazed Gurkhas wearing Walkmen (presumably the compact Clansman PRC 349) who ran through minefields shooting their own wounded, cut off men's heads and laughed as they killed and died. The problem with a reputation for unbridled ferocity is that while it encourages anticipatory flight, once battle is joined it may reinforce the autonomic fight response instead. Just such a reaction occurred on Longdon, where many fled, but a number of trapped men correctly judged there was no point in trying to surrender, and fought to the death.

Although *Avenger* left the gunline at 0245, having fired 150 shells, A Company's Collett could count on a great deal more fire support than Argue had enjoyed, and made full use of it. Not only was he able to work out a more thorough artillery fire plan with Patrick, but the Mortar Platoon was now at full strength, after battalion 2i/c Major Paton brought the vehicle group across Murrell Bridge without waiting for 45 Commando to clear North Sister. Major Dennison and CSM Caithness of Support Company were also at the summit, and with the advent of Colbeck's and Mason's mixed SFMG/Milan groups, the mid-ridge was at last swept clear of the enemy, although the further effectiveness of the fire support base was limited by the topographical limitations mentioned earlier. A large 'what if' hangs over this reorganization, however: while A and Support Coys were getting ready there were about 150 men packed into the area immediately around the summit. If Jofre, who prayed God to forgive him for bombarding the still-disputed summit of Harriet, had prayed a little harder and done the same for the long-lost peak of Longdon, it might have crippled 3 Para. He did not because Carrizo Salvadores could not bring himself to write off Baldini's men and, I suspect deliberately, misled his superior about the course of the battle.

Collett ordered his men to strip down to weapons and combat kit with ammunition stuffed into their pockets, and to advance along the base of the northern rock face on their bellies. Corporal Sturge's section led all the way to Full Back, using up their own grenades and 66s and then those of the following section. Only one man was wounded, by his own grenade, during the two-hour advance. Sturge himself took point during the first hour when the section crawled alongside the second bowl, taking out two machine-guns and outflanking the Marine HMGs on the slope below.

OF ALL THE ACTS OF bravery I have described, Sturge's sustained act of courage impresses me most. Every 66 he fired advertised his location, every grenade he threw invited others in return and at every turn of rock or fold of earth there could have been an enemy soldier waiting to shoot him. Although Collett, who received an MC, later tried to disown him, at the time he rewarded Sturge with a .45 automatic pistol he found in Carrizo Salvadores' command post. Some time later, when A Company with some prisoners was clearing the enemy dead to a burial pit on the northern side of the hill, Sturge arrived with a wounded Argentine, shot in the leg a little earlier by CSM Munro. 'What shall I do with this one?' Sturge asked. 'Put him with the others,' replied Munro and Sturge shot him in the head with the .45 automatic. The Support Company hierarchy was nearby and rushed to disarm him. When Mason asked him why he had done it, Sturge babbled that the man was a sniper, so perhaps his over-stressed mind saw it as revenge for the deaths of Hope and Jenkins on Wing Forward. Once Bramley's first book spilled the beans, the Maroon Machine closed ranks and although a fatuous police enquiry dug up the burial pit and went to Argentina to appeal for witnesses, it concluded there was no chance of a successful prosecution. There wasn't from the start: any competent lawyer would have got Sturge off on grounds of diminished responsibility. The real question is what diminished it, and the answer to that question is all-embracing.

BRAMLEY AFFIRMS THAT only two of the GPMGs lined up just below the western summit were able to maintain sustained fire. Colbeck disagrees, but whatever the case the fire support base was compelled to suspend fire at about 0500 because A/1 Platoon was about to cross over the ridge. But now the leading sections could bring their own firepower to bear and at 0530 Carrizo Salvadores radioed Jofre that he could no longer raise his head because the enemy was in among his HQ Platoon positions and pouring constant machine-gun fire on his command post. A little later he reported a Milan hit in the rocks behind his command post (it could not have been a Milan – it was probably a 66 fired by Sturge's section at a nearby heavy machine-gun sangar) and received permission to abandon the hill. He retreated with some of his dead and many wounded. Most of the seventy-eight fit men he brought away were Eng 10 Sappers: it follows that the bulk of RIM 7/B, including company commander López, must have leaked down the slope towards Moody Brook when the second bowl was abandoned. Twenty-one RIM 7/Cs returned to Rum Punch with Castañeda and, as we saw, fourteen of Dachary's men survived. Twenty-nine dead (all S/C 62s or older, including the senior conscript on the islands, S/C 54 Gattoni) and about fifty prisoners remained on Longdon.*

Before they pulled back the RIM 7/Cs – instrumental in prolonging the defence for three hours – landed one last blow on 3 Para. At about 0500 Colbeck, on the right of the fire support base line, thought he could see the emplacement of an enemy 105mm rocket launcher and asked Dennison for clearance to engage it. Not wishing to fire the awesome Milan anywhere near the leading sections of A Company, and unaware that the rocket launcher Colbeck could see was actually on the other, southern side of the hill, Dennison denied him permission, with tragic consequences. Abandoned by its crew, the rocket launcher was brought back into action by Lance Corporal Medina of Castañeda's platoon, who fired a last rocket at the fire support base at about 0600 and hit McCarthy's Milan team, killing him, Privates Hedicker and West, and wounding two others. Either the rocket launcher in question or its twin, abandoned in the face of Shaw's assault nine hours earlier, can still be seen close to the memorial block of granite adorned with bronze poppies that marks the western end of the summit bowl.

The fall of Longdon was a terrible blow to Jofre, and not solely because it involved men of his own brigade. A violent bombardment of the GA 3/C battery seemed to presage a further enemy advance towards Wireless Ridge.

---

* RIM 7 lost thirty-six killed during the war, twenty-one on Longdon, most of the remainder on Wireless Ridge. Six Marines, one Eng 10 and the forward observer Ramos were also killed on Longdon.

If Wireless Ridge fell, not only would the GA 3/C battery be lost, but Jofre's reserve infantry units – EX 10 in the valley and RIM 6/B making its way towards Tumbledown – would be outflanked. Jaimet of RIM 6/B reported that he was being closely pursued by the enemy and Jofre ordered GA 3/C to fire a reverse rolling barrage to cover the retreat from North Sister. When RIM 6/B angled away from the track to climb the flank of Tumbledown, the barrage continued down the valley and landed on the EX 10 position at about 0530, killing Staff Sergeant Ron of EX 10 and wounding several others, including RI 4's Pérez Grandi, who had the back of a thigh torn off. His men insisted on carrying him back to the hospital in Stanley and, astonishingly, the leg was saved. RIM 6/B was in place on Tumbledown by about 0700 and after Carrizo Salvadores reported his group at Wireless Ridge at about 0730, Jofre ordered the rest of GA 3 to fire at the eastern end of Longdon, while GA 3/C continued to cover the valley. GAA 4, as we have seen, was pounding Harriet. It seems Jofre was so fixated on the southern coast road and on the Moody Brook valley that if 45 Commando had advanced from the Two Sisters, as Whitehead wished, the Marines would have arrived at Tumbledown not only under the cover of a thick morning mist, but also completely unharassed by artillery.

The mist cloaked the dawn so well that the men of 3 Para never realized EX 10 was in the valley below them. The only contact seems to have been an incident reported by Bramley, when the mist cleared to reveal a man in a trench some distance down the south-eastern slope, whom they thought might be an enemy forward observer. They fired at him enthusiastically and this may be the phantom attack Soloaga reported repelled at 1200, after which he was given permission to fall back on Wireless Ridge. On arrival EX 10 took the left flank of the new defensive formation put together by Giménez, CO of RIM 7. Jofre also sent the Machine-gun Platoon of RI 2, with eight MAGS and two heavy machine-guns, which had flown in from the mainland during the night of 10–11 June. He also sent the Combat Aviation 601 helicopters to evacuate Mount Low, flying the HQ Platoon of RI 4/A directly to the centre of Wireless Ridge. Although still expecting another British landing, during the night Jofre ordered Lieutenant Colonel Comini of RIM 3, facing the coast south of Stanley, to shift the axis of his regiment from east–west to north–south. Comini put Major Berazay in charge of what would become the new right wing at Moody Brook, which was accomplished by moving RIM 3/A from the left wing of the old position. Captain Zunino, the company commander, tried to speed up the process by using trucks. Unfortunately, the temperature dropped below freezing that night (presaging the early arrival of an unusually severe winter) and vehicular chaos ensued. It took the company over five hours to reach its new position on Moody Brook, forming a rough line across the valley with RIM 6/B and EX 10 on either flank. You can walk the distance in less than one.

3 Para had its collective head well down throughout 12 June, because Longdon is clearly visible from Stanley and when the mist cleared the Argentine artillery began to work the ridge over with a vengeance, joined by sniper, heavy machine-gun and 105mm rocket launcher fire from Tumbledown. The renewed bombardment killed 9 Independent Squadron Sapper Corporal Wilson (brother-in-law of Sergeant McCarthy, who died at the summit) and two eighteen-year-olds: Private Bull of A Company and Private Absolon of Patrols, who was awarded a posthumous MM for his pre-battle infiltrations. Spotters on the crest of Tumbledown were now able to direct the fire of BIM 5's 106mm mortar battery and 'walked' bombs from the summit down the western slope, where the RAP was. Either a shell or a bomb in this area killed REME Craftsmen Shaw and Jones, and tore a leg off Connick, who had stopped to chat to them. Twenty-three British soldiers were dead, nine of them NCOs, and forty-seven wounded. Two of the dead were medics, three were stretcher bearers. Greater love hath no man than this, that a man lay down his life for his friends.

Jones and Shaw were not the last to die on the hill. In the RAP a wounded Argentine drew a pistol and was shot to death even as the medics were working to save his life. Elsewhere, a wounded Argentine grabbed Bramley's leg and was dispatched by Sergeant Pettinger. Another wounded soldier was found to have a primed phosphorus grenade in his hand when turned over and was shot before he could throw it. Corporal Carrizo, whom last we saw hiding in the rocks as Shaw's platoon attacked the tents, crawled out at first light: 'I remember standing up. Suddenly I was confronted by two English soldiers. I was shot in the head as I tried to surrender.' He awoke on the *Uganda,* where two bullets were removed from his skull for the loss of an eye. As far as I know he still believes he was 'executed', and he was one of

the few veterans to register a complaint about British treatment of prisoners
with the Metropolitan Police enquiry. His account coincides exactly with a
vivid memory that haunted Sergeant French of A Company, as told to Hugh
McManners in *The Scars of War*. French was following Collett when an
Argentine suddenly emerged from the rocks:

> I shot him twice on the head [with a pistol – he would not have
> survived two high velocity headshots from a rifle] and although
> I didn't stop to check he was dead, I knew he was. I ask myself now,
> did I have to do that? Could I not maybe have taken him and handed
> him back? If I had ignored him, would he have shot [Collett]? We
> knew they'd waved the white flag at Goose Green and then killed
> people. It was a stupid thing they did . . . we weren't going to take
> any chances. In some ways he was a victim of one of his own side's
> mistakes. At the time I was quite happy with what I did. But it's
> funny how as the years go on, when I have a quiet moment, I always
> think of him . . . I've said a lot of prayers to his family – I mean that.
> I'm not proud of what happened, but I'd do it again if I had to, for a
> just cause. But if I had a chance to take him prisoner I would. We're
> not here to destroy each other, it's wrong.

15 Tumbledown/William

THE BATTLE FOR TUMBLEDOWN is, to date, the last battalion-sized 'forlorn hope' assault* carried out by the British Army, appropriately by one of its oldest regiments, the Scots Guards. There is no social animus in my earlier comments on the folly of sending the two Guards battalions to the Falklands. They are good troops, possessed of an admirable *esprit de corps.* Their officers, known variously as 'debutante's delights', 'chinless wonders', and so forth, have a tradition of nurturing outstanding savagery under a suave exterior: a matter unexplored in *Tumbledown,* a TV film based on the story of Guards Lieutenant Robert Lawrence MC, who lived despite a rifle-shot to the head that destroyed half his brain. The other half retained an appalling memory of what the anodyne term 'hand-to-hand fighting' really involves:

> I stuck my bayonet into the back of his arm, dug it right in because I had run out of ammunition. He spun wildly on the ground and my bayonet snapped. And as he spun, he was trying to get a Colt 45 out of an Army holster on his waist. So I had to stab him to death. I stabbed him and I stabbed him, again and again, in the mouth, in the face, in the guts, with a snapped bayonet. It was absolutely horrific [retrospectively – at the time he recalls crying out 'Isn't this fun?' not long after this incident]. Stabbing a man to death is

★ From the Dutch *verloren hoop* (lost troop), 'forlorn hope' was the designation adopted by the British in the seventeenth century for those sent to storm a breach in the walls during an assault on a fortress.

not a clean way to kill somebody, and what made it doubly horrific was that at one point he started screaming '*Please* . . .' in English to me. But if I had left him he could have ended up shooting me in the back. I took his rifle, moved on, shot a sniper, picked up his and moved on again.

The 2nd Battalion, Scots Guards (2 SG) was on ceremonial duty in London when advised on 5 April that they might be going to war. The CO, Lieutenant Colonel Mike Scott, and Captain Spicer his Operations Officer (also Training Officer and Support Company commander and much later author of *An Unorthodox Soldier*) had to scramble in order to obtain even basics like rucksacks and Clansman radios. 2 SG was also understrength, but volunteers from the Grenadier, Coldstream and Irish Guards soon made up the deficit. As was to be demonstrated again in the 1991 Gulf War, the British could only put a fully (but not properly) equipped division in the field at short notice by cannibalizing stores across the whole Army.

Like most soldiers, Spicer blames government parsimony. In fact the armed forces were over-officered to an almost Ruritanian degree and were probably the least cost-effective component of the British public sector. The Guards battalions should not have been sent because they were not combat-ready and other regiments were. Their unpreparedness delayed departure and also made them less able to make up for lost time when they arrived. That was not something forced on the defence establishment by politicians, nor was the lack of contingency planning, military intelligence, inventory control, logistical expertise, familiarity with key weapons systems and so on down the list. None were expensive – merely essential. The Guards had five weeks to make good their deficiencies before embarkation on 12 May. Was it supposed the Warsaw Pact would give as much notice of its intention to roll over Western Europe?

We have seen how 2 SG nearly became the victim of what would have been the bluest of blue-on-blues in British military history on 6 June. Had it been left to Brigadier Wilson, their reprieve would have proved temporary. On 9 June, the day following the *Galahad* disaster, he summoned his battalion commanders to a meeting at Fitzroy, which to their astonishment was filmed by the BBC, by now regarded by most as an enemy fifth column. It was an attempt to put a brave face on things for the benefit of the folks back home and he said nothing of operational matters until the journalists were gone. One wishes they had stayed to film the faces of the COs and their staff as Wilson outlined his plan: once 42 Commando seized Harriet, the Gurkhas were to 'patrol aggressively' along the line of the coast road towards Tumbledown and William in the hope that the defenders would flee. Failing that, on 12 June the Gurkhas and 2 SG would attack William and Tumbledown simultaneously – in daylight – from the point on the road known as Ponies Pass.

Few things are absolutely certain in war, but barring day-long blanketing mist this was a recipe for a catastrophe that would have relegated the tragedy at Fitzroy to a footnote in the history books. The two hills were known to be held by a battalion of Argentine Marines, normally based in Tierra del Fuego and therefore well equipped for the conditions, who had been in place for two months and were set up to counter an attack from precisely the direction Wilson proposed. William, which would have to be taken first because it flanked the approach to Tumbledown, was not only heavily defended but was close to the road from Stanley, along which Argentine reinforcements could be rushed. Even if the Gurkhas were able to draw all the fire from William, 2 SG would still have to cross a minefield, then a large stone run followed by two smaller ones before assaulting into a broadside of machine-gun fire from much the largest and most complex of the Stanley hills. The slope was almost a defender's dream and the enemy had built sturdy bunkers within the stone runs to cover the areas of dead ground.

FRONTAL ASSAULT ON the enemy's strongest point – does this sound familiar? It should. It is the hallmark of the personality type dissected in Norman Dixon's *On the Psychology of Military Incompetence.* 'But General Walpole took no trouble to reconnoitre; and, without even a cursory examination of the position, launched his men in a blundering and haphazard manner against the strongest face . . . ' The incident described was at Fort Rooyah during the Indian Mutiny, but any one of a dozen general officers' names from the Crimean, Boer and the two World Wars could be substituted for Walpole's. Wilson's scheme held out at best the prospect of a Pyrrhic victory, at worst a loss of momentum and a morale boost for the enemy that might have doomed the entire campaign. According to his chief Sapper, Wilson's reason for proposing a headlong attack was that he was under intense pressure to win 'the race for Stanley' – yet there are still those who feel he was unjustly treated after the war and 'cruelly' hustled into retirement. While conceding that whoever was exerting the pressure from London richly deserved to precede him into professional oblivion, it is an established principle of international jurisprudence (except, as we have seen, in Argentina) that a soldier not only should but *must* disobey criminal orders. If the knowing, needless sacrifice of lives on the altar of inter-service rivalry is not a premeditated crime then the term has no meaning.

FORTUNATELY MIKE SCOTT (no familiarity intended – there were several Scotts among the Scots) had the moral courage to rebel, quietly but firmly. Here serendipity once more worked to British advantage because the CO of a Guards battalion may courteously accept suggestions from lesser beings, but takes orders only from the great Guardsman in the Sky or his senior earthly representatives. In addition, although the First Battalion, 7th Gurkha Rifles (1/7 Gurkhas) was the strongest infantry unit in the Falklands, it was politically impossible to give them the primary role in 5 Brigade's offensive. The Welsh Guards were out of it and should have been withdrawn to San Carlos to release 40 Commando, instead of borrowing two companies from it to maintain an illusion of participation. Wilson either led with 2 SG or did not lead at all, and power therefore devolved to Scott. The brigadier was gradually shut out of the decision-making process until, during the battle, Spicer took it upon himself to shut down the radio link with Brigade to stop Wilson 'pestering' Scott. Once the Para battalions were taken from Wilson's brigade it was an error to leave him in command. It would have been better to honour the custom that two Guards battalions demand a Guards brigadier, but no British tradition is more sacred than 'Buggins's turn'.

The staff of 2 SG quickly discarded the daylight attack option, and after Scott's chief sapper, Lieutenant Peter McManners, advised him that it would take all night to locate and breach the minefield, so was the approach from the south-west. Scott therefore recommended an attack during the night of 12–13 June from a staging area between Harriet and Goat Ridge, assuming

42 Commando gained control of them on the 11th–12th. The line of advance was the one 45 Commando envisaged and was straining at the leash to pursue in the morning of the 12th, but neither Scott nor Wilson appear to have been told that 3 Commando Brigade might follow through. The lack of coordination and inter-communication that Division was supposed to ensure was not Moore's fault: he lacked the staff and the communications equipment, and despite donning a neutral Afrika Korps-style cap was presumed guilty of favouring the Marines even when what he proposed was manifestly the correct military solution. It was a command shambles created by old men in London squabbling over the limelight like pantomime queens.

Scott's scheme, rubber-stamped by Wilson on the 11th, was for 2 SG to attack Tumbledown from the west. Once it was secure 1/7 Gurkhas would pass around it to attack William from the north, across the saddle between the two features. The Welsh Guards/40 Commando battalion was to be in reserve in the lee of Harriet ready to exploit forward to Sapper Hill. The attack was to coincide with an assault on Wireless Ridge by 2 Para, now back under command of 3 Commando Brigade. Tumbledown towered over Wireless Ridge and until 2 SG could silence the support weapons and drive the Argentine artillery observers off it, 2 Para was likely to have a thin time of it. But at the same time 2 Para's attack would prevent Argentine forces in the valley from reinforcing Tumbledown, so the two operations were inter-dependant. In the absence of time to conduct ground reconnaissance of his own, Scott gratefully accepted Thompson's offer of the M&AW Cadre members who had set up on Goat Ridge on 8–9 June to guide 2 SG and the Gurkhas to their start lines east of Goat Ridge.

A cartoon published in London at the time showed two Argentine soldiers huddled in a trench, one saying: 'No, no, you've got it all wrong. It's the Gurkhas who cut your throat with a big knife – the Scots do it with a broken bottle.' The 5th Marine Infantry Battalion (BIM 5) on Tumbledown and Mount William was to have the dubious distinction of being attacked by both, although in the event William was abandoned before the Gurkhas got there. The Argentine Marines on the Falklands were in most respects inde-pendent of the Army, enjoying as they did their own logistics airlift plus organic artillery, air defence and sapper support. To their credit, at the command level Marine Colonel Moeremans' staff were fully integrated with

Jofre's, and inter-service rivalry was not a factor in the battle of Tumbledown. The CO of BIM 5, Lieutenant Colonel Robacio, broke ranks six years after the war, when he dishonestly alleged his battalion only fell back from Tumbledown and William because Jofre ordered it to do so, after the Army had been driven from Wireless Ridge. Robacio was provoked by press denigration of the Navy's role in the Falklands debacle, but it was still a sad and demeaning coda to one of the few examples of cooperation among the services in Argentine history.

In the expectation that the British would renew their offensive during the night of 12–13 June, Jofre's hasty redeployments created a decidedly messy command and control situation in Moody Brook valley. He retained personal command of the three companies in the valley, when EX 10 on the western end of Wireless Ridge should have been put under RIM 7's Giménez, and RIM 6/B on the north-eastern extension of Tumbledown under BIM 5's Robacio. The rest of RIM 3 (bar C Company, plonked in the middle of BIM 5 under Robacio's command for no obvious reason) should have been brought forward under its CO Lieutenant Colonel Comini to form a coherent reserve force in Moody Brook. The result of not doing so was that the defenders were never able to make their greater numbers and firepower count: there was no tactical coordination, so each unit fought its own battle and was defeated piecemeal.

After the war Jofre admitted his generalship was unbalanced by a fixation on the threat of a British attack from the south, but the fundamental flaw was to have ignored the principle of concentration. Now the range had closed, however, he hoped the Army artillery, under Brigade command, would break up any enemy attack before it closed with the infantry. The gunners had defied all efforts to knock them out, making a virtue of the regular necessity to re-site their self-burying weapons by leaving mock-ups behind to draw enemy fire. Akhurst, the Battery Commander attached to 45 Commando, ruefully admitted that he wasted much of his counter-battery fire on old tires and sections of drainpipe under camouflage nets.*

Robacio's sector was, on paper, a tough nut to crack. He had the Marine battery of howitzers plus four 105mm rocket launchers, four 120mm, six

---

* Before 13–14 June British air attacks, naval gunfire and land counter-battery fire disabled no mortars, no rocket launchers and only one gun each in GA 3, GAA 4 and the Marine battery.

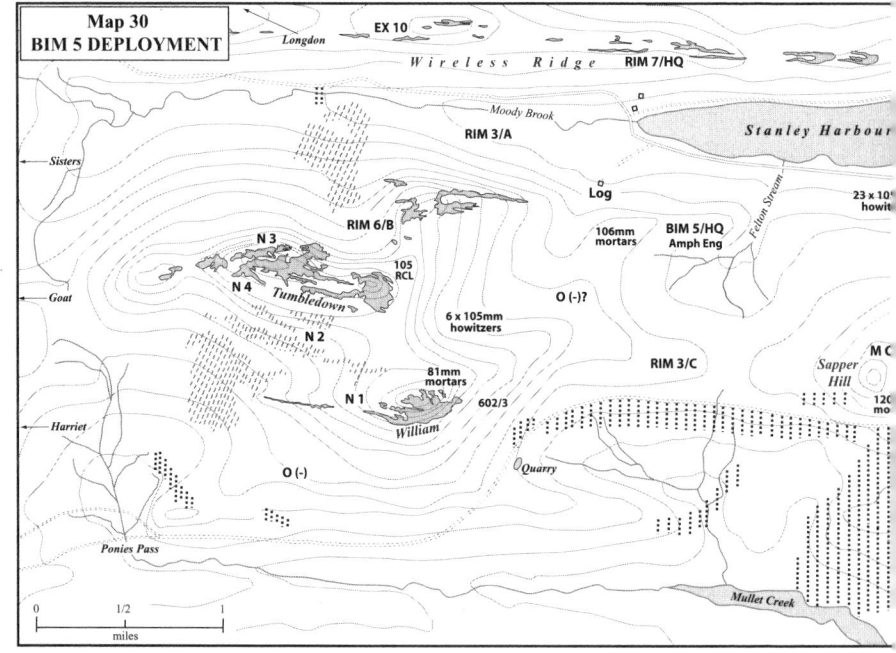

Map 30
BIM 5 DEPLOYMENT

Longdon

EX 10

Wireless Ridge RIM 7/HQ

Moody Brook

RIM 3/A

Stanley Harbour

Sisters

Log

23 x 10'
howit

RIM 6/B

106mm
mortars

BIM 5/HQ
Amph Eng

Felton Stream

N 3

105
RCL

N 4 *Tumbledown*

O (-)?

Goat

6 x 105mm
howitzers

N 2

RIM 3/C

M C

*Sapper
Hill*

81mm
mortars

N 1

602/3

120
mo

Harriet

William

O (-)

Quarry

Ponies Pass

Mullet Creek

0   1/2   1
miles

106mm and six 81mm mortars under his direct command. Two more rocket launchers, six 60mm mortars, two Bantam anti-tank missile groups, eight heavy machine-guns and two dozen MAGs were under platoon command on Tumbledown/William. However his HQ at Felton Stream was too far back, an error compounded by having the Amphibious Engineers under Major Menghini co-located. Robacio was far too concerned with countering a possible attack from the south, and his rifle companies were therefore spread too thin. One company, even one with four rifle platoons like Captain Villarraza's command (N Company), could not adequately defend both Tumbledown and William. Captain Cionchi's M Company on Sapper Hill was behind wide belts of mines that required only a machine-gun platoon to cover them. The rifle platoons should have gone with the 81mm Mortar Platoon when it was sent to William, permitting N Company to concentrate on Tumbledown. The battalion reserve – O Company under battalion 2 i/c Major Pernías – was probably on the reverse slope at a point central to the whole defensive scheme, where the two hills offered some protection from naval gunfire and land artillery. Pernías sent a platoon under Sub-Lieutenant Quiroga reinforced by a section of Sappers, a total of thirty-seven men, to a position in front of William, covering Ponies Pass, where it was to play an equivocal and, from the British point of view, crucially important part in the battle.

Villarraza's scheme for the defence of Tumbledown/William was inflexibly set up to counter an attack from the south (see **Map 31**, p. 290). Most of his firepower eggs were in the basket of Sub-Lieutenant Bianchi's platoon on William, with Sub-Lieutenant Oruezabala's platoon in support from the military crest down among the stone runs. His third platoon, under Staff Sergeant Lucero, was posted to cover Moody Brook valley from an isolated position close against the northern cliff face of Tumbledown. When Robacio gave him another twenty-seven-man platoon from HQ Company, Villarraza sent it to the western end of Tumbledown, but told 2nd Lieutenant Vázquez his task was to bring the expected attack from the south under flanking fire. It is easy to see why he discounted an attack from the west: that end of Tumbledown is narrow, dauntingly steep and any advance up the hill is channelled into a narrow defile between rock walls, at the foot of which a twenty-five-man platoon of Marine Sappers under 2nd Lieutenant Miño was located. An outcrop further to the west was not judged worth defending because an enemy advance from there would run into fire from Miño's position, which overlooked it, while the flanks were covered by MAGs at the western ends of Lucero's and Vázquez's positions. The position was further strengthened in the early morning of the 12th when Silva arrived with his fifteen-man RI 4 section from South Sister, and readily agreed to cover the gap between Miño's men and Vázquez's right flank.* The ground in the area was well drained, permitting the defenders to construct deep dug-outs with steps up to narrow exits within strong sangars, some under overhanging boulders.

Nobody would have attacked here – knowing it to be so strongly held – without smothering the defenders with artillery, but Scott was not granted the time to recce the objective and the outcrop prevented direct sight of the western end of Tumbledown from Goat Ridge. He also lacked the artillery

---

* Mosterín from Harriet and Llambías from South Sister also arrived at Vázquez' position before continuing, respectively, to William and Sapper Hill.

resources to perform all the fire missions that such a large objective merited. He could call on nine 105mm light guns, three with newly arrived 97 Battery, 4th Field Regiment RA and the six of her sister 29 Battery, which had been on the island as long as the three batteries (7, 8 and 79) of 29 Commando Regiment RA. Additional support came from his own, 1/7 Gurkhas' and 42 Commando's mortars, plus the four enemy 120mm mortars captured on Harriet. The problem was ammunition, and with severe weather hampering resupply and priority given to restocking the batteries in action on the 11th–12th, it was not until the 13th that he could order a general 'softening up' of the objective. Jaimet, who was at the relatively sheltered north-eastern end of Tumbledown, described what it was like at the receiving end:

> British artillery fire . . . went up and down the mountain [which] quaked and shuddered under the impacts. The [phosphorus] shells were like flying kerosene tins filled with hot metal fragments . . . I saw them hit some soldiers near me and they burned through the thickest clothing, parkas, jackets, pullovers, everything, through to the flesh. I heard the cries of the wounded . . . calling for their comrades . . . twelve men before nightfall. We thought we had suffered before, but what luxury and comfort compared to this.

Without specific targeting information, Scott really had no choice but to order a silent advance to contact. Once battle was joined he would be able to call on naval gunfire from the three 4.5-inch guns of *Yarmouth* and *Active* in the gun line to the south. Unfortunately he took the advice of his inexperienced Battery Commander, Major Gwyn, over that of Naval Gunfire Observer Captain Brown, outranked but fresh from outstanding success in close support of 45 Commando on the Sisters, and before that at South Georgia and Pebble Island. During the battle Gwyn lost radio contact with his forward observers, but continued to believe he could target his guns more accurately than the Naval Gunfire Observer: an absurdity when the ships enjoyed the benefit of the computers and modern gunnery aids the RA had been obliged to leave behind. The result was that although Gwyn's fire plan successfully isolated the western end of Tumbledown, and divided William from Tumbledown, the close support the infantry needed was denied to them for many hours. For his part, Vázquez had the utmost difficulty persuading

MoD does the buying, servicemen do the dying. The final agony of defenceless HMS *Antelope* in Ajax Bay. (Rex Features)

SIGHTS OF STANLEY
Why the Foreign Office failed to sell them out

Above left: Great War gun with 1982 inscription. Above right: Jubilee Villas on Stanley waterfront.
Below left: 1914 memorial. Below right: 1982 memorial. (Author's collection)

an Carlos yesterday: capture of Platoon Sergeant Colque (left) and Marine Lt Commander
`amiletti (right) by 3 Para and 40 Commando on 21 and 23 May 1982. (Camera Press)

an Carlos Water today: 2 Para entrenchments in the foreground. (Author's collection)

Corporal Matthews of 3 Para standing in Corporal Carrizo's mortar pit, Longdon. (Military Picture Library)

Strongpoint held by PFC Claudio Scaglione on the northern flank of Longdon. McKay attacked up hill on the other side of the crest between the two rock formations on the left. (Author's collection)

Where Sergeant McCarthy's Milan team died near the crest of Longdon.
(Military Picture Library)

One of the most evocative images of this or any war: Tom Smith's photograph of the bunker where Sergeant McKay fell, with the Murrell River in the background. (Daily Express)

Argentine .50-calibre machine gun mount on Harriet still overlooking the long slope up which L Company, 42 Commando, attacked during the night of 11–12 June 1982. (Author's collection)

The crest of Tumbledown. Three of the six men who stormed it with Kiszeley were wounded at the far side, looking out over Stanley. (Author's collection)

The vital Murrell bridges today: ruins of the old bridge in front of the wartime replacement flown from Bluff Cove. (Author's collection)

Falkland Islanders celebrating their liberation in front of Government House. (Camera Press)

Argentine nationalism yesterday, today and forever. (Corbis)

ARGENTINE

5th Marine Infantry Battalion (BIM 5)

CO – Lt Col Robacio,   RSM Hernández

2i/c – Lt Col Ponce,   Ops – Maj Pernías

M Company (Sapper Hill) – Capt Cionchi

(RIM 3/C's 4 x 120mm mortars, 3 HMG, 6 MAG)

  RI 4 Group – Sub-Lt Llambías

RIM 3/C (under BIM 5 command) – Lt Binotti

N Coy (Tumbledown/William) – Capt Villarraza

CSM Nuñez   Forward Observer – 2Lt de Marco

  1 Platoon – Sub-Lt Bianchi

  (2 Bantam AT, 2 x 105 RCL, 3 HMG, 6 MAG)

  RI 12 Group – Sub-Lt Mosterín

  Mortar Platoon (from M Company) – WO Cuñé

  (6 x 81mm mortars)

  2 Platoon – Sub-Lt Oruezabala (2 HMG, 3 MAG)

  3 Platoon – SSgt Lucero (60mm mortar, 3 HMG)

  4 Platoon – 2Lt Vázquez/Sgt Fochesatto

  (60mm mortar, 3 MAG)

  RI 4 Group – 2Lt Silva

  Amph Eng 5 Platoon – 2Lt Miño

O Coy – Maj Pernías

  Ponies Pass Platoon – Sub-Lts Quiroga/Calmels

  (3 x 60mm mortars, 4 MAG)

  Amph Eng 1 section – 2Lt Valdéz Zabala

Heavy Weapons Group – 2 Lt Galluzzi

  (6 x 106mm mortars, 4 x 105 RCL)

6th Mech Inf Regiment (RIM 6) – Maj Jaimet

B Coy – Lt Abella

  1 Platoon – Sub-Lt de la Madrid

  2 Platoon – Sub-Lt Franco

Comando 602/3 Platoon – Capt Ferrero

Artillery Support

  Marine Batt (6 x 105mm) – 2Lt Abadal

  GA 3 (12 x 105mm)

BRITISH

2nd Battalion, The Scots Guards (2 SG)

CO – Lt Col Scott,   RSM MacKenzie

2i/c – Maj Mackay-Dick,   Ops – Capt Spicer

HQ Coy – Maj Bethell/CSM Braby (Ponies Pass)

G Coy – Maj Dalzell-Jobs

  7 Platoon – Lt Johnson

  8 Platoon – Lt Page

  9 Platoon – 2Lt Blount/Sgt McDonald

LF (Left Flank) Coy – Maj Kiszely/CSM Nicol

  Forward Observer – Capt Nicol

  13 Platoon – 2Lt Stuart/Sgt Simeon

  14 Platoon – Lt Fraser

  15 Platoon – Lt Mitchell

RF (Right Flank) Coy – Maj Price/CSM Amos

  Forward Observer – Capt Miller

  1 Platoon – 2Lt Dalrymple

  2 Platoon – Lt Lawrence/Sgt Robertson

  3 Platoon – 2Lt Mathewson/Sgt Jackson

  (with Company 2i/c Capt Bryden)

Support (F) Coy – Capt Spicer

  Anti-Tank Platoon – Capt Campbell-Lamerton

  Recce Platoon – Capt Scott/Sgt Allum

  Mortar Platoon (Harriet) –

  (6 x 81mm mortars, 6 x HMG)

42 Commando and 1/7 Gurkhas

  6 x 81mm mortars each

9 Para Sq RE – Maj Davies/SSM Walker

  3 Troop – Lt McManners

Blues and Royals (2 Scorpions/2 Scimitars)

  4 Troop – Lt Coreth

Artillery support

  29/97 Batts, 4 Field Regt RA (9 x 105mm)

  Battery Commander – Maj Gwyn

  Active and *Yarmouth* (3 x 4.5-inch)

  Naval Gunfire Observer – Capt Brown

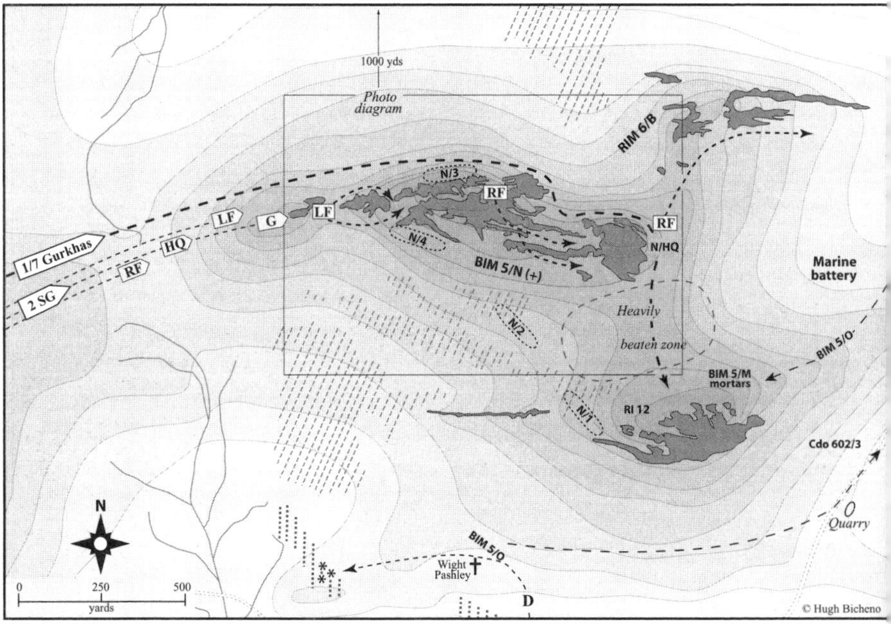

Map 31: TUMBLEDOWN & WILLIAM

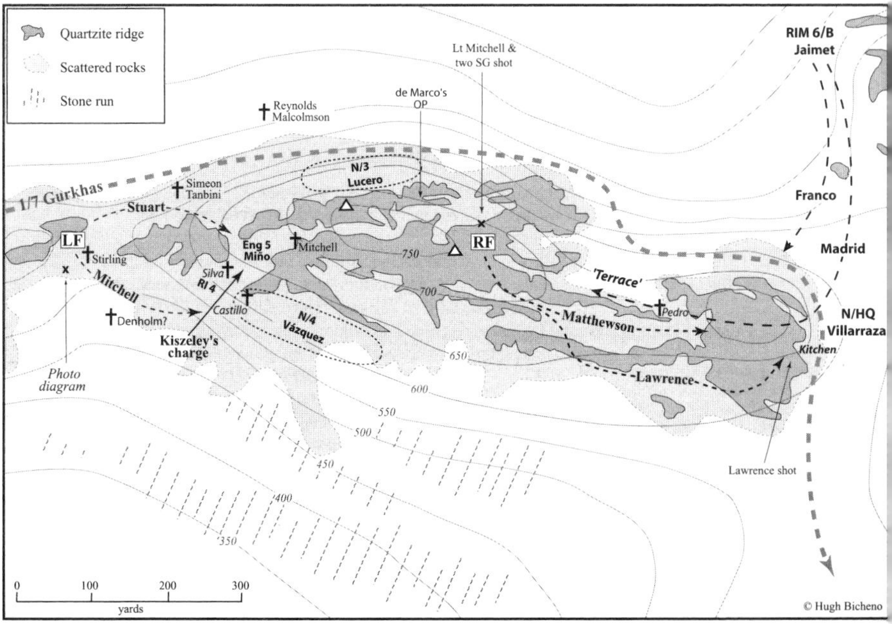

Labels on upper map (Map 31):
1000 yds · Photo diagram · RIM 6/B · N/3 · RF · RF · 1/7 Gurkhas · LF · G · LF · RF · HQ · N/4 · BIM 5/N (+) · N/HQ · 2 SG · N/2 · Marine battery · Heavily beaten zone · BIM 5/O · BIM 5/M mortars · RI 12 · N/1 · Cdo 602/3 · N · Quarry · BIM 5/Q · Wight Pashley · D · 0 250 500 yards · © Hugh Bicheno

Labels on lower map:
- Quartzite ridge
- Scattered rocks
- Stone run

RIM 6/B Jaimet · Lt Mitchell & two SG shot · Reynolds Malcolmson · de Marco's OP · N/3 Lucero · 1/7 Gurkhas · Stuart · Simeon Tanbini · Franco · LF · Stirling · Eng 5 Mino · Mitchell · 750 · RF · Madrid · x · Mitchell · Silva RI 4 · 'Terrace' · N/HQ Villarraza · Denholm? · Castillo · N/4 Vázquez · 700 · Matthewson · Pedro · Kitchen · Kiszeley's charge · 650 · Photo diagram · 600 · Lawrence · 550 · 500 · Lawrence shot · 450 · 400 · 350 · 0 100 200 300 yards · © Hugh Bicheno

290

From the North

Secondary summit

Summit

Saddle

Peat bank

Lucero

Slope to summit

13 Platoon

Photo Diagram 31: TUMBLEDOWN

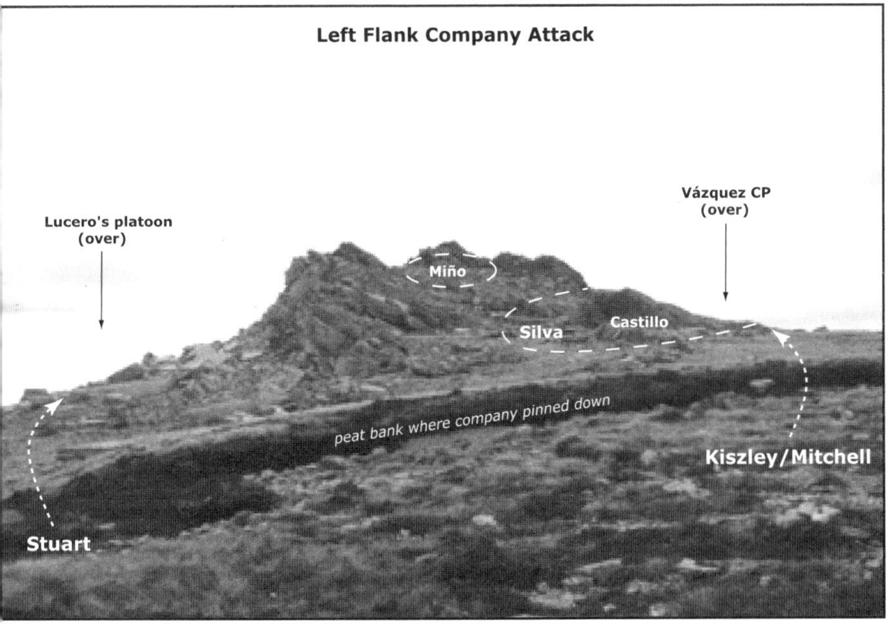

Left Flank Company Attack

Lucero's platoon (over)

Vázquez CP (over)

Miño

Silva

Castillo

peat bank where company pinned down

Kiszley/Mitchell

Stuart

291

his own gunners and mortar men to fire on his position – the enemy was in the open, his men safe in their dug-outs. He did not finally get the desired response until in exasperation he sent the gunners a request (via battalion commander Robacio, no less) to perform an unnatural act on themselves with their gun tubes.

Scott's scheme, given to his company commanders at 1530 on 11 June, was for a three-phase operation the following night, with G Company leading to take the western outcrop, Left Flank Company (LF) the main ridge as far as the twin summit peaks, and Right Flank Company (RF) the rest, including a large rock formation to the north-west of the main ridge overlooking an enemy logistics distribution point.* The main assault was to be preceded by a diversionary attack led by HQ Company commander Major Bethell, supported by a troop (two Scorpions and two Scimitars) of the Blues and Royals from the south-west, intended to keep the enemy's attention fixed in the wrong direction.

2 SG and the Gurkhas spent the 12th waiting for the promised helicopter lift. It was not until 1600 that Wilson advised the COs that a higher priority had been given to resupplying 3 Commando Brigade after the battles of the night before. Scott demanded a twenty-four-hour postponement to ensure that Gwyn's gunline should also be fully stocked. Furthermore, anxious as Moore was to relieve the pressure on the forward battalions, it would have been utter folly to attack without even giving the Guards and Gurkhas a chance to eyeball their objective. Early on the 13th troop commanders down to section level were flown to Goat Ridge and spent the day studying Tumbledown/ William. The rank and file were brought to the assembly area behind the ridge throughout the day, under intermittent shelling that wounded a lance sergeant.

Bethell's thirty-man group consisted of two sections from the Recce Platoon under Sergeant Coull, an HQ Company section including Drill Sergeant Wight, armed with converted Bren guns (LMG) and led by CSM Brady, and two 9 Parachute Squadron Sappers. They started from Port Harriet House and met up with the tanks on the road south-west of Harriet at about 1700. They rode forward with them until at 1830 they dismounted to advance on foot, skirting south of Ponies Pass. The battalion advance was scheduled

---

* 'Left Flank' and 'Right Flank' are survivals from the days of red coats and linear battlefield manoeuvres.

to start at 2100 but it was not until 2045 that Bethell arrived at the enemy position he intended to attack: a cluster of above-ground bunkers built with peat-filled fuel drums, from which members of the O Company/Sapper group under Quiroga had been observing the British advance through passive night goggles for half an hour. The Argentine position was tiered, with the riflemen holding the first line, four MAGs and the command post 100 yards behind them, and three 60mm mortars 150 yards further back. The reason why Bethell's group was permitted to get so close seems to have been because Quiroga twisted his ankle and held fire until Sub-Lieutenant Calmels arrived to replace him.

One of the MAGs opened up at point-blank range and the Brens promptly returned fire. Drill Sergeant Wight and Sapper Lance Corporal Pashley were killed in the first exchange and S/C 62 Iñiguez mortally wounded, the only Argentine fatality in this engagement. Five Guardsmen and about the same number of Argentines were wounded over the next hour and a half, during which the diversion drew fire from all BIM 5's mortars and the Marine battery. Calmels reported he was under attack by two companies and at 2220 received permission to retreat, while for his part Bethell decided at about 2230 that his men had done enough. So it was that the two groups disengaged at about the same time, but not before a grenade wounded Bethell and Piper Duffy. Carrying their casualties the diversion group then walked into a minefield and four men were crippled, leaving barely enough fit men to help the wounded and not enough to carry the dead, who were abandoned amid heavy, but fortunately peat-dampened mortar fire.

Bethell lost radio contact early with Lieutenant Coreth of the Blues and Royals, who drove toward the sound of the guns when the action started until, skirting a crater in the road, he drove over an anti-tank mine that lifted his Scorpion several feet in the air, dismounted the engine and shredded a track, but did not breach the hull or injure the crew. The remaining tanks did their bit for the diversion by taking it in turns to fire at William and Tumbledown as they reversed towards Harriet, also under heavy fire. At some point they emerged from the radio black hole and Coreth was able to re-establish contact with Bethell, at the time on hands and knees with Sapper Lance Corporal Foran and Piper Duffy, using a torch to identify mines. It was not until 0200 that they made it back to the road, where Coreth picked up the wounded and rushed them to the 42 Commando RAP south-west of Harriet.

The diversion cost two of the nine British killed and eleven of the forty-three wounded during the battle. Its success can be measured by the fact that when Jofre published his apologia in 1987, he still believed a full battalion attack with armoured support was launched out of Ponies Pass (see **Diagram 7**, p. 313). Perhaps more to the point Robacio, Pernías and Villarraza believed it at the time, which is a good part of the reason why Vázquez's, Silva's and Miño's men at the western end of Tumbledown were left to fight the main body of 2 SG on their own. Foran got an MM for mine clearing under fire, but Bethell only a Mention in Despatches for devising and executing a brilliantly successful operation that saved many lives, in which he repeatedly risked his own to attack enemy positions and recover his wounded.

Leading the main attack, Major Dalzell-Jobs' G Company advanced a mile without alerting the enemy. The temperature had fallen below freezing and the night was darkened by snow flurries driven by fierce winds into the back of the advancing Guards – and into the eyes of the defenders on Tumbledown. It was not until Major Kiszeley's LF Company passed through, entering the relatively sheltered saddle between the western outcrop and Tumbledown proper at about 2230, that Miño's and Silva's men spotted them. They held fire until the two leading platoons were in the middle of the saddle and then a stunning volume of fire drove the Guards to cover, behind a peat bank they were extraordinarily lucky not to have crossed before the firing started. 'Everybody got down because the initial firefight was incredible, it was like being at the wrong end of a machine-gun range,' Lieutenant Mitchell of 15 Platoon recalled. 'Bullets at close range cracked like a whip over your head. The air was full of bits of lead and chunks of rock, which were being broken off and were flying around all over the place . . . You had the feeling that if you raised your hand slightly in the air it would be shot off.' Guardsman Stirling was killed and 15 Platoon Sergeant Jackson wounded in the initial fusillade. Newly graduated 2nd Lieutenant Stuart's 13 Platoon was out of the immediate line of fire and ran forward to hook around Miño's northern flank, only to run into accurate rifle fire, possibly from Lucero's platoon. Platoon Sergeant Simeon and Guardsman Tanbini were killed and when CSM Nicol and Lance Corporal Eyre went to their aid they were wounded: Nicol by a bullet that struck the barrel of his rifle, held across his chest, and ricocheted through his hand. He thought it likely they were all victims of a single sniper.

LF Company was now in the same situation as 3 Para/B after the first rush ran out of momentum on Longdon, with the deadly difference that here the enemy was firmly in control of the high ground. The company was stuck for over three hours, although on the left 13 Platoon retained its lodgement in the rocks to the right of Miño's position, from which Lance Sergeants Davidson and McGuiness chipped away at the Argentine Sappers' resolve with anti-tank rockets and phosphorus grenades. Lacking similar cover, attempts by Mitchell's platoon to outflank right brought them progressively further into the prepared arcs of fire from the Silva/Vázquez position. Eventually all progress stopped, despite several daring forays by Guardsman Reynolds.* Kiszeley became separated from his forward observer, Captain Nicol, during the first firefight and once they found each other they also found they were in an area of very poor radio reception. The result was that Vázquez won the race to obtain close artillery support, and when Nicol and Gwyn finally got back in contact it was no longer possible to differentiate between own and enemy shells. BIM 5's guns and mortars also beat up the outcrop, wounding a number of G Company men including 9 Platoon Sergeant McDonald, while beyond it Scott's HQ group was bracketed by successive salvos. The HQ group ran forward to take cover in the outcrop as a third salvo tore up the ground where they had been. This may have been the work of the Argentine 155s: Spicer describes an explosion too powerful to have been caused by mere 105s, which excavated the peat bank behind which the HQ Group had been sheltering.

The breakthrough started at about 0200 when Gwyn at last started dropping shells close enough, permitting Mitchell's platoon to get in among Vázquez's men, at about the same time that Miño, outflanked by Stuart's platoon and deserted by most of his men, abandoned his position and retreated up the hill. The telephone cables were cut and the British were jamming his radio so Miño sent a runner, who never arrived, to warn Vázquez. The first that the men facing Mitchell's platoon knew about Miño's

---

★ Guardsman Denholm died on this flank, the place and cause unspecified in any account I have found.

departure was when they came under GPMG and anti-tank rocket fire from above and behind, which wounded several and killed the gallant Silva. The Argentine Army's citation for Oscar Silva's posthumous MVC says he died on Two Sisters: fighting alongside the Marines, it seems, did not count.

McGuiness, in charge of the ten men of Stuart's platoon highest up the hill, recalled: 'we definitely took them by surprise and could see them dodging about, trying to get into cover. This allowed the rest of the company to go forward; we could see them and kept moving our fire ahead of them.' Stuart's men fell back after this, to get out of the way of Gwyn's barrage, and the slope was stormed by a group of Mitchell's men, led by Company Commander Kiszeley. 'Are you with me Jock?' he called out.* Silence. He tried again and someone replied resignedly 'Och aye, sir, I'm wi'you,' and another, 'Aye sir, I'm fuckin' wi' you as well.' Gwyn was to fire three salvos and then stop while the infantry stormed the hill, and to the relieved surprise of the men who went 'over the top' they burst through Vázquez's line without loss. With Miño's men gone and Vázquez's left behind, it must have been Silva's orphaned men who made the Scots fight for every inch of the defile to the summit, killing section leader Lance Sergeant Mitchell and wounding several others. Four RI 4s in addition to Silva died on Tumbledown, Kiszeley himself shooting two and bayoneting a third. In return he had his beret shot off and was hit by two bullets, stopped by his compass and a spare magazine.

Vázquez believed the British fell back after the attack, but in fact the Kiszeley/Mitchell party continued towards the summit and the lull Vázquez experienced was because the rest of 15 Platoon waited for Lieutenant Fraser's 14 Platoon to join them before mopping up along the base of the hill. For Vázquez the turning point was when the MAG manned by Warrant Officer Julio Castillo and two others (in a particularly strong position tucked under a large boulder, still plainly identifiable) was silenced at about 0230. Castillo held the right flank of Vázquez's position for four hours against repeated British attacks, and continued to fight when surrounded. He was awarded a posthumous CHVC. Vázquez surrendered at dawn, and when he called out to his men to stop fighting and come out with their hands up he was shocked that only four men responded. Eight of his men were dead, five wounded and all the survivors captured save one: S/C 62 Jorge Sánchez

* As all Paras are 'Toms', so all Scots soldiers are 'Jocks'.

made a daring escape under fire to Oruezabala's position. Vázquez himself was lucky to survive, because he seems to have been identified as the mythic sniper who 'put bullets through the cap badges of [variable number] men'. Spicer writes of a captured officer who boasted of having done this, and since Vázquez was the only officer captured he must have been the man thus demonized, although with better luck than the alleged sniper on Longdon.

I have a soft spot for Vázquez. He admits that he stopped praying to God to spare his life, realizing: 'what I'm asking is stupid. Everyone asks the same, but in a war not everyone will survive. I'm wasting a prayer. Besides, the Englishman to my front is making the same petition and there is only one God.' So he prayed instead, 'God, all I ask is that when the moment comes I may face it with dignity.'

If obliged to choose one terrain feature on the Falklands that most compels awe at the courage of the men who stormed it, my vote goes to the defile leading to the small peat plateau within the high crags at the summit of Tumbledown. A 60mm mortar section occupied the plateau early in the battle, but the many craters still visible in the area make it clear why it was abandoned. Also still to be seen is the almost impregnable artillery observation post built by 2nd Lieutenant de Marco, BIM 5/N's forward observer, overlooking the sheer northern face with an unrivalled view of Longdon, Wireless Ridge and the Moody Brook valley: a further reminder of how vital Tumbledown was for the Argentine defence. The peak was taken by Kiszeley, Mitchell and five Guardsmen including the intrepid Reynolds: the bulk of LF Company was still below, mopping up, guarding prisoners and evacuating their own and enemy wounded. Kiszeley's group paused, skylined, at the eastern end of the plateau, amazed to see Stanley lit up as though in peacetime, and a burst of automatic fire from the broad hollow below, known as the 'Terrace' to the Argentines, wounded three of them, including Reynolds and Lieutenant Mitchell, who was shot in both legs.

Hours later a mortar bomb hit a stretcher-bearer group evacuating the wounded from the summit. Reynolds and Guardsman Malcolmson, carrying Mitchell, were killed, eight others wounded or re-wounded and the stretcher shredded, but Mitchell was miraculously spared to hobble back to the RAP at Goat Ridge, using a rifle as a crutch. LF Company lost seven men killed and twenty-one wounded. It is hard to imagine what reasons there may have been not to award Kiszeley the VC, but he got an MC instead. Reynolds, meanwhile, received a many-times earned DCM, as did CSM Nicol for continuing to recover the wounded, despite his own wound, throughout the period when the company was stalled at the foot of the hill. There was nothing for either of the Mitchells, Davidson or McGuiness, not for the same reasons that other brave men went undecorated on Longdon but because it would have been 'unfair' to award one company or battalion significantly more medals than any other. Kindergarten reasoning, typical of MoD.

Kiszeley's group reached the summit no more than ten minutes ahead of Sub-Lieutenant de la Madrid's RIM 6/B/1 Platoon, guided by de Marco and Miño who were anxious to make amends for having given up the feature in the first place. The fault was not really theirs. Despite repeated pleas over four or five hours – and no less repeated assurances that reinforcements were on their way – the men at the western end of Tumbledown were left unsupported to the end. Robacio and Villarraza had their minds closed to the possibility that Vázquez might be facing the main attack, and that the battalion attack they thought they had defeated in the south-west was the diversion. Pernías sent the O Company reserve to the saddle behind William, where, along with the rest of N Company, it was isolated by Gwyn's dissecting fire plan. Much later, Robacio ordered M Company to move forward from Sapper Hill (although RIM 3/C was nearer), but when he learned that Miño had retreated, the only troops that could intervene in time were the men of Jaimet's RIM 6/B. Jaimet, in turn, sent only one platoon under a green sub-lieutenant instead of ordering senior Lieutenant Arbella to lead a company attack, or better still leading it himself.

De la Madrid says: 'I spread my men out behind the men who were still fighting' in the Terrace area, which is something of a puzzle: either they were stragglers from Miño's platoon (unlikely) or there had been an unrecorded sortie by some of Villarraza's HQ Group. Braving the fire of two machine-guns and a 'missile launcher' firing down from the summit, de la Madrid went forward until he heard English voices above and behind him. He spotted a group of twelve men through his night goggles and fired a rifle grenade at them. Fraser's 14 Platoon, newly arrived to support Kiszeley's tiny group, reported two NCOs wounded by a grenade at about this time. For the next hour or so the two groups sniped at each other across the Terrace. Thanks to the die-hards of Vázquez's platoon it was not until about 0600 that Major Price's RF Company came up to resume the offensive, and during that period a company attack might have won back the summit. It was the last clear chance the Argentines had to inflict a significant check on the British.

We must now return to the battle for Wireless Ridge, which greatly influenced the end-game on Tumbledown. Although 2 Para's Chaundler refused an appeal from Mike Scott to release some of his artillery support to help 2 SG, the tremendous fire-power unleashed on Wireless Ridge in fact helped the Scots considerably. A glance back at **Map 31** (p. 290) will show how Lucero's platoon on the north side of Tumbledown was ideally placed to counter-attack Stuart's flanking move, which drove off Miño's Sappers and unlocked the western defences of the hill, or failing that to redeploy to the summit via the steep peat slope to its right. Lucero did neither because his allotted task was to support Wireless Ridge with his mortar and heavy machine-guns, and you did not become an SNCO in the Argentine Navy by questioning orders. Nor was there any reason to do so. Both Lucero and Jaimet, who was also supporting the men on Wireless Ridge with his mortars, could plainly see their compatriots being chewed up to their front. As we have seen, Villaraza and Robacio were confident they had defeated the main enemy attack until they learned of Miño's retreat, and until that moment nothing Lucero or Jaimet could see and hear on the radio warned them that, behind them, Tumbledown was falling to the enemy. However, once they did realize their peril, Robacio and Jaimet failed to respond adequately. Both later claimed they wanted a fight to the death in Stanley – but if their concept of honour demanded more bloodshed, why not their own, leading their men on Tumbledown?⋆

⋆ Robacio and Miño (!) got Navy-sponsored CHVCs, but not Vázquez. The Army gave Jaimet an MVC.

16 Victory

WIRELESS RIDGE IS AT once the closest and least accessible of the Stanley battlefields. The two hills north of the ridge, named 'Rough Diamond' and 'Apple Pie' by Chaundler, are like half-filled basins floating in the marshy sea of what my guide informed me is the worst going to be found anywhere on the islands (see **Map 32**, p. 304). Jofre's new defensive line involved abandoning Rough Diamond (3 Para's 'Rum Punch'). After Castañeda's men fell back from Longdon, RIM 7/C was withdrawn to reinforce RIM 7/A on Apple Pie, freeing up a platoon to guard the eastern flank from a hill surrounded on three sides by the Murrell river. A section under a sergeant, which included Anglo-Argentine S/C 62s Alan Craig and Michael Savage, was left behind to man the mortars on Rough Diamond and spent a miserable day on 12 June under accurate mortar fire directed from Longdon.* One of the survivors from Castañeda's foray to Longdon was killed and several wounded only a few feet away from Savage. That night the group carried the wounded back to Stanley and themselves out of the war, despite exhortations to return from 'very clean-looking' officers who did not offer to lead them back to the front line. Bad though it was on Rough Diamond, the unfortunates on Apple Pie had it even worse – they were shelled ferociously and at 2200 Lieutenant Calvo, the local commander, reported six MAGs destroyed and three men wounded.

* Savage's father fought in the RAF during World War II.

Convinced by Armour Liaison Officer Captain Field that the Scimitars and Scorpions of Lieutenant Innes-Kerr's 3 Troop, Blues and Royals could handle the terrain, Chaundler decided to send the tanks and two rifle companies straight at Apple Pie from the north, through one of the principal marshy areas. On the eve of battle he learned of a minefield in the path of B Company, but after consulting with Crosland decided it was too late to change the plan. Fortunately the pressure pads on the mines were frozen solid. The key role in the attack was assigned to Neame's D Company, tasked to take Rough Diamond and then, after A and B Coys had taken Apple Pie and C (Patrols) Company had secured the hill next to the river, to hook wide along the base of Longdon and attack Wireless Ridge itself from west to east, with fire support from Apple Pie. Major Rice, the Battery Commander, and his forward observers with the rifle companies, were to direct fire from the two land batteries in close support of the operation, while naval gunfire from *Ambuscade* would concentrate on the main ridge. The attack was to be as 'noisy' as possible, with every gun and mortar plastering the Argentine positions for half an hour before the infantry set out.

The attack was delayed for twenty-four hours for the logistical reasons we have seen, compounded on the northern front when, late on the 12th, the Murrell Bridge collapsed under the weight of the Samson armoured recovery vehicle, loaded with ammunition for 8 Battery, which had been flown forward that day to a new firing position about 2,000 yards west of Longdon. The accident also cut the only land supply route for the Bandwagons to reach 2 and 3 Para, and without the time or materials to construct another the only solution was to use the bridge section built to repair the partially demolished causeway at Fitzroy. One of the two heavy-lift Chinooks (the sole survivor from *Atlantic Conveyor* was joined by one from *Atlantic Causeway* on 4 June) was taken off resupply duties to carry the section to the Murrell and to lift the capsized but still functional Samson out of the stream.* The delay worked to British advantage, because the morale of the men on Apple Pie and Wireless Ridge was even more undermined by the lull on 13 June than it had been by the previous day's bombardment. The enemy was obviously gathering strength and, compelled by the high water table to occupy peat shelters entirely above ground, the defenders felt horribly vulnerable.

---

* The bridge is still there, although the dangerously rotten timbers make crossing it an adventure.

At 2115 the lull ended when Chaundler's preliminary bombardment crashed down on the defenders. D Company advanced quickly to find Rough Diamond abandoned. Although they were supposed to stay put until A and B Coys seized Apple Pie, Neame's men did not linger after an unusually concentrated Argentine barrage tore up the hill. There were still a few brave souls on Apple Pie who tried to make a fight of it when Farrar-Hockley's and Crosland's men advanced, but they were soon discouraged by renewed artillery and mortar fire, punctuated by Milans guided by terrifyingly accurate tracer fire from the tanks. They were equipped with third generation night sights and so not blinded, as the defenders were, by the sinister colour-denying light from a steady rain of parachute flares. Calvo and García, the other lieutenant on Apple Pie, were wounded along with several of their men and, leaving behind thirty-seven men who preferred to surrender, the rest left the hill and retreated to Stanley with their wounded.

2 Para's first fatality of the night came as A and B Coys approached their objective and ran into an Argentine artillery barrage, which killed Colour Sergeant Findlay of A Company HQ Group and wounded several others. They encountered little resistance on Apple Pie itself but came under heavy artillery fire once GAA 4 was advised the feature had fallen and, like Neame's men, found it necessary to advance off their objective. The next phase was for C Company, still led by Roger Jenner – who had refused casualty evacuation after being wounded on Darwin Hill – to take the hill next to the Murrell. The Paras thought they heard weapons cocked as they approached, but if so the defenders thought better of it and decamped. The feature was not shelled by the Argentines, but one of the British guns had gone rogue and for a while every salvo fired at Wireless Ridge included a shell that dropped with unnerving precision on C Company's new position. The gunners were compelled to fire each gun individually until the culprit could be identified, and in the midst of doing so were further distracted when a raid on Camber Peninsula by the SAS in the assault craft of 1st Raiding Squadron RM came unstuck, requiring the artillery to shift fire to cover their retreat.

IN BREACH OF THE parole given when she was permitted to enter the area of operations, the supply/hospital ship *Bahía Paraíso* in Port William had on board a group of Gendarmería Special Forces intending to use her for a

ARGENTINE

7th Mechanised Infantry Regiment (RIM 7)

CO – Lt Col Giménez

Forward Observer – Maj Nani (W)

HQ Coy – Maj Pérez Cometto (Ops) (W)

  Recce Platoon – 2Lt Galíndez (W)

A Coy – Lt Calvo (W)

  3 Platoons

C Coy – Lt García (W)

  2 Platoons

3rd Mechanised Infantry Regiment (RIM 3)

OC – Maj Berazay (Ops officer)

A Coy – Capt Zunino

  1 Platoon – Lt Rodríguez (W)

  2 Platoon – Sub Lt Aristegui (W)

  3 Platoon – 2Lt Monez (W)

  Support Platoon – 2Lt Dobroevic

4th Infantry Regiment (RI 4)

A Coy – Lt Moughty (W)

2nd Infantry Regiment (RI 2)

  MG Platoon

Armoured Recce Regt 10 (EX 10)

OC – Capt Soloaga

  Platoon – Lt Bertolini (W)

  Platoon – 2Lt Harrington (W)

From Tumbledown

Mortars of RIM 6/B (Jaimet)

Mortar and HMG of BIM 5/N/3 (Lucero)

Artillery Support

GAA 4 (13/14 x 105mm)

GA 3/D (2 x 155mm)

BRITISH

2nd Battalion, Parachute Regiment (2 Para)

CO – Lt Col Chaundler, 2 i/c – Maj Keeble

Battery Commander – Maj Rice

Naval Gunfire Observer – Capt Arnold

A Coy – Maj Farrar-Hockley/CSM Price

  As before

B Coy – Maj Crosland/CSM Richens

  As before

C (Patrols) Coy – Maj R Jenner/CSM Geddis

  As before

D Coy – Maj Neame/CSM Greenhalgh

  As before except:

  12 Platoon – Lt Page/Sgt Meredith

Support Coy – Maj H Jenner/CSM Cotton

  As before

59 Ind. Commando Squadron RE

  Recce Troop – Lt Livingstone

Blues and Royals – Capt Field (liaison)

3 Troop – LT Innes-Kerr

(2 Scorpions/2 Scimitars)

Artillery support

7 and 8 Batteries, 29 Commando Regt RA

(12 x 105mm)

HMS *Ambuscade*

(1 x 4.5-inch)

From Longdon

3 Para's mortars

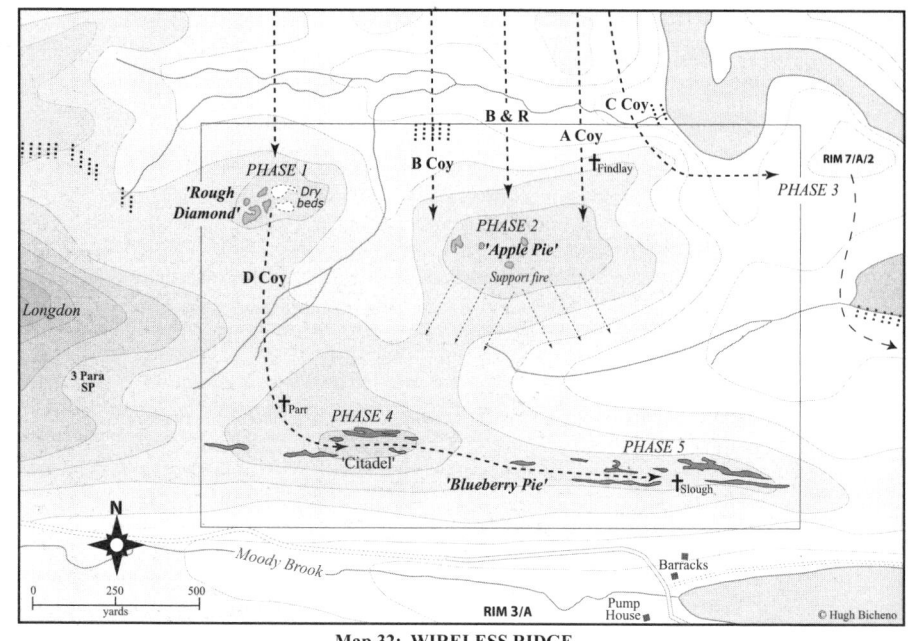

Map 32: WIRELESS RIDGE

Looking West

Kent · Longdon · Estancia · Vernet

3 Para

10 EX

RI 2/MG

2 Para/D

RIM 7/Recce

Photo Diagram 32: WIRELESS RIDGE

Looking East

Hearnden Water · Camber Peninsula · Stanley · Moody Brook

Comandos

RIM 7/HQ

RIM 3/A

2 Para/D

landing behind British lines. At about 2340 one of the Gendarmes spotted the assault craft and lit them up with the ship's searchlight. The raiders were fired on by the Marines and anti-aircraft artillery on Camber Peninsula, and fled back towards and around *Bahía Paraíso*, which was hit by friendly fire. One of the boats was lost and three SAS and a Raiding Squadron Marine NCO wounded. The raid has received a bad press. The military historian Martin Middlebrook attributes it to SAS glory-seeking and Thompson quotes a member of his staff saying 'Bloody Special Forces; the whole world has to stop for them I suppose.' The comment was, to say the least, ungracious. Like Bethell's effort at Ponies Pass, the raid on Camber Peninsula was an entirely successful diversion, as proved by the Argentine Army's official history and by Jofre's 1987 memoir, in which he insists it was a full-blown amphibious landing attempt. It made him feel more beset, and less inclined to continue the struggle.

WHILE THE ARTILLERY was blasting Camber Peninsula, 2 Para's advance was sustained by its own support weapons. Determined to maintain effective fire, the Mortar Platoon set up on rocky outcrops to overcome the self-burying phenomenon and men stood on the baseplates to keep the weapons from moving after every discharge. Four of them suffered cracked ankles, but it worked. By the time the guns (less the rogue) shifted back to Wireless Ridge, the unscheduled advance to the forward (southern) end of Apple Pie by 2 Para's main force had broken up the westward-facing defensive scheme set up by RIM 7's Giménez, with the last active RI 4 platoon (brought back from Mount Low on the 12th) and RIM 7's Recce Platoon covering the ground between Apple Pie and Wireless Ridge. Outflanked and with their commanding officers wounded they decamped to Stanley, cursed as they went by RIM 7's Ops Officer, Major Pérez Cometto, who was himself wounded not long afterwards. As an encore, 2 Para's Support Platoon and Innes-Kerr's tanks 'shot in' D Company's next objective: the western end of Wireless Ridge, held by EX 10. Soloaga, the company CO, described the effect in an almost admiring tone:

> The astonishing precision of the enemy's fire, even though it was
> night, is burned in my memory. From the beginning all kinds of
> tracer ammunition had a constant and crushing effect on our troops,

and the enemy's use of explosive shells in their automatic weapons [from the Scorpions and Scimitars] made the situation steadily worse, especially as my unit drew the greater part because it was the only one returning fire.

The rocky Citadel around the highest point on Wireless Ridge was held by the machine-gun platoon of RI 2, Argentina's premier airborne infantry regiment. The RI 2s had two HMG and six MAGs, and should have been able to provide strong support for EX 10. It is not certain how long the RI 2s stuck with it, but it is perfectly clear why they departed: photographs of the ridge immediately after the battle show craters along its entire extent. Today most of the scars have healed – but not around the Citadel, which is littered with rusting shards of shrapnel and where the vegetation still has not fully recovered. Two dual-purpose HMG mountings remain in the Citadel, and there is also a rusting 105 rocket launcher further west in the position held by EX 10, which was fired at Apple Pie by some very brave men, to no effect but at very great peril of their lives.*

The final straw may have come at about 0430 when Soloaga, acting as his own forward observer and experiencing great difficulty in getting GAA 4 to fire close enough, adjusted fire onto his own position. How many casualties this caused is impossible to verify, but unfortunately EX 10 was not dug in. During two hours of combat the unit suffered five killed and about fifty wounded, including many NCOs and all the officers except Soloaga himself, until at about 0500 the cavalrymen fell back, with permission from Jofre and in good order, carrying their wounded. At almost the same time as Soloaga's mishap, Neame's forward observer committed a similar error and a British barrage dropped on the place where D Company was forming up to assault the ridge, killing Private Parr. Perversely, the delay caused by the blue-on-blue may in fact have saved lives because when D Company finally attacked, the enemy was gone. The Paras secured the Citadel at 0600, just as RF Company resumed 2 SG's assault on Tumbledown.

ENDGAME ON TUMBLEDOWN was relatively short and very sharp. When RF Company's Price arrived at the summit Kiszeley briefed him on the location of the enemy he had been duelling with on the other side of the

---

* They may have been Sergeant Cabrera and Acting Lance Corporal Alberto Chávez, killed at about this time.

Terrace. Price decided to outflank de la Madrid's men and sent his 2i/c Captain Bryden with 2nd Lieutenant Matthewson's 3 Platoon along the southern side of the ridge that frames the Terrace. Lieutenant Lawrence's 2 Platoon was sent even further right, south of the main quartzite formation altogether. Second Lieutenant Dalrymple's 1 Platoon formed a fire base with the remains of LF Company at the summit. This became the only support fire for 2 and 3 Platoons because by now 1/7 Gurkhas had moved up the northern cliff-face of Tumbledown (they were almost level with the Guards, on the other side of a large outcrop and some 300 feet below them). Because of uncertainty about the exact location of the Gurkhas, neither the guns nor the mortars could be safely registered on new targets. Lance Corporal Rennie of 3 Platoon described what followed:

> Our assault was initiated by a Guardsman killing a sniper, which was followed by a volley of 66 anti-tank rounds. We ran forward in extended line, machine-gunners and riflemen firing from the hip to keep enemy heads down . . . Halfway across the open ground 2 Platoon went to ground to give covering fire, enabling us to gain a foothold on the enemy position. From then on we fought from crag to crag, rock to rock, taking out pockets of enemy and lone riflemen, all of whom resisted fiercely.

The eastern end of Tumbledown is more broken than **Map 31** (p. 290) conveys. It is full of rocky alcoves and patches of peat interspersed among the quartzite formations: micro-terrains where a single determined man might hold out almost indefinitely against averagely cautious troops – not, unfortunately for de la Madrid's men, a description that could be applied to the men of RF Company. The Scots pepper-potted forward with grenades, rifle and bayonet in a relentless progression that won the dispassionate approval of de la Madrid: 'they thinned out and came round our flanks; their deployment was good. They also engaged us with light mortars and missile launchers. This went on for a long time, and we suffered heavy casualties; we had eight dead and ten wounded. We started to run short of ammunition, particularly for the MAGs.'

3 Platoon Sergeant Jackson and Guardsman Pengelly won the MM and Lawrence the MC for individual acts of heroism during the advance, which

gradually worked around behind de la Madrid's men. Jaimet sent another platoon under Sub-Lieutenant Franco, but by the time it arrived at the back of Tumbledown, Corporal Campbell's section was established in the rocks above and Franco withdrew after losing three killed by machine-gun fire. Meanwhile, the laconic de la Madrid managed to extract the remains of his platoon from under the noses of Matthewson's men and 2 Platoon (led by Sergeant Robertson following Lawrence's near-fatal wounding):

> I could see we were outflanked, with the British behind us, so we were cut off from my company. Some of my men had been taken prisoner. I regrouped and found I was down to sixteen men. I started to retreat. The British above me were firing MAGs, but we passed close to the rocks, actually under their fire. I left six men in a line with one MAG to cover our retreat, but really we were fighting all the time; we could not break contact. They came on us fast, and we fell back; it was starting to get light. The whole hill had fallen by then, and we were on lower ground, south of Moody Brook. We eventually got through to Stanley, through what I must say was a perfect barrage fired by the Royal Artillery. We had to wait for breaks in the firing, but I still lost a man killed there.*

The last Argentine to die on Tumbledown itself was 'Pedro', whom I mentioned in the Introduction. He kept firing and moving to new positions until some members of the fire support team advanced around the base of the Terrace to acquire a better firing angle. British accounts state that Pedro was killed by Lance Corporal Tyler of LF Company with a 66, but in fact he fell to the machine-gun fire that followed the rocket, with a bullet through the forehead. The incident took place at least an hour after de la Madrid and the rest of the Argentine troops retreated. In *5th Infantry Brigade in the Falklands,* Nicholas van der Bijl reports that Captain Campbell-Lamerton of 2 SG's Anti-Tank Platoon persuaded an Argentine officer to appeal to Pedro to surrender, but I have not been able to establish who the officer was – it cannot have been Vázquez, who surrendered at about this time at the far end of Tumbledown, and Argentine sources admit to no other officer captured.

---

* Assistant Sgt Aguilar, whose helmet was taken as a souvenir and returned to his grave on the 20th anniversary. De la Madrid, yet another of the recent Academy graduates, was awarded the MVC.

If the Argentines care to do so, they may be able to establish who the officer was, and through him and de la Madrid perhaps identify and honour the memory of a very brave man lying in an anonymous grave in Darwin Harbour cemetery.

Covered by Campbell, Robertson led 2 Platoon along the rock-free north-eastern spur to the quartzite outcrop overlooking BIM 5's logistics DP (see **Map 30**, p. 286). Miller, the forward observer, joined him and called in artillery strikes on the retreating enemy until ordered to stop firing to permit surrender negotiations to take place. One of the forward observers with the Gurkhas, while moving along the cliff face and driving Lucero's platoon ahead of them, was shot in a blue-on-blue by a member of 2 SG Reconnaissance Platoon. The Gurkhas then had eight men wounded by Argentine artillery as they regrouped below the Terrace, called in by the forward observer de Marco.* A group of Sappers under Sergeant Wrega, who won the MM, cleared a path across the heavily shelled saddle from Tumbledown, but when the Gurkhas advanced they found William abandoned.

BACK ON WIRELESS RIDGE, no sooner did D Company occupy the rocky Citadel than it had to beat off the only company-sized counter-attack of the war, as RIM 3/A advanced from its position across Moody Brook in textbook formation. Jofre ordered Major Berazay, Ops Officer of RIM 3 and sector commander, to cover the retreat of EX 10 and of the last remnant of RIM 7, the HQ Group where only Giménez and one member of his staff remained unwounded. Berazay ordered RIM 3/A company commander Captain Zunino to set up a fire base with Lieutenant Dubroevic's mortars at the Pump House, and then the rifle platoons attacked towards the Citadel, with 2nd Lieutenant Rodríguez's and Sub-Lieutenant Aristegui's platoons in the lead and 2nd Lieutenant Monez's in support. S/C 62 Horacio Benítez of Aristegui's platoon (who was to survive a shot that passed through his helmet, grazing his head, and recovered consciousness to find he had been dumped on a pile of corpses) recalled that after weeks of shelling, 'we were like savages, eager to kill, completely degraded . . . in the last days we would be out sunbathing or listening to music while we were being shelled . . . I felt

---

* To do so he must have remained behind when de la Madrid retreated, which makes him a possible candidate for the captured officer referred to by van der Bijl.

as though I had always lived that way, as though I had been born there.' So much for green troops breaking under bombardment. He felt exaltation when ordered to attack, even though it was a daunting prospect:

> There were no trees, no rocks, no cover of any kind . . . everything
> was flying, machine-gun tracer crossing between the two sides,
> mortars, rocket-launchers . . . when we reached the foot of the ridge,
> the British fired star-shells, which turned night into day. We could
> see the British had three machine-gun posts that opened fire on us,
> then they came out in the open and were firing small hand-held
> missiles. From below they were like a ball of fire coming at us . . .
> It was so desperate that some of the men rushed back; the British
> fire followed them. They didn't know which way to run.

Benítez was one of a small number that reached the top, but the attack lost momentum after Aristegui was shot in the neck and Platoon Sergeant Vallejos in the stomach, and then 2 Para/D advanced from the Citadel to drive the survivors off the ridge. Meanwhile, Rodríguez's platoon angled east to try to make contact with any RIM 7s who might still be holding out, but according to Berazay the men came under artillery fire from both sides and after Rodríguez was wounded the platoon fell back on Moody Brook barracks. Some of the RIM 3s remained behind and attacked 12 Platoon, leading D Company's advance, from the rear. Private Carter recalled thinking they were being fired on by their own 10 and 11 Platoons:

> We asked [Neame] to come over and check our position. He
> bimbled across seeming oblivious to tracer all around him, then
> wandered back. We thought, 'silly bugger'. Then our platoon
> commander [Lieutenant Page] stood up, shouted to everyone to
> keep down and was knocked over himself, hit in the leg. He was
> screaming and shouting, but when the medic stripped him off
> there was no wound, just massive bruising where the round had
> hit his ammunition pouch.

The fire-fight lasted two hours, but as dawn broke there was nothing to stop the Paras occupying the rest of Wireless Ridge. As 12 Platoon moved into the area previously occupied by RIM 7/HQ, a sniper firing from the Pump

House at the bottom of Moody Brook valley shot and killed Private Slough. Sergeant Meredith, who took over platoon command after Page was injured as he had after Barry was killed at Goose Green, succeeded in firing an 84 at the building. The repairs are still plainly visible, and whoever inflicted the last British combat fatality of the war did not fire again.*

The Argentines made one final, pathetically brave effort. At about 0900 a group of about fifty RIM 7s, many of them B Company survivors, were rallied by Carrizo Salvadores and an Army Chaplain outside the Catholic Church in Stanley. They marched along the harbour front road singing the *Malvinas March,* among them the extraordinarily brave Félix Barreto and fierce Santiago Gauto, who recalled:

> Major Carrizo asked a colonel for a radio and was refused. We watched them arguing. Carrizo told him: 'We'll never win a war like this.' He was right. Then he turned to us and said 'Let those with balls follow me.' We advanced. Men around me had tears running down their faces. We knew we were not going to get very far, we were going to die, we were marching to death. The British were firing down on us with machine-guns, mortars, artillery. It was like advancing through the gates of hell itself.

The attack caused considerable alarm among the men of D Company, who were short of ammunition and now fixed bayonets. Chaundler was up with them by now and personally called in a last fire mission from guns now down to a few shells each. It was enough. After what Neame called 'quite a sporting effort, but one without a sporting chance' Carrizo Salvadores and his men fell back and joined the rest of RIM 7 and RIM 3/A along Felton Stream, where Jofre sent Military Police 181 Company backed by a Comando 601 platoon to prevent them returning to Stanley. A wild rumour about SAS infiltrators dressed as Argentine officers and encouraging retreat also led Jofre to order anyone doing so to be shot on the spot. The Wireless Ridge survivors were outraged and for about two hours the few unwounded RIM 7 and RIM 3 officers and NCOs struggled to keep the tense situation from exploding into fratricidal violence against the MPs.

---

* Meredith was awarded the DCM. Crosland and Farrar-Hockley received the MC but Neame (whose namesake grandfather won the VC in the Great War) unconscionably received no recognition.

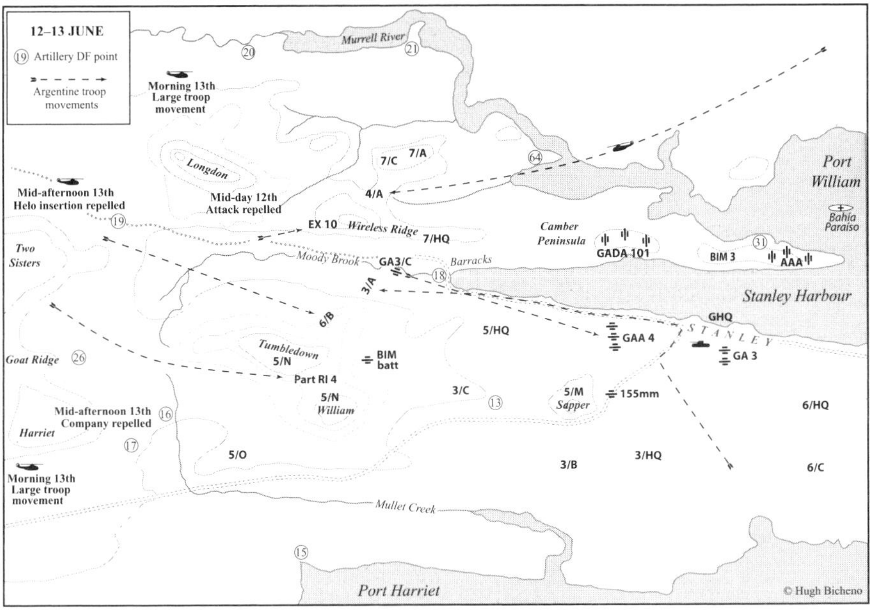

Diagram 7: JOFRE'S BATTLE

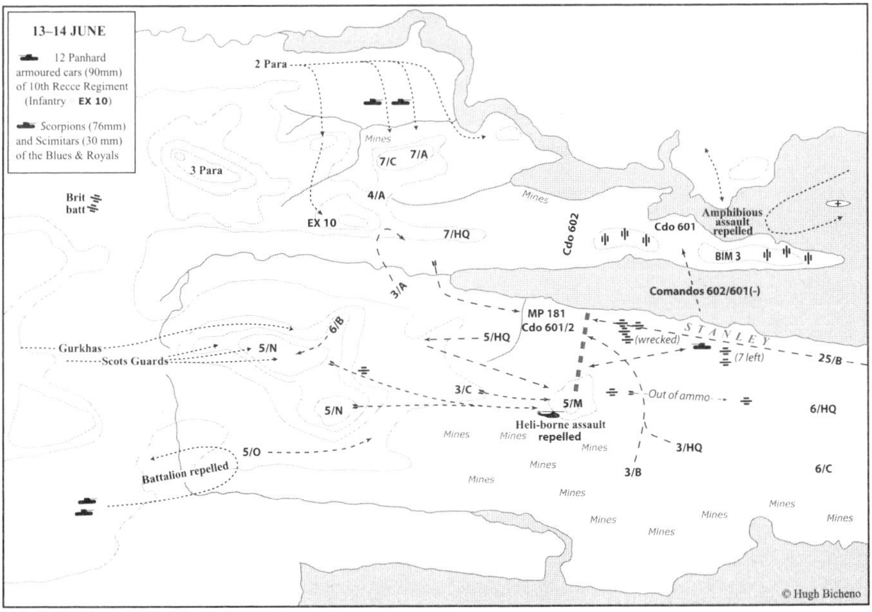

313

At some point during the confrontation the rest of RIM 3 came up from the south and an RI 25 company arrived from the airport peninsula, perhaps 1,000 men to form a last-ditch defensive line in front of the now silenced guns of GAA 4 on the racecourse. Jofre ordered the armoured cars of EX 10 to advance to a position north of Sapper Hill, but recalled them after they came under artillery fire. **Diagram 7** is drawn from the maps and text in Jofre's memoir *Malvinas: la defensa de Puerto Argentino* to show how the last three days looked from his point of view. British accounts tend to treat the surrender on the 14th as the inevitable outcome of the battles of Tumbledown and Wireless Ridge, but serious fighting might have continued. It would have been a bloodbath, because once Wireless Ridge was gone the British only had to advance along Camber Peninsula on the other side of the harbour to bring Stanley within rifle range. Further resistance could only be justified by an essentially political decision to sully the British victory by forcing them to fight their way into Stanley, to 'destroy the town in order to save it' as a US Marine colonel infelicitously put it during the 1968 Tet Offensive in Vietnam. Some credit is due to Jofre and Menéndez for preventing useless slaughter.

They were too late to prevent the last and most pointless deaths of the war, when two Sea Kings bringing forward 9 Troop, 40 Commando, under Welsh Guards command, dropped them in error at the foot of Sapper Hill. The Sea Kings were badly damaged before they could escape and in the ensuing brief but fierce firefight four Commandos were wounded (two more, including Troop Commander 2nd Lieutenant Cooper, later trod on mines). On the other side, three of Cionchi's BIM 5/Ms were killed and several more wounded when 2nd Lieutenants Koch and Davis rashly launched their men in a frontal attack in broad daylight. Among those involved was Llambías from South Sister, whose most vivid memory of the skirmish was his uncontrollable fury as he tried to shoot the helicopters out of the sky. Not long afterwards the defenders were ordered to withdraw from the hill and a *de facto* ceasefire took hold across the fighting front.

Humanitarian concerns may have been uppermost in the minds of Jofre and Menendez, but it is nonetheless the case that their military situation was untenable. There was now nothing to stop the British siting a battery within visual range of the airfield and there could be no more flights. But the crucial factor was that after *Lycaon* and other vessels brought every VT shell from the stores of the Army in Germany, the British artillery advantage awaited only adequate airlift to become a crushing reality. The airlift arrived with the aircraft ferries *Atlantic Causeway* and *Contender Bezant*, along with Royal Fleet Auxiliaries *Fort Grange* and *Engadine* (see **Appendix C**). The additional helicopters did not immediately resolve the logistics bottleneck because of the bad-tempered arrival of General Winter, but as the newly-arrived aircrews became more accustomed to foul weather flying, so the Argentines faced an enemy rapidly growing in strength as their own ebbed away. At the ceasefire there were only seven Argentine guns still functioning and they were down to their last few shells, but the Argentine Army's war log recorded a pronounced change for the worse as early as 10–11 June (paraphrased):

> Extraordinarily intense concentrations of fire from enemy field and naval guns reach all parts of the position, particularly around the artillery and communications centres. The men are practically unable to move and logistics flow is seriously reduced. Casualties are mounting, although fortunately not in proportion to the magnitude of the bombardment. Our own guns reply but cannot reach the enemy. Telephone lines are severed and units can only communicate by radio. Radar is shut down because the enemy evidently knows where it is and for the same reason radio communications are kept to the minimum.

At sea things did not look so rosy. On 13 June Woodward sent Northwood and Moore a signal saying that half his escorts were down to zero capability and his carriers virtually defenceless because the three Sea Wolf frigates (*Andromeda* and the two Type 22s) were decomposing. The fleet was also running out of shells (having fired around 8,000 during the campaign) and resupply was ten days away. He wrote in his diary: 'we are now on the cliff edge of our capability [and] if the Args could only breathe on us, we'd fall over! Perhaps they're in the same way: one can only trust so, otherwise we're in for a carve-up.'

In some manner, carefully not investigated after the war, the Argentines knew about Woodward's state of mind. On the 14th Galtieri told Menéndez that he had categorical intelligence to the effect that all the Stanley garrison had to do was hold on for a few more days, because the British were at the end of their tether. Although deliberate treason cannot be ruled out, the most likely source was off-the-record briefing against the war by British politicians and civil servants determined to undermine Thatcher's insistence on outright victory: which does not greatly narrow the field. The mechanism is well illustrated by the post-war performance of MoD official Clive Ponting, who, while responsible for preparing Defence Secretary Michael Heseltine's replies to Parliamentary questions, made sure the questions would be damaging by leaking confidential information to disgruntled Labour MP Tam Dalyell.

Galtieri's information was good but his hopes were misplaced. At this late stage the outcome of the war would not have been unduly affected by the departure of the carriers. In terms of maintaining an adequate Harrier Combat Air Patrol over the islands the forward airstrip at Port San Carlos, tragically out of action on the day of the *Galahad* disaster because of a flying accident, offered a superior alternative to the distant carriers. In addition, the second generation Type 42 *Exeter* revealed the full capability of Sea Dart on 7 June by shooting down a reconnaissance Learjet at 40,000 feet, as she was to do again during the night of 13–14 June against one of two Canberras flying the last Argentine combat mission of the war. During the same incident *Exeter* was also the most likely source of a fortunately aborted missile attack on *Penelope,* subject of much the most successful of the MoD's Falklands cover-ups.*

The Argentine Air Force could still mount dangerous attacks, notably on 13 June when three Grupo 5 Skyhawks dropped para-retarded bombs close to 3 Commando Brigade HQ on Mount Kent, at the time hosting Moore and his staff. The HQ had stayed in one place far too long, allowing Argentine electronic intelligence to pin-point the location, and only the peat prevented one more entry in the register of military disasters attributable to underestimating the enemy. But for every air raid that got through, four or five turned back when advised by Stanley radar of the presence of a Harrier Combat Air Patrol, which was about to become almost continuous once the Port San Carlos airstrip became fully functional. As their raids became more

* See the article by Michael Potter in the Bibliography.

infrequent, so the loss rate became more intolerable, and the Argentine aircraft were also suffering a rising rate of mechanical problems. Meanwhile, only one sortie by the Harriers, known to the Argentine troops as *Muerte Negra* (Black Death), had to be cancelled because of non-combat unserviceability, and with the advent of the US 'Paveway' laser-guided bombs they were about to become an order of magnitude more deadly.

But beyond technical and tactical considerations, Argentine morale was broken. Internal desertion was rising along with the incidence of self-inflicted wounds, as was the feeling of impotence among those still prepared to fight but worn down by six weeks of air and sea bombardment. Survivors returning from the battles for the hills brought horror stories and no man in the Stanley peninsula chamber pot could doubt what was coming down on him: the only question was when, and how unpleasantly. The metaphor is more than usually appropriate because a bizarre manifestation of the breakdown of discipline was that some of the Argentine troops took to defecating in any unguarded house or public building, as they had done at Goose Green. The practise continued on board the British ships that ferried them back to their country. Far from being ashamed of themselves, they boasted of it.* A desire to *cagar* (shit on/harm) the Kelpers as the cause of their humiliation began to spread, and for Jofre the moment of truth came when Major Dalton, his Brigade Ops Officer, reported:

> that many soldiers were in a strange state and the Kelpers were
> bound to get hurt. One RIM 3 platoon was told to go into the houses
> and kill Kelpers by a fanatical lieutenant. I will never forget that
> moment. It was as though a lightning bolt hit me. It was becoming
> evident to me that I was no longer in control. I told General
> Menendez and he realized that there was no question of fighting
> any further. He told me that he wished to talk to Galtieri to arrange
> a ceasefire. I agreed. It was all over. Fighting on Sapper Hill was
> out of the question.

Max Hastings interviewed a RIM 3 conscript identified only as 'Santiago', who confirmed the report: 'Nobody really knew what the orders were,

---

* See Edgardo Esteban, *Iluminados por el fuego*. However, most behaved well and were grateful for good treatment.

whether we should go on fighting or not. Many of the junior officers were disoriented because we had lost our company commander and couldn't find him anywhere . . . We were all very nervous after all we had lived through. Our platoon commander [Lieutenant Frecha] told us to take positions in the houses: "Don't be afraid of anyone," he said. "Go into the houses and if a Kelper resists, shoot him."' So it came back in the end to where it all began, the affront to Argentine Nationalism posed by the fact that no inducement or threat could overcome the contempt in which the islanders held everything Argentina stood for. Let us close, therefore, with a brief review of how the Kelpers handled the occupation, and how a few genuinely patriotic Argentine officers quietly ensured that while their own cause might be defeated, it would not also be sullied with non-combatant blood.

17 The Islanders' War

DURING THE NIGHT OF 11–12 June the home of John Fowler, Superintendent of Education, and his schoolteacher wife Veronica was riddled by a shell fired by *Avenger*. The house was close to the 1914 Victory Monument, a firing position for one of the Argentine 155mm guns, and was directly in front of the GAA 4 guns on the Racecourse. It should have been evacuated long before. The Fowlers received minor wounds and their two children were unharmed, but others sheltering in their house were not so lucky. Schoolteacher Susan Whitley was killed and her husband Steven, the Government Veterinary Surgeon, was seriously wounded.[*] Public Works Surveyor Harold Bonner was unharmed but his wife Doreen was killed. Eighty-five-year-old Mary Goodwin was mortally wounded. Doreen's mentally handicapped daughter and Mary's son Laurie survived unharmed. The names of the three women, two of them contract personnel from Britain, and Mary, a Kelper who had never left the islands, are on the Liberation Memorial in front of the Secretariat building: the only British civilians to die in the war.

Among the first to arrive at the scene were two unsung heroes of the occupation: Argentine Air Force Group Captain Carlos Bloomer Reeve, General Secretary of Menéndez's civil administration, and Navy Captain Barry Melbourne Hussey, Health, Education and Social Services Secretary.

[*] Susan Whitley is buried on Sea Lion Island. Her family established a Trust in her name with donations from the people of Llandrindod Wells in Wales, her home town, which sponsors an annual Arts and Crafts exhibition.

They lived nearby in what has been since 1989 the Stanley Museum, a building constructed in 1981 for the Argentine Air Force officers who ran the air service to Buenos Aires set up in the 1972 Anglo-Argentine Communications Agreement. John Fowler recalled Hussey saying, 'First we took your home, now we are killing you,' and replying that he should prevail on Menéndez to 'call it off' and prevent more deaths among the people he had supposedly come to liberate. Bloomer Reeve and Hussey did precisely that, preparing the Governor's mind for the last straw, which was Jofre's warning of the dangerously vengeful mood among his defeated troops. It did not need much preparing – Menéndez was a very civil administrator, who showed great sensitivity towards the outraged and humiliated Kelpers, even refusing to permit the removal of portraits of the Queen and Prince Philip from Government House 'because they are a loved and respected family'. He knew his career was over and he was not prepared to go down in history as the man responsible for the destruction of the community. At Stanley, as at Goose Green, the British had shown they were prepared to kill Kelpers in order to win. The plain subtext was that if the Argentines forced them to do so, they could expect no mercy.

There is a passage in Admiral Woodward's memoir where he writes of his anger towards Menéndez for not 'packing it in' as soon as the British landed, moderated in hindsight by contemptuous gratitude for his incompetence: 'It would not have taken much effort on his part to spin the land campaign out another ten days – and that would have finished us, not him.' Woodward's previously cited 'cliff edge of capability' diary entry suggests that ten days was an optimistic estimate, yet somehow the warships remained on station, despite being hit by hurricane-force winds on the night of the 14th. It is sad that even on reflection he did not understand the dynamics of the land campaign. Like Moore, Menéndez discovered that one of his two brigade commanders was unsatisfactory, but there was nothing either could do about it. They had to play the cards they were dealt and Menéndez knew he only held enough to bluff. He could not 'pack it in' when the British called, and at the end he could only have extended the war for one or two more days, during which hundreds of his men would have fallen to the wolves coming down from the hills. A more typical Argentine general might have done so with an eye to a political career as the 'hero of Puerto Argentino', and

Menéndez deserves honour, not contempt, for resisting the temptation, as well as a direct order to continue fighting from Galtieri, his Commander-in-Chief.

Menéndez's moderation is the more remarkable because he spoke no English and had no previous exposure to the bloody-mindedness for which islanders are famed, and which 150 years of hardship and metropolitan British indifference had distilled to a high concentration in the Kelpers. Much credit is due to Bloomer Reeve, who spoke perfect English and, while posted to Stanley in 1975–76 (in representation of LADE, the Air Force-run airline that ran twice-weekly flights to Buenos Aires), made many friends and came to admire the little community.*

If Bloomer Reeve was the bright shining head of the Argentine coin, Major Patricio Dowling was the dirty tail. A fourth generation Irish-Argentine with chips on both shoulders, he arrived with the invasion force as the head of the intelligence section of Military Police 181, complete with dossiers on all potential trouble-makers. He rushed around acting tough for two weeks until Bloomer Reeve persuaded Menéndez to send him home. Reports of Dowling's doings – but not of his departure – reached Britain with the individuals expelled from the islands in the first week of the Argentine occupation, including information that Dowling's section had taken over the top floor of the Police Station. The floor in question was demolished and Dowling's less theatrical successor badly wounded by a wire-guided missile on 11 June, one of two fired by a Wessex helicopter from the Murrell Peninsula. The wire on the other cut and it careered all over the harbour before plunging into the water. Most accounts allege the hit on the Police Station was a near-miss of the Town Hall, said to be the true target because the British believed it to be a meeting place for the Argentine top brass. Not so. The SAS had recce'd Stanley thoroughly and British commanders certainly knew where Jofre and Menéndez had their HQs, which were prominent and easily identifiable targets (see **Maps 33–34**, pp. 322–323). I believe it was a carefully targeted assassination attempt on the man most clearly identified with a hard line towards the islanders,

---

* Hussey was also bilingual and, as an officer in the Massera/Anaya navy, his respect for the islanders was even more remarkable. Happily it did not harm his career and he retired as a vice-admiral.

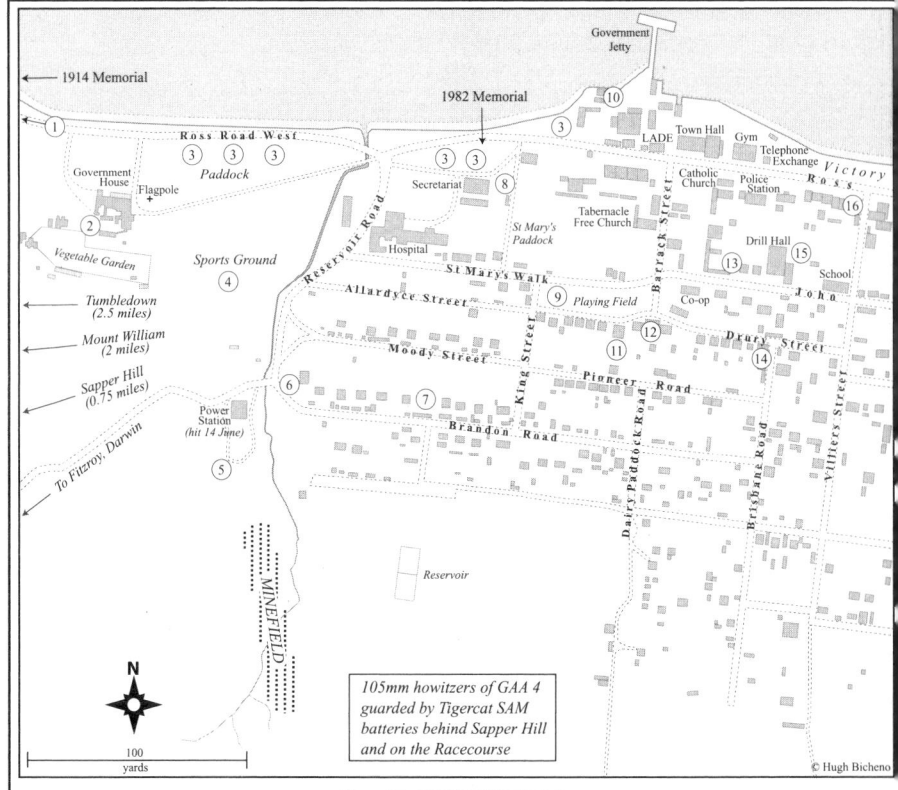

Map 33: WEST STANLEY

1. Night of 11–12 June NGS kills Susan Whitley, Doreen Bonner and Mary Goodwin in the Fowler house, destroys uninhabited Bryson house nearby on Racecourse Road.
2. Courtyard where Captain Giachino mortally wounded, 2 April.
3. Half-buried food and clothing containers.
4. Main troop assembly point and helipad.
5. Roland AA missile battery guarded by 3 x 20mm AAA.
6. George Butler's house (ammunition dump) burned by Major de Urquiza 14 June.
7. Home of Reynaldo Reid, possible Argentine intelligence agent.
8. Menendez's General Headquarters (GHQ).
9. 2 x twin 30mm Hispano-Suiza AAA and radar control.
10. Public Works garage (ammunition dump) burned by Major de Urquiza 14 June.
11. 2 x twin 30mm Hispano-Suiza AAA behind John Smith's house.
12. Historic Marine Barracks (Argentine Marines admin).
13. Falkland Islands Broadcasting Station (FIBS).
14. Rose Hotel (FAA Intelligence sleeping quarters).
15. Squash court (ammunition dump) burned 14 June.
16. Upland Goose Hotel (Army Intelligence sleeping quarters).

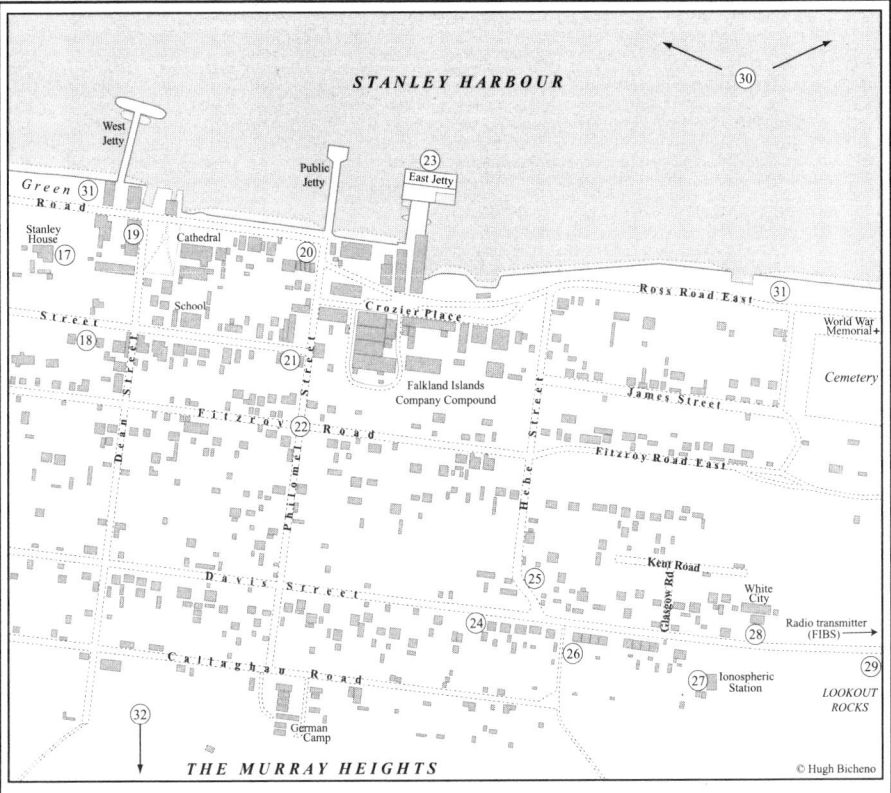

Map 34: EAST STANLEY

17. Jofre's GHQ. Garden was the last position of the last functioning 155mm gun.
18. Home of Fred Gooch – clandestine radio equipment found in attic post-war.
19. West Store – last refuge/rallying point for civilians 12–14 June.
20. Jubilee Villas (19th century prefabs – look like Sidcup-on-Sea).
21. Globe Store looted and burned 14 June.
22. Panhard armoured cars abandoned on Philomel Hill.
23. *Cabo San Antonio* loads Amtraks and BIM 2 on 4 April. Mooring of *Bahía Paraiso* hospital ship.
24. Location of Panhards until nearby Newman house shelled, gas cylinder explodes 13 June.
25. Shed containing ammunition burned 14 June.
26. Firing position of 155mm gun against naval targets.
27. Ionospheric Station attacked with rockets during invasion.
28. Location of FAA long range radar unsuccessfully attacked with Shrike 31 May.
29. Argentine APC destroyed near here, 2 April. Buildings shot up.
30. Greatest concentration of SAM and AAA on Airfield and Camber peninsulas.
31. AAA batteries.
32. 105mm howitzers of GA 3 on Stanley Common.

intended as a warning to other Argentine officers to behave themselves, because Nemesis was at hand.

The point about Dowling is that he was sent home for doing in the Falklands what earned him his rank during the Dirty War. The Argentines entertained the hope there could be a negotiated settlement almost until the end, and any peaceful solution would have had the islands crawling with neutral observers. Dowling's thuggish stupidity damaged the legitimacy the Argentines were anxious to establish before the world, and also subverted the hearts and minds approach to the islanders that Menéndez, Bloomer Reeve and Hussey were appointed to administer. In *Falkland Islanders at War,* Graham Bound says Dowling 'melted into the mist that hides many who once exercised illegitimate power in Argentina'. My internet browser pierced the mist. In 1998 a group of 200 Irish-Argentines addressed a petition to the Irish Minister for Justice, Equality and Law Reform, which stated that their great-grandparents emigrated in search of a better life, but now 'the economic and social situation in Argentina does not allow the descendants of those emigrants and their families to wholly fulfill the dreams of their forefathers regarding the access to basic levels of security, health and education [and] would like to have the opportunity to live and work in Ireland, just as Argentina offered the same opportunities to Irish people in the past'. Among the signatories are fourteen Dowlings, including Patricio.

For a full account of the many ways in which the islanders tried the patience of the Argentines I refer the reader to Bound's book, while John Smith's diary of *74 Days* (from which my map of Stanley) paints a vivid picture of what it was like to live in Stanley during the occupation and the siege. This is a military history, so I hope the many who contributed to their liberation in countless acts of defiance, which never let the Argentines forget they were unwelcome invaders, will forgive me if I concentrate on the few who put their lives on the line in direct support of British forces. The prize for sustained, cold-blooded courage goes to the Cape Pembroke lighthouse keeper, Reg Silvey, a radio ham who used his steel core washing line as an aerial to transmit information on Argentine troops and weapons locations to Britain throughout the occupation. The Falklands were under martial law and he would probably have been shot as a spy if the Argentine radio location vans had discovered his operation. His only protection was a stolen notice signed by Menéndez declaring his cottage cleared by military police and off limits to Argentine soldiers. Among other contributions he advised that there were no civilians on Stanley Airport peninsula, thus enabling the Black Buck raids. Mario Zuvic, a Chilean resident and a refugee from Stanley staying with the Short family at Port Louis, used their radio to jam the transmissions of Argentine forward observers, an extraordinarily dangerous activity. Neither of these very brave men received post-war honours.

Nobody ever accused ex-Police Chief Terry Peck of cold blood. He began his campaign of resistance by wandering around with a drainpipe, in which he concealed a telephoto-lensed camera, taking pictures of Argentine anti-aircraft artillery and missile sites that were smuggled out by people leaving the islands, all at risk of their liberty and possibly their lives. Warned that Dowling was looking for him, he left Stanley on a motorbike and travelled to Green Patch. After three homes he visited were raided by heliborne Comando 601 squads – conducting a bizarre campaign to overawe the outlying settlements and not, in fact, looking for him – he slept rough for ten days until he arrived at Brookfield Farm, where Trudi McPhee ordered him to take a bath. After he was immersed she threw him a rubber duck, which became his *nom de guerre*.

When Terry learned of the San Carlos landings he set out to meet the British troops on a wide route to the north that took him across Salvador Water (see **Map 18**, p. 192). He was guided from Salvador to San Carlos by fourteen-year-old Saul Pitaluga, whose father Robin was arrested on 1 May for radio communication with *Hermes* and subjected to a mock execution in Stanley. On arrival at San Carlos Terry was thoroughly debriefed by 3 Commando Brigade intelligence and provided them with maps of Argentine dispositions. He then teamed up with Butler's 3 Para Patrols Company, and guided the battalion through Teal Inlet to Tony and Ailsa Heathman's Estancia House. On 30 May, with Pike's hopes for a prompt assault on Longdon stalled by a lack of transport to bring up support weapons and stores, Terry radioed Brookfield Farm and asked Trudi to come to Estancia with as many vehicles and drivers as she could gather.

Trudi organized a caravan of Landrovers and tractors, including an old but powerful and 'incredibly noisy' caterpillar tractor driven by her partner Roddy McKay. Drivers who followed her through what was still enemy territory were Vernon Steen, a Stanley refugee at her farm, Claude Molken-buhr and Bruce May from Johnson's Harbour, Keith Whitney from Rincon Grande, Andres Short and Trevor Browning from Port Louis, Terence Phillips from Mount Kent, Neil Watson and Mike Luxton from Long Island and, from the residents and refugees at Green Patch, Raymond Newman, Pat Whitney, Maurice Davis, Terry Betts, Mike Carey, Peter Gilding, Patrick and Alastair Minto (see **Map 20**, p. 195). On arrival at Estancia they put themselves at the disposal of Paton, 3 Para's 2i/c, who was struggling with logistics and regarded them as manna from heaven. 'I don't know how we could have managed without them,' he said. 'It was something we hadn't really thought through – how we were going to move this stuff around. Trudi was the focal point. It needed someone to get a grip and she took it upon herself to do so.' Indeed. Another officer wryly commented that 'such was her strength of character, it was not always clear who was giving orders to whom.'

The Kelper Logistics Force not only shuttled supplies from Teal Inlet (the first convoy came perilously close to being shot up by the Blues and Royals) but also ran a twenty-four-hour transport service to and from 3 Para's forward positions between Mounts Estancia and Vernet, coming under fire from the Argentine 155s and from the 120mm mortars on Longdon, with occasional high level night bombings from Argentine Air Force Canberras and one ground attack (on McKay's tractor) by a Skyhawk. They also provided a taxi service to the Murrell Bridge for Butler's patrols, while Terry and Steen actually guided some of the Longdon infiltrations.

On the night of the battle most of them set out to carry the main force to Furze Bush Pass along a route nobody had driven before. Trudi led the way on foot, wearing white gloves to signal to the following drivers, but most bogged down. Vehicles driven by Trudi, Patrick Minto and Pat Whitney made it as far as the mortar line, while Terry and Steen helped guide A and B Coys to their start lines (see **Map 24**, p. 216). Terry, a 44-year-old with only militia training, went further and actually took part in the battle with A Company. 3 Para elected him the right marker for their victory march to the cathedral in Stanley and made him an honorary member.* Whitehall in its munificence awarded him an MBE and Steen a BEM, while 3 Para was able

---

* Terry is the Falklands representative of the South Atlantic Medal Association. He has crippling arthritis and remains haunted by the horror of Longdon, which he can see from his lounge.

to obtain Commendations from Commander-in-Chief Admiral Fieldhouse for Trudi and seven others. The Heathmans were inexplicably not on the list. To put this in perspective, large landowners who were helpful to the forces received OBEs.

MBEs and BEMs were also awarded to individuals for doing their jobs and subtly undermining the occupiers in often very dangerous conditions. They included Patrick Watts, who manned the Falkland Islands Broadcasting Station throughout and refused to bend the knee, Terence Carey and Leslie Harris at the Power Station and Derek Rozee at the Water Treatment Plant, who from time to time cut off supply to sectors occupied mainly by the Argentines. Some credit is due to Argentine Army Engineer Lieutenant Colonel Manuel Dorrego, in charge of Public Works, who must have known what the civilian engineers were doing – the blame for which landed firmly on his head – but refrained from punishing them. When one considers that all the Argentine officers were, at minimum, accomplices in the institutional kidnapping, torture and murder of the Dirty War – Carrizo Salvadores, for example, ran one of the 'processing centres' – and that most of them treated their own men worse than cattle, it must be said that with few exceptions their behaviour towards the Kelpers was astoundingly restrained.

This said, they undoubtedly made use of civilians as shields. Piaggi at Goose Green massed the residents, including forty-three children, at the heart of his defensive screen, close and equidistant from his HQ, the Oerlikon anti-aircraft battery and his 120mm mortar. As a prisoner he was outraged to be housed with his men amid ammunition dumps in the Ajax Bay Forward Maintenance Area, sharing a building with UXBs and taking exercise in a muddy sheep pen. His protests were met with variations on the theme that if he knew of a better 'ole he should go to it, and even the Red Cross representatives told him that he could not expect the British to observe the niceties of the Geneva Convention when their tents and most other field amenities were at the bottom of the ocean on the *Atlantic Conveyor.* The excuse was disingenuous – the prisoners did not have to be housed within such a high value target for air attack, but their captors can be forgiven for a little *schadenfreude* at the expense of officers responsible for littering the Goose Green isthmus with unmarked mines and sadistically ingenious booby traps.

Maps 33 and **34** do not convey how Stanley used to nestle on the steep slope leading down from the Murray Heights to the harbour, making it an almost impossible target for naval gunfire from the south.* It will be noted that the generals were not foolish in the location of their GHQs – Menéndez chose a building in the lee of the Secretariat and the Hospital, and Jofre took over a building previously in use as a dormitory for schoolchildren from the outlying settlements, close to the main General Store and the Cathedral. Anti-aircraft guns were placed among inhabited houses and the 155mm guns used the few paved roads to make rapid changes of location. But once the gunships began to fire from the north (see **Diagram 4**, p. 109), directed by SBS spotters on Beagle Ridge, property along Ross Road began to look less desirable; and after the missile attack on the Police Station, there went the neighbourhood. However, the principal destruction from British guns was around the perimeter of the town, concentrated around the areas used by the 155s to fire at the gunships and for counter-battery fire to the west. The islanders had a touching faith in the accuracy of the British gunners – when the Newman House on Ross Road was hit, Leslie Harris's wife Jill went towards it to look for her son, one of the local firemen. Argentine troops urgently beckoned her to take cover, but she replied: 'No, they're trying to get you, not me.'

Most of the damage to civilian premises was done by Argentine incendiarists. Half a dozen places were deliberately fired, including several in use as ammunition stores, which failed to result in the lethal explosions hoped for by the perpetrators. Such people are usually keen to remain anonymous, but to emphasize how close the whole situation was to the precipice Major Luis de Urquiza (about as aristocratic a surname as Argentine history records) of Logistics 10 proudly admitted his responsibility after he returned to the mainland. Be it noted that his exploits took place *after* he was informed that his Commanding Officer had ordered a ceasefire. He set booby traps around Government House and set fire to the Public Works garage at Government Jetty, and to George Butler's house near the Power Station, both in use as ammunition dumps. He also claims to have fired his rifle at British troops on the outskirts of Stanley in the hope of provoking them to break the ceasefire, although one may fairly doubt that one such as he would have dared draw attention to himself in this manner. He also said he

* Stanley has now grown over the heights to the new ring road, and the balance of the town is completely altered.

took down the national flag outside Government House and hid it inside his coat, when in fact it was entrusted to Soloaga of EX 10. The fact that Urquiza boasted of these actions, and that it was printed in a compendium along with accounts by genuinely brave men who actually fought for their country, illustrates the cultural gulf better than any words I could write.

Had there been more like Urquiza, innocence like Jill Harris's would have led to many more civilian deaths – and journalist Max Hastings's walk along Ross Road to be 'the first man in Stanley' would have been his last. It was Menéndez's responsibility to assure their safety and he did not do so opportunely: guilt for which was another weight tipping the scales in favour of surrender. The preliminary negotiations were handled by Dr Alison Bleaney, who until a few days previously had been permitted to maintain a radio doctor service for the settlements. In the morning of the 14th she tuned her portable radio to the 4.5 MHz civilian channel band and heard a message from the bilingual Marine Captain Rod Bell, who was trying to make contact with the Argentine authorities. She went to find Hussey, who accompanied her while she reassembled the recently disabled radio transmitter, and together they listened to what Bell had to say. Hussey then went to find Bloomer Reeve and they asked Menéndez for permission to respond. The two officers were not allowed to talk to Bell directly, but the terms of a meeting were agreed through Alison, her baby gurgling happily on her hip as she made history. She received an OBE, but insisted the two officers deserved the credit for persuading Menéndez to do the right thing. As we have seen, by this time he had more than enough reason to grasp the lifeline thrown to him by Bell, who was unconscionably omitted from the post-war honours list.

Stanley Museum is on Holdfast Road, so named because it was the line where Moore ordered 2 Para to halt while Lieutenant Colonel Rose of the SAS flew forward with Bell (in a helicopter trailing a large white flag) to arrange a meeting between Moore and Menéndez. As he had at Goose Green, Bell vehemently argued that face-saving concessions should be granted, so photographers were excluded (the screams of outrage from the hacks echoed for years) and the term 'unconditional' was crossed out on the surrender document. Moore's signal to London was admirably brief, dignified and said all that was needed: 'The Falkland Islands are once more under the government desired by their inhabitants. God save the Queen.'

Conclusion

40 AND 42 COMMANDO, and Z Company 45 Commando arrived in Southampton on 11 July to rapturous popular acclaim, with Union Jacks everywhere, girls flashing their breasts and 'Rule Britannia' bellowed loud enough to crack windows. The crews of *Hermes* and *Broadsword* received a similar welcome at Portsmouth on the 21st. It would be remarkable if the incidence of post-traumatic stress disorder (PTSD) was not markedly lower among those who experienced these spontaneous outpourings of love and pride than among the Paras and the rest of 45 Commando, who flew home a few days earlier from Ascension to isolated airfields, or in 5 Infantry Brigade, which flew back in late July and early August. The Task Force ships dribbled back, *Invincible* not until 17 September when she was met by the Queen, who came to welcome her son Prince Andrew. On 12 October there was a Victory Parade in London, more decorous than the jamborees at the ports but no less thunderously supportive. Meanwhile, popular interest in the war fed on a flood of books, magazines and articles, hence the contemporary quip 'never in the history of human conflict has so much been written by so many about so few.'

Argentine troops returning from the islands on British ships, professional cadre and conscripts alike, were treated like a contagious disease by their own authorities and shunned by the public. I have been unable to find the source of press reports that more soldiers, on both sides, subsequently committed suicide than were killed in the war: but even if true it cannot be assumed that PTSD was the common denominator. Among the British, alcoholism has a stronger claim, a genetic predisposition notably less common among Argentines, who would also be less affected by PTSD because their family structures are so much stronger. If there has been a higher than normal incidence of suicide among the Malvinas veterans, being treated as 'losers' by their society in the American style probably had much to do with it. The genuinely worthless individuals responsible for initiating the war did not have the decency to shoot themselves. Nor were they executed after court martial, although the armed forces' own internal enquiry, presided over by retired Lieutenant General Benjamín Rattenbach, recommended they should be.* However, nothing could now save the PNR or, ultimately, the armed forces' claim to represent the soul of the nation. So great was their loss of prestige that even in 2001–02, when civilian politicians achieved the greatest *quilombo* (whorehouse; sordid mess) in Argentine history with five presidents in ten days amid economic meltdown, the armed forces remained quietly on the sidelines despite going unpaid for months. One lesson learned, at least.

In Britain returning COs were not even officially debriefed because, it was said, the war was a one-off from which nothing important could be learned: and nobody was promoted out of turn because it would be 'unfair' to those who did not take part in the war. Sigh. In Argentina the armed forces embarked on a process known as *desmalvinización* (de-Falkandization) with the same objective: the reaffirmation of the sacred promotion escalator. One of my favourite anecdotes – possibly a factoid but illuminating an eternal verity nonetheless – is of a Guards RSM greeting the end of World War I with the comment that now the Army could get back to 'real soldiering'. Peter Dunn, the American author whose summary of the positive military lessons of the war I quote in Chapter 5, concluded that: 'when all is said and done, *the* lesson of the Falklands is that lessons from history must be learned – not briefed, heard, read or debated, nor optimised, bulletized, sanitized or summarized – but *learned*.' Indeed: but as an historian and sometime intelligence officer, I am not holding my breath.

One hopes that a latter-day Admiral Anaya would not now be so easily

---

* The report only became public, via a smuggled photocopy, in 1987.

tempted to draw the wrong conclusion. He would know that British politicians got a shot across the bow from the 'real country' in 1982, and will not soon forget it. A willingness to think things through remains elusive, however: witness the current imbalance between British military commitments and available forces. Outright pacifism – the rejection of violence even in self-defence – is ethically defensible. But if you accept that there will be times when the threat or the use of force will be necessary to deter or punish aggression, then it is deeply unethical to fudge *si vis pacem, para bellum* ('if you desire peace, prepare for war'). That means being fully prepared mentally as well as physically. Not timidly, apologetically, half-heartedly, symbolically, ceremonially or on the cheap – fully. As Julian Thompson says:

> The main lesson . . . was a failure of deterrence, and that we must be absolutely clear in future times, so we never get ourselves into that situation. . . . It is very important to realize that you cannot run away from war, you have to face it if it has to be. You don't stop wars by running away from them, you stop them by making it plain to the person on the other side that you are not going to be pushed any further and that the results are going to be pretty awful if he starts pushing you.

Let there be no doubt that the deterrent effect of the war was enhanced by the ferocity of the British troops and the ruthlessness of their commanders: not a novel phenomenon. It was, after all, English Parliamentary leader John Hampden (1594–1643) who said 'the essence of war is violence, moderation in war is folly.' There is a paradox here that much better minds than mine have wrestled with for centuries without achieving a satisfactory resolution: assuming your cause is just, must you also wage war in a just manner, even if by doing so you weaken yourself in the face of an unjust and unconstrained opponent? The lawless usually perceive moderation as a weakness to be exploited: in 1982 the Argentine Navy gambled that British nuclear attack submarines would be too constrained by the niceties of international law to strike first. They would have been certain of it had they known that when Prime Minister Callaghan sent *Dreadnought* to the South Atlantic in 1977, her captain had secret orders drafted by MoD lawyers not to respond if attacked but to 'surface or withdraw at high speed submerged'.

Government lawyers exist to provide a legal justification for what their political masters wish to do, and Callaghan simply wanted to establish the alibi he flourished in 1982, not to deter aggression. His successor had to deal with the consequences, but even though the MoD lawyers found accordingly, they still managed to make a dog's breakfast of the 200-mile Total Exclusion Zone around the Falklands announced in April 1982, tacking on the proviso that warships could be attacked anywhere only after it was pointed out that *25 de Mayo* could launch her aircraft from well outside the Zone. The announcement should have been redrafted to lead with the operative proviso. Unfortunately, lawyers in Common Law societies grow rich on ambiguity and have no incentive or training to draft laws – or pronouncements – in terms comprehensible to the laity. The political consequences when *Belgrano* was sunk included the US newspaper headline 'Britannia Waives the Rules,' Nott's lily-gilding statement to Parliament and the pious humbug of the British left ever since.

In much the same way, legal doubts about British sovereignty over the Falklands that were excavated by Foreign Office lawyers in support of the policy of sell-out have now, thanks to Freedman's *Official History,* gained a new lease of life. The sole purpose of the original findings was to provide a fig leaf of shysterish justification for a deeply dishonourable policy. Everybody knew it at the time, but once the imprimatur of legal justification is obtained it is much easier to persuade people that black is white. Civil Service lawyers are by definition second-raters, their opinions rendered worthless by institutional bias and the concern about their pensions that keep such people in line. They should not be used as cover for essentially political decisions, particularly in times of war when confusion can have fatal consequences.

A thousand mostly young Britons were killed or wounded in the war and it is right to lament the suffering and the extinction of so much human potential. But during the same period many tens of thousands more were denied timely and appropriate medical treatment by the National Health Service and millions of lives were blighted by endemic institutional failure in the social services, education, policing and the administration of the law. All these largely anonymous casualties were – are – caused by bureaucrats high and low pursuing their self-interest in the teeth of overwhelming evidence that by doing so they harm the rest of society and sap the vitality of posterity. Yet the myth of an impartial and 'fair' public service persists. By all means let us be indignant about the appalling human waste of war – but why stop there?

If not lives, then what about money? Ironically, the war saved the British government far more than it cost. In November 2001 Argentina declared the largest sovereign (and private dollar denominated) debt default in history: $132 billion, three or four times greater than the previous record set by Russia in 1998. British banks and companies, particularly the state-symbiotic arms industry, were fully behind the policy of sell-out in 1966–82 and, until the default, never ceased whining about being shut out of the lucrative Argentine market as a result of the Falklands dispute. Their virtual exclusion from the corrupt and unsustainable Argentine investment bonanza of the 1990s has spared them the monumental bath taken by French, German, Italian and above all Spanish investors, many of whom will claim their losses from their governments through the equivalent of the British Export Credits Guarantee Programme. Armaments deals, to the winning of which British diplomacy was unsuccessfully devoted during the 1970s, have proved to be particularly bad investments: the bribes paid to win them are unrecoverable, the equipment is now valueless, and the contracts have been denounced on moral and repudiated on legal grounds.

I doubt there will ever be an 'Official History' of the war in Northern Ireland, which cost far more lives and money than the Falklands and where a vastly greater military commitment failed to produce a conclusive result. While the Falklands War was fought, between 1 April and 15 June 1982 Northern Irish gangsters committed nineteen murders, ten of British troops, and a child was killed by a plastic bullet fired by a British soldier. On 25 June 1982 the heroes of the IRA killed eight unarmed soldiers on ceremonial duty in London. In the first incident a car bomb in Hyde Park killed two Household Cavalry troopers and seven horses, wounding a further twenty-three people. In the second, a bomb under the Regent's Park bandstand killed six Royal Greenjackets bandsmen and wounded twenty-four spectators. Poignantly, the Greenjackets had been earmarked to go to the Falklands until the Household Division stamped its feet.

What followed illustrated why there was always a leavening of intelligent but viciously contemptuous individuals among the dull sectarian thugs. First of all the Mayor of London, Ken Livingstone, welcomed spokesmen for the IRA to his city as honoured guests.* Then, in 1987 Gilbert McNamee was convicted on planted evidence as the bomb maker. The real culprit was Desmond Ellis, who admitted responsibility. He was *acquitted* by a British court in 1991 because the police only produced evidence that had been used to send him to jail in Ireland. No need to wonder why they did that – they dared not expose their own investigation of the London bombings to public scrutiny. McNamee was released in 1998 under the Good Friday agreement but persisted in clearing his name, and in December of the same year the Court of Appeals found his conviction 'unsafe'.

John Lawrence's harrowing account of his treatment on return from the Falklands with half his brain blown away ends with the thought:

> . . . if this was happening to me, an officer with a supportive forces family [his father and co-author was an RAF Wing Commander], what the hell was happening to the injured Guardsman whose father was an out-of-work shipbuilder in Glasgow, or an out-of-work miner in Wales? . . . I will, I have no doubt, be accused of being bitter. I am. Not about the war, the injury or my disability, but bitter about the pretence of real care and above all bitter about the small-mindedness which stops us changing as a society or a race.

The war produced several other blinding glimpses of the obvious, this from the future best-selling author Robert Harris:

> The instinctive secrecy of the military and the Civil Service; the prostitution and hysteria of sections of the press; the lies, the misinformation, the manipulation of public opinion by the authorities; the political intimidation of the broadcasters; the ready connivance of the media at their own distortion . . . all these occur as much in normal peacetime in Britain as in war.

---

* An act of crawling appeasement he repeated in 2004 by inviting a prominent Islamic defender of suicide-bombings to visit London. In 2005 over fifty Londoners were killed by practitioners of the technique.

In 2001 the BBC's star war reporter John Simpson waddled into the Afghan capital and proclaimed himself 'the first man into Kabul', only to discover that even if he had lost all sense of the ridiculous, the viewing public had not. He then claimed it was irony, intended to mock Max Hastings's exploit at Stanley in 1982. In 1985, two years after the Argentine military regime had fallen, Simpson no less fearlessly wrote and starred in *The Disappeared,* a programme about the Dirty War. I briefed his colleagues on it during the Amnesty International visit nine years earlier, but that did not stop the BBC adopting a position of moral neutrality in 1982.

In fairness, the islanders I spoke with were grateful to the BBC for running the twice weekly radio news magazine 'Calling the Falklands' and were surprised to learn my views on the World Service. I found this puzzling until I realized they only dared tune in sparingly, because they were supposed to have surrendered their radios to the Argentines. It was also a generational thing – I remember my father, a lifelong employee of Cable & Wireless who spent most of his career abroad, tuning in every evening to the rousing strains of 'Lilli Burlero',* a habit and a tune carried over from World War II when the BBC moderated the truth with patriotic discretion.

The class, or perhaps more precisely the type of person whose attributes led Anaya to think he could get away with stealing the Falklands was bitchily outraged when Thatcher proved him – and them – wrong. Steven Berkoff's 1986 play *Sink the Belgrano,* much celebrated by the left and favourably reviewed by the BBC, featured 'Scratcher' for Thatcher, 'Nit' for Nott and 'Pimp' for Pym. Possibly the ease with which Berkoff's own name can be – and no doubt often has been – turned to descriptive pejoratives inclined the author to that sophisticated line of wit. Meanwhile, Ian Curteis's *The Falklands Play,* filmed the same year for the BBC, was not broadcast because it was judged 'too partisan'. When it was finally screened in 2002 (on viewed-by-few BBC 4), taxpayers were graciously permitted to see what they paid for sixteen years earlier: a factually accurate dramatisation of what went on in Downing Street during the war, including Thatcher's tears when she learned of the loss of *Sheffield.*

Although there is no objective evidence of an electoral 'Falklands factor', belief that there was is sacred dogma among Progressives. Oddly, the one

* A non-PC ditty, to put it mildly. See *www.contemplator.com/ireland/lilli.html*

political lesson well and truly learned from the Falklands War – the imperative need to be a loyal ally to Uncle Sam – has done Prime Minister Blair far more harm than blatant contempt for his party, Parliament and the Constitution put together. It is sad that this rare example of Blair giving his word and keeping it has been the only action for which he has paid a significant political penalty. The wonderful, even hilariously amusing paradox is that those who denounce him for subservience to American cultural imperialism have themselves slavishly adopted every 'Progressive' social engineering fad to come out of the United States for many years: mixed ability school classes; release into the community of the mentally disturbed and of the handicapped into the general school population; political correctness; and the strident cults (as opposed to the pre-existing low-key practice) of environmentalism and multi-culturalism.

But that is a subject for another book. Militarily, in contrast to the EuroFighter project, which has dragged on since 1983 through repeated French efforts to sabotage it, the submarine-launched cruise missiles acquired from the USA in 1995 have been operational with the Royal Navy since 1998. The Royal Navy is also acquiring 150 Joint Strike Fighters (the US armed forces have ordered 3,000, so the unit cost of a superior aircraft will be significantly lower than the EuroFighter) to replace the Harriers. The Pentagon awarded the contract for the Joint Strike Fighter in 2001 and the first operational aircraft will be delivered in 2008. If Britain wants to 'punch above its own weight', the most cost-effective way lies in commonality with the US armed forces. It is most unlikely the promised super aircraft carriers announced in 2003 will ever be built, given the financial constraints sure to follow the unsustainable increase in the Labour government's payroll vote. A more realistic alternative would be a less gold-plated joint venture with the three-dimensional US Marine Corps, which provides a template to which Britain's bickering armed forces might aspire.

Trudi McPhee is right to suspect that the Falkland Islands are a problem Whitehall will try to get rid of in some underhand way once memories have dimmed, but wrong to believe the Foreign Office will take the lead. The islands are now mainly 'a pain in the arse' to the MoD. The road from Stanley to the military base and international airport at Mount Pleasant is built along a ridiculously high and occasionally lethal causeway, allegedly because annual rainfall was taken as the monthly figure during the planning stage. However, the project went ahead as planned even after the error in calculation was pointed out, and the politest explanation is that the man in Whitehall still thinks he knows best. A more sinister interpretation is that it was a deliberate decision to enable the military presence to cut itself off from the society it is supposed to be protecting. While it may be true that Mount Pleasant had to be constructed well away from Stanley for social as well as geological reasons, it borders on the insane to have left the island's sole significant population centre without close-quarter defence. Should the town and its airport fall to an Argentine *coup de main* in the future, there is no chance the Commander British Forces will receive political clearance 'to destroy the town in order to save it'. The door to another round of *ocupar para negociar* has been, perhaps only subconsciously, left open.

While the imbalance of economic and military power between Britain and Argentina is now far greater than in 1982, the possibility of a raid hailed by drumbeating hordes in the Plaza de Mayo can never be ruled out. The Argentines never cease to proclaim that they were the victims in 1982, and their Constitution now proclaims the Falklands to be 'an integral part of the national territory'. Few in the islands trust the British government's promise not to discuss sovereignty without their consent because the Foreign Office has learned nothing from past failures, as seen most recently over Gibraltar. If you enter into negotiations with a party whose rock-bottom minimum demand is greater than the maximum concession you are able to make, all you do is raise the other party's expectations and signal your own infirmity of purpose. The Argentines – and the Spanish – should grow up, certainly. But since that is going to happen right after pigs are observed flying around Big Ben in formation, the Foreign Office does ministers no favours by encouraging them to believe a London-driven compromise is possible.

Admiral Carlos Büsser, operational commander of the 2 April 1982 invasion, has been reliving the high point of his career ever since. In his 1999 book *Malvinas: conflicto vigente* (Falklands: Ever-Present Conflict) there is a priceless prologue by a Dominican friar with the splendidly multicultural name of Aníbal Fosbery. It is worth reading in full, but the nub of the prelate's argument is that: 'Anglo-Saxon imperialism has fused into a hegemonic power that seeks to establish a new international order based on democracy, free trade and international law, globalizing justice as it has consensualised it [?] by means of the Pinochet case.' This, it seems, is a very wicked thing. He concludes that although Argentina must bear the new reality in mind, 'when the dignity and decorum of the people and national sovereignty is involved we must not equivocate out of naivety, treachery or effeminacy.' *Pax vobiscum, frater.*

The 'Pinochet case' was the house arrest of the old Chilean dictator in 1998–2000, ordered by British Home Secretary Jack Straw, on a warrant issued by Spanish Examining Magistrate Baltasar Garzón. At the time it was assumed Straw acted to punish Pinochet for having helped Thatcher win the Falklands War, possibly also to provoke the Chileans into cutting off the islands' air link through their territory. The aim, so this theory went, was to squeeze the islanders into permitting Blair to discuss sovereignty during his planned visit to Argentina in 2001. Ockham's Razor cuts to a simpler explanation: Pinochet still had a considerable following in his own country and the arrest kept him away while an alliance of Chilean leftist parties narrowly won the December 1999–January 2000 general elections. By a strange coincidence and despite a ruling by the House of Lords that Garzón's warrant was valid, immediately after the Chilean elections Straw's house lawyers found Pinochet too ill to stand trial and he was released. Net result: good relations with the new Chilean regime and encouragement to Latin American judges to go after their ex-dictators. Both, however incidentally, beneficial to the long-term interests of the Falklanders.

One tends to forget that people who reach high office are probably rather good at politics. I have despised Straw since he was a more than usually obnoxious student activist and then Harold Wilson's confidential assistant, but I have to admit his sleight of hand in the Pinochet case was masterful, making him the natural choice for Foreign Secretary when Robin Cook resigned over the 2003 Iraq War. I do wonder, though, whether someone with a Security Service file as thick as Straw's must be was the right choice to shepherd a Freedom of Information Act through the bureaucracy.

Far be it from me to argue in favour of naivety, treachery or effeminacy when the dignity and decorum of the people and national sovereignty is at stake, but if Fra Fosbery believes those attributes lay behind the Pinochet case, and have served the 'consensualising' Brits so well, would the Argentine national interest not be better served by learning from them rather than carrying on and on with the same breast-beating Nationalist rant? If there were an ounce of genuine patriotism within Argentine Nationalism, they might have learned much more from the war. 'Fabian E', one of Daniel Kon's *Los chicos de la guerra* (The War Kids), hid in the rocks on Longdon near where Baldini died and was fortunate to remain undiscovered until he crawled out the next day. Like other Argentine prisoners he was struck by the easy familiarity among British officers and men, but the full cultural impact came later:

> I watched the English Army at work while I was a prisoner and no one shouted, but each one carried out his particular duty. Things were done well in an orderly fashion like that. When they gave us food on the ship or in the sheep-pens, they shared it out equally; everything was organized so that no one was eating more than the next man; even they ate the same food as we did. One day, in the sheep-pens, they handed over the food so that we could divide it up among ourselves, and there was such a row, such a lack of organiza- tion, that some people ended up eating nothing at all. Those are the things where I make comparisons. It seems we Argentines are almost always looking for a way to come out on top, to get some personal profit out of every situation.

Regrettably, the Argentine political nation has no interest whatever in drawing the right conclusions from either the Falklands or the Dirty War. After 1982 wounded Nationalism became the only game in town, its tattered banner fought over by the Radical Party and the Peronistas while all competed to beat their drums with the bones of the dead. One result was that until 2004 the Argentines who died on the islands (there are 240 graves, some con- taining multiple remains; 109 of them named and the rest are 'Known to God') lay in a cemetery built and maintained by the British. It was at last transformed by private subscription of the relatives of the fallen, after a long struggle to overcome attempts by their own government to turn the event into a bombastic reaffirmation of Argentine sovereignty. Jimmy Burns and Nicholas van der Bijl, among others, blamed the islanders for the impasse;

I hope they did so only from ignorance of the fact that the Argentine authorities were cynically exploiting the issue.

Lest we should think the Argentine armed forces are permanently out of the picture, it is as well to examine the text of a TV speech by Army Chief of Staff General Martín Balza, CO of GA 3 during the Falklands War and one of the few senior officers to emerge with credit from the debacle. The speech came in the wake of a flurry of revelations that began with the televised confession of retired Navy Captain Adolfo Scilingo in March 1995.* While Balza did not use the usual weasel word 'excesses', he fastidiously spoke of 'illegitimate means of obtaining information, including the suppression of life' and in general glossed over the harsh realities of the Dirty War, rounding it off with a new and improved version of the Argentine armed forces' claim to represent the soul of the nation, for good or ill:

> To be just we must recognize that in this conflict among Argentines
> almost all of us are guilty, by commission or omission, by our
> presence or our absence, by recommending or passively allowing it
> to happen . . . Even though we might wish to deposit the guilt with
> the few, in truth the guilt resides in the collective unconscious of the
> entire nation.

The collective unconscious, of course, cannot be brought to trial. The only meaningful sentence passed on any of the uniformed murderers was on the conscience-stricken Scilingo, who was rash enough to travel to Spain. He is so far the only fish caught in the net of the law associated with Examining Magistrate Garzón, whereby people can be prosecuted in Spanish courts for offences committed outside Spain. Scilingo is now serving 640 years in a Spanish jail after being convicted in 2005 of crimes committed during the Dirty War. Presumably the intention is to keep him under lock and key for use in future trials of bigger fish, made doubly necessary by the certainty that nobody else, now, will be stupid enough to confess.

Within Argentina, impunity for crimes committed in 1974–83 was won by Aldo Rico and Mohamed Alí Seineldín. During Easter Week 1987, Rico led a group of cammed-up Falklands veterans (hence *carapintadas* – painted faces) who seized control of the great military base at Campo de Mayo in

---

* See Horacio Verbitsky (trans. Esther Allen), *The Flight: Confessions of an Argentine Dirty Warrior*.

protest against a judicial summons for Major Barreiro, an unabashed Nazi and chief torturer in the La Perla concentration camp, and a fellow member of Seineldín's Jew-hating 'Integralist Lodge'. Rico demanded the dismissal of Army Chief Ríos for handing Barreiro over to the courts. Radical President Raúl Alfonsín (1983–89) found the Army would not suppress the rebellion and was compelled to negotiate with Rico in person. Ríos was replaced and the Due Obedience Law passed a month later, which admitted the 'just obeying orders' defence. In January 1988 Rico and his *carapintadas* again defied the authorities in arms, but this time the new Army Chief sent troops against them. Rico declared he would fight to the death but surrendered without a shot being fired. In 1990 he and Barreiro formed the 'Movement for Dignity and Independence'. In 1991, in alliance with right-wing Peronistas, Rico was elected Mayor of San Miguel in Buenos Aires. He then formally joined the Peronista Party and unsuccessfully tried, twice, to become the party's presidential candidate. His most recent initiative is a proposal that Argentina should declare economic war on the USA.

Seineldín, whom the Argentine Army High Command had prudently posted to Panamá, returned secretly and on 3 December 1988 led a *carapintada* revolt demanding not only a blanket amnesty but also formal praise for all crimes committed during the dictatorship.* The rebels were surrounded by troops loyal to the government and surrendered on the 4th. In addition to the Integralist Lodge, Seineldín had organized a secret civilian militia known as the 'Dignity Battalion', one of whose members told reporters (secrecy being a very relative matter in Argentina): 'In the world we admire [Libyan dictator] Khaddafi and [Panamanian dictator until overthrown by US invasion in 1989] Noriega. The principal enemy is not Russia because Marxism is dying. The principal enemy, not counting Zionism, is the United States and England.' Peronista President Saúl Menem, elected in May 1989, pardoned all involved in these uprisings as well as 280 Army and Police officers convicted by Argentine courts of crimes against humanity, plus the surviving Montoneros leadership and, bizarrely, a number of dead people.

Not included in the pardons were a group self-identified as the 'All for the

---

* Rico's second revolt and Seineldín's first involved forting up with support from RI 4 and RI 5 respectively, in Corrientes (see **Map 2**). Probably the result of posting disaffected officers away from Buenos Aires.

Fatherland Movement' (MTP), which on 22 January 1989 seized the arsenal of RIM 3 at La Tablada, Buenos Aires, and surrendered that evening following a day-long gun-battle in which thirty-nine were killed and sixty wounded. Here's where we step completely through the looking glass. The leader of the ultra-Nationalist MTP was Enrique Gorriarán Merlo, previously a leader of the 4th International (Trotskyist) ERP, who in 1980 led the hit squad that assassinated ex-dictator Anastasio Somoza, in Paraguay, on behalf of the Nicaraguan Sandinistas. Not to be outdone, on the second anniversary of his earlier revolt Seineldín and associates seized the barracks of the Argentine Guards Regiment 'Patricios' (RI 1) and a prominent downtown building in Buenos Aires, in an operation code-named 'Virgin of Luján' (Patron Saint of Argentina – a miraculous effigy dating from 1630). They surrendered that evening after a battle with the police in which fifteen were killed and thirty-five wounded.

All involved in these two risings were pardoned in a 'Decree of Necessity and Urgency' signed by Peronista interim President Duhalde in May 2003, before handing over to fellow Peronista Néstor Kirchner. In late 2003 Eduardo de la Cruz, Attorney-General of Buenos Aires Province, revealed that his staff had been using a system called Excalibur to monitor and trace the telephone calls of the criminal gangs terrorizing the nation's capital. They found a significant and constant volume of calls to and from the Presidential Palace, primarily from Kirchner's private office, and also to and from Army Communications Battalion 601. The criminals alone, said de la Cruz, could not organize a birthday party: they depended on 'people permanently entrenched in branches of government' for information, weapons, infrastructure and cover for their activities. Shortly afterwards Kirchner demanded an apology from Britain for having sent ships carrying nuclear weapons to the South Atlantic, some of which supposedly went down with the three frigates (*Ardent, Antelope* and ?) and three 'cruisers' (*Sheffield, Coventry* and ?) sunk during the war. As always the Falklands are trotted out whenever the Peronistas wish to distract attention from their crimes.

It is to this utterly rotten society that the Progressive London *Guardian* proposes the Falkland Islands should be 'negotiated away'. It reminds me of my trepidation when calling on Lorenzo Miguel, head of the Peronista '62 Organizations' and at the time running the Triple A, to give him an engraved invitation to attend the annual conference of the British Trade Union Congress (TUC). They even offered to pay his airfare, when he controlled the country's pension system and, had he wished it, the national airline would have put a Boeing 707 at his disposal. Intimidated by traversing the largest office I have ever seen, I was relieved to find him charming and the soul of courtesy – although I imagine he cried with laughter when he told his cronies about my visit. The point? The TUC conference organizers were told their Argentine brother was a murderous gangster and did not care, any more than the *Guardian* cares that criminal gangs are run from the private office of what it regards as the 'Social Democrat' Kirchner.

Lee Kuan Yew, Prime Minister of Singapore 1959–90, once urged a BBC interviewer to bear in mind that Singapore was not Bloomsbury.* Nor is Argentina. The Falkland Islands are now, barring defence, a little nation, self-governing and run on redistributionist principles that British lefties can only dream of. But that reality makes no impact on the Guardianista mindset. It will not have escaped the reader's notice that the denunciation of Anglo-Saxon hegemony, etc., by the monk Aníbal Fosbery and the anonymous member of Seineldín's 'Dignity Battalion' could just as easily have been taken from a *Guardian* or *New Statesman* editorial. I suspect the striking convergence of Progressive with Fascist utterances is the reason I did not find, in all the academic literature on the Falklands War, a single book in English that explores the social and cultural currents that move politics like flotsam in the Gulf Stream. And war, as Clausewitz observed long ago, 'is nothing but the continuation of politics with the admixture of other means'.

In trying to correct the deficiency and to relate the deep background to the conduct of the war, my eyes were fully opened to how dangerously misleading the old ideological labels have become. The true dividing line is between those prepared to work with humanity as it is, in all its chaotic and exasperating diversity, and those possessed of the intrinsically genocidal conceit that there should be – and that they can create – a 'New Man'. The right of the Falkland Islanders to live as they wish without harming others is a good litmus test. Between the overt, strident Nazi-Fascists of Argentina who deny them that right and the furtive Fabio-Fascists of Britain who want to 'negotiate it away' there is only a difference of degree.

* Described by R.H. Tawney in *Equality* as 'not the geographical area, but the mental disease . . .'

APPENDIX A

Ideologies

Communism is an ideal of a world without states, property, money or social classes, in which people come together voluntarily to carry out projects in response to the needs of the human community. In the wake of the Marxist–Leninist (*q.v.*) tyranny in the Soviet Union and similar regimes elsewhere, the term came to describe totalitarian (*q.v.*) regimes, in which all of human activity is subject to the unlimited coercive power of a self-selected élite.

Conservatism is a belief that customs and institutions shaped by time embody a profound collective wisdom and therefore rejects attempts to remodel society according to theoretical blueprints. Thus, properly speaking, it is an anti-ideology – but see Neo-Conservatism (*q.v.*).

Corporati(vi)sm is a late 19th century Roman Catholic doctrine proposing a Third Way between Socialism (*q.v.*) and Liberalism (*q.v.*), implemented through a legislative body in which labour, management and capital are represented by syndicates known as Corporations. It is the organizing principle of the Economic and Social Committee of the European Community.

Fabianism was the contemporary British equivalent of Progressivism (*q.v.*), highly influential in the development of the Labour Party and the founding philosophy of the London School of Economics.

Fascism is a totalitarian (*q.v.*) ideology associated with Benito Mussolini (1883–1945) that elevates the nation over all other loyalties. It calls for the creation of a 'new man' purged of individualism and materialism. It celebrates masculinity, youth and the regenerative power of violence. It seeks to unify the nation under the leadership of a supreme leader in struggle against internal and external enemies.

Liberalism in the classical definition stands for limited government by consent, individual autonomy, economic freedom and religious toleration – thus strongly associated with anticlericalism in mainland Europe. In the USA the term has become one of abuse directed at those espousing policies roughly corresponding to European Social Democracy (*q.v.*).

Marxism–Leninism is a totalitarian (*q.v.*) ideology developed by Vladimir Lenin (1870–1924) on the premise that the industrial working class (proletariat) can only achieve the revolutionary consciousness believed by Karl Marx (1818–1883) to be historically inevitable through the efforts of a 'revolutionary vanguard', such as Lenin's Bolsheviks in the Russian Revolution of 1917.

Nazism (National Socialism) is a totalitarian (*q.v.*) ideology associated with Adolf Hitler (1889–1945), based on the premise that a nation is the highest creation of a race, and great nations an expression of militarily powerful races possessed of good genes. It shares with fascism a belief in violence, the 'leader principle' and hostility towards Liberalism (*q.v.*), Socialism (*q.v.*) and globalization.

Neo-Conservatism is an ideology associated with disenchanted US 'liberals' (*q.v.)* who became influential within the Republican Party during the latter part of the twentieth century, based on faith in the power of markets and prices to order human affairs, irrespective of culture, politics and institutions. Unlike true Conservatism (*q.v.*), it favours the selective use of big government in the pursuit of a Messianic foreign policy and a re-moralizing domestic agenda.

Oligarchy means rule by the few, which being a description of all governments requires further qualification. Historically, oligarchies were based on military prowess, thence to birth, wealth, ability or more usually a combination of all three. In bureaucratic oligarchies professional civil servants set the agenda to which their democratically elected masters generally conform.

Progressivism was a US movement of the late nineteenth and early twentieth centuries to increase the power of the state and to professionalize government, associated with a belief that a self-selecting élite should weed out the less favoured through eugenics and bestow enlightenment on the remainder. Term later appropriated by the Communist Party of the Soviet Union to describe itself and like-minded political movements. Now the preferred alternative title used by British Social Democrats (*q.v.*) – but see Fabianism (*q.v.*).

Socialism in the absolute is an intermediate stage preparing the way for the withering away of the state in Communism (*q.v.*). The widespread association of the term with anti-democratic movements and totalitarian regimes led reformist socialist parties to rename themselves Social Democrats. Common to all is a commitment to socio-economic outcomes predetermined by an élite that believes itself, alone, correct-thinking, and bureaucracy-intensive redistributionist policies.

Totalitarianism is any philosophy that claims to have the answers to all the questions of existence and which seeks to impose that philosophy through indoctrination as well as coercion. It is distinguished from authoritarianism by its determination to control people's thoughts as well as their actions.

Argentine & British Orbats Disembarked Troops

It took me only a week to put together the Argentine orbat, with only a few blanks, from sources published in 1982–84; for the British I abandoned the struggle after many months of trying to obtain the same anodyne information. This included an extraordinary performance by supposedly expert researchers who strung me along for ten weeks before breaking off contact when it was too late for me to hire anyone else. I have left greyed out the data boxes they were supposed to fill.

In 1982 the Argentines calculated (for pension purposes) 14,218 participants in the war (10,001 Army; 3,119 Navy; 1,029 Air Force; 40 Gendarmería; 29 Prefectura Naval). By 1999 this had risen to 22,200 (Army 10,306; Navy 10,321; Air Force 1,478; Others 95). The increase may reflect the addition of support elements on the mainland, or simply corruption. The British awarded 29,682 South Atlantic Campaign Medals, indicating about 16,000 in support of 13,500 personnel disembarked or in permanent close support, broken down as follows:

Royal Navy	12,927
Army	6,968
Royal Marines	3,729
Royal Fleet Auxiliary	1,960
Royal Air Force	2,008
Merchant Navy	2,010
NAAFI	80

ARGENTINE ORBAT
30 May

Unit	Location	Officer Commanding	Total	KIA	WIA
Governor (Civil)	Stanley	Brig Gen Menendez	24	-	-
Military Staff	Stanley	Brig Gen Daher	11	-	-
Combined Ops	Stanley	Col Cáceres	12	-	1
Logistics Ops	Stanley	Col González	12	1	1
Engineer 181/601	Dispersed	Maj Etienot	209	2	10
CAB 601	Dispersed	Lt Col Scarpa	74	6	2
Intelligence 181/602	Stanley	Col Cervo	38	1	1
Communications 181	Stanley	Lt Col Andujar	44	1	2
Military Police 181	Stanley		64	-	2
Hospital Group	Stanley		63	-	-
		Total	**551**	**11**	**19**

3 INFANTRY BRIGADE

Unit	Location	Officer Commanding	Total	KIA	WIA
HQ	Stanley	Brig Gen Parada	232	4	13
Comms 3	Stanley/Port Howard		23	-	1
Engineers 3	Stanley/Port Howard	Maj Lima	172	-	3
Medical 3	Stanley/Port Howard		104	2	5
RI 4	Hills N & W of Stanley	Lt Col Soria	678	24	122
RI 5	Port Howard	Col Mabragana	847	8	67
RI 12	Goose Green	Lt Col Piaggi	733	35	72
		Total	**2789**	**73**	**283**

9 INFANTRY BRIGADE

Unit	Location	Officer Commanding	Total	KIA	WIA
HQ	Stanley	Brig Gen Daher	7	-	-
Logistics 9	Stanley		108	-	2
Comms 9	Stanley/Fox Bay		9	-	3
Engineers 9	Stanley/Fox Bay	Maj Lima	130	-	-
RI 8	Fox Bay	Lt Col Repossi	837	5	51
RI 25	Airfield/Goose Green	Lt Col Seineldín	681	13	53
		Total	**1772**	**18**	**109**

10 MECHANIZED INFANTRY BRIGADE

Unit	Location	Officer Commanding	Total	KIA	WIA
HQ	Stanley	Brig Gen Jofre	179	3	4
Logistics 10	Stanley		135	3	5
Comms 10	Stanley	Maj Tomatis	245	1	5
Engineers 10	Stanley/Longdon	Maj Matalón	272	2	17
RIM 3	South of Stanley	Lt Col Comini	930	5	84
RIM 6	West of Stanley	Lt Col Halperín	562	12	35
RIM 7	Longdon/Wireless Ridge	Lt Col Giménez	826	36	152
RI 1 Coy	Harriet/Stanley	1Lt MacDonald	188	1	7
* RI 2 MG Coy arrived 10/11 June: to Wireless Ridge 12 June		**Total**	**3337**	**63**	**309**

MARINES

Unit	Location	Officer Commanding	Total	KIA	WIA
HQ	Stanley	Col Moeremans	28	-	-
Logistics	Stanley	Maj Arena	80	1	-
Amph. Engineers	Pebble Is/Tumbledown	Maj Menghini	168	3	-
BIM 5	Tumbledown	Lt Col Robacio	743	16	4
BIM 2 Coy	Pebble Is	Capt Marega	130	-	-
HMG Gun Coy	Dispersed	Lt Dachary	136	8	7
BIM 3 Platoon	Camber Peninsula	2Lt Gazzolo	38	-	1
K 9 (14 dogs)	Felton Stream	Lt Paz	23	-	-
		Total	**1346**	**28**	**12**

Unit	Location	Officer Commanding	Total	KIA	WIA
FAA Infantry	Goose Green		57	3	-

BRITISH ORBAT
3 Commando Brigade (21 May)

Unit	Officer Commanding	Total	KIA	WIA	Other
HQ	Brig Thompson		-	-	-
Bde Signals Sq RM	Maj Dixon		-	2	3
Y Signals Troop RM	Capt Corbett		-	-	-
Field Records RM	Capt Hancock		-	-	-
Detachment, Postal & Courier Regt			-	-	-
Bde Air Sq RM	Maj Cameron	56	4	4	-
Flight, 656 Sq AAC	*See 5 Brigade*		-	-	-
605, 611, 612, 613 Tac Air Control	Maj Hughes		2	-	-
Logistics Regt RM	Lt Col Helberg		1	7	3
8 Detachments, 17 Port Regt RCT			-	-	-
Detachment, 47 Air Dispatch Sq RCT			-	-	-
Detachment, 81 Ordnance Coy RAOC	*See 5 Brigade*		-	-	-
Surgical Support Teams RN	Lt Cdr Jolly		-	-	-
Troop, 16 Field Ambulance RAMC	*See 5 Brigade*		-	-	-
Cdo Forces Band (medical orderlies)	Capt Ware	36	-	-	-

INFANTRY

Unit	Officer Commanding	Total	KIA	WIA	Other
40 Commando RM	Lt Col Hunt		1	6	8
42 Commando RM	Lt Col Vaux		2	23	22
45 Commando RM	Lt Col Whitehead		12	23	23
2 Battalion Parachute Regt	Lt Col Jones		18	39	48
3 Battalion Parachute Regt	Lt Col Pike		20	56	20

SPECIAL FORCES

Unit	Officer Commanding	Total	KIA	WIA	Other
D & G Squadrons, 22 SAS	Lt Col Rose	128	15	4	-
264 Signals	Maj Butler		4	-	-
2, 3 & 6 Sections, SBS	Maj Thomson	85	1	-	-
M & AW Cadre, RM	Capt Boswell		-	3	-
1 Raiding Squadron, RM	Capt Baxter	31	-	-	-

ARMOUR

Unit	Officer Commanding	Total	KIA	WIA	Other
B Squadron, Blues & Royals	Capt Field		-	1	1

ROYAL ARTILLERY

Unit	Officer Commanding	Total	KIA	WIA	Other
29 Commando Regt	Lt Col Holroyd-Smith		-	4	5
29 Bty, 4 Field Regt	Maj Rice		-	1	-

AIR DEFENCE

Unit	Officer Commanding	Total	KIA	WIA	Other
AD Troop RM	Lt Dunn	50	-	-	-
T Bty, 12 AD Regt RA	*(CO: Lt Col Bowden)*		-	-	3
Troop, 32 Guided Weapons Regt RA	Capt Dickey		-	-	1

ROYAL ENGINEERS

Unit	Officer Commanding	Total	KIA	WIA	Other
59 Independent Commando Sq	Maj Macdonald		3	7	-
11 Field Sq, 38 Eng Regt	*(CO: Lt Col Field)*		-	-	2
49 EOD Sq, 33 Eng Regt			1	-	-
EOD Party (RAF)			-	-	-
Troop, 9 Parachute Sq	*See 5 Brigade*		-	-	-

| | Approx Total First Wave | 7500 | 84 | 180 | 139 |

ARGENTINE ORBAT
30 May (cont'd)

Unit	Location	Officer Commanding	Total	KIA	WIA
SPECIAL FORCES					
Comando 601	Stanley/Moody Brook	Maj Castagneta	79	1	2
Comando 602	Stanley/Moody Brook	Maj Rico	50	5	7
Gendarmería SF	Stanley/Moody Brook	Cdr Spadaro	40	7	8
Air Force SF	Airfield	▬▬▬▬▬	35	-	-
		Total	204	13	17
ARMOUR					
Cavalry HQ/Comms	Stanley	Maj Carullo	53	-	-
Armoured Recce 10	Moody Brook	Capt Soloaga	216	6	68
Armoured Recce 181	Stanley	▬▬▬▬▬	34	1	2
		Total	303	7	70
ARTILLERY					
GA 3	Stanley Common	Lt Col Balza	258	2	21
GAA 4	Racecourse/Goose Green	Lt Col Quevedo	368	3	42
Marine battery	Behind Tumbledown	Lt Abadal	85	2	2
		Total	711	7	65
ANTI-AIRCRAFT					
GADA 601	Dispersed	Lt Col Arias	462	6	23
GADA 101	Cortley Peninsula	Maj Monje	112	3	9
Marine AA	Cortley Peninsula	Capt Silva	308	2	-
Air Force AA	Airfield/Goose Green	▬▬▬▬▬	200	-	-
		Total	1082	11	32
AIR/SEA OPERATIONS					
FAA	Airfield/Goose Green	▬▬▬▬▬	900	10	1
CANA	Pebble Is	Capt Gaffolio	50	4	-
Naval	Stanley	VAdm Otero	673	31	-
		Total	1623	45	1
	Total Argentine Forces in the Falkland Islands		13775	279	917

Of which elsewhere than Stanley Peninsula

Goose Green (1100 men)   RI 12 (-) plus C Coy, RI 25 (122), RI 8 section (37), Engineers 601 (11), GAA 4 (45), GADA 601 (33) & 202 FAA personnel

Port Howard (955 men)   RI 5 plus Engineers 3 (89), Comms 3 (8) & Medical 3 (11)

Fox Bay (930 men)   RI 8 plus part Comms 9 & Engineers 9

Murrell Peninsula (225 men)   A & part C Coys, RI 4 until 31 May-12 June

Pebble Is (180 men)   H Coy BIM 3 plus Amph Engineers & CANA personnel

In addition 373 men were killed at sea or operating from mainland air bases

General Belgrano	323
Mainland FAA & CANA	41
Alférez Sobral	8
Narwal	1

BRITISH ORBAT
5 Army Brigade (1 June)

Unit	Officer Commanding	Total	KIA	WIA	Other
HQ	Brig Wilson		2	-	-
Bde Signals (264 Signal Sq)	Maj Forge		4	-	-
656 Sq AAC	Maj Sibun		4	1	-
407 Road Transport Troop RCT	Maj Gardner		-	-	-
16 Field Ambulance RAMC	Lt Col Roberts		3	4	1
81 & 91 Ordnance Coys RAOC	Maj Thomas/Maj Smith		-	-	2
421 EOD Coy RAOC	Maj Welch		-	-	-
10 Field Workshop REME	Maj Ball		-	-	-
REME (att. Welsh Guards & 3 Para)			4	-	-
Army Catering Corps			4	-	-
Part 160 Provost Coy RMP	Capt Barley		-	-	-
8 Field Cash Office Army Pay Corps			-	-	-

INFANTRY

Unit	Officer Commanding	Total	KIA	WIA	Other
2 Battalion Scots Guards	Lt Col Scott		8	39	14
1 Battalion Welsh Guards	Lt Col Rickett		33	28	9
1 Battalion 7th Gurkha Rifles	Lt Col Morgan		1	15	-

ROYAL ARTILLERY

Unit	Officer Commanding	Total	KIA	WIA	Other
HQ & 97 Bty, 4 Field Regt	Lt Col Holt		-	1	3
Troop, 21 AD Bty			-	-	-
Troop, 32 Guided Weapons Regt	*See 3 Cdo Bde*		-	-	-

ROYAL ENGINEERS

Unit	Officer Commanding	Total	KIA	WIA	Other
9 Parachute Sq	Maj Davies		4	3	2
20 Field Sq, 38 Eng Regt	*See 3 Cdo Bde*		-	20	-
Approx Total Second Wave		3500	67	111	31
Approx Total British Forces on the Falkland Islands		11000	151	291	170

**EMBARKED PERSONNEL IN PERMANENT
CLOSE SUPPORT OF GROUND OPERATIONS**

Unit		Total	KIA	WIA	Other
Royal Fleet Auxiliary		1960	7	2	-
LPD (casualties LCU 4)			6	-	-
Approx Total		2500	13	2	-
Approx total British Forces in ground operations and close support		13500	164	293	170

In addition 94 men were killed in combat or operational accidents on RN or MN ships

HMS *Ardent*	22
HMS *Sheffield*	20
HMS *Coventry*	19
HMS *Glamorgan*	14
MV *Atlantic Conveyor*	13
HMS *Invincible*	3
HMS *Argonaut*	2
HMS *Antelope*	1
HMS *Hermes*	1

Naval Task Force

By date of arrival in war zone

* Major conversion
MN = Merchant Navy RFA = *Royal Fleet Auxiliary* RMA = Royal Maritime Auxiliary RN = *Royal Navy*

	Name	Type	In service	tons	knots	Notes	Fate
25/3	*Endurance*	RN ice patrol	1968	3600	15	2 Wasp	Scrapped 1991
11/4	*Spartan*	RN nuclear submarine	1979	4500	30		In service 2005
11/4	*Splendid*	RN nuclear submarine	1981	4500	30		Decomm 2003
12/4	*Conqueror*	RN nuclear submarine	1971	4900	30	Sank *Belgrano* 2/5	Decomm 1992
19/4	*Courageous*	RN nuclear submarine	1971	4900	30		Decomm 1992
21/4	*Antrim*	RN destroyer (County)	1970	6200	30		To Chile 1984
21/4	*Plymouth*	RN frigate (Rothesay)	1961	2800	28	Damaged 8/6	Museum 1988
21/4	*Tidespring*	RFA tanker	1963	27400	-		Decomm 1991
22/4	*Brilliant*	RN frigate (Type 22)	1981	4000	30	Damaged 21/5	To Brazil 1996
22/4	*Brambleleaf*	RFA tanker	1980	40200	15		In service 2005

SOUTH GEORGIA OPERATIONS 21–25 APRIL

	Name	Type	In service	tons	knots	Notes	Fate
27/4	British Tay	MN tanker	1974	15650	-		
30/4	*Alacrity*	RN frigate (Type 21)	1977	3250	30	Exocet missed 30/5	To Pakistan 1994
30/4	British Tamar	MN tanker	1974	15650	-		
30/4	British Trent	MN tanker	1974	15650	-		
1/5	*Appleleaf*	RFA tanker	1979	40200	15		To Australia 1989
1/5	*Arrow*	RN frigate (Type 21)	1976	3250	30		To Pakistan 1994
1/5	*Broadsword*	RN frigate (Type 22)	1979	4000	30	Damaged 21/5	To Brazil 1995
1/5	*Coventry*	RN destroyer (Type 42)	1978	4100	30		Sunk 25/5
1/5	*Glamorgan*	RN destroyer (County)	1966	6200	30	Damaged 10/6	To Chile 1986
1/5	*Glasgow*	RN destroyer (Type 42)	1979	4100	30	Damaged 15/5	In service 2005
1/5	*Hermes*	RN aircraft carrier	1959	28700	28	12 Harrier/18 Sea King	To India 1987
1/5	*Invincible*	RN aircraft carrier	1980	19810	28	8 Harrier/15 Sea King	In service 2005
1/5	*Olmeda*	RFA tanker	1965	36000	-		Decomm 1994
1/5	*Sheffield*	RN destroyer (Type 42)	1975	4100	30		Burned out 4/5
1/5	*Yarmouth*	RN frigate (Rothesay)	1960	2800	28		Sunk (target) 1987

FIRST AIR ATTACKS 1 MAY

	Name	Type	In service	tons	knots	Notes	Fate
3/5	*Fort Austin*	RFA fleet storeship	1979	23600	22	4 x ASW Sea King	In service 2005
5/5	British Test	MN tanker	1973	15650	-		
7/5	*Onyx*	RN submarine	1967	2410	17	Used for SBS ops	Museum 1990

Date	Name	Type	Year	Tonnage	No.	Role	Fate
7/5	Salvageman	MN tug	1981	1568	-		
8/5	Shell Eburna	MN tanker	1980	19763	-		
10/5	Alvega	MN tanker	1978	33000	-		
11/5	Uganda	MN liner	1953	16907	17	Hospital ship	Wrecked 1986
12/5	Fort Toronto	MN water tanker	1982	19982	-	Sole water source	
12/5	Regent	RFA fleet storeship	1967	22890	-		Decomm 1992
13/5	Plumleaf	RFA tanker	1960	26480	-		Decomm 1985
14/5	British Dart	MN tanker	1973	15650	-		
14/5	British Esk	MN tanker	1974	15650	-		
14/5	Hecla	RFA survey ship	1965	2733	14	Casualty ferry	To Ireland 1997
15/5	Anco Charger	MN tanker	1974	15568	-		
15/5	British Wye	MN tanker	1975	15650	-	C-130 bombed 29/5	
16/5	Europic Ferry	MN Ro-Ro ferry	1969	4190	-	*Helo deck	
16/5	Fearless	RN sssault Ship	1965	12120	21	4 LCU/ 4 LCVP/4 Sea King	Decomm 2002
16/5	Intrepid	RN assault Ship	1967	12120	21	4 LCU/ 4 LCVP/5 Wessex	Decomm 2003
16/5	Pearleaf	RFA tanker	1960	25790	-		To Saudi 1985
16/5	Stena Seaspread	MN oil rig tender	1981	6061	-		
16/5	Stromness	RFA fleet storeship	1967	16792	22		To USA 1983
16/5	Valiant	RN nuclear submarine	1966	4900	30		Decomm 1994
18/5	Atlantic Conveyor	MN container ship	1971	14946	-	Aircraft ferry	Burned out 25/5
18/5	British Avon	MN tanker	1973	15650	-		
18/5	Canberra	MN liner	1963	44807	27	Helo deck	Scrapped 1998
18/5	Dumbarton Castle	RN fisheries protection	1982	1427	20		In service 2005
18/5	Sir Bedivere	RFA Logistics	1967	5674	17		In service 2005
18/5	Tidepool	RFA tanker	1963	27400	-		To Chile 1982
19/5	Ardent	RN frigate (Type 21)	1977	3250	30		Sunk 21/5
19/5	Argonaut	RN frigate (Leander 2)	1967	3200	28		Scrapped 1993
19/5	Balder London	MN tanker	1977	19976	-		Later RFA Orangeleaf
19/5	Elk	MN Ro-Ro ferry	1978	5463	-	Ammunition ship	
19/5	Exeter	RN destroyer (Type 42)	1980	4100	30		In service 2005
19/5	Hydra	RFA survey ship	1966	2733	14	Casualty ferry	To Indonesia 1986
19/5	Sir Galahad	RFA Logistics	1966	5674	17		Burned out 8/6/82
19/5	Sir Geraint	RFA Logistics	1967	5674	17		Decomm 2003
19/5	Sir Lancelot	RFA Logistics	1964	5550	17		To Singapore 1992
19/5	Sir Percivale	RFA Logistics	1968	5674	17		Decomm 2005
19/5	Sir Tristram	RFA Logistics	1967	5674	17		In service 2005
20/5	Norland	MN Ro-Ro ferry	1975	12988	-	Helo deck	
21/5	Leeds Castle	RN fisheries protection	1981	1427	20		In service 2005

SAN CARLOS BAY LANDING 21 MAY

Date	Name	Type	Year	Tonnage	No.	Role	Fate
22/5	Ambuscade	RN frigate (Type 21)	1975	3250	30		To Pakistan 1993
22/5	Antelope	RN frigate (Type 21)	1975	3250	30		Sunk 24/5
23/5	Resource	RFA fleet storeship	1967	22890	22		Decomm 1997
23/5	Saxonia	MN freighter	1973	12000	-		
24/5	Irishman	MN tug	1979	689	-		
24/5	Yorkshireman	MN tug	1979	689	-		
25/5	Active	RN frigate (Type 21)	1977	3250	30		To Pakistan 1994
25/5	Andromeda	RN frigate (Leander 3)	1968	2962	28		To India 1995
25/5	Avenger	RN frigate (Type 21)	1978	3250	30		To Pakistan 1994
25/5	Bayleaf	RFA tanker	1982	40200	15		In service 2005
25/5	Blue Rover	RFA tanker	1970	11522	19		To Portugal 1993
25/5	Bristol	RN destroyer (Type 82)	1973	7100	30		Training hulk 1993
25/5	Herald	RFA survey ship	1974	2945	14	Casualty ferry	To Ireland 2001
25/5	Olna	RFA tanker	1966	36000	-		Decomm 2001
25/5	Penelope	RN frigate (Leander 2)	1963	3200	28		To Ecuador 1991
26/5	Cardiff	RN destroyer (Type 42)	1979	4100	30		In service 2005
26/5	Minerva	RN frigate (Leander 2)	1966	2860	28		Decomm 1992
27/5	Goosander	RMA salvage		900	-		

27/5	Typhoon	RMA tug	1960	1380	-		Sold 1989
27/5	Cordella	MN trawler	1982	1238	-	Minesweeper	
27/5	Farnella	MN trawler	1982	1207	-	Minesweeper	
27/5	Junella	MN trawler	1982	1615	-	Minesweeper	
27/5	Northella	MN trawler	1982	1238	-	Minesweeper	
27/5	Pict	MN trawler	1982	1478	-	Minesweeper tender	
27/5	QE 2	MN liner	1969	67140	32	*Helo deck	In service 2005
28/5	Lycaon	MN freighter	1977	11804	-	Ammunition ship	
29/5	Atlantic Causeway	MN container ship	1970	14946	-	Helicopter ferry	
30/5	Iris	MN tele-cable ship	1977	3874	-		
1/6	Baltic Ferry	MN Ro-Ro ferry	1979	6500	-		
3/6	Fort Grange	RFA fleet storeship	1978	23600	22	4 x ASW Sea King	In service 2005 as Fort Rosalie
3/6	Nordic Ferry	MN Ro-Ro ferry	1975	6500	-		
6/6	Engadine	RFA helicopter support	1967	8960	-		Decomm 1989
8/6	Wimpey Seahorse	MN tug	1983	1599	-		
10/6	Contender Bezant	MN container ship	1982	11445	-	Helicopter ferry	Later RFA Argus
12/6	Tor Caledonia	MN Ro-Ro ferry	1978	10000	-		

SURRENDER 14 JUNE

15/6	St Edmund	MN Ro-Ro ferry	1974	9000	-		
16/6	Astronomer	MN container ship	1977	27867	28	Helicopter ferry	Later RFA Reliant
18/6	British Enterprise	MN oil rig tender	1966	1595	-		
18/6	Scottish Eagle	MN tanker	1981	33000	-		
20/6	G. A. Walker	MN tanker	1974	18774	-		
20/6	Myrmidon	MN freighter	-	11804	-	Ammunition ship	
21/6	Geestport	MN freighter	1983	7730	-		
21/6	Stena Inspector	MN oil rig tender	1981	6061	-	Forward repair ship	Later RFA Diligence
1/7	Avelona Star	MN refrigerator ship	1975	9784	21		
3/7	Laertes	MN freighter	1977	11800	-	Ammunition ship	
10/7	Brecon	RN minesweeper	1980	725	15		In service 2005
10/7	Ledbury	RN minesweeper	1981	675	15		In service 2005
10/7	St Helena	MN freighter	1964	3150	-	Minesweeper tender	

SUMMARY

50 Merchant Navy
15 tankers
7 Ro-Ro ferries
6 freighters
5 trawlers
4 container ships
4 tugs

3 liners
3 oil rig tenders
1 refrigerator ship
1 tele-cable ship
1 water tanker

2 Royal Maritime Auxiliary
1 tug
1 boom defence

38 Royal Navy
15 frigates
8 destroyers

5 nuclear submarines
2 aircraft carriers
2 assault ships
2 fisheries protection
2 mine counter measures
1 ice patrol ship
1 diesel submarine

25 Royal Fleet Auxiliary
10 tankers
6 logistics landing ship
5 storeships
3 survey ships
1 helicopter support s

APPENDIX D

Air Defence & Aviation Assets

ARGENTINE AD ASSETS

Army AD Group 601 (GADA 601)
    1 x Cardion TPS-44 long-range radar
    1 x Roland Radar/SAM battery
    6 x Skyguard fire control radars
    3 x Tigercat SAM batteries
    12 x twin 35mm Oerlikon AAA
    3 x twin 20mm Oerlikon AAA
Army B Battery, AD Group 101 (GADA 101)
    8 x 30mm Hispano-Suiza AAA
Army & Marine Infantry Units
  Blowpipe and SA-7 'Grail' SAM
Marine AD Battalion 1 (AAA)
    3 x Skyguard radar
    3 x Tigercat SAM batteries
    12 x 30mm Hispano-Suiza AAA
FAA AD Group (GDA)
    1 x Westinghouse TPS-43F long-range radar
    1 x Superfledermaus fire control radar
    1 x Elta short-range radar
    4 x twin 35mm Oerlikon AAA
    9 x twin 20mm Rheinmetall AAA

BRITISH AD ASSETS

Blowpipe SAM – 2 Troops, 32 Guided Weapons
  Regt RA; Troop, 21 AD Bty, 27 Field Regt RA;
AD Troop RM
Stinger SAM – SAS
12 Rapier SAM Units – T Battery, 12 AD Regt RA
12 Rapier SAM Units – 63 Sq, RAF Regt (June)
HMS *Brilliant, Broadsword, Andromeda*
  2 x 6 Sea Wolf SAM, 2 x 40mm AAA
HMS *Bristol*
  1 x 2 Sea Dart SAM, 4 x 20mm AAA
HMS *Invincible, Cardiff, Coventry, Exeter,*
Glasgow, Sheffield
  1 x 2 Sea Dart SAM, 2 x 20mm AAA
HMS *Fearless, Intrepid*
  4 x 4 Seacat SAM, 2 x 40mm AAA
HMS *Argonaut, Minerva, Penelope*
  3 x 4 Seacat SAM, 2 x 40mm AAA
HMS *Hermes*
  2 x 4 Seacat SAM, 10 x 40mm AAA
HMS *Antrim, Glamorgan*
  1 x Seaslug, 2 x 4 Seacat SAM, 2 x 20mm AAA
HMS *Active, Alacrity, Ambuscade, Antelope,*
Ardent, Arrow, Avenger, Plymouth, Yarmouth
  1 x 4 Seacat SAM, 2 x 20mm AAA
RFA *Sir Bedivere, Geraint, Lancelot, Tristram*
  2 x 40mm AAA
RFA *Sir Galahad, Percivale*
  1 x 40mm AAA

BRITISH AVIATION

Type	Squadron	War Base	Deployed	Lost
FIXED WING				
Sea Harrier FRS1	800	HMS *Hermes*	16	2
	801	HMS *Invincible*	12	3
	809	HMS *Hermes* & *Invincible*	8	1
Harrier GR3 (RAF)	1	HMS *Hermes*	10	3
		Sub-total embarked fixed wing aircraft	*46*	*9*
Vulcan B2	44/54/101	RAF Ascension Island	4	0
Victor K2	55/57	RAF Ascension Island	20	0
Nimrod MR1/2	120/201/206	RAF Ascension Island	10	0
Phantom FGR2	29	RAF Ascension Island	3	0
Hercules C1/3	Several	RAF Ascension Island	Unknown	0
		Sub-total fixed wing aircraft Ascension Island	*37+*	*0*
		Total fixed wing aircraft (of which strike aircraft)	83+ (50)	9 (9)
HELICOPTERS				
Lynx	815	Frigates	24	3
Sea King	820	HMS *Invincible*	11	0
	824	RFA *Fort Grange, Olmeda*	5	0
	825	SS *Atlantic Causeway*, RMS *QE II*	10	0
	826	HMS *Hermes*	11	2
Wasp	829	HMS *Active, Endurance, Hecla, Herald, Hydra,*		
		Plymouth, Yarmouth	11	0
		Sub-total ASW helicopters	*72*	*5*
Wessex	845	RFA *Fort Austin, Resource, Tidepool, Tidespring*	18	2
Sea King (Cargo)	846	HMS *Hermes, Fearless* & *Intrepid* SS *Canberra,*		
		MV *Norland, Elk*	14	5
Wessex	847	RFA *Engadine*, SS *Atlantic Causeway*	27	0
	848	RFA *Olna, Regent* SS *Atlantic Conveyor*	11	4
Chinook (RAF)	18	SS *Atlantic Conveyor*	4	3
		Sub-total heavy lift helicopters	*74*	*14*
Gazelle		3 Commando Brigade Air Squadron	10	2
	656	Army Air Corps	6	1
Scout		3 Commando Brigade Air Squadron	9	1
	656	Army Air Corps	7	0
		Sub-total light helicopters	*32*	*4*
		Total helicopters	178	23
		TOTAL (of which strike aircraft)	**261 (50)**	**32 (9)**

ARGENTINE AVIATION

Type	Grupo	War Base	In Service	Deployed	Lost
AIR FORCE (FAA)					
Lockheed C-130	1	Comodoro Rivadavia	7	7	1
Lockheed KC-130	1	Comodoro Rivadavia	2	2	0
Boeing 707	1	Buenos Aires	3	3	0
Fokker F-27	1	Comodoro Rivadavia	11	11	0
Fokker F-28	1	Comodoro Rivadavia	5	5	0
Learjet	1	Comodoro Rivadavia	4	4	1
Canberra B62	2	Trelew	10	9	2
Pucará	3	Stanley/Pebble/Goose Green	60	24	24
Skyhawk A-4C	4	San Julián	16	12	9
Skyhawk A-4B	5	Río Gallegos	36	24	10
IAI Dagger	6	San Julián	33	18	11
Bell Jet Ranger	7	Stanley	8	2	2
Boeing Chinook	7	Stanley	2	2	0
Mirage IIIEA	8	Río Gallegos	15	6	2
Twin Otter	9	Comodoro Rivadavia	6	6	0
		Sub-total (of which strike aircraft)	*218 (170)*	*135 (93)*	*62 (58)*
ARMY AIR BATALLION (CAB 601)					
Aérospatiale Puma		Stanley	12	5	5
Agusta Hirundo		Stanley	9	3	3
Bell Iroquois		Stanley	20	9	9
Boeing Chinook		Stanley	2	2	2
Aeritalia G-222		Buenos Aires	3	3	0
		Sub-total (of which strike aircraft)	*46 (9)*	*22 (3)*	*19 (3)*
NAVAL AIR COMMAND (CANA)					
Beech Turbo Mentor	1	Stanley/Pebble	15	4	4
Lockheed Neptune	2	Río Grande	2	2	0
Grumman Tracker	2	Río Grande	5	5	0
Embraer AEW	2	Río Grande	2	2	0
Sikorsky Sea King	2	Bahía Blanca/*25 de Mayo*	5	5	0
Super Etendard	3	Río Grande	5	5	0
Skyhawk A-4Q	3	Río Grande	8	8	3
Aérospatiale Alouette	3	Bahía Blanca/*General Belgrano*	9	9	1
Westland Lynx	3	*Santíssima Trinidad/Hércules*	2	2	1
Aermacchi MB-339A	4	Stanley	10	6	5
Lockheed Electra	5	Comodoro Rivadavia	3	3	0
Fokker F-28	5	Río Grande	5	5	0
		Sub-total (of which strike aircraft)	*71 (40)*	*56 (25)*	*14 (13)*
COAST GUARD (PNA)					
Aérospatiale Puma		Stanley	3	1	1
Shorts Skyvan		Pebble/Stanley	5	2	2
		Sub-total	*8*	*3*	*3*
		TOTAL (of which strike aircraft)	**343 (219)**	**216 (121)**	**98 (74)**

Awards For Military Valour

In order of precedence

BRITAIN

In 1982 British awards were fragmented and complex. Since 1993 the DSO is awarded for distinguished leadership at any rank. The Conspicuous Gallantry Cross (CGC) was created to replace the DSO, DCM and CGM and is the second highest award for gallantry after the VC. The DSC subsumed the DSM, the MC the MM, the DFC the DFM and the AFC the AFM.

VC	Victoria Cross (all ranks, all services)
DSO	Distinguished Service Order (commanding officers)
DSC	Distinguished Service Cross (officers, sea)
DCM	Distinguished Conduct Medal (other ranks, land)
MC	Military Cross (officers, land)
DFC	Distinguished Flying Cross (officers, air)
AFC	Air Force Cross (officers, air)
CGM	Conspicuous Gallantry Medal (officers, sea and air)
DSM	Distinguished Service Medal (other ranks, sea and air)
MM	Military Medal (other ranks, land)
QGM	Queen's Gallantry Medal (military or civilian)
DFM	Distinguished Flying Medal (other ranks)
AFM	Air Force Medal (other ranks)

ARGENTINA

There are four awards 'From the Argentine Nation'. The highest is the 'Cross for Heroic Valour in Combat' (CHVC) and the second is 'Medal for Valour in Combat' (MVC). There are also automatic medals for those killed or wounded.

Bibliography

*recommended

ENGLISH (*London unless otherwise specified*)

Acosta-Alzuru, Carolina & Elli Lester-Roushanzamir, *All You Will See is the One You Once Knew: Portrayals from the Falklands/Malvinas War in US and Latin American Newspapers* (Athens, GA, 2000)

Adams, Valerie, *The Media and the Falklands Campaign* (1986)

Adkin, Mark, *Goose Green* (2000)

Amnesty International, *Report of the Mission to Argentina* (1977)

Amnesty International, *Testimony on Secret Detention Camps in Argentina* (1980)

Amnesty International, *The Disappeared of Argentina: History of Cases reported to Amnesty International November 1975–December 1979* (1980).

*Anderson, Martin, *Argentina's Desaparecidos and the Myth of the 'Dirty War'* (Boulder 1993)

*Andreski, Stanislav, *Parasitism and Subversion: the Case of Latin America* (1966)

Andreski, Stanislav, *Military Organization and Society* (1968)

*Andrew, Christopher & Vasili Mitrokhin, *The Mitrokhin Archive: the KGB in Europe and the West* (2000)

Andrew, Christopher, *Secret Service: the Making of the British Intelligence Community* (1992)

Arcangelis, Mario de, *Electronic Warfare* (Poole 1985)

*Arthur, Max, *Above All, Courage* (1985)

Aulich, James, *Framing the Falklands War: Nationhood, Culture and Identity* (1992)

Barker, Nick, *Beyond Endurance* (Barnsley 2002)

Barnett, Anthony, *Iron Britannia* (1982)

Beck, Peter, *The Falkland Islands as an International Problem* (1988)

Belgrano Action Group, *The Unnecessary War* (Hampstead 1986)

Benn, Tony, *On the Falklands War* (1982)

Betts, Terence, *A Falkland Islander Till I Die* (Lewes 2004)

Bijl, Nicholas van der & Paul Hannon, *Argentine Forces in the Falklands* (1992)

Bijl, Nicholas van der, *Nine Battles to Stanley* (Barnsley 1999)

*Bijl, Nicholas van der & David Aldea, *5th Infantry Brigade in the Falklands* (Barnsley 2003)

Billière, Peter de la, *Looking for Trouble* (1994)

*Bilton, Michael & Peter Kosminsky (eds.), *Speaking Out* (1989) – see TV Documentaries

Bishop, Patrick & John Witherow, *The Winter War* (1982)

Blakeway, Denys, *The Falklands War* (1992) – see TV Documentaries

*Bound, Graham, *Falkland Islanders at War* (Barnsley 2002)

*Bramley, Vincent, *Excursion to Hell* (1991)

*Bramley, Vincent, *Two Sides of Hell* (1994)

Bransby, Guy, *Her Majesty's Interrogator* (1996)

Braybrook, Roy, *Battle for the Falklands: Air Forces* (1982)

Brody, Reed, *Contra Terror in Nicaragua* (Boston 1985)

*Brown, David, *The Royal Navy and the Falklands War* (1987)

Brown, Timothy, *The Real Contra War: Highlander Peasant Resistance* (Norman 2001)

Burns, Jimmy, *The Land That Lost Its Heroes: Argentina, the Falklands and Alfonsín* (1987)

Callaghan, James, *Time and Chance* (1987)

Cameron, Sue, *The Cheating Classes* (2002)

Carlson, Eric, *I Remember Julia: Voices of the Disappeared* (Philadelphia 1996)

Carrington, Peter, *Reflect on Things Past* (1988)

*Cawkell, Mary, *The History of the Falkland Islands* (Oswestry 2001)

Chandler, David (ed.), *The Oxford History of the British Army* (Oxford 2003)

Charlton, Michael, *The Little Platoon* (Oxford 1989)

Child, Jack, *Geopolitics and Conflict in South America: Quarrels among Neighbours* (New York 1985)

*Clapp, Michael & Ewen Southby-Tailyour, *Amphibious Assault Falklands* (1997)

Clark, Fred, *Airloss: Falklands conflict 1982* (Stanley n.d.)

Coase, Ronald, *British Broadcasting: a Study in Monopoly* (1950)

*Colbeck, Graham, *With 3 Para to the Falklands* (2002)

Coll, Alberto & Anthony Arendt (eds.), *The Falklands War: Lessons for Strategy, Diplomacy and International Law* (Boston 1985)

Connor, Ken, *Ghost Force: the Secret History of the SAS* (2002)

Cooksey, Jon, *3 Para Mount Longdon: the Bloodiest Battle* (Barnsley 2004)

Cordesman, Anthony & Abraham Wagner, *The Lessons of Modern War*, Vol 3 (Boulder 1990)

Cornwall, Rupert, *God's Banker* (1984)

Craig, Chris, *Call for Fire: Sea Combat in the Falklands and the Gulf War* (1995)

Critchley, Julian, *Westminster Blues* (1985)

Critchley, Mike, *Task Force Portfolio*, 2 vols. (Liskeard n.d.)

Crozier, Brian, *Free Agent: the Unseen War 1941–1991* (1993)

Curtis, Mike, *CQB: Close Quarter Battle* (1997)

*Dale, Iain (ed.), *Memories of the Falklands* (2002)

Dalyell, Tam, *One Man's Falklands* (1982)

Dalyell, Tam, *Thatcher's Torpedo* (1983)

*Danchev, Alex (ed.), *International Perspectives on the Falklands Conflict: a Matter*

of Life and Death (Basingstoke 1992), of which the following:
  Calvert, Peter, 'The Malvinas as a Factor in Argentine politics'.
  Danchev, Alex, 'The Franks Report: a Chronicle of Unripe Time'.
  Ellerby, Clive, 'The Role of the Falklands Lobby'.
  Noguera, Felipe & Peter Willetts, 'Public Attitudes and the Future of the Islands'.
  Sanfuentes, Felipe, 'The Chilean Falklands Factor'.
Dartford, Mark (ed.), *Falklands Armoury* (Poole 1985)
David, Saul, *Military Blunders: the How and Why of Military Failure* (1997)
Dillon, G. M., *Public Opinion and the Falklands Conflict* (Lancaster 1984)
Dillon, G. M., *The Falklands, Politics and War* (1989)
Dillon, Martin, *The Dirty War* (1991)
Dinges, John, *The Condor Years: How Pinochet and his Allies Brought Terrorism to Three Continents* (New York 2004)
Dixon, Norman, *On the Psychology of Military Incompetence* (1976)
Dobson, Christopher, John Miller & Ronald Payne, *The Falklands Conflict* (Falmouth 1982)
Drinan, Robert, S.J., *The Mobilization of Shame* (Yale 2001)
Eddy, Paul, Magnus Linklater & Peter Gillman (Sunday Times Insight Team), *The Falklands War* (1982)
English, Adrian & Anthony Watts, *Battle for the Falklands: Naval Forces* (1982)
Escudé, Carlos, *Foreign Policy Theory in Menem's Argentina* (Gainesville 1997)
Feitlowitz, Marguerite, *A Lexicon of Terror* (New York 1998)
Ferguson, Niall, *Empire: How Britain Made the Modern World* (2003)
*Fitz-Gibbon, Spencer, *Not Mentioned in Despatches* (Cambridge 2001)
Fowler, William, *Battle for the Falklands: Land Forces* (1982)
Fox, Robert, *Eyewitness Falklands* (1982)
Freedman, Lawrence, *Britain and the Falklands War* (Oxford 1988)
Freedman, Lawrence & Virginia Gamba-Stonehouse, *Signals of War* (1990)
Frost, John, *2 Para Falklands: the battalion at war* (1984)
Foster, Kevin, *Fighting Fictions: War, Narrative and National Identity* (1999)
Fursdon, Edward, *The Falklands Aftermath: Picking up the Pieces* (1988)
Garvin, Glenn, *Everybody Had His Own Gringo* (McLean 1992)
Gavshon, Arthur & Desmond Rice, *The Sinking of the Belgrano* (1984)
Geraghty, Tony, *Who Dares Wins: the Sory of the SAS 1950–1992* (1992)
*Gibran, Daniel, *Falklands: Britain Versus the Past in the South Atlantic* (Jefferson 1998)
*Goebel, Julius (Intro & Preface J.C.J. Metford), *The Struggle for the Falkland Islands: a Study in Legal and Diplomatic History* (Yale 1982)
Goñi, Uki, *The Real Odessa: Smuggling the Nazis to Perón's Argentina* (2002)
Gough, Barry, *The Falkland Islands/Malvinas: the Contest for Empire in the South Atlantic* (1992)
Gough, Richard, *Falklands 1914* (Penzance 2003)
Graham-Yooll, Andrew, *A State of Fear: Memories of Argentina's Nightmare* (1986)
Graham-Yooll, Andrew, *Committed Observer: Memoirs of a Journalist* (1995)
Graham-Yooll, Andrew, *Imperial Skirmishes: War and Gunboat Diplomacy in Latin America* (New York 2002)
Graziano, Frank, *Divine Violence: Spectacle, Psychosexuality and Radical Christianity in the Argentine Dirty War* (Portland 1992)

Greenberg, Susan & Graham Smith, *'Rejoice!': Media Freedom and the Falklands* (1983)

Grossman, David, *On Killing* (Boston 1996)

Grove, Eric, *Vanguard to Trident: British Naval Policy since World War II* (1987)

*Guest, Iain, *Behind the Disappearances: Argentina's Dirty War Against Human Rights and the United Nations* (Philadelphia 1990)

Gurwin, Larry, *The Calvi Affair* (1984)

Haig, Alexander, *Caveat: Realism, Reagan and Foreign Policy* (1984)

Hanrahan, Brian & Robert Fox, *'I counted them all out and I counted them all back': the Battle for the Falklands* (1984)

Harris, Robert, *Gotcha! The Media, the Government and the Falklands Crisis* (1983)

Hastings, Max & Simon Jenkins, *The Battle for the Falklands* (1983)

Hayek, Friedrich, *The Constitution of Liberty* (1960)

Healey, Denis, *The Time of My Life* (1989)

*HMSO (ed. Tim Coates), *War in the Falklands, 1982* (2001)

HMSO, *The Falklands Campaign: the Lessons* (1982)

Higgitt, Mark, *Through Fire and Water* (Edinburgh 2001)

*Hobson, Chris with Andrew Noble, *Falklands Air War* (Hinckley 2002)

*Holmes, Richard, *Firing Line* (1985) republished as *Acts of War* (2004)

Honeywell, Martin & Jenny Pearce, *Falklands/Malvinas: Whose Crisis?* (1982)

Hopkinson, Nicholas, *War and the Media* (1992)

Hough, Richard, *Falklands 1914* (2003)

Hughes-Wilson, John, *Military Intelligence Blunders and Cover-Ups* (2004)

Hunt, Rex, *My Falkland Days* (Newton Abbot 1992)

*Inskip, Ian, *Ordeal by Exocet* (2002)

*Jennings, Christian & Adrian Weale, *Green-Eyed Boys* (1996)

Jolly, Rick, *The Red and Green Life Machine: a Diary of the Falklands Field Hospital* (1983)

Jolly, Rick, *Ajax Bay: a Visitor's Guide* (Stanley n.d.)

Kakar, Hassan, *Afghanistan: The Soviet Invasion and the Afghan Response, 1979–1982* (Berkeley 1995)

Kinney, Douglas, *National Interest, National Honor: the Diplomacy of the Falklands Crisis* (New York 1989)

Koburger, Charles, *Sea Power in the Falklands* (New York 1983)

Lane, Andrew, *Royal Marine Commandos in the Falklands War* (Tiverton 2000)

*Lawrence, John & Robert, *Tumbledown: When the Fighting is Over* (1997)

Leach, Henry, *Endure No Makeshifts* (1993)

Leigh, David, *The Wilson Plot: the Intelligence Services and the Discrediting of a Prime Minister 1945–1976* (1988)

*Lukowiak, Ken, *A Soldier's Song* (1999)

McCart, Neil, *Canberra: the great white whale* (Cambridge 1983)

*McManners, Hugh, *The Scars of War* (1993)

*McManners, Hugh, *Falklands Commando* (2002)

Macksey, Kenneth, *For Want of a Nail: the Impact on War of Logistics and Communications* (1989)

Manley, Michael, *Jamaica: Struggle in the Periphery* (1982)

Maritime Books, *Falklands: Task Force Portfolio*, Part 1 (Liskeard n.d.)

Maritime Books, *Falklands: Task Force Portfolio*, Part 2 (Liskeard n.d.)

Marshall Cavendish Ltd., *The Falklands War* – 14 part serial (1983)

Marshall Cavendish Ltd., *Falklands Aftermath: Forces '85* (1984)

Mercer, Derrik, Geoff Mungham & Kevin Williams, *The Fog of War: the Media on the Battlefield* (1987)

*Middlebrook, Martin, *Task Force* (1987)

*Middlebrook, Martin, *The Fight for the 'Malvinas'* (1989)

*Milsted, David, *Brewer's Anthology of England and the English* (2001)

Moir, G.D., *The History of the Falklands* (Biggin Hill 1998)

Monaghan, David, *The Falklands War: Myth and Countermyth* (1998)

Morrison, David & Howard Tumber, *Journalists at War: the Dynamics of News Reporting during the Falklands Conflict* (1988)

Moyano, María José, *Argentina's Lost Patrol: Armed Struggle 1969–1979* (Yale 1995)

Munro, Richard, *Place Names of the Falkland Islands* (Huntingdon 1998)

Norden, Deborah, *Military Coups in Argentina* [post 1983] (Lincoln 1996)

North, Douglass, *Institutions, Institutional Change and Economic Performance* (Cambridge 1990)

Oakley, Derek, *The Falklands Military Machine* (Staplehurst 2002)

Olson, Mancur, *The Rise and Decline of Nations: Economic Growth, Stagflation and Social Rigidities* (Yale 1982)

Owen, David, *Time to Declare* (1992)

Parker, John, *SBS: the Inside Story* (1997)

Parsons, Michael, *The Falklands War* (Stroud 2000)

Paul, T.V., *Assymetric Conflicts: War Initiation by Weaker Powers* (Cambridge 1994)

*Perkins, Roger, *Operation Paraquat* (Chippenham 1986)

Perl, Raphael, *The Falkland Islands Dispute in International Law and Politics: a Documentary Sourcebook* (New York 1983)

Perrett, Bryan, *Weapons of the Falklands Conflict* (Poole 1982)

Ponting, Clive, *The Right to Know: the Inside Story of the Belgrano affair* (1985)

Quarrie, Bruce, *The World's Elite Forces* (London 1985)

Ratcliffe, Peter, N. Botham & B. Hitchen, *Eye of the Storm: Twenty-Five Years in Action with the SAS* (2000)

Reagan, Ronald, *An American Life* (1990)

Reynolds, David, *Task Force: The Illustrated History of the Falklands War* (Stroud 2002)

Richards, Phil, *The Falkland Islands: Offshore Geology and Exploration* (Edinburgh 2003)

*Richardson, Louise, *When Allies Differ: Anglo-American relations during the Suez and Falklands crises* (1996)

*Rock, David, *Authoritarian Argentina: the Nationalist movement, its History and its Impact* (Berkeley 1993)

Rosenberg, Tina, *Children of Cain* (1992)

Samuel, Raphael (ed.), *Patriotism: the Making and Unmaking of British National Identity*, 3 vols. (1989)

Schoeck, Helmut, *Envy: a Theory of Social Behaviour* (New York 1969)

Seear, Mike, *With the Gurkhas in the Falklands* (Barnsley 2003)

Simpson, John & Jana Bennet, *The Disappeared* (1985)

Sklar, Holly, *Washington's War on Nicaragua* (Boston 1988)

*Slessor, Tim, *Ministries of Deception* (2002)
*Smith, John, *74 Days: an Islander's Diary of the Falklands Occupation*
    (Old Basing 2002)
Southby-Tailyour, Ewen, *Reasons in Writing* (1993)
Stavridis, Stelios and Christopher Hill (eds.), *Domestic Sources of Foreign Policy:*
    West European reactions to the Falklands conflict (Oxford 1996)
Stavridis, Stelios, *The Constraints of an International 'Double Vocation': the reaction*
    in Spain to the Falklands War of 1982 (Bristol 1992)
Stewart, Nora Kinzer, *Mates & Muchachos* (McLean 1991)
Stone, Phil & Don Aldiss, *The Falkland Islands: Reading the Rocks*
    (Nottingham 2000)
Stone, Phil & Don Aldiss, *Stone Runs – Rock in the Landscape* (Nottingham 2001)
Stone, Phil & Don Aldiss, *Fossils from the Falkland Islands* (Nottingham 2002)
Sunday Express Magazine Team, *War in the Falklands: the campaign in pictures*
    (1982)
Sunday Times Insight Team – see Eddy, Paul
Thatcher, Margaret, *The Downing Street Years* (1993)
*Thompson, Julian, *No Picnic* (rev. ed. 2001)
*Thompson, Julian, *The Lifeblood of War* (1991)
Thornton, Richard, *The Falklands Sting* (1998)
Tinker, David, *A Message from the Falklands* (Harmondsworth 1983)
Tosches, Nick, *Power on Earth* (Westminster, MD 1986)
Trickett, Paul, *UKREP and the Falklands Conflict: Driving the Machine*
    (Leicester 1999)
*Underwood, Geoffrey, *Our Falklands War* (Liskeard 1983)
*Vaux, Nick, *March to the South Atlantic* (1986)
Villar, Roger, *Merchant Ships at War: the Falklands Experience* (1984)
Vistica, Gregory, *Fall from Glory* (New York 1997)
Wagstaff, William, *Falkland Islands: Bradt Travel Guide* (2001)
Walker, Thomas (ed.), *Revolution and Counterrevolution in Nicaragua*
    (Boulder 1991)
Ward, 'Sharkey', *Sea Harrier over the Falklands* (2000)
*Washington, Linda (ed.), *Ten Years On: the British Army in the Falklands War* (1992)
*Watson, Bruce & Peter Dunn (eds.), *Military lessons of the Falklands Islands War:*
    Views from the United States (Boulder 1984)
Weinberger, Caspar, *Fighting for Peace: Seven Critical Years at the Pentagon* (1990)
*West, Nigel, *Secret War for the Falklands* (1997)
*Weston, Simon, *Going Back: Return to the Falklands* (1992)
*Wigglesworth, Angela, *Falkland People* (1992)
Williams, Philip with Maurice Power, *Summer Soldier* (1990)
Winton, John (ed.), *Signals from the Falklands* (1995)
*Woodward, Sandy with Patrick Robinson, *One Hundred Days* (1992)
Woolf, Cecil & Jean Moorcroft Wilson, *Authors Take Sides on the Falklands* (1982)
Wright, Peter, *Spycatcher* (New York 1988)
Yallop, David, *In God's Name* (New York 1984)
Young, Hugo, *One of Us* (1989)
Young, Michael, *The Rise of the Meritocracy* (1958)

TRANSLATION (*London unless otherwise specified*)

CONADEP (Argentine National Commission on Disappeared People) with an Introduction by Ronald Dworkin), *Nunca Más (Never Again): A Report* (1986)

Cardoso, Oscar, Ricardo Kirschbaum & Eduardo Van der Kooy (trans. Bernard Ethell), *Falklands: the Secret Plot* (East Molesey 1987).

Dabat, Alejandro & Luis Lorenzano (trans. Ralph Johnstone), *Argentina: the Malvinas and the End of Military Rule* (1984)

*Kon, Daniel (trans. David Bolt Assocs), *Los Chicos de la Guerra: the Boys of the War* (1983)

Latin American Newsletters (in both languages), *The Falklands War: the official communications of the British and Argentine governments* (1983)

Mignone, Emilio (trans. Philip Berryman), *Witness to the Truth: the complicity of Church and dictatorship in Argentina* (Maryknoll 1988)

Moro, Rubén (trans. Michael Valeur), *The History of the South Atlantic Conflict* (New York 1989)

Partnoy, Alicia (trans. & with Lois Athey & Sandra Braunstein), *The Little School: Tales of Disappearance and Survival in Argentina* (1988)

Revolutionary Communist Party, *Malvinas are Argentina's* (1982)

Timerman, Jacobo (trans. Tody Talbot), *Prisoner without a Name, Cell without a Number* (1981)

Verbitsky, Horacio (trans. Esther Allen), *The Flight: Confessions of an Argentine Dirty Warrior* (New York 1996)

SPANISH (Buenos Aires unless otherwise specified)

Abete, Hugo, *¡El buen combate!: la guerra de las Malvinas según el método de estudio de la historia militar* (1998)

Ageitos, Stella, *Historia de la impunidad* (2002)

*Aguiar, Félix et. al., *Operaciones terrestres en las islas Malvinas* (1985)

Aldana, Norberto, *Malvinas a prueba de fuego* (1988)

*Andrada, Benigno, *Guerra aérea en las Malvinas* (1983)

Asociación Madres de Plaza de Mayo, *Massera el genocida* (n.d.)

*Balza, Martín, *Malvinas: relatos de soldados* (1983)

Balza, Martín, *Malvinas: gesta e incompetencia* (2003)

Bardini, Roberto, *Tacuara* (2003)

Becerra, Alfredo (ed.), *Protestas por Malvinas 1833–1946* (1998)

Benedetto, Fernando, *A-4B/C Skyhawk* (2002)

Berger, Martín, *El rescate de las Malvinas* (1982)

Betts, Alexander with Peter Bate, *La verdad sobre las Malvinas, mi tierra natal* (1987)

Blaustein, Eduardo & Martín Zubieta, *Decíamos ayer* (1998)

*Boccazzi, Joaquín, *Compilación Malvinas* (2004)

Büsser, Carlos et. al., *Operación Rosario* (1984)

Büsser, Carlos, *Malvinas: conflicto vigente* (1999)

Cabanillas, Rubén, *No apagues la luz cuando te vayas* (2004)

Calloni, Stella, *Los años del lobo* (1999)

Canclini, Arnoldo, *Malvinas: su historia en historias* (2000)

*Carballo, Pablo, *Dios y los halcones* (1983)

Camps, Ramón, *El poder en la sombra: el affaire Graiver* (1983)

Cerón, Sergio, *Malvinas: ¿gesta heroica of derrota vergonzosa?* (1984)

Círculo Militar, *In Memoriam* (1998)

CONADEP, *Definitivamente - nunca más* (1985)

Costa, Eduardo, *Guerra bajo la Cruz del Sur* (1988)

Duhalde, Eduardo, *El estado terrorista argentino* (1983)

Editorial Oriente, *La guerra de las Malvinas*, 2 vols. (1987)

Ejército Argentino (occupation newsheet), *La Gaceta Argentina* (Stanley 1982)

*Ejército Argentino, *Conflicto Malvinas*, 2 Vols (1983)

Escudé, Carlos, *Gran Bretaña, Estados Unidos y la declinación argentina 1942–1949* (1983)

*Escudé, Carlos, *Argentina vs. las grandes potencias: el precio del desafío* (1986)

*Escudé, Carlos, *La declinación argentina* (1996)

Esteban, Edgardo & Gustavo Romero, *Malvinas: diario del regreso* (1993)

Estrada, Marcos de, *Una verdad sobre las Malvinas* (1982)

Fitte, Ernesto, *Martín García: historia de una isla argentina* (1971)

Foulkes, Haroldo, *Los kelpers en las Malvinas y en la Patagonia* (1983)

Gamba, Virginia, *Malvinas confidencial: un análisis global* (1982)

Gamba, Virginia, *El peón de la reina* (1984)

Gambini, Hugo (ed.), *Malvinas: crónica documental*, 3 vols. (1982)

García Lupo, Rogelio, *Diplomacia secreta y rendición incondicional* (1983)

Gasparini, Juan, *Montoneros: final de cuentas* (1988)

*Gilbert, Abel & Miguel Vitagliano, *El terror y la gloria: la vida, el fútbol y la política en la Argentina del Mundial 78* (1998)

Gobierno Argentino, *Las Malvinas: ¡Argentinos a vencer!* (1982)

*Goñi, Uki, *Judas: la verdadera historia de Alfredo Astiz el infiltrado* (1996)

Guttman, Daniel, *Tacuara* (2003)

Hernández, Pablo, *Conversaciones con el Teniente Coronel Aldo Rico* (1989)

*Jofre, Oscar & Félix Aguiar, *Malvinas: la defensa de Puerto Argentino* (1987)

Kanaf, Leo, *La batalla de las Malvinas* (1982)

Kazanzew, Nicolás, *Malvinas a sangre y fuego* (1982)

López Echagüe, Hernán, *El enigma del General Bussi* (1991)

Massera, Emilio, *El camino a la democracia* (1979)

Matassi, Pío, *Probado en combate* (1997)

Mayorga, Horacio, *No vencidos: relato de las operaciones navales en el conflicto del Atlántico Sur* (1998)

Méndez, Eugenio, *Confesiones de un Montonero* (1988)

Miguens, José Enrique, *Los neo-fascismos en la Argentina* (1983)

Mittelbach, Federico & Jorge, *Sobre áreas y tumbas* (2000)

Montenegro, Néstor & Eduardo Aliverti, *Los nombres de la derrota* (1982)

Muñoz, Jorge, *Misión cumplida: epopeya de los barcos mercantes argentinos en la guerra de las Malvinas* (2000)

Morelli, Lilian, *Los héroes olvidados* (1990)

Otegui, José María, *La isla Trinidad: la otra cara de las Malvinas* (1984)

Perdía, Roberto Cirilo, *La otra historia: testimonio de un jefe Montonero* (1997)

*Presti, Marisa, *Ana Frank es argentina* (2004)

*Rattenbach, Emilio, *Informe Rattenbach* (2000)

Rodríguez Mottino, Horacio, *La artillería argentina en Malvinas* (1984)

*Rodríguez Muñoz, Chacho (ed.), *Malvinas: 20 años 20 héroes* (2003)

Ruiz Moreno, Isidoro, *Comandos en acción: el ejército en Malvinas* (1986)

Russell, Roberto (ed.), *América Latina y la guerra del Atlántico sur* (1984)

Salguero, Ricardo, *Todo sobre el Beagle* (1979)

Seineldín, Mohamed Alí, *Malvinas: un sentimiento* (1999)

*Simeoni, Héctor, *Malvinas: contrahistoria* (1984)

Solanas Pacheco, Julia, *Malvinas: Y ahora . . . ¿qué?* (1996)

Solari Yrigoyen, Hipólito, *Malvinas: lo que no cuentan los ingleses* (1998)

*Túrolo, Carlos, *Así lucharon* (1982)

*Túrolo, Carlos, *Malvinas: testimonio de su gobernador* (1983)

Vargas, Salvador, *Malvinas: historias breves y sentimientos* (2002)

Vásquez, Juan, *Los comandos anfibios el 2 de abril* (2002)

Vázquez, Enrique, *PRN la última: origen, apogeo y caída de la dictadura militar* (1985)

Verbitsky, Horacio, *La posguerra sucia* (1985)

*Verbitsky, Horacio, *Malvinas: la última batalla de la tercera guerra mundial* (2002)

Villarino, Emilio, *Exocet* (1986)

*Villarino, Emilio, *Batallón 5* (1992)

Villegas, Osiris, *El conflicto con Chile en la Región Austral* (1978)

Viola, Oscar, *La derrota diplomática y militar de la República Argentina en la guerra de las Malvinas* (1982)

Waispek, Carlos, *Balsa 44: relato de un sobreviviente del crucero ARA Belgrano* (1994)

ARTICLES

Akhurst, Gerald, 'A Gunner's Tale', *Field Artillery Journal* (March–April 1984)

Aldea, David, 'Blood and Mud at Goose Green', *Military History*, 19:1 (April 2002)

Bolia, Robert, 'The Falklands War: the Bluff Cove Disaster', *Military Review*, 84:6 (November/December 2004)

Brett, Bernard, 'Action Lynx!', *The Elite*, 55 (1986)

Burley, Peter, 'Fighting for the Falklands in 1770', *History Today* 32:6 (June 1982)

Chapman, P, 'Operation Corporate – The Sir Galahad Bombing', *Journal of the Royal Army Medical Corps*, 130, 84–88 (1984)

Chaundler, David [CO 3 Para], 'Night Attack', *The Elite*, 7 (1985)

Conference of 8 April 2003, *Royal Air Force Historical Society Journal*, No. 30 (Oxford 2003)

Cooper, David [Chaplain 2 Para], '2 Para: Ready for Anything', *The Elite*, 1 (1985)

Corum, James, 'Argentine Airpower in the Falklands War', *Air & Space Power Journal*, 16:3 (Fall 2002)

Costa Mendez, Nicanor [Argentine Minister of Foreign Affairs], 'Beyond Deterrence: The Malvinas-Falklands Case', *Journal of Social Issues*, 43:4 (1988)

Craig, R, 'Military Cold Injury During the War in the Falkland Islands: an evaluation of possible risk factors', *Journal of the Royal Army Medical Corps*, 130, 89–96 (1984)

Dorman, Andrew, 'John Nott and the Royal Navy: the 1981 Defence Review Revisited', *Contemporary British History*, 15:2 (Summer 2001)

Dunbar-Miller, R., Alcohol and the Fighting Man – An Historical Review (2 parts) *Journal of the Royal Army Medical Corps*, 130, 12–15 & 117–121 (1984)

Escudé, Carlos, 'The Malvinas Conflict' (4 parts), *The Buenos Aires Herald*, (November 1985)

Escudé, Carlos, 'Argentine Territorial Nationalism' *Journal of Latin American Studies* 20 (1988)

Ethell, Jeffrey, 'Bomb Alley', *The Elite*, 66 (1986)

Ethell, Jeffrey, 'Exocet', *The Elite*, 67 (1986)

Falkland Islands Association – *Newsletter*

Feldman, David, 'The United States Role in the Malvinas Crisis 1982: Misguidance and Misperception in Argentina's Decision to Go to War', *Journal of Interamerican Studies and World Affairs*, 27:2 (1985)

Ferguson, Gregor, 'Top Malo', *The Elite*, 29 (1985)

Finlan, Alastair, 'British Special Forces and the Falklands conflict', *Defense & Security Analysis*, 18:4 (December 2002)

Fonfe, Michael, 'RAF Regiment deploys ex-Argentine AA guns', *Air Clues* (August and September 1990)

Fowler, Will, 'Falklands Kit', *The Elite*, 2 (1985)

Franklin, William, 'Gunners at War', *The Elite*, 32 (1985)

Freedman, Lawrence, 'Intelligence Operations in the Falklands', *Intelligence and National Security*, Vol 1:3 (September 1986)

Gilbert, Adrian, 'Hand to Hand Combat', *The Elite*, 8 (1985)

Gilbert, Adrian, 'The Voyage of the Conqueror', *The Elite*, 75 (1986)

Gooch, A, 'The Falklands War and a Very Special Relationship: the Hispanic World and the Anglo-Saxon World, Parts 1 & 2, *Contemporary Review*, 257:1498/1499 (1990)

Goyret, José, 'El Ejército Argentino en la guerra de las Malvinas', *Armas y Geostrategia*, Vol 2:6 (May 1983)

Groom, A. & J. Coull, 'Army Amputees from the Falklands – Review', *Journal of the Royal Army Medical Corps*, 130. 114–116 (1984)

Grove, Eric, 'The Falklands War and British Defense Policy', *Defense & Security Analysis*, 18:4 (December 2002)

Hamilton-Russell, James, 'Scorpion and Scimitar', *The Elite*, 42 (1985)

Hart Dyke, David [Captain, *Coventry*], 'Lessons from the Falklands – An Operator's View', *The Naval Review*, 72:1 (January 1984)

Head, Daniel, 'The 2nd Parachute Battalion's War in the Falklands: Light Armor Made the Difference in South Atlantic Deployment', *Armor* (September–October 1999)

Holroyd Smith, Michael, 'The Falkland Islands Campaign – the Perceptions of a Gunner CO' *R.A. Historical Society Proceedings*, 5:2 (January 1984)

Horne, Alistair, 'A British Historian's Meditations', *National Review* (July 23, 1982)

Hughes-Wilson, John, 'The Falklands War: How the Devil Did You Do It?', *Battlefields Review* 18 (2002)

Huntington, Samuel P., 'The Clash of Civilizations', *Foreign Affairs* 72:3 (Summer 1993)

Jones, Mark, 'Questioning Menem's way', *Current History* (February 1998)

King, David, 'Intelligence Failures and the Falklands War', *Intelligence and National Security*, Vol 2:2 (April 1987)

Kirkpatrick, Jeane [US Ambassador to the UN], 'My Falklands War and Theirs', *The National Interest* (Winter 1989/90)

Lane, Richard [Ops Officer, *Coventry*], The Fog of War: Personal Experience of Leadership', *Journal of the Royal United Services Institute for Defence Studies*, 143:6 (December 1998)

Lynch, Tim, 'Going Back Down South', *Battlefields Review* 24 (2003)

Macdonald, Peter, 'Assault Squadron', *The Elite*, 115 (1987)

McLaughlin, John, 'Falklands Soul Searching', *National Review* 34:12 (1982)

McManners, Hugh, 'Fire Support', *The Elite*, 46 (1985)

McManners, Hugh, 'Avenger', *The Elite*, 97 (1986)

McManners, Hugh, 'Choppers at War', *The Elite*, 104 (1986)

McManners, Hugh, 'First In Last Out [9 Para Squadron RE]', *The Elite*, 107 (1987)

McManners, Hugh, 'Talking Logistics', *The Elite*, 117 (1987)

Maisch, Christian, 'The Falkland/Malvinas Islands Clash of 1831–32: U.S. and British Diplomacy in the South Atlantic', *Diplomatic History*, Vol 24: 2 (Spring 2000)

Marshal Cavendish, *The Falklands War*, 14 part serial (1983)

Moore, Jeremy & John Woodward, 'The Falklands Experience', *Journal of the Royal United Services Institute for Defence Studies*, 128:1 (March 1983)

Morgan, M. J., 'Naval Gunfire Support for Operation Corporate, 1982', *Royal Artillery Journal*, 110:2 (September 1983)

Parsons, Anthony, 'The Falklands crisis in the United Nations 31 March–14 June 1982' *International Affairs*, 59: 2 (1983)

Parsons, Michael, 'The South Atlantic Coflict of 1982: a Test for Anglo-American Relations', *Revue Française de Civilisation Britannique*, 12:1 (2002)

Penguin News – Falkland Islands weekly newspaper

Pike, Hew [CO 3 Para], 'With Fixed Bayonets', *The Elite*, 20 (1985)

Pike, Hew, 'The Other Side of the Hill', *Pegasus* (April 1988)

Potter, Michael, 'Blue-on-Blue in the Falklands', *Proceedings of the United States Naval Institute*, Vol. 126:10 (October 2000)

Price, Alfred, 'Falklands Air Strike', *The Elite*, 3 (1985)

Price, M., 'The Falkands: rate of British psychiatric casualties compared to recent American wars', *Journal of the Royal Army Medical Corps*, 130, 109–113 (1984)

Prince, Stephen, 'British Command and Control in the Falklands campaign', *Defense & Security Analysis*, 18:4 (December 2002)

Ridlon, David, 'Shots in the Dark: British tactical intelligence in the Falklands War', *Military Intelligence* (July–September 1989)

Ryan, Patrick, 'Falklands Fallout', *Marine Corps Gazette*, 67:6 (1983)

Sanders, David, et al., 'Government Popularity and the Falklands War: a reassessment', *British Journal of Political Science*, 17 (1987)

Sheridan, Guy [OC South Georgia], 'Operation Paraquet', *The Elite*, 56 (1986)

Smith, E.D., 'Gurkhas in Command', *The Elite*, 35 (1985)

Southby-Tailyour, Ewen, 'Corporate Decision', *The Elite*, 114 (1987)

Speller, Ian, 'Delayed Reaction: UK Maritime Capabilities and the Lessons of the Falklands Conflict', *Defense & Security Analysis*, 18:4 (December 2002)

Strawson, John, 'SAS: Falklands Battlefield', *The Elite*, 109 (1987)

Thompson, Julian [CO 3 Cdo Bde], 'Falklands: With Hindsight', *Army Quarterly and Defence Journal*, 122:3 (July 1992)

Thompson, Julian, 'Battle of Goose Green; New Arguments are Flawed', *Army Quarterly and Defence Journal*, 125:3 (July 1995)

Tothill, David, 'In Argentina at the Time of the Falklands War', *Diplomacy and Statecraft*, 12:3 (September 2001)

Tripodi, Paolo, 'General Matthei's Revelation and Chile's Role During the Falklands War', *Journal of Strategic Studies*, 26:4 (December 2003)

Train, US Adm Harry. 'Analysis of the Falklands/Malvinas Islands Campaign', *Naval War College Review*, 41 (Winter 1988)

Trainor, US Lt Gen Bernard, 'Reflections on the Falklands', *Marine Corps Gazette* (January 1989)

Tustin, Maj T.J., 'The Logistics of the Falklands War' 2 Parts, *The Army Quarterly and Defence Journal* Vols 114:3 & 114:4 (July/October 1984)

US Navy Department of Program Appraisal, 'Lessons of the Falklands: Summary Report' (1983)

Vaux, Nick [CO 42 Cdo], 'Marine Assault', *The Elite*, 28 (1985)

Whalen, Robert, 'Bimble in the Dark: Tactical Intelligence in the Falklands War', *Marine Corps Gazette*, 82:3 (March 1998)

Whitehead, Andrew [CO 45 Cdo], 'Yomp to Victory', *The Elite*, 31 (1985)

VIDEOS

Granada, *Battle for the Falklands* (1982)

BBC, *Task Force South* (1982)

BBC, *The Price of Victory* (1983)

Services Sound and Vision Corp., *Falklands, the Land Battle*, 4 vols (1983)

Yorkshire TV, *The Falklands War: the Untold Story* (1987) – see Bilton & Kosminsky

ITN, *Wars in Peace: the Falklands – Special Forces* (1991)

Channel Four, *The Falklands War* (1992) – see Denys Blakeway

ITN, *The Falklands War: A Close Run Thing* (1995)

Sky News, *Falklands 20 Years On* (2002)

Touch Productions, *Simon's Heroes* (2002)

Channel 5, *War in the Falklands* (2002)

The History Channel, *Port Stanley 1982* (2002)

The History Channel, *History's Raiders: The Falklands Campaign – SAS* (2004)

WEBSITES

General:

www.sama82.org/index.htm – SAMA 82 site.

www.comcen.com.au/~raiment – photo-memoir of the *Canberra*.

www.britains-smallwars.com/Falklands – excellent general site.

www.naval-history.net/NAVAL1982FALKLANDS.htm – best of the on-line general histories, based closely on Gordon Smith's book.

www.falklandswar.org.uk – useful database.

www.iwm.org.uk/upload/package/3/falklands/falkext.htm – interviews.

www.nuncamas.org/document/militar/rattenbach/rattenbach00.htm – the Rattenbach report

ar.geocities.com/laperlaaustral/historia.htm – comprehensive Argentine site on the war with biographies, memoirs, and a surprisingly limited amount of hyperbole.

www.argentina-rree.com/12/12-08.htm – Anglo-Argentine diplomatic relations 1976–1981.

Technical:

www.geocities.com/Pentagon/Fort/2839/Barrie/Air-Reconnaissance.htm – contemporary aerial reconnaissance photos.

www.multied.com/navy/cruiser/Phoenix.html – history of the USS *Phoenix*/*General Belgrano*.

www.thunder-and-lightnings.co.uk/tsr2/history.html – the TSR2 saga.

British media:

news.bbc.co.uk/hi/english/static/in_depth/uk/2002/falklands/default.stm – BBC's 20-year retrospective.

keywords.dsvr.co.uk/freepress/body.phtml?category=&id=238 – Kim Sabido on the war at the Campaign for Press and Broadcasting Freedom site.

www.channel4.com/science/microsites/G/going_critical/hms_coventry/index_t.html – summary of the errors leading to the loss of HMS *Coventry*.

www.guardian.co.uk/Thatcher/Story/0,2763,400983,00.html – a representative example of contemporary *Guardian* journalism.

www.sterlingtimes.co.uk/gotcha1.htm – infamous 'Gotcha' headline from *The Sun*.

www.telegraph.co.uk/news/main.jhtml?xml=%2Fnews%2F2002%2F03%2F13%2Fn ot13.xml – revealing interview with John Nott.

Falkland Islands:

www.falklands-malvinas.com – bilingual discussion forum

www.falklands.gov.fk – Falkland Islands Government site.

www.army.mod.uk/bffi/home.htm – British Forces Falkland Islands.

Dirty War:

www2.gwu.edu/~nsarchiv/index.html – National Security Archive maintained by George Washington University. Documents obtained under the Freedom of Information Act.

ar.geocities.com/victorbevi/listas_de_los_asesinados_por_fue.html – terrorist activities by subversive groups.

www.yendor.com/vanished/index.html – *desaparecidos* site.

www.desaparecidos.org/arg/conadep/lista-revisada/main.html – list of *desaparecidos*.

www.derechos.org/nizkor/arg/eng.html – military torturers and kidnappers.

www.impunidad.com/cases/rodolfo_fernandezE.htm – case of Rolo Fernández Pondal.

ukinet.com/media/text/index.htm – site maintained by the great journalist Uki Goñi.

www.lafogata.org/proyecto/dictadura.htm – Clergy involved or complicit in the Dirty War.

www.namebase.org/nbhome.html – vital tool for all conspiracy theorists.

Index

Graf Spee, the (German pocket battleship) 42
Grandi, Sub-Lieutenant Pérez 235, 241–2, 244
Gray, Private 225, 266, 269
Great Britain: erosion of international respect
24–7; Argentine assessment of 25, 92–3;
homosexual/espionage scandals 26–7;
appeasement policy 27–8, 44, 82; intellectual failure 28; Falkland Islands policy
29–30, 43–5, 94; post-war 35; industrial
relations 39; right of abode 39–40; and the
1968 Memorandum 43–5; failure to
reinforce Falkland Islands 59–60; withdrawal of Argentine ambassadors 59;
six-frigate deal with Argentine Navy 69;
relations with America 77–82, 337; shame
84–5; economic failure 85–7; decline
85–92, 97; bureaucratization 86–7; Civil
Service 86–7; justice system 87–8; political
scene pre-Thatcher 88–92; 'brain drain'
89–90; Welfare State 90–1; education 91;
local government 91; National Health
Service 91, 333–4; journalism 91–2; and
Thatcher 93–4; defence cuts 95, 96; 'word'
95–6; general election, 1983 96–7; Royal
Navy's role 98; skilled improvisation
99–100; leaks 316; troops return 330;
debriefings 331; cost of war 333–4
Great Britain, the 43
Green-Eyed Boys (Jennings and Weale) 272
Green Patch 143
Greenland, Ken 176
Greenwood, Private 223
Grey, Sergeant 223
Gringham, Private 273
Grose, Private 226
Grupo Fahrenheit 52
Grytviken, action at 123
Guerrico (Argentine corvette) 123
Guest, Ian 50, 66–7
Guildford Four, the 88
Gwyn, Major 288, 295, 296
Gypsy Cove 40

Haddow, Lieutenant 253
Hagelin, Dagmar 51
Hagyard, Marine 258
Haig, Al 80
Halkett, Sergeant 234
Hamilton, Captain 191
Hardman, Corporal 175
Harriers: at San Carlos 149–50, 154, 155;
losses 155; at Darwin/Goose Green 187–8;

action at Choiseul Sound 206; cancelled
operation 317
Harriet 220, 241
Harriet, assault on: terrain 248–9; defenders
249–50; Goat Ridge 249, 253, 264; Wall
Mountain 249, 251–2; attacking force
250–2; preparations 252–4, 258; casualties
33, 253, 264–5; order of battle 255; 42
Commando attack 259–65; and the battle of
Longdon 259
Harris, Captain 204
Harris, Jill 328
Harris, Leslie 327
Harris, Robert 335
Hastings, Max 28, 97, 317–8, 329
Hayek, Friedrich 90
Hayward, Private 213
Heath, Edward 30, 77–8, 89
Heaton, Corporal 225
Hedicker, Private 34
helicopters Chinook 137, 301; Identification
Friend/Foe 143; Gazelles 148; at
Darwin/Goose Green 158–9; 180
Henríquez, Cardinal Raúl Silva 53
Hermes, HMS 158, 203, 330
Higgs, Lance Corporal 274
Hobson, Chris 139
Holman-Smith, Private 181
Holmberg, Elena 66
Hooker's Point 42, 202, 203
House of Commons 119, 121
Howard, Sergeant 267
Hulme, Lieutenant Commander 154
Hunt, Corporal 244
Hunt, Sergeant 234
Hunt, Governor Rex 118, 121
Huntington, Samuel 58
Hussey, Captain Barry Melbourne 319–20,
321, 329

Illingworth, Private 171
Immigration Act, 1971 39
Inflexible, HMS 40–1
intelligence 158, 159–60, 230–1, 315–6,
324–5
international anarchy 74
interrogation techniques 70
Intrepid, HMS 150, 202, 203
Invincible, HMS (aircraft carrier) 41, 138–9,
139, 330
Invincible, HMS (WWI battlecruiser) 40–1
IRA 334–5